Shakespearean
Educations

Shakespearean Educations

Power, Citizenship, and Performance

Edited by
Coppélia Kahn, Heather S. Nathans,
and Mimi Godfrey

UNIVERSITY OF DELAWARE PRESS
Newark

Published by University of Delaware Press
Co-published with The Rowman & Littlefield Publishing Group, Inc.
4501 Forbes Boulevard, Suite 200, Lanham, Maryland 20706
www.rlpgbooks.com

Estover Road, Plymouth PL6 7PY, United Kingdom

British Library Cataloguing in Publication Information Available

Library of Congress Cataloging-in-Publication Data
Library of Congress Cataloguing-in-Publication Data on file under LC#2010013488
ISBN: 978-1-61149-028-2 (cl. : alk. paper)
eISBN: 978-1-61149-029-9
The paper used in this publication meets the minimum requirements of American
National Standard for Information Sciences—Permanence of Paper for Printed
Library Materials, ANSI/NISO Z39.48-1992.

Printed in the United States of America

Contents

Illustrations

Acknowledgments

THE VOLUME YOU HOLD IN YOUR HANDS REPRESENTS THE CULMINATION of an extraordinarily fruitful and significant time at the Folger Shakespeare Library. *Shakespearean Educations: Power, Citizenship, and Performance* is a book that has flourished through the generous efforts and support of many individuals and institutions.

In 2004, preparations began at the Library to mark what would be, in 2007, the seventy-fifth anniversary of the founding of the Folger. Dr. Barbara A. Mowat, Director of Research, and Dr. Kathleen Lynch, Executive Director of the Folger Institute, noted that the Folger's celebrations would coincide with the four-hundredth anniversary of the successful permanent settlement at Jamestown; they began discussions with the Institute's Central Executive Committee on how best to bring these two histories together. Dr. Theodore Leinwand, a member of the committee, joined with them to plan a scholarly conference under the aegis of the Institute's Center for Shakespeare Studies. It was designed to gather Shakespeare scholars, as well as specialists in American studies and the histories of education and rhetoric, to consider how Shakespeare's plays became integral to Americans' cultural literacy, moral education, and civic formation.

The result of their visionary efforts was "Shakespeare in American Education, 1607–1934," held 16 to 17 March 2007. This highly successful gathering drew on perspectives from the histories of university, primary, and secondary school education from the colonial period through the twentieth century, using original archival research carried out at the Folger and throughout the country; commentary was provided by Arthur N. Applebee, Michael Bristol, John Guillory, and Michael Warner. We regret that participant Peggy O'Brien had previous commitments that prevented her from being able to revise her conference presentation for publication in this collection.

We would like to express our deep appreciation of the many ways in which the Folger Shakespeare Library supported the conference and this volume. Dedicated fellowships permitted our participants to carry out their work at the Folger, for instance. We gratefully acknowledge the additional generosity of Morrison DeS. Webb and of our corporate sponsors, Barnes & Noble Booksellers, Simon & Schuster, and W. W. Norton.

Further support from the National Endowment for the Humanities (NEH) was crucial. The NEH awarded the Institute a collaborative research grant that supported additional archival research in libraries and archives across the United States. The grant allowed the Institute to bring the speakers together for a workshop, and it funded grants-in-aid for teachers across the country to participate in the conference discussions. The NEH designated the conference as a *We the People* project, for its potential to encourage and strengthen the teaching, study, and understanding of American history and culture. We thank the Endowment for its generous support, but also acknowledge that any views, findings, conclusions, or recommendations expressed during the conference or in these essays do not necessarily reflect those of the National Endowment for the Humanities.

Those familiar with the Folger Shakespeare Library know firsthand the generosity and professionalism of its staff, but we would like to single out several people without whom the conference and this volume would never have left the planning stages. Essence Newhoff, Director of Major Gifts, Development, worked closely with Dr. Owen Williams, Assistant Director of the Folger Institute, in the initial search for underwriting and other support. Garland Scott, Head of External Relations, drew on the findings of the conference and a concurrent exhibition to mount a permanent Web site, "Shakespeare and American Life," and a companion radio documentary of the same name, and to produce the Folger's first podcasts. Virginia Millington and Caryn Lazzuri, successive program assistants for the Institute, ensured that the workshop and conference ran smoothly. Kathleen Lynch and Owen Williams continued to provide steadfast support and guidance throughout the development of this collection. The Institute defrayed photography and editorial expenses at critical junctures. Dr. Williams made the work of revision immeasurably easier by providing, through the Folger Institute, an online site for the editors and authors to post documents and other materials. He also answered questions and solved problems with his customary grace and élan. Last but hardly least, we tender most appreciative thanks to Aaron Tobiason, who swiftly and expertly compiled the bibliography, and to Bernice Eisen, who created the index.

Shakespearean
Educations

Introduction

Coppélia Kahn and Heather S. Nathans

"O THIS LEARNING, WHAT A THING IT IS!" CRIES THE DODDERING AND foolish Gremio in William Shakespeare's *Taming of the Shrew*.[1] Gremio hopes that by surrounding himself with men of education he will appear wiser himself. He also believes that he may school his ladylove, Bianca, to be the ideal docile and decorative wife. Of course, Gremio's plans go sadly awry as the characters in the play absorb very different kinds of education from the ones that he imagines might be contained in the books and instruments he provides. Nor does his mere proximity to men of learning manage to make him into a scholar. In the end, both Gremio and the audience realize that knowledge cannot be compassed within Latin texts or lessons learned by rote. Characters in the play apply their knowledge in unexpected ways. For example, Kate and Bianca use their newly acquired learning to renegotiate women's traditional roles, while Tranio employs his knowledge, gleaned from study with his master, to transcend class boundaries (albeit temporarily).

Much the same might be said of the development of Shakespeare in American education and culture over the past several hundred years.[2] While some might assume that mere association with Shakespeare's works has always conveyed instant wisdom and social status, the processes by which Shakespearean educations evolved in America were long, complicated, and often contentious. Given that America was conceived in self-conscious opposition to British monarchy and aristocracy, while Shakespeare's plays are populated with kings and queens, dukes and duchesses, it could hardly be otherwise. Yet citizens of the new republic maintained their cultural ties to Britain and their sense of British identity for decades after the War of Independence.[3] As a distinctively American culture emerged, however, so did a restive impatience with British cultural hegemony. In 1808, Philadelphia playwright and future mayor James Nelson Barker complained that audiences were too quick to censure fledgling American authors for emulating Shakespeare.[4] In 1838, Orestes

13

Brownson, the American essayist and political activist, lamented, "Our literature is tame and servile, wanting in freshness, freedom, and originality. We write as Englishmen, not Americans."[5] Exactly at midcentury, Herman Melville challenged "this absolute and unconditioned adoration of Shakespeare," asking, "[W]hat sort of belief is this for an American, a man who is bound to carry republican progressiveness into Literature, as well as into Life?"[6]

Yet Shakespeare's presence in American education was always strong. In myriad complex ways, Shakespeare was appropriated, challenged, or transfigured by diverse groups in American culture—all struggling to create their own sense of how an appreciation of his works could be fitted into the education of American citizens and harmonized with republican values. For some, Shakespeare belonged to the classroom; others found their way to Shakespeare by reading on their own or through clubs and societies. Some viewed that education as part of formal classroom experience. Others used knowledge of Shakespeare's texts to combat oppression; and some imagined that familiarity with the Bard would confer the rights and privileges of citizenship.

Since the 1600s, some form of a Shakespearean education has been a constant in American intellectual and cultural life. This study examines how and why Shakespeare's works shaped the development of American education, from the colonial period through the Chicago World's Fair of 1934, taking the reader up to the years before the Servicemen's Readjustment Act of 1944 (popularly known as the GI Bill), coeducation, and a nascent civil rights movement would alter the educational landscape yet again. Our scope is chronological (although it cannot, of course, cover every period), and it is our hope that these essays will inspire other scholars and critics to uncover still more narratives on how Shakespeare has been yoked to American education. In these scholarly essays, we cross the professional and pedagogical realms of theater and book, stage and page. We provide snapshots of the theories and varied practices of Shakespearean education in diversified social, cultural, and political milieus over three hundred years. In each case, we ask what constitutes *education* and what constitutes *Shakespeare*; cumulatively, we query the nature of education, the nature of citizenship in a democracy, and the roles of literature, elocution, theater, and performance in both.

Expanding the notion of "education" beyond the classroom to literary clubs, private salons, public lectures, libraries, primers, and theatrical performance, this collection challenges scholars to consider how different groups in our society have adopted Shakespeare as part of a specifically "American" education. *Shakespearean Educations* maps the ways in which former slaves, Puritan ministers, university leaders, and working-class theatergoers used Shakespeare not only to educate themselves about literature and culture, but also to educate others about their own experience.

Unlike other recent works such as Frances Teague's *Shakespeare in American Popular Culture* (2006) or Kim Sturgess's *Shakespeare and the American Nation* (2003),[7] which provide broader investigations of Shakespeare's transformation into an American cultural icon, this collection crafts a series of microhistories, each of which explores the diverse educational processes that equipped many Americans to use Shakespeare to shape their national identities and establish their citizenship at critical junctures in American history. Today, most Americans first encounter Shakespeare in school (and many *never* encounter him in the theater). Yet scholars have generally overlooked the vital role that a Shakespearean education has played in creating a kind of *lingua franca* for different American communities over the centuries. Schoolboys of eighteenth-century Boston studied the same speeches that escaped slaves recited in their private literary clubs some seventy years later. Nineteenth-century female readers covertly learning about Shakespeare in their fathers' libraries encountered the same passages that Harvard professors would bring to the attention of their students in the early twentieth century.

Numerous Shakespearean phrases or allusions omnipresent in the news media, such as "sea change," "protesting too much," and "the better part of valor" have made their way into the contemporary American lexicon. But few Americans could identify the sources of these now-familiar phrases. That Shakespeare has become so enmeshed in our national vocabulary testifies to a widespread process of indoctrination. But the fact that the genealogy has largely disappeared in the process suggests that many Americans are no longer entirely sure *why* they learn Shakespeare. Is it an inherited obligation? Does it still convey cultural currency? Can it still be an act of defiance? A brief overview of the shifting educational contexts in which Americans have encountered Shakespeare may help to illuminate the case studies included in this volume, as well as suggesting areas for future study.

SHAKESPEARE IN PERFORMANCE

The debate over whether Shakespeare was an author to be read or a playwright to be performed haunted the colonies from the late seventeenth century until the eve of the American Revolution. Two of America's early colonial settlements—Pennsylvania and Massachusetts—openly disdained live theatrical performance as an activity that corrupted the morals of godly citizens. Part of that dislike of theater sprang from the perceived need among the Quaker and Puritan populations to reject the cultural, religious, and intellectual sway of Anglican English culture.[8] Both colonies firmly embedded antitheatrical prohibitions into their frames of government, thus helping to ensure that any Shakespearean educations in those regions would remain text based, rather than focused on the medium of performance. Colonies such as Virginia, Maryland, and South Carolina, on the other hand, sustained much more direct and cordial cultural ties with Anglican Britain.[9] In those regions, live theatrical performances offered a means of reaffirming cultural connections, of alleviating homesickness by allowing colonists to imagine that they were sharing in the cosmopolitan pleasures of their London counterparts some three thousand miles away. Touring companies traveled the circuit from Jamaica to New York, bringing Shakespeare's works (including *Hamlet, Richard III, Macbeth, The Merchant of Venice, Romeo and Juliet, Othello,* and *Julius Caesar,* as well as eighteenth-century adaptations of *The Taming of the Shrew* and *Cymbeline*) to enthusiastic audiences.[10] While these performances offered opportunities to indoctrinate colonial Americans into the works of Shakespeare, they also underscored the sharp boundaries that some colonists drew around what did or did not constitute a Shakespearean education. In a famous incident from 1766, theater manager David Douglass tried to bring Shakespeare's *Othello* to the colony of Rhode Island (which had issued a ban on theatrical entertainments the year before). Douglass sought to circumvent the law by claiming that he was presenting a "moral lecture on jealousy." This transparent ploy fooled no one, and he was forced to withdraw in defeat.[11] While this incident may seem a trivial example of a canny theater manager trying to trick local authorities, it can also point to a larger intellectual debate already being waged concerning the proper "sphere" and context for a Shakespearean education in American culture. If the citizens of Rhode Island, Massachusetts, and Pennsylvania rejected the theater as both the site and the medium for this education, where *was* the right setting and who would have control over the content and the delivery?

The coming of the American Revolution meant a temporary suspension of American theatrical entertainments (with bans issued by the Continental Congress in 1774 and again in 1778). The aftermath of the war brought pressing questions about how American culture would be reimagined. Could Americans still claim the cultural products of Great Britain, while eschewing its cultural authority? How could Americans uncouple the works of Shakespeare from their implicit identification with English citizenship?

The newly created country thus embarked on a long process of reinventing the meaning of Shakespeare in the classroom, in performance, and in everyday life. The urgent need to claim their own intellectual and cultural identity prompted Americans to imagine how they might perform their American-ness not merely *with* Shakespeare, but *through* Shakespeare, so that his works became the medium through which they enacted lessons of power and rituals of belonging.

Shakespeare experienced a revival on the American stage, as fledgling early national playhouses staged familiar prewar favorites. Old plays took on new meanings, as some read lessons of partisan politics in *King John,* or as others looked to plays such as *The Merchant of Venice* to debate the rights and status of Jewish American citizens after the war.[12] After their brief suppression during the Revolution, Shakespeare's plays reemerged triumphant, and they have occupied a prominent place in the American theater scene ever since—whether the plays were being performed in luxurious upper-class playhouses or cellar rooms in taverns, whether they were adapted into operas or transmogrified into minstrel shows. As scholars from Lawrence W. Levine to Michael D. Bristol have argued, Americans have developed a kind of literacy in Shakespeare strongly tied to our performance traditions.[13] Perhaps more significantly, Americans developed early on the habit of appropriating those aspects of Shakespeare they found particularly relevant to their own experiences into the vocabulary of their daily lives.

Witnessing a performance, however it might inspire emulation or admiration, does not automatically constitute an education. How was Shakespeare's work integrated into the other educational venues, models, and sources to which diverse populations of American citizens, slaves, and immigrants might have access?

SHAKESPEARE IN SCHOOL BEFORE THE CIVIL WAR

Prior to the American Revolution, each colony (and often each city or town) assumed responsibility for educating its citizens.[14] Certain topics, such as Latin and arithmetic, were widely considered to be part of a basic education. Some cities (such as Boston) established well-run schools for the most prominent young men in town—young men who would later seek further education at Harvard. Other regions, less wealthy, faced greater challenges in establishing strong school programs and networks. Yet the prevailing understanding, no matter the region, seems to have been that education was intended to fit a male citizen to occupy his destined role in society—one that would be shaped by his race, gender, and class. Thus the prewar system, whether delivered by schoolmasters in a small Latin school in New England or by a tutor on a Virginia plantation,[15] seems to have reinforced rather than challenged the dominant social hierarchies. Young men who might be expected to deliver political addresses in the Virginia House of Burgesses or before the governor of Massachusetts learned to model their oratory on the style of Roman political figures and Shakespeare's classical heroes, such as Brutus or Julius Caesar.

However, as historian Robert H. Wiebe notes, by the 1830s and 1840s, the "institutional web" of public education had meshed with the conviction that every American had " 'the *absolute right* to an education.' "[16] This democratization of public education meant greater access to opportunity among free black populations, among recent immigrants, and among women. Perhaps more importantly, it shifted the role of education from that of merely preparing a citizen to become a "republican machine," to equipping him (or her) to play an active role in American society.

In many ways, American education seems to have declared its independence from traditional systems of patronage and philanthropy in the early decades of the nineteenth century. The net effect rendered American educational institutions at once more homogenous and yet idiosyncratic. Wiebe notes that the uncoupling of educational systems from church, federal, or private philanthropies produced a population that regulated educational practices according to their local preferences and/or prejudices. While the broader goals may have included fitting pupils for citizenship, the path that each student would take might vary widely; perhaps more importantly, so would his final destination. Imagining education as a means to social transformation distinguished this new model from its prewar and early national forerunners. Shakespeare's work remained both visible and significant throughout this process of transformation.

SHAKESPEARE IN PRINT AND SHAKESPEARE ALOUD

Until 1795, Americans read their Shakespeare in books edited by British scholars and printed in Britain. In that year, publishers

Bioren and Madan of Philadelphia issued "the first complete edition of Shakespeare to be produced outside of Britain and Ireland." Its text, however, was based on a British edition.[17] Noting that the poet is "as yet but imperfectly known on the western shore of the Atlantic," the anonymous author of the preface spends most of it defending Shakespeare against charges of immorality, first by accusing Restoration playwrights of far worse. In contrast to Macheath or Horner, he declares, "The fools of Shakespeare are always despised, and his villains are always hated. . . . and while *The Country Wife* concludes with a dance of cuckolds, the abortive gallantry of Falstaff ends with a marriage."[18] Displaying as thorough a knowledge of eighteenth-century Shakespeare editors as of English drama, the author proclaims independence from the "inconvenient bulk" of emendations, notes, and commentary in British editions. This one will include only a single note by Dr. Johnson at the end of each play, and a glossary of obsolete words, because "an American reader is seldom disposed to wander through the wilderness of verbal criticism. An immense tract of excellent land, uncultivated, and even unexplored, presents an object more interesting to every mind than those ingenious literary trifles, that in Europe command so much attention."[19] By addressing itself to an American reader with distinct preferences and sensibilities, this edition links knowledge of Shakespeare to the idea of an American identity.

Other American editions quickly followed. In 1813, the first single-volume edition, affordable and portable, appeared. *The Illustrated Shakespeare* that issued from Harper and Brothers, New York, in 1847, a three-volume edition bound in red, gold-embossed leather and enriched by hundreds of etchings, marked a distinct moment in American Shakespeare scholarship. The editor, Gulian Crommelin Verplanck, a New York lawyer and congressman, used John Payne Collier's 1842–44 edition as a base but boldly recast Collier's text, notes, biography of Shakespeare, and other apparatus according to his own researches and opinions, thus "directing the attention of the American student [to the] progress of . . . the greatest and most original mind in our literature."[20] Not at all deferential to English forerunners, an American scholar lays claim to a common Anglo-American literature and to the learned institution of Shakespeare scholarship that originated in England.

A handwritten inscription in one American Shakespeare demonstrates that his works accompanied pioneers to the frontier: "This Volume left for California March 15, 1849 via the Way of the plains and arrived here the 17th day May 1851. Boneta."[21] Americans read Shakespeare on board whaling ships, as well as on the plains: one

Lincoln Colcord, "born at sea, the son of a shipmaster," notes that during his childhood voyages, the only books on board were "a Bible, a copy of Shakespeare, and a couple of cheap copies of *David Copperfield* and *Bleak House*."[22] For those far from a classroom, Shakespeare, like Dickens and the Bible, offered spiritual, moral, and sentimental education.

What in Shakespeare might have appealed specifically to these intrepid American pioneers and voyagers? Esther Cloudman Dunn speculates that as "a playwright of melodrama, oratory, and blood-stirring violence," Shakespeare was popular with those accustomed to rugged scenery and the physical struggles endemic to frontier life.[23] The social historian Lawrence Levine believes that the individualism of Shakespeare's heroes—their bold confrontations with authority and tradition—resonated with Americans: "Shakespeare's characters—like the Davy Crocketts and Mike Finks that dominated American folklore and the Jacksons, Websters, Clays, and Calhouns who dominated American politics—were larger than life: their passions, appetites, and dilemmas were of epic proportions. . . . All of them could be seen as the architects of their own fortune, the masters of their own fate."[24] The popularity of Edwin Forrest's muscular portrayals of frontier figures, native Americans, and Shakespearean monarchs alike offers perhaps the best example of American audiences' superimposing their own sense of rugged individualism on almost any heroic role during this period. Forrest transformed Macbeth, Othello, Richard III, and King Lear into models of *American* masculinity.[25]

Americans' growing affinity for Shakespeare during the nineteenth century can also be explained by a kinship between the long-established role of oratory, in both schools and public life, and Shakespeare's fine declamatory speeches, with their piling up of parallel phrases and emotional climaxes. Walt Whitman recalls "declaiming some stormy passage from Julius Caesar or Richard" as he rode down Broadway in an omnibus.[26] Shakespeare may have been published in the form of complete plays and complete works, but he was often memorized and recited in the form of single speeches. For an illiterate or semiliterate audience on the high seas or the frontier, hearing Shakespeare declaimed in the prevalent high, florid style exemplified the power of language at its highest.

Shakespeare was a key figure in the elocutionary movement that shaped American education throughout the eighteenth and nineteenth centuries. The oratorical manuals that circulated both inside and beyond schools used his speeches out of context as models of eloquence and persuasive power. Generations of grade-school and high-school children learned to declaim Polonius's advice to Laertes or Iago's strictures on jealousy as exemplars of how to evoke and mold the passions in elegant English and, by implication, as lessons in moral conduct. Neither the speaker's merits nor the dramatic context of his advice was considered relevant. Rather, the point was to abstract from the plays what was useful to ordinary Americans. While this denaturing of Shakespeare's work might initially seem to diminish his power and authority, it allowed his texts to become a kind of palimpsest upon which Americans continually reinscribed new notions of identity and belonging.

Thus, Shakespeare's language, quite apart from his plays as aesthetic objects or theatrical performances, became an oral and aural means of training Americans to use their native language as an instrument of self-improvement and as cultural capital. Lectures about Shakespeare were part of this phenomenon, too. Audiences paid to hear preachers, teachers, and public intellectuals on lecture circuits discuss Shakespeare as a moral, religious, and political thinker. Most famously, Ralph Waldo Emerson included Shakespeare in a lecture series that was later published as *Representative Men* in 1850. Henry N. Hudson, editor of an eleven-volume *Complete Works* that sold well for more than thirty years, also lectured on Shakespeare to large audiences. His talks could be tantamount to dramatic performance. A contemporary account portrays Hudson as "charged with a kind of electric light, burdened with a kind of volcanic energy, struggling to find exit in flashes or volumes of expression . . . by tones, emphasis and accent, gestures, contortions and gyrations . . . inspiring his hearers and pupils with his own enthusiasm."[27] Even unschooled Americans who did not go to the theater or read Shakespeare on their own could thus learn of his significance and experience his power as a literary artist. A related form of Shakespearean education could be obtained through attending readings of the plays. In 1849, Fanny Kemble, daughter of the renowned English Shakespearean actor Charles Kemble and niece of the equally famous actress Mrs. Siddons, read entire plays aloud at the Stuyvesant Institute in New York three evenings a week and at noon on Mondays, drawing enraptured crowds of six or seven hundred.[28]

Toward the end of the nineteenth century, as millions of non-English speaking immigrants arrived, knowing Shakespeare became one way of establishing a new national identity. In 1895, twenty-six different ethnic groups lived within the thirty blocks nearest to Hull House, the Chicago center founded by Jane Addams in 1889 to promote immigrant education and social advancement.[29] There, prospective American citizens took courses in subjects ranging from Dante to needlework, attended lectures and performances, and participated in special interest clubs. The Shakespeare Club flourished continuously for sixteen years.[30] Shakespeare's plays were performed by several Hull House dramatic groups, along with Ibsen's works, Greek tragedy, and new plays by the immigrants themselves. In 1901, for example, the Lincoln Club, consisting of fourteen Jewish teenagers, put on a production of *The Merry Wives of Windsor.* Madge Jennison, who directed it, commented, "We rehearsed until eleven o'clock, and then sometimes we sat and talked of the play until midnight. . . . I never told them to read the notes and commissaries [*sic*], but they did; there came this hunger to understand."[31] The performers learned correct English pronunciation, enjoyed a camaraderie that broke down the isolation of long workdays, and gained a certain entrée into American culture—through Shakespeare. They brought their own knowledge and experiences to the text, believing them to be as valid as any scholarly commentary. Unlike others, Jane Addams and her colleagues advocated a cosmopolitan standard of cultural values, and did not hold Shakespeare to be the icon of an Anglo-Saxon culture fundamental to American identity.[32]

Percy MacKaye, author and director of the "community masque" *Caliban by the Yellow Sands,* did. Performed in New York in 1916 and in Boston in 1917, before audiences totaling more than 300,000, *Caliban* dramatizes the education of its titular hero, a surrogate for the millions of nonnative speakers pressing for citizenship. That education consists of learning to love Shakespeare as personified by Prospero, who conjures up a panoply of scenes from Shakespeare's plays that civilizes the ignorant, rebellious Caliban. In one of the play's many huge spectacles, immigrant groups carrying banners representing their original countries celebrate the bard's universal preeminence.[33] Although this construction of an Anglo-Saxon Shakespeare by no means prevailed, it did persist. When Joseph Quincy Adams, "Supervisor of Research" for the newly founded Folger Shakespeare Library, gave his inaugural speech in 1932, he called immigration "a menace to the preservation of our long-established English civilization" and portrayed the study of Shakespeare from grade school on as "the cornerstone of cultural discipline."[34] Fortunately, Americans' engagement with Shakespeare has been far less the cultural discipline than Adams thought it was, and far more a series of contestatory, innovative reinventions.

SHAKESPEARE IN THE TRANSFORMATION
OF AMERICAN EDUCATION

In the aftermath of the Civil War, higher education in America was gradually systematized, professionalized, and diversified, both locally and nationally. Before the war, college teaching had been a branch of genteel amateurism, ranking far below law or the ministry and requiring private income to supplement meager salaries. An ideology of "mental discipline" drove the curriculum, in which Greek, Latin, mathematics, and moral philosophy were taught through drill, recitation, and oral quizzes, with emphasis on developing "character" and little attention to content and meaning. Science, modern languages, modern literature such as Shakespeare, and modern history were not included: it was assumed that gentlemen would already be conversant with literature.[35]

During the 1870s and 1880s, colleges and universities began to follow new European models, whether that of the German research university devoted to training specialized scholars along scientific lines, or that based on an ideal of liberal culture aiming for breadth of knowledge and the formation of taste and sensibility. By around 1900, either model required a professoriate trained abroad, preferably with a doctoral degree from a German university.[36] In line with these developments, for the first time Shakespeare became an object of formal study rather than an extracurricular source of knowledge and cultural enrichment.

This important cultural relocation did not come about easily or transparently. In defining themselves, English departments struggled to find a balance between the quasi-scientific philological study of the historical development of *language,* and a humanistic approach to *literature* as "a moral and spiritual force and a repository of 'general ideas' which could be applied directly to the conduct of life and the improvement of national culture."[37] In this struggle between philologists and belletrists, Shakespeare could be a bargaining chip as curricula were designed and revised: Shakespeare often showed up in the ambiguous second year of "new, 'literary' subjects—those which were *neither* rhetoric and composition *nor* historical linguistics."[38] In an 1895 article, Charles Mills Gayley, chair of the English department at the University of California at Berkeley, explains that "literary science [*sic*] is in a transitional stage. . . . The study of literature in the sentimental, the formally stylistic, or the second-hand-historical fashion, is out of date. Scholars in philology—narrowed to linguistics—have set a new pace by making of their branch a genetic study . . . of sources, causes, relations, movements, and effects." Then, mindful of humanistic claims, he cautions that "the method . . . is not necessarily of universal applicability" and diplomatically recommends a "synthesis of the courses and methods of a department" to form "a system."[39] Gayley himself straddled the line: while presiding over Berkeley's meticulously systematic English curriculum, he gave spellbinding lectures on Shakespeare that stressed not philology but poetry, character, and ethical values.

Concurrently, the institutions of Shakespeare scholarship arose, fostered more by a tradition of genteel antiquarianism than by the professoriat. The Shakespeare Society of Philadelphia, founded in 1852, was the first formal organization in America dedicated to the study of Shakespeare. Meeting every month to read and discuss plays (and to enjoy fine dinners of several courses), lawyers and gentlemen dealt with the same textual variants, cruces, and emendations as did scholarly editors, and a small reference library was established for this purpose. Out of this society grew the *New Variorum Shakespeare,* a series of single volume editions comprehending all previous scholarship, edited by Horace Howard Furness. A lawyer by training, Furness devoted his time entirely from 1872 on to editing the series and to accumulating early editions of Shakespeare, criticism, and theater records, as well as works by other sixteenth- and seventeenth-century writers. As Michael Bristol notes, at this point, "Shakespeare was the concern of well-educated individuals with sufficient wealth and leisure to devote to such a highly specialized ensemble of secular interests" (this description also applies to Henry Clay Folger, who founded the Folger Shakespeare Library).[40] But Furness went on to establish a Department of English at the University of Pennsylvania; today, the Furness collection is housed at that university, for the use of students, faculty, and independent scholars.

Even as Shakespeare entered the hallowed halls of the Ivy League or became enshrined in collections such as those of Folger or Furness, he penetrated the most pervasive form of American "education" of the late nineteenth and early twentieth centuries: advertising. Shakespeare became a collectible product, whose images, characters, and quotations appeared on everything from candy wrappers to calendars to greeting cards. These new forms—not contained within the covers of leather-bound books or enclosed within the four walls of a playhouse, lyceum, or classroom—allowed Americans to "write" their own versions of Shakespeare by decorating scrapbooks, toy chests, walls, or keepsake boxes. In these objects, Americans created what

Ellen Gruber Garvey labels "indexes of the heart."[41] Where half a century earlier, Melville had bemoaned America's obsession with Shakespeare, by the beginning of the twentieth century, Shakespeare had become firmly entrenched in almost every aspect of American life. Yet Americans had demonstrated that they would read, hear, and engage with Shakespeare on their own terms, not those of their erstwhile British rulers.

SHAKESPEAREAN EDUCATIONS

Shakespearean Educations is divided into four sections. Part I, "Educating Citizens," traces the presence of Shakespeare in colonial, early national, and antebellum America. These essays explore the range of educational options open to groups who aspired to enjoy American citizenship to its fullest, whether black, white, female, immigrant, or working class. They also investigate the obstacles presented by religious opposition, geographical isolation, or racial, ethnic, gender, or class prejudice. Jennifer Mylander undertakes the challenge of finding traces of Shakespeare in colonial America, when antitheatrical prejudice ran high in New England and when theatrical activities in those regions had to be undertaken clandestinely (if at all). Heather S. Nathans describes how former slaves sometimes proffered their Shakespearean education as proof of their fitness to participate in white American culture, and the struggle of white artisan-class workers to establish their own educational venues in which to enjoy Shakespeare. Sandra M. Gustafson's essay examines the use of Shakespeare in the development of American political and racial rhetoric, observing that by the mid-nineteenth century Frederick Douglass had begun to use Shakespearean texts ironically, against his white oppressors.

Part II, "Moral and Practical Educations," features essays that examine Shakespeare's role in the shaping and standardizing of American education in the nineteenth century. Jonathan Burton suggests that books such as the widely used *McGuffey Readers* used Shakespeare to teach moral lessons (continuing a tradition of the eighteenth-century stage). Like Nan Johnson, he argues that a Shakespearean education in antebellum America was used by some to establish boundaries, not necessarily of class, but of moral and intellectual participation in the young nation.

Part III, "Ivy-Covered Shakespeare," charts the first forays into formalizing a Shakespearean education in the nation's colleges and universities. Elizabeth Renker argues that by the end of the nineteenth century, institutions of higher education began to "de-democratize" Shakespeare, appropriating him as a guardian for the intellectual (if not economic) elite. Denise Albanese investigates how Shakespeare became a kind of "historical sedimentation" in higher education—the foundation upon which advanced studies were presumed to be built. Dayton Haskin and Coppélia Kahn explore Shakespeare's transformation into a "custodian of culture," as faculty at Harvard integrated him into the college curriculum and, at Berkeley, used professorial cachet to move Shakespeare *outside* academia.

Part IV, "Back to the Future," examines Shakespeare's reemergence from the classroom. His successful incorporation into the American educational system at the end of the nineteenth century fundamentally transformed the ways in which Americans between the world wars imagined and absorbed their Shakespeare, whether in or out of the classroom. Marvin McAllister recounts the history of Howard University's first amateur dramatics club, which chose *The Merry Wives of Windsor* as its inaugural production—identifying it not as a play embedded in issues of racial identity, but as one that offered African American students the opportunity to demonstrate their scholarly and artistic grasp of the form. Interestingly, McAllister notes that the club also selected the play because the club's selection committee thought that its middle-class characters and engaging prose (rather than poetic) dialogue might be more accessible and interesting to students. Rosemary Kegl discusses the World's Fair of 1934, with its massive reconstruction of Shakespeare's Globe, imagined as a draw for the city's teachers and the nation's adoring Shakespeare fans. The World's Fair Globe was conceived as a site where families (presumably already familiar with Shakespeare) might congregate to experience "live" what they had only learned about in school.

Shakespearean Educations concludes with an afterword by Theodore Leinwand, speculating on how contemporary educators might approach the challenge of integrating Shakespeare into the classroom. Leinwand suggests that modern educators should exercise the same freedoms that so many of our predecessors did in reinventing the definition of a Shakespearean education for a new kind of student. What emerges from the essays overall is a debate over the ways in which Shakespearean educations continue to shape culture and our contemporary notion of what constitutes a "real" education.

NOTES

1. William Shakespeare, *The Taming of the Shrew*, in Stephen Greenblatt, gen. ed., *The Norton Shakespeare, Based on the Oxford Edition* (New York: W.W. Norton, 1997), 1.2.153.

2. This project emerged from a national conference on 16 to 17 March 2007, sponsored by the Folger Shakespeare Library and the National Endowment for the Humanities. Scholars collaborated over a twelve-month period to fashion essays that would speak to one another across a diverse range of fields, from American history and American studies, to theater, rhetoric, and English.

3. For more on the development of American cultural identity in relation to a British one, see Susan Harris Smith, *American Drama: The Bastard Art* (Cambridge: Cambridge University Press, 1997); Leonard Tennenhouse, *The Importance of Feeling English: American Literature and the British Diaspora, 1750–1850* (Princeton: Princeton University Press, 2007); and Michael Warner, *The Letters of the Republic: Publication and the Public Sphere in Eighteenth-Century America* (Cambridge: Harvard University Press, 1990).

4. See a discussion of Barker's work in *When They Weren't Doing Shakespeare: Essays on Nineteenth-Century British and American Theatre*, ed. Judith Fisher and Stephen Watt (Athens: University of Georgia Press, 1989).

5. Orestes Brownson, "Specimens of Foreign Standard Literature," *Boston Quarterly Review* (1838), rpt. in *Americans on Shakespeare 1776–1914*, ed. Peter Rawlings (Aldershot, UK: Ashgate, 1999), 72.

6. Herman Melville, "Hawthorne and His Mosses, by a Virginian Spending a July in Vermont," *Literary World* 7 (1850), rpt. in *Americans on Shakespeare*, 165.

7. See Frances Teague, *Shakespeare and the American Popular Stage* (Cambridge: Cambridge University Press, 2006); and Kim Sturgess, *Shakespeare and the American Nation* (Cambridge: Cambridge University Press, 2004).

8. For more on colonial and early American antitheatricalism, see Heather S. Nathans, *Early American Theatre from the Revolution to Thomas Jefferson: Into the Hands of the People* (Cambridge: Cambridge University Press, 2003).

9. For a discussion of performances in theater-friendly colonies in the pre-Revolutionary period, see Odai Johnson, *Absence and Memory in Colonial American Theatre: Fiorelli's Plaster* (New York: Palgrave Macmillan Press, 2006); and Hugh F. Rankin, *The Theater in Colonial America* (Chapel Hill: University of North Carolina Press, 1965).

10. Notices of these performances may be found in contemporary American newspapers. They also appear in published daybooks of the colonial and early national theaters, including George C. Odell, *Annals of the New York Stage*, 15 vols. (New York: Columbia University Press, 1927–49); Thomas Clark Pollock, *The Philadelphia Theatre in the Eighteenth Century, Together with the Day Book of the Same Period* (New York: Greenwood Press, 1968); and Eola Willis, *The Charleston Stage in the XVIII Century: With Social Settings of the Time* (Columbia, SC: State Co., 1924).

11. Rankin, 93–94.

12. Nathans, *Early American Theatre*, 158; and Heather S. Nathans, "A Much Maligned People: Jews On and Off the Stage in the Early American Republic," *Early American Studies* 2.2 (2004): 310–42.

13. See Michael D. Bristol, *Shakespeare's America, America's Shakespeare: Literature, Institution, Ideology in the United States* (London: Routledge, 1990); and Lawrence W.

Levine, *Highbrow/Lowbrow: The Emergence of Cultural Hierarchy in America* (Cambridge: Harvard University Press, 1988).

14. For more on how the colonies structured their early schooling systems (including issues of regionalism), see Jack P. Greene, *Pursuits of Happiness: The Social Development of Early Modern British Colonies and the Formation of American Culture* (Chapel Hill: University of North Carolina Press, 1988).

15. For more on the life and experiences of a private tutor in the Southern colonies, see *Journal & Letters of Philip Vickers Fithian, 1773–1774: A Plantation Tutor of the Old Dominion*, ed. Hunter Dickinson Farish (Williamsburg, VA: Colonial Williamsburg, Inc., 1943).

16. Robert H. Wiebe, *The Opening of American Society: From the Adoption of the Constitution to the Eve of Disunion* (New York: Random House, 1984), 309 (emphasis in the original).

17. Andrew Murphy, *Shakespeare in Print: A History and Chronology of Shakespeare Publishing* (Cambridge: Cambridge University Press, 2003), 145–46.

18. "Preface to the American Edition," in *The Plays and Poems of William Shakespeare* (Philadelphia: Bioren and Madan, 1795), rpt. in Kim C. Sturgess, *Shakespeare and the American Nation* (Cambridge: Cambridge University Press, 2004), 212–14.

19. "Preface," in *Shakespeare and the American Nation*, 216.

20. Gulian Crommelin Verplanck, "Preface," in *The Illustrated Shakespeare*, 3 vols. (New York: Harper and Brothers, 1847), x.

21. Virginia Mason Vaughan and Alden T. Vaughan, eds., *Shakespeare in American Life* (Washington, DC: Folger Shakespeare Library, 2007), 138 (catalog of the exhibition of the same name at the Folger Shakespeare Library, March 8–August 18, 2007).

22. Esther Cloudman Dunn, *Shakespeare in America* (New York: Macmillan Company, 1939), 6.

23. Dunn, 175.

24. Levine, 41.

25. Much has been written of Forrest's aggressively masculine style, and of his habit of re-writing well-known plays to suit his needs. For two strong overviews of Forrest's importance to the development of nineteenth-century masculinity in performance, see David Grimsted, *Melodrama Unveiled: American Theatre and Culture, 1800–1850* (Berkeley: University of California Press, 1968); and Bruce A. McConachie, *Melodramatic Formations: American Theatre and Society, 1820–1870* (Iowa City: Iowa University Press, 1992).

26. Walt Whitman, *Specimen Days* (Boston: David R. Godine, 1971), 10.

27. Murphy, 152.

28. Dorothy Marshall, *Fanny Kemble* (New York: St. Martin's Press, 1977), 220.

29. Victoria Bissel Brown, ed., "Introduction," in *Twenty Years at Hull-House, with Auto-Biographical Notes by Jane Addams* (New York: Bedford/St. Martin's Press, 1999), 18.

30. *Twenty Years at Hull-House*, 198.

31. Quoted in Shannon Jackson, *Lines of Activity: Performance, Historiography, Hull-House Domesticity* (Ann Arbor: University of Michigan Press, 2000), 217. See also Thomas Cartelli, *Repositioning Shakespeare: National Formations, Postcolonial Appropriations* (London and New York: Routledge, 1999), 46–62; and Stuart Hecht, *Hull-House Theater: An Analytical and Evaluative History* (Ann Arbor, MI: University Microfilms International, 1991).

32. Jackson, in *Lines of Activity*, 224.

33. For interpretations of MacKaye's pageant, see Cartelli, 63–83; and Coppélia

Kahn, "Caliban at the Stadium: Shakespeare and the Making of Americans," *Massachusetts Review* 42.2 (2000): 256–84.

34. Joseph Quincy Adams, "Shakespeare in American Education" (excerpt from his address at the dedication of the Folger Shakespeare Library) in *Shakespeare for Students* (New York: Houghton Mifflin, n.d.). In addition to a portion of Adams's address, this fifteen-page pamphlet contains advertisements for Shakespeare books published by Houghton Mifflin.

35. See Laurence Veysey, *The Emergence of the American University* (Chicago: University of Chicago Press, 1965), 9, 24.

36. Veysey, 283.

37. Gerald Graff and Michael Warner, eds., *The Origins of Literary Study in America: A Documentary Anthology* (London: Routledge, 1989), 6.

38. Ibid., 12.

39. Charles Mills Gayley, "English at the University of California," in *Origins of Literary Study*, 58–59.

40. Bristol, 67.

41. Ellen Gruber Garvey, "Scissoring and Scrapbooks: Reading, Remaking, and Recirculating," in *New Media, 1740–1915* (Cambridge: MIT Press, 2003), 207–28, esp. 214.

I
Educating Citizens

Instruction and English Refinement in America: Shakespeare, Antitheatricality, and Early Modern Reading

Jennifer Mylander

FROM THEIR FIRST VOYAGES TO AMERICAN LANDS, EARLY MODERN ENGLISH men and women packed books for the long journey across the Atlantic. The earliest evidence of English books in America exists in a record that notes only their destruction. In 1590, when John White returned belatedly to the Roanoke settlement with supplies, he found the colony abandoned, with no sign of the settlers except for the word "Croatoan" carved into a tree. White's record of this voyage, later printed in Hakluyt's *Principal Nauigations,* details what remained of the settlement: "about the place many of my things spoyled and broken, and *my bookes torne from the covers . . .* this could bee no other but the dede of the Savages our enemies at Dasamongwepeuk."[1] White attributed this destruction as the malicious act of angry "enemies" who knew the items were valued by the English. Nearly a century later, English books were again targets, as minister John Eliot notes that copies of the "Indian Bible" printed in Algonquian were destroyed during King Philip's War, probably because, as Jill Lepore concludes, "Algonquians hostile to Christianity seized the books as a symbol of the pernicious influence of English culture and destroyed any they came upon."[2] Among the "praying Indians" converted through English missionary projects, printed books took on additional significance as grave goods, as evidenced by the recovery of a page from a printed Bible in a Native American grave; orthodox New England settlers used a similar custom of pinning printed elegies to the funeral hearse. Even in their absence, books were culturally significant, as in Jamestown in 1608 when colonists accused the leader Edward Maria Wingfield of being an atheist because he did not have a Bible.[3] These stories suggest that the transatlantic pan-English culture was a culture of the book and that the Algonquian and Iroquoian peoples that lined the American coast recognized the importance of this feature.

While books were, in bare practical terms, luxury items, significant evidence suggests that they were indispensable for English colonists of a wide range of wealth and status levels. The vast majority of the printed books in British America before 1725 were English imprints that served as valuable markers of English culture in the unfamiliarity of the "New World"; in this role, they were instrumental to colonists who continued to identify themselves not as "Americans" but as the English in America.[4] Driven by fear of degeneration due to exposure to supposedly "savage" lands and peoples, colonists sought to fix a stable, invulnerable English identity. Competition and, eventually, conflict with indigenous Americans were essential in budding constructions of English "civilized" society, as can be inferred from Cotton Mather's description of profane colonial lifestyles as becoming "Indianized."[5] For some English colonists, most notably John Eliot and his colleagues in the New England mission, printed books were quite literally symbolic of English culture. As Matthew Brown shows, writers for the mission construct tales of indigenous peoples expressing "awe" at book technology, yet these stories convey English, not Native American, "bibliophilia": printed books "are figured as monuments, as products of civilization, products that symbolize its antiquity and record its history in iconic, totemic terms."[6]

Like John White returning to Roanoke, historians of reading in early America face limited textual and material traces of early colonial book culture. Wills, probate inventories, and letters of individual book owners offer the best records of what English books were present in the colonies during the seventeenth century. These materials can be supplemented with records from the surviving letter book of John Usher, one of the most successful Boston booksellers in the 1670s and 1680s.[7] Complicating any investigation of a particular author's circulation, such as Shakespeare's, in this early period is the fact that most records of private ownership simply list "books" or "a parcel of books" rather than identifying each by title or author, although the monetary values given to these bundles can vary widely.[8] Surviving records suggest that copies of Shakespeare's works were scarce in seventeenth-century English colonies, with only two records that confirm colonists reading Shakespeare for the entire century. Elnathan Chauncey, son of a Harvard College president, quoted from *Venus and Adonis* in his commonplace book in 1661, although study of his selections throughout this journal has revealed that he likely encountered Shakespeare only through a printed miscellany of verse filled with anonymous excerpts. The only confirmed book of Shakespeare in the seventeenth-century colonies, therefore, is the copy of *Macbeth* listed in the 1699 probate inventory of Arthur Spicer of Richmond County, Virginia.[9] And yet, not long after, in 1723, the complete six-volume edition of Shakespeare's *Works* was cataloged in the library of Harvard College, enshrined as a valuable collection for advanced readers alongside the classical and theological works that dominated the collection. This reference is matched by several records of private libraries containing Shakespeare in the early eighteenth century: William Bladen of Maryland, Cotton Mather of Massachusetts, and Edmund Berkeley of Virginia are just a few of the colonial readers who owned Shakespeare's complete plays before 1725.[10] The first recorded North American colonial production of a Shakespeare play was put on a few years later, with an amateur performance of *Romeo and Juliet* in New York in 1730.[11]

How do we account for the respect and authority conveyed by Harvard's acquisition of Shakespeare's *Works* by 1723 if we interpret the *absence of records* of Shakespeare's texts in the preceding century to mean that his texts were themselves absent? The dramatic increase in records mentioning Shakespeare may indicate that the earlier absence of references to Shakespeare in the seventeenth century tells us more about the lack of cultural value placed on printed playbooks than it does about their circulation. Lacking the cultural and literary value we place on these texts today, Shakespeare's playbooks were measured in this early period by their minimal resale value: small playbooks of individual plays by Shakespeare were often clustered with other small unbound quartos in early modern library inventories. Even in library catalogues that detail valuable volumes, inexpensive books were often left unidentified, as in the Salem, Massachusetts, inventory of Rebekah Bacon in 1655 that includes "Calvins Institutions, Luther upon the Galatians, M' Shepards Morality of the Sabath . . . & 10 smal bookes."[12] Although this discrepancy may seem odd, it reflects attitudes not entirely unfamiliar. A catalog of a private person's library written today would not likely be an objective record of all reading materials: instead, it might focus on works of cultural or historical value (first editions, autographed copies, hard covers, et cetera) while giving lower priority to books deemed less culturally significant (children's books, cookbooks) and likely omitting entirely reading materials considered ephemera (magazines, newspapers) or physically damaged.[13] Book catalogs from the early modern period similarly replicate colonists' attitudes about the comparative value of dramatic and other texts; as a result, most of the records of Shakespeare ownership before 1740 are records of the *Works* or *Complete Plays* rather than less prestigious, more affordable (and likely more common) individual playbooks. Single-text playbooks were often marketed in the period through title-page advertisements of theatrical productions, and, as a result, were more closely aligned with rates of theatrical performances than large-format collections of a playwright's works; as a result, single-text playbooks would be more subject to the antitheatrical attitudes that prevailed in the seventeenth-century colonies.[14]

While the value of dramatic *texts* varied in this period, the comparative value of *books* stayed fairly consistent: larger volumes (such as Shakespeare's multiple-play volumes or collected *Works*) were consistently assessed at higher values and were, therefore, more frequently cataloged.[15] The significant increase in records referring to Shakespeare's texts in the early eighteenth century confirms that his collected *Works* circulated more widely in this period, but it does not preclude the possibility that single-text playbooks circulated but were not recorded.

THE CIRCULATION OF ENGLISH IMPRINTS IN COLONIAL AMERICA

Literary studies of Shakespeare in early America usually focus on the first complete edition of the plays in America, printed in Philadelphia in 1795. This edition is significant for the early national period both economically and culturally, but evidence like this from the history of printing should not be taken as transparent evidence of the history of reading.[16] Arguments that assume that English imprints of Shakespeare's plays must have been expensive, exotic, or hard to come by before the 1795 Philadelphia printing underestimate the significance of the transatlantic book trade and misrepresent the dominant colonial book culture.

Although the combined products of North American presses were important new hybrids born of colonial print culture, in terms of circulation they fulfilled a minor supplemental role before 1750. I estimate that books printed in Massachusetts accounted for only ten percent of the books identified in library inventories in New England before the eighteenth century. American imprints are even less prominent outside of this region, and it is not unusual to come across a private book catalog without any American imprints listed.[17] Even assuming that most book owners in the period would have also owned a locally printed almanac, this factor would not substantially shift the average relative percentage of English to American imprints. One of the primary reasons for the American colonial presses fulfilling only a supplemental role in this early period is that they had to import their paper, so it was often most cost efficient to import a printed book. The first paper mill in English America was founded in 1690, but the American colonies did not produce enough paper for their needs until the Revolutionary War disrupted trade with Great Britain.[18]

Reading practices were more complex and social in the colonial period than is sometimes recognized, and the range of reading materials was fairly broad. As I have suggested, colonial readership was far from limited to the products of the colonial presses: books imported from England formed the core of domestic and circulating libraries, well into the eighteenth century. Hugh Amory, comparing English books exported to the North American colonies with the American imprints compiled in the North American Imprints Program, concludes that there were approximately ten times more English imprints than American imprints circulating in the colonies until the mid-1770s.[19] Readers might pick up a *New-England Primer* and a locally printed almanac from the same bookstore where they bought the English-printed devotional guides, conduct books, and other books that were, according to David Hall, "at the very center of traditional literacy" because they sold steadily throughout the colonial period.[20] In addition to stocking steady sellers, colonial bookstalls and their hawkers supplied a range of novelty books such as a single-text playbook by Shakespeare. Thomas Goddard Wright confirms that colonists were "at no greater handicap than if they had been living in some remote place in the north or west of England."[21] In order to convey the scope of the transatlantic trade, James Raven analyzed the eighteenth-century custom totals in the port books at the English Public Record Office, estimating that at least five percent of the total English production was shipped to the mainland colonies for booksellers. Based on these and other records, Raven concludes that the steady demand for English books increased throughout the late seventeenth and into the eighteenth centuries; by the late eighteenth century this demand outstripped population growth.[22] Actual circulation of English imprints in British America must be even higher than the totals of official trade since thousands of books were brought in the personal luggage of immigrants or shipped by individuals in England as gifts, donations, and inheritances.

In her study of the first American printing of Shakespeare's complete *Plays and Poems,* Kim Sturgess analyzes the significance of this 1795 edition without first establishing what Shakespeare editions colonists would have read in the decades preceding this printing.

Sturgess implies that consumers had only been reading Shake-speare's plays in multitext compilations during the colonial period. As a result, she argues that the 1795 edition made Shakespeare more popular by "reduc[ing]" the "cost of access" to Shakespeare's texts for American readers, although this is difficult to establish without comparative prices. She suggests that prohibitively high costs have previously been a "barrier to a wider acceptance of the text" and that this obstacle is lifted by the publishers of the Philadelphia edi-tion, but does not address the significance of the edition as multi-text—if early national publishers had wanted to reach the widest possible audience by creating an inexpensive edition of a Shake-speare text, a single-text playbook of *Romeo and Juliet* or *Richard III* would have been more affordable than even a single volume of the collected plays. In many ways, Sturgess makes a strong case for the importance of prefatory and other paratextual features for interpre-tation of Shakespeare's cultural value for early national readers, but her interesting account of the 1795 Philadelphia edition would be strengthened by additional consideration of the role of English imprints in colonial reading.[23]

Much recent work is indebted to Lawrence Levine's suggestion that the reading of Shakespeare was "confined to a relatively small, educated elite" in the eighteenth century, while performances of the plays were more inclusively popular. Levine focuses on the devel-opment of popular theatrical entertainments based on Shakespeare in American venues, but his attention to the circulation of perform-ances need not exclude the possibility of the circulation of Shake-speare's plays in printed books. While Levine's conclusion about the reading of Shakespeare as "confined" and "elite" is surely accurate in the sense that not all colonists were literate in the period, it hints at a sense of reading as the studious, silent reading practiced by colo-nists who could afford expensive folios and elegant parlors in which to read them.[24] However, printed books often stretched beyond the reading literate in the colonial period because reading was often aloud or in groups; while education was surely one purpose for read-ing, so was entertainment: Virginian William Byrd, for example, describes passing the time during inclement weather reading *The Beggar's Opera* for listeners.[25]

BOOKSELLER JOHN USHER AND ANTITHEATRICALITY

Closer examination of John Usher's successful colonial booksell-ing business in the 1680s offers a glimpse into the English imprints regularly imported in orthodox New England.[26] Usher was one of the most successful Boston book merchants in the 1670s and 1680s, at a point when the Boston trade was rapidly expanding: Boston employed as many as fifteen booksellers in the thirty years from 1669 to 1699.[27] This total does not count the approximately dozen publishers of this period who were employed as merchants otherwise but participated (probably as investors) in the publication of one or more Massachusetts imprints. Even if we account for possible rapid turnover among these merchants, it seems safe to estimate that the Boston book market was able to sustain eight to ten book specialists at a time in the last quarter of the seventeenth century.

Surviving records from John Usher's business in the 1680s show that a colonial bookdealer's business was by no means small, even in comparison with London standards. When John Dunton came to Boston in the 1680s to sell excess stock he described Usher as "very Rich, adventures much to sea; but has got his Estate by Bookselling."[28] After Usher offered to buy Dunton's entire stock, Dunton describes him with the respect he would offer a colleague, on par with London bookdealers. Invoices in Usher's letter book give us a detailed look at the range of English imprints imported regularly in the years 1682 to 1685. In March of 1683/4, Usher imported approximately seven hundred and fifty copies of seventy-one English titles. Usher paid London stationer Richard Chiswell £61 5s. 6d. for these volumes and spent an additional £50 17s. 0d. on stationery in the same shipment. Only two and a half months later, Usher purchased more books and stationery totaling £40 3s. 7d. This inventory records forty-eight English imprints in over three hundred copies.[29] Looking at these records Hugh Amory concludes, "between 3,500 and 4,000 volumes were annually exported to Boston in the 1680s, and . . . they sold out, since orders would not otherwise have continued." Usher's London supplier Robert Boulter sent shipments valuing £445 11s. 6d. between 1679 and 1683, and Richard Chiswell sent a total of £567 in the first five years of the 1680s.[30]

Generic analysis of Usher's invoices confirms much of what we know about English bookstalls and literary value in the early modern period, showing colonial cultural standards similar to (or in emulation of) the metropolis. One significant difference between Usher's stock and the range of English production, for the purposes of this study, is the lack of English-language dramatic texts such as Shakespeare. Usher's stock is dominated by English imprints and his inventories resemble contemporary London book shops with the exception of the antitheatrical bias of his imports. Texts that we would classify as literary today, English-language poetry and narra-

tive prose, make up only five percent of imports. Of literature now
recognized as canonical, Usher imported four copies of *Paradise
Lost,* one copy of the *Arcadia,* and two copies of the Earl of Rochester's poems. While much of the literature he imports is related to
Protestantism, like Benjamin Keach's *War with the Devil,* which is an
engaging narrative dialogue of a youth's moral quandaries, he does
import a few items that may seem surprising in "Puritan" New
England, such as three copies of the erotic novel, anti-Catholic piece
Venus in the Cloyster. The large volume of Usher's business suggests
that he may have been involved in some wholesale bookselling to
owners of general stores throughout British America. But even if
Usher's sales far outweighed those of his Boston bookseller competitors, Usher did not dominate the business to the extent that he
squeezed other merchants out of bookselling, which speaks to a
thriving book market even at this early period.[31]

Significantly, Usher's selections suggest an antitheatrical bias:
although surviving records from Usher's business are from a decade
before Massachusetts's 1699 ban on theater (and this later legislation is directed at the prevention of performances rather than
explicitly at reading or owning dramatic texts), Usher does not
import Shakespeare or any other English-language dramatic texts in
the five years of records that survive from his business.[32] Usher's
omission of vernacular theatrical texts may have been the result of
his personal values or a concession to the marketplace he served,
but it is worth noting that he did import classical drama. In April of
1685 Usher received "12 Lattine Terrence," most likely a collection
of Terrence's greatest comedies, as part of a shipment that also
included "12 Hoolls Terrence" along with books explicitly focused
on teaching Latin and Greek like "100 Hoolls Sententia" and "10
Greek Gramers." This order reflects an ongoing desire for Latin
dramatic texts, as Usher had received "12 Terrences" and "6 sene-
cas" from a London bookseller only three years previously.[33] This
receptivity to Latin-language drama suggests that antitheatrical attitudes could vary depending on the context or audience for the text.
Within recent years, theater historians have begun transforming our
concept of antitheatricality in colonial British America. Rather than
blanket notions of stereotypical Puritan aversion to all forms of representation, antitheatricality is better understood as a discourse in
flux, subject to economic and political attitudes, as well as Protestant
ones, and sometimes specific to particular types of theater. Odai
Johnson and William J. Burling have shown that amateur and collegiate performances, for example, were not generally subject to the
same restrictions as professional companies, as in the case of the

Pennsylvania ban on theater in 1759, shortly after the arrival of a professional acting troupe, when only two years previously local newspapers had advertised and praised a collegiate production. Precisely because colonists, in the words of Tice Miller, "wanted to import British cultural institutions to bring refinement to their communities," the "British" association with English-language drama like Shakespeare eventually became problematic in the 1760s and 1770s for those colonists who would later support the Revolution.[34]

PLAYBOOKS AND COLONIAL INSTRUCTION

Given the limitations of surviving records, what can be said about the reading of Shakespeare in British America in the transformative years from 1675 to 1725? This period has been identified by scholars such as Richard Bushman and Richard Gildrie as significant, as an era when civility was "redefin[ed]" and a new era of refinement had begun.[35] Given the importance of Shakespeare as cultural currency near the end of the colonial period, what evidence, if any, might illuminate the prehistory of Shakespeare's role in American education?

While Harvard University did not place Shakespeare's plays within the formal curriculum until the nineteenth century, the appearance of his *Works* in the 1723 college library marks a significant shift in attitudes about the use of reading dramatic texts. To investigate the relationships among dramatic reading, instruction, and the emerging culture of refinement, I want to examine one private book catalogue of what may be an "average" colonist, as a case study of what can be found by reading between the lines of taciturn early modern evidence. This is the book list from the probate inventory of schoolmaster Nathaniel Hill of Henrico County, Virginia, taken shortly after his death in 1691:

1 large Bible
16 Play books
2 old books of Arithmatic [*sic*]
3 Latin books
1 book of letters
1 Clerk's Guide[36]

Records like this one tantalize us with what they leave untold—which plays and Latin texts did Hill own and, more importantly, how might he have used them as part of instruction? In what follows, I use this brief inventory to speculate on Hill as an educator and on his relationship to broader discourses of civility emerging between 1675 and 1725.

Hill seems to have been a fairly typical schoolmaster for a private school in colonial Virginia. He began his teaching career in the Chesapeake sometime before 1683 when a Gloucester, Virginia county court ordered that he be made exempt from the taxes taken of all free men for one year to encourage "able tutors" like Hill to teach in Virginia.[37] Hill is next recorded in Henrico County, where his belongings were inventoried after his death in 1691. "[B]ooks of Arithmatic," "book of letters," and "Clerk's Guide" show that he offered his services as a "writing master," teaching writing and arithmetic to students who came to him after achieving reading literacy at home or at a "dame school." The books traditionally used for teaching reading—primers, catechisms, and psalters—are not listed here; although the Bible was used for training students to read, it was the final text in a sequence of advancing difficulty, a text that marked a kind of "graduation" in achieving reading literacy of vernacular print. Although children in the United States may now learn reading and writing simultaneously and are often encouraged to recognize, spell, and write their names to combine these diverse developmental skills, early modern education separated reading from writing literacy. While writing literacy rates for British colonial women tended to improve throughout the eighteenth century, in 1680s Virginia writing was still a primarily male skill, introduced to boys by a male instructor after they had left the domestic, female world of the "dame school" behind.[38] The "Clerk's Guide" in Hill's inventory is a copybook that teaches cursive writing through model script to emulate (not unlike the dotted guidelines that allow preschoolers to trace out letters). The "book of letters" might refer to another copybook belonging to Hill or a textbook on the writing of epistles, with rhetorical advice and sample letters for a range of social and business occasions. In these books, letters tended to be included in full, categorized by situation, and presented as a comprehensive reference so that a reader could extract what he found appropriate. Compilations of model letters became increasingly fashionable in this period, because by the second half of the seventeenth century, "facility in letter writing was aligned with good manners and civility rather than with [academic] rhetoric."[39] As such, a wider set of English men and women, on both sides of the Atlantic, sought to improve themselves in this venue that allowed for public display of graces. As Richard L. Bushman explains, colonists "with no prospect of publication themselves were conscious as they wrote letters that they were undertaking small literary performances. . . . The act had to be adorned with the proper gestures and carried off with aplomb and style."[40] While these two kinds of books would be used at different moments in a student's development, each is applicable to Hill's task as a teacher of writing.

Based on the reference to "3 Latin books," Hill seems to have also run a traditional "grammar" school in the early modern sense: a school focused on learning to read and write Latin (and sometimes Greek) in preparation for entrance to English universities. In colonial settings, schoolmasters commonly taught students at varying skill levels simultaneously, charging different fees for each child depending on the skills sought. Hill likely taught a number of students who, after a training for a year or more to achieve basic writing and numeracy skills, left school for apprenticeships, while also teaching a more select group of young men who had already achieved vernacular writing literacy in the more traditional English grammar school education.[41] Entrance requirements for both British American and British colleges were consistent throughout this period in expecting reading and writing knowledge of classical languages. "Double translation" was a common method for this training: a student would translate a single Latin text into English and then, based on his translation (and not the original text), translate the text back into Latin so that, when complete, the student could compare his own Latin to the original.[42] Instructors chose texts for their students from a canon of frequently used, easily accessible classical texts, while likely also consulting their own expertise by teaching the texts they themselves had mastered. Based on Usher's import lists, grammar school students in British America were using a beginning Latin textbook entitled *Sententiae Pueriles* (Sentences for Boys), but were also translating Erasmus, Horace, Ovid, Terrence, and Seneca from Latin and, for advanced students, the New Testament in its original Greek.[43]

The most intriguing aspect of Hill's book list is the presence of a large collection of "16 Play books." If Hill himself attended university in England, he may have read plays and participated in theatrical productions as part of his schooling—and it does seem likely that Hill was trained in England. Most private schoolmasters in the Chesapeake in this period were educated in England, often sponsored by the Bishop of London for their transatlantic voyage.[44] Cambridge University records a student named Nathaniel Hill who was admitted as a subsizar to Trinity College in 1665.[45] Little else is recorded about this student that might allow us to verify if this Nathaniel Hill is the schoolmaster in the Chesapeake twenty-five years later, except that the student Hill did not complete his degree. This information, rather than discrediting the connection between the two records, corroborates it: one of the reasons for a shortage of schoolmasters in early colonial America is that those who had completed degrees from universities often left teaching to become parish ministers in order to earn a larger salary, so Hill's continued work as a writing master suggests that he was not qualified to be a minister. His experience as student at an English university may account for the Gloucester County court identifying Hill as an "able tutor" worthy of being courted with a tax break. Another telling detail is that the Trinity College Nathaniel Hill was a "subsizar," a student on scholarship rather than a gentleman of means. Economic limitations may have shortened his time at Cambridge and may have spurred on a decision to move to Virginia, since most of those who made the transatlantic voyage in the seventeenth century did so as long-distance subsistence migrants, seeking new ways to support themselves.[46]

If the "16 Play books" Hill owned were Latin-language dramas, they were likely the plays of Seneca, Plautus, and Terrence, who were the most frequently read classical dramatists in early modern England. Usher's consistent importation of Latin plays like "12 Terrences" confirms a broader pattern in early modern English education at grammar schools: the consistent use of Latin-language drama as texts for translation and sometimes performance to engage and motivate otherwise reluctant students. Ben Jonson satirized anti-theatrical suspicion through his close-minded character Censure who rants, "They make all their scholars playboys! . . . We send them to learn their grammar and their Terence, and they learn their playbooks!" (Like most of Jonson's posturing Puritans, Censure speaks out of ignorance, in this case seemingly unaware of the fact that Terrence's works are dramatic literature.)[47] Texts that might have been considered racy in the vernacular, like Ovid and Seneca, were common within all-male classrooms made up of the social elite (or those who aspired to the social elite). From the perspective of language acquisition, the use of comedies makes sense: the ability to understand and enjoy another culture's jokes signals a rich kind of fluency. But if reading Latin-language drama was common at grammar schools, the tradition of both reading and performance of plays was well established at English universities, including Trinity College, where Hill may have been a student. By the sixteenth century, students at colleges at Cambridge and Oxford were not only performing classical drama, they were also composing new English- and Latin-language plays for performances. University scholars produced plays like *Gammar Gurton's Needle,* which was notorious for the bawdy humor that accompanied its classically inspired themes, as well as more serious theatricals, such as Cambridge's Senecan-style Latin-language history play about Richard III and the Tudor myth.[48]

Collegiate dramatic performances, in both England and its American colonies, seem to have been exempt from antitheatrical attitudes for all but the strictest opponents of representation. Administrators at Cambridge University fought to ban traveling professional acting troupes, claiming that their presence caused disobedience and licentiousness among the university's scholars, while simultaneously allowing continued theatricals within the colleges.[49] Odai Johnson and William J. Burling find this pattern in colonial British America as well: "The most frequent assembly of amateurs were students who performed at the early colonial colleges. Entries occur for such 'young scholars' from 1690 on through to the closing of the theatres in 1774. . . . These productions were hosted by colleges throughout the colonies . . . including Harvard and Yale Colleges in colonies that were otherwise hostile theatre marketplaces."[50] Collegiate performances were considered first and foremost educational. Harvard students seem to have produced a play written by one of their own in 1690, although the performance was probably not open to public spectators. In 1702 at the College of William and Mary students publicly performed two "pastoral colloquies," perhaps both in English and Latin; the texts the students performed may have been written by the faculty of the College. By 1736, the "Young Gentlemen" of William and Mary had produced two plays, *Cato* and *The Drummer,* in full-scale public productions.[51] For generations, the translation and performance of dramatic texts were established methods for teaching classical languages, but this was not the only pedagogical goal of this study—for advocates of collegiate theatricals, rehearsing performances also taught declamation, inculcating appropriate gesture, timing, and confidence. As early as 1616, Thomas Heywood commended this training in that it "emboldens a scholler to speake, but instructs him to speake well, and with judgement. . . . to fit his phrases to his action."[52] In his study of British America, Richard L. Bushman argues that "the refinement of America began around 1690" and that refinement in conversation became increasingly important throughout the colonial period.[53]

It is within this connection—the continued education of privileged students and the study of dramatic literature aimed at refinement—that provides the context that may make Nathaniel Hill's book inventory legible. Although the most commonly used dramatic texts in pedagogical situations were Latin-language plays, the phrase "16 Play books" suggests that those taking down the inventory were looking at sixteen small books, likely inexpensive single-text quarto editions, more immediately recognizably by their genre than their author. If the "Play books" had been bound together they would probably have been recorded as a "collection of plays," as they were in other period libraries. In Usher's inventories, Latin-language plays were usually grouped and bound together in large folios or quartos organized by author, as in the record "12 Terrences," or twelve copies of Terrence's collected plays. Instead, those taking down Hill's probate inventory distinguish the "Play books" from the "Latin books." Although the colonists noting Hill's inventory were both reading and writing literate, these recorders may not have been able to read Latin themselves in order to identify the three "Latin books" more specifically. The language used by the recorders in the inventory suggests that the "Play books" may have been English-language texts because they were clearly differentiated from the "Latin books." It is possible, of course, that the sixteen books are sixteen copies of a single play text, but this seems unlikely given early modern attitudes toward printed books; throughout the early modern period, and in colonial Chesapeake in particular, books were valuable items that readers were used to sharing. Because of the expense of purchasing multiple volumes of the same text, it seems more likely that a writing master would ask students to write out their own copies of a speech or the complete "sides" of play for a performance. Furthermore, this rewriting would not seem an extraordinarily arduous one: some Harvard students copied out complete textbooks by hand in the late seventeenth century.[54]

Although we will likely never be able to verify which dramatic titles Nathaniel Hill owned, we can produce reasonable estimates of the plays most likely represented in his collection, based on reprint totals for English presses in the seventeenth century. During the period from 1550 to 1700, the anonymous *Mucedorus and Amadine,* Shakespeare's *Richard III* and *Hamlet,* Kyd's *Spanish Tragedy,* Marlowe's *Dr. Faustus,* and Beaumont and Fletcher's *Philaster* were among the most frequently reprinted single-text playbooks. We might also add Shakespeare's *Romeo and Juliet* and Beaumont and Fletcher's *Maid's Tragedy.* If we narrow the focus to 1660 to 1690 (five years before Hill entered Trinity College to one year before his death), Restoration playwrights join the list, with Dryden's *Indian Emperor* and *Sir Martin Mar-all,* Etherege's *Comical Revenge,* and Wycherley's *Plain Dealer* each reprinted at least five times in this period. But the period from 1660 to 1690 was also an important time for reprinting of Shakespeare's plays, although many of these were Restoration-era revisions. In these thirty years, *Hamlet*'s popularity increases significantly with four new editions, Dryden's adaptation of *The Tempest* goes through five editions, and *Macbeth* is the most frequently reprinted Shakespearean text, with seven total editions.[55] Based on these records, it is reasonable to estimate that as many as twenty-five percent of Hill's playbooks would have been Shakespearean plays. It is extremely likely, then, that at least one of his "16 Play books" was written by Shakespeare. Although the surviving probate inventory limits our ability to verify which plays Hill read in Virginia, it does provide a provocative glimpse into the world of early colonial education.

Ultimately, the limited records available about Hill make it impossible to prove that he used Shakespeare or other English language drama to teach refined declamation of the sort well established for a century later. The surviving record cannot absolutely confirm which plays Hill read or even if he was, in any sense, an "average" colonial writing master as I have speculated here. And yet, dramatic texts— even, I believe, plays by Shakespeare—may have been used in early colonial America as part of continued education for those who had already mastered reading literacy and basic devotional training. While historians trace the emergence of a refined colonial culture between 1675 and 1725 through material culture as well as textual history, for the colonists' concepts of refinement and civility were subject to competition and debate. Defined, in part, against discourses of Native American "savagery," civility became an increasingly important component of English colonial identities for the rapidly expanding market class of the eighteenth century. In the hands of private teachers like Nathaniel Hill, an English playbook by Shakespeare may have become a tool for inculcating the speech and gesture of the metropolis to students who would come to embody the refined culture of the colonial elite.

NOTES

1. Richard Hakluyt, *The Principal Nauigations, Voyages, Traffiques and Discoueries of the English Nation* (London, 1599–1600), sig. Bb1r (emphasis added).

2. Jill Lepore, *The Name of War: King Phillip's War and the Origins of American Identity* (New York: Alfred A. Knopf, 1998), 43.

3. David D. Hall, "Introduction," in *The Colonial Book in the Atlantic World*, ed. Hugh Amory and David D. Hall (Cambridge: Cambridge University Press, 2000), 25; Matthew P. Brown, *The Pilgrim and the Bee: Reading Rituals and Book Culture in Early New England* (Philadelphia: University of Pennsylvania Press, 2007), 146–62;

Richard Beale Davis, *Intellectual Life in the Colonial South 1585–1763* (Knoxville: University of Tennessee Press, 1978), 501.

4. Hugh Amory, "Reinventing the Colonial Book," in *The Colonial Book in the Atlantic World,* 28. References to "America" were used to refer to the land and the peoples indigenous to that land, as in Roger Williams' title *A Key into the Languages of America;* when referring to themselves and their plantations, settlers consistently described themselves as English.

5. Lepore, 197; Karen Ordahl Kupperman, "Fear of Hot Climates in the Anglo-American Colonial Experience," *William and Mary Quarterly* 41 (1984): 214; John Wood Sweet, "Introduction: Sea Changes," in *Envisioning an English Empire: Jamestown and the Making of the North Atlantic World,* ed. Robert Appelbaum and John Wood Sweet (Philadelphia: University of Pennsylvania Press, 2005), 9; Anna Bryson, *From Courtesy to Civility: Changing Codes of Conduct in Early Modern England* (Oxford: Clarendon Press, 1998), 277–78. Early modern Englishness was not only opposed to American "savagery": English colonial ventures were haunted by deep-seated concerns of inferiority to Spanish and, later, Dutch success in the Atlantic sphere. The English positioned themselves as benign colonizers and missionaries opposed to the "Black Legend" of Spanish cruelty. This stance concealed envy and emulation of continental colonial modes, especially visible in England's adoption of African slavery and Spanish plantation styles. See Joyce E. Chaplin, "Race," in *The British Atlantic World, 1500–1800,* ed. David Armitage and Michael J. Braddick (New York: Palgrave Macmillan, 2002), 155; April Lee Hatfield, *Atlantic Virginia: Intercolonial Relations in the Seventeenth Century* (Philadelphia: University of Pennsylvania Press, 2004), 1–3; Eric Griffin, "The Specter of Spain in John Smith's Colonial Writing," in *Envisioning an English Empire: Jamestown and the Making of the North Atlantic World,* ed. Robert Appelbaum and John Wood Sweet (Philadelphia: University of Pennsylvania Press, 2005), 111–12; Laura M. Stevens, *The Poor Indians: British Missionaries, Native Americans, and Colonial Sensibility* (Philadelphia: University of Pennsylvania Press, 2004), 34–38; and Thomas Scanlan, *Colonial Writing and the New World 1583–1671: Allegories of Desire* (Cambridge: Cambridge University Press, 1999), 1–3.

6. Brown, 179–80.

7. Survival rates increase significantly as we move later in the period, with more records of private ownership, bookselling, and even circulating libraries in the early eighteenth century. The survival rates for such documents can vary widely by region; they are especially low for Southern colonies like Virginia, Maryland, and the Carolinas due to the United States' Civil War–era fires. The most famous libraries of early British America are the large collections of learned, high-status men such as Simon Bradstreet, Thomas Teackle, and Cotton Mather. But although their private libraries were remarkable, with an impact that extended beyond a single owner as books were lent and discussed, the contents of any particular "average library" are, paradoxically, harder to ascertain since average libraries were less likely to receive careful cataloging. Thomas Goddard Wright, *Literary Culture in Early New England 1620–1730* 2nd ed. (New York: Russell & Russell, 1966), 44; Worthington Chauncey Ford, *The Boston Book Market 1679–1700* (New York: Burt Franklin, 1918), 4–5, 23; Jon Butler, "Thomas Teackle's 333 Books: A Great Library on Virginia's Eastern Shore, 1697," *William and Mary Quarterly* 49 (1992): 449–91; and Patricia Scott Deetz, Christopher Fennell, and J. Eric Deetz, *The Plymouth Colony Archive Project,* 2000–2006, online at http://etext.virginia.edu.

8. In his survey of books and education in colonial Virginia, Phillip Bruce concludes that the term "parcel" could commonly include "several dozen volumes at

the lowest." See R. B. Davis, 498; and Philip Alexander Bruce, *Institutional History of Virginia in the Seventeenth Century* (New York: G. P. Putnam's Sons, 1910), 423. My own comparison with records from Essex County, Massachusetts, confirms that "books" could be used to refer to a substantial library. The March 22, 1675 probate record of Jonathan Gage, for example, begins "weareing apparel linen & woollen, 3li. 15s.; bed & beding, 3li., books, 6li." At £6, a library worth twice the value of a bed is a remarkable collection in an era when a bedstead was frequently one of the most valuable pieces of furniture in the home. The only inventory listings more valuable than his books are his cattle and his land. Another Essex County inventory from the same year values a "bible and a psalm book"—books that might traditionally be among the largest and most expensive in a modest home—at six shillings, a fraction of the worth of Gage's collection. Although Gage seems to have had a particularly valuable library, comparison of the nine records listing books for the year 1675 reveals an average Essex collection valued at nearly £2, and yet none of these records list the titles or authors of the books. Perhaps Gage was the first to own Shakespeare's *Richard III* or *Hamlet* in Massachusetts, but the record remains frustratingly silent. *The Probate Records of Essex County, Massachusetts Volume 3: 1675–1681* (Salem: The Essex Institute, 1920), 1, 45.

9. Edwin Elliott Willoughby, "The Reading of Shakespeare in Colonial America," *Papers of the Bibliographical Society of America* 31 (1937): 50; and R. B. Davis, 508–9.

10. W. H. Bond and Hugh Amory, ed., *The Printed Catalogues of the Harvard College Library 1723–1790* (Boston: Colonial Society of Massachusetts, 1996), 101; R. B. Davis, 531–32, 548; and Willoughby, 49.

11. Odai Johnson and William J. Burling, *The Colonial American Stage, 1665–1774: A Documentary Calendar* (Madison, NJ: Fairleigh Dickinson University Press, 2001), 107; and Tice L. Miller, *Entertaining the Nation: American Drama in the Eighteenth and Nineteenth Centuries* (Carbondale: Southern Illinois University Press, 2007), 6–7.

12. Heidi Brayman Hackel, *Reading Material in Early Modern England: Print, Gender, and Literacy* (Cambridge: Cambridge University Press, 2005), 266; and *The Probate Records of Essex County, Massachusetts. Volume 1: 1635–1664* (Salem: Essex Institute, 1916), 229–30.

13. Note that in terms of resale value a book that has been damaged through neglect may be assessed similarly to a book that has been literally read to pieces. For a historian of reading, these books represent different cultural values, even though they might each be assessed as similarly worthless in monetary terms.

14. It is an oversimplification to conclude from this evidence that small-format playbooks were exclusively theatrical while collected plays were solidly literary, since even Ben Jonson's *Works* combine marketing based on literary authorship with advertisements of the texts' theatrical connections. Furthermore, over the course of the seventeenth century both theatrical *and* authorial title-page attribution rates rose on printed playbooks, which suggests that early modern booksellers did not constitute the "theatrical" and the "literary" as absolute and opposed categories.

15. Alan B. Farmer and Zachary Lesser, "Vile Arts: The Marketing of English Printed Drama, 1512–1660," *Research Opportunities in Renaissance Drama* 39 (2000): 82–91. This project is therefore similar to Odai Johnson's work on recovering colonial theater through "the evocation of absent or immaterial evidence." See *Absence and Memory in Colonial American Theatre: Fiorelli's Plaster* (New York: Palgrave Macmillan, 2006), 9.

16. Andrew Murphy, *Shakespeare in Print: A History and Chronology of Shakespeare Publishing* (Cambridge: Cambridge University Press, 2003), 337, 142–45; Lawrence Levine, "William Shakespeare in America," in *Popular Culture in American History*,

ed. Jim Cullen (Malden: Blackwell Publishers, 2001), 35; and Christopher D. Felker, "The Print History of *The Tempest* in Early America," in *The Tempest: Critical Essays,* ed. Patrick M. Murphy (New York: Routledge, 2002), 497.

17. It must be noted, however, that this percentage has limitations, since it can be based only on those records that include titles. Even widely circulated genres like primers and almanacs were seldom listed by title in booklists, if mentioned at all.

18. Hellmut Lehmann-Haupt, *The Book in America: A History of the Making, the Selling, and the Collecting of Books in the United States* (New York: R. R. Bowker, 1939), 16–23. Because the northern colonies held a dominant position in the production and distribution of printed books in British America, it has long been assumed that New England retained a bookish culture, while Chesapeake-region Maryland and Virginia did not. These assumptions fit logically with other common narratives of the early colonies' cultural values: the New England colonies are reified as "the city on the hill," purified of economic motivations and connected to the democratic influence of the printing press, while the southern colonies stay mired in associations with commodity crops and African slavery. While attention to the *production* of printed books in British America supports these narratives, study of the *consumption* of printed books does not. While the differences among the American colonies before 1725 were multiple and complex, studies of private book collections show an unexpected degree of continuity in the genres and even the specific titles that dominated these collections. New England colonies do seem to have had increased access to printed books, and this accessibility is reflected in a higher percentage of households owning some printed books, but the differences between north and south are more of degree than kind. The increased access to books in New England is comparable to the situation in the counties immediately surrounding London—although both in England and America, the spread of books was more dependent on terrain and roads (the real time for a hawker) than on specific spatial proximity. Readers in commercial hubs throughout British America experienced greater access when compared to their inland or rural neighbors. See Jennifer Mylander, "Early Modern 'How-To' Books: Impractical Manuals and the Construction of Englishness in the Atlantic World," *Journal for Early Modern Cultural Studies* 9 (2009): 123–46; and Louis B. Wright, "The Purposeful Reading of Our Colonial Ancestors," *English Literary History* 4 (1937): 87.

19. Hugh Amory, "A Note on Statistics," in *The Colonial Book in the Atlantic World,* 514.

20. David D. Hall, "The Uses of Literacy in New England, 1600–1850," in *Cultures of Print: Essays in the History of the Book* (Amherst: University of Massachusetts Press 1996), 61–62.

21. Lehmann-Haupt, 52; and T. Wright, 61.

22. James Raven, "The Importation of Books in the Eighteenth Century," in *The Colonial Book in the Atlantic World,* 183–87. For an analysis of the substantial Atlantic circulation of books between individuals, see David Cressy, *Coming Over: Migration and Communication between England and New England in the Seventeenth Century* (Cambridge: Cambridge University Press, 1987). British America supported a rapidly expanding book market, with Boston becoming the most significant hub for books by the Restoration, and Philadelphia supplanting that role by the mid-eighteenth century. Throughout the colonial period merchants of all sizes carried English books, with the smallest dealers likely carrying hornbooks, Bibles, and small devotional manuals. By the end of the seventeenth century, some Boston bookdealers were almost surely functioning as middlemen, wholesaling selections of books to

merchants in other parts of English America. In the Chesapeake, where plantations were positioned to be as close as possible to navigable water, merchants likely offered books and other finished products for sale out of the boats into which they packed tobacco. As in England, hawkers were distributors of books to more remote regions, with record of them in the 1680s although they likely existed earlier. By the early eighteenth century, some chapmen at least were working with, and possibly employed by, Boston booksellers. See Stephen Botein, "The Anglo-American Book Trade before 1776: Personnel and Strategies," in *Printing and Society in Early America,* ed. William L. Joyce et al. (Worcester, MA: American Antiquarian Society, 1983), 55–56.

23. Kim C. Sturgess, *Shakespeare and the American Nation* (Cambridge: Cambridge University Press, 2004), 60. Sturgess lists the price for each volume in the Philadelphia edition at $1 but does not offer a comparative price for a single volume of an imported edition to contextualize this cost.

24. Levine, 35. Most owners of the *Works* likely owned the octavo or duodecimo editions that conserved paper (and so conserved cost) that were frequently printed in London. See Murphy, 311–29.

25. Brown, 5; and Jane Carson, *Colonial Virginians at Play* (Charlottesville: University Press of Virginia, 1965), 45.

26. Usher's business was first established by his father Hezekiah Usher, who was the first British colonial merchant to have a significant trade in books, with a shop in Cambridge, Massachusetts, by 1639 that moved to Boston in 1642. Although the elder Usher also supported himself through large-scale trade of commodities, he was a significant bookdealer who, like many London stationers, also functioned as a publisher. By 1669, he stopped trading in books, making way for his sons Hezekiah and John Usher to take over the trade. Jill Lepore argues that it is Hezekiah Usher, not John, who should be regarded as the recipient of London shipments preserved in John Usher's letter book, though she does not provide evidence to warrant countering the consensus opinion of Amory and others. Presumably she refers to the second Hezekiah Usher, John's brother. See Jill Lepore, "Literacy and Reading in Puritan New England," in *Perspectives on American Book History: Artifacts and Commentary,* ed. Scott E. Casper, Joanne D. Chaison, and Jeffrey D. Groves (Amherst: University of Massachusetts Press, 2002), 40.

27. Benjamin Franklin, ed. *Boston Printers, Publishers, and Booksellers: 1640–1800* (Boston: G. K. Hall & Co., 1980), 473–78; Lehmann-Haupt, 44–45; Hugh Amory, "Printing and Bookselling in New England, 1638–1713," in *The Colonial Book in the Atlantic World,* 96–100; George Emery Littlefield, *Early Boston Booksellers 1642–1711* (New York: Club of Odd Volumes, 1900), 67–68. For the total of fifteen, see Franklin. This total includes one person whose status as a bookseller is debated; Amory records Mary Woodmansey Tappin Avery as a publisher of two tracts but not a bookseller, while Franklin identifies her as a bookseller in Boston for the period 1678 to 1707. See Franklin, 20; and Amory, "Printing," 98.

28. Lehmann-Haupt, 45; and Amory, "Printing," 90.

29. Ford, 121–39.

30. Amory, "Printing," 104–5.

31. The largest segments of Usher's stock are devoted to works of divinity, devotional manuals, and textbooks. In both inventories, books of divinity aimed at the clergy make up around 25 percent of imported titles; if these books are grouped together with devotional guides for laypersons, they make up approximately 42 percent of imported titles. Textbooks—comprising everything from copybooks to Latin grammars—make up an additional 18 percent of the titles in both shipments.

Usher surely carried the ubiquitous books of what John Locke called the "ordinary road" of early modern English vernacular education: readers progressed through the cycle from hornbooks, primers, catechisms, prose psalters, and, finally, complete Bibles. For those who would learn to write as well as read, Usher carried copy books and spelling books. For those (almost exclusively) young men who would proceed to study of classical languages, Usher imported a range of Latin and Greek texts, both in their original languages and in translation as guides for students. Practical manuals (primarily books of husbandry, law, medicine, navigation, and military discipline) make up the next largest segment if categorized as a group, although some of these might also be broadly considered textbooks as well (based on an analysis of Ford, 121–39).

32. Davis, 19; and Heather S. Nathans, *Early American Theatre from the Revolution to Thomas Jefferson: Into the Hands of the People* (Cambridge: Cambridge University Press, 2003), 19–22.

33. T. Wright, 224–26, 234–37.

34. Johnson and Burling, 25; Miller, 3; Peter A. Davis, "Puritan Mercantilism and the Politics of Anti-Theatrical Legislation in Colonial America," in *The American Stage: Social and Economic Issues from the Colonial Period to the Present,* ed. Ron Engle and Tice L. Miller (Cambridge: Cambridge University Press, 1993), 18–19; Nathans, 2; and Johnson, 4–11, 129–34.

35. Richard P. Gildrie, *The Profane, the Civil, and the Godly: The Reformation of Manners in Orthodox New England, 1679–1749* (University Park: Pennsylvania State University Press, 1994), 15; and Richard L. Bushman, *The Refinement of America: Persons, Houses, Cities* (New York: Alfred A. Knopf, 1992), xii–xv.

36. "Books in Colonial Virginia," *Virginia Magazine of History and Biography* 10 (1902–3): 405.

37. Mary Newton Stanard, *Colonial Virginia: Its People and Customs* (Philadelphia: J. P. Lippincott, 1917), 271.

38. E. Jennifer Monaghan, *Learning to Read and Write in Colonial America* (Amherst: University of Massachusetts Press, 2005), 384–85.

39. Bushman, 90–96; Gary Schneider, *The Culture of Epistolarity: Vernacular Letters and Letter Writing in Early Modern England, 1500–1700* (Newark: University of Delaware Press, 2005), 44–45; Bryson, 157–58.

40. Bushman, 90.

41. Louis H. Manarin and Clifford Dowdey, *The History of Henrico County* (Charlottesville: University Press of Virginia, 1984), 67–68, 96.

42. Richard M. Gummere, *The American Colonial Mind and the Classical Tradition* (Cambridge: Harvard University Press, 1963), 56–63; T. Wright, 18–22.

43. T. Wright, 224–237.

44. Stanard, 271.

45. W. W. Rouse Ball and J. A. Venn, *Admissions to Trinity College, Cambridge Volume II 1546–1700* (London: Macmillan, 1913), 474. Neither *Alumni Oxonienses* nor *Sibley's Harvard Graduates* lists a Nathaniel Hill for the period.

46. Stanard, 271; and Allison Games, "Migration," in *The British Atlantic World, 1500–1800,* 34–41.

47. Henry W. Simon, *The Reading of Shakespeare in American Schools and Colleges: An Historical Survey* (New York: Simon and Schuster, 1932), 1–5. It is possible that Hill only read his playbooks for personal entertainment. Based on the tradition of using dramatic texts for advanced students in early modern English education, however, there is good reason to consider the playbooks within an instructional context.

48. Frederick S. Boas, *University Drama in the Tudor Age* (New York: Arno Press, 1978), 69–81, 111–19.

49. Boas, 220–27. While there were college members at sixteenth–century Cambridge that opposed performances on campus, they remained in the minority and theatricals continued. For collegiate theatricals at Yale College, see Jason Schaffer, "'Great Cato's Descendants': A Genealogy of Colonial Performance," *Theatre Survey* 44 (2003): 5–28.

50. Johnson and Burling, 25. Studying seventeenth-century printing and reprinting rates of play books, Alan Farmer and Zachary Lesser note a similar distinction between professional and amateur/collegiate drama: "most of the dramatic publications [after the 1642 ban on performances in England] . . . were not plays from the professional stage. . . . [D]rama in general may have continued to be printed, [but] stationers in the 1640s were investing in *professional* plays less often than they had in any period since the 1580s." Alan B. Farmer and Zachary Lesser, "Canons and Classics: Publishing Drama in Caroline England," in *Localizing Caroline Drama: Politics and Economics of the Early Modern English Stage, 1625–1642*, ed. Adam Zucker and Alan B. Farmer (New York: Palgrave Macmillan, 2006), 24–25.

51. Johnson and Burling, 95–97, 116–19; R. B. Davis, 1284; Hugh F. Rankin, *The Theater in Colonial America* (Chapel Hill: University of North Carolina Press, 1960), 18–19.

52. Boas, 235–36, 350–51.

53. Bushman, xii, 83–89.

54. John Tufts, *A Compendium of Logick According to Ye Modern Philosophers* Extracted from Legrand and Others Their Systems: by Mr. Brattle (1705), Harvard Archives.

55. Farmer and Lesser, "Canons," 28–37; Alan B. Farmer and Zachary Lesser, *DEEP: Database of Early English Playbooks,* online at http://deep.sas.upenn.edu; and *English Short Title Catalogue,* online at http://estc.bl.uk.

"A course of learning and ingenious studies": Shakespearean Education and Theater in Antebellum America

Heather S. Nathans

In 1788, MATHEW CAREY'S POPULAR PHILADELPHIA JOURNAL, THE *AMERI-can Museum,* printed a letter from a black author who called himself "Othello," exhorting the nation's white citizens to fulfill the Revolution's promise and abolish slavery. Appropriating the dignity and authority of Shakespeare's martial leader, the author warned that if white Americans continued to flout the laws of nature by holding slaves, they would bring down divine justice from "a Creator, whose vengeance may be now on the wing, to disseminate and hurl the arrows of destruction."[1] The following year, the *American Museum* printed another letter on the subject of slavery by an anonymous author who also borrowed Shakespearean rhetoric to support his argument. Describing himself as a former slave, he paraphrased Shakespeare's *Merchant of Venice,* begging justice for the nation's black citizens: "Has not a negro eyes? Has not a negro hands, organs, dimensions, senses, affections, passions?"[2] In 1798, Boston's white working-class population angrily protested a production of Shakespeare's *King John,* on the grounds that its content was too politically charged for a nation divided into pro- and anti-French factions. The newspaper description of the event does not provide a synopsis of the play or an extended analysis of its political meaning. Instead, it takes for granted that working-class audiences would be able to read contemporary political events through the lens of one of the Bard's (admittedly) less frequently performed works.[3] In 1799, one of the popular manuals published for the education of young women featured several poems *based* on Shakespeare's plays, including a sonnet on Ophelia and one on Oberon, but no actual Shakespearean text. The content of the sonnets seems to assume that the young ladies would already have sufficient familiarity with *Hamlet* and *A Midsummer Night's Dream* to understand the two poems.[4]

Each of these instances points to the author's, reader's, and audience's Shakespearean education. Some basic indoctrination into Shakespeare's works allowed his texts to become the *lingua franca* of these various racialized, classed, and gendered discussions. In the absence of formal "teaching," since, as the other essays in this collection suggest, Shakespeare was not taught as a specific subject until later in the nineteenth century, how might eighteenth-century and antebellum Americans have acquired their Shakespearean education, and how did they understand its usefulness?

The consistent presence of Shakespeare in American culture throughout this period and in this diverse range of venues highlights the fluid notion of "education" in eighteenth-century and antebellum American culture. Did education consist merely of what one learned in the classroom, or might an individual who studied outside a formal school setting be considered "educated" as well? What educational structures had the power to confer authority on the interpretation of texts and knowledge? Could the theater itself be considered a "school" for manners, elocution, and textual exploration for those who might be excluded from more traditional educational settings? This essay explores the ways in which traditionally marginalized groups in the new nation embraced Shakespeare's texts and the theatre as tools for civil and cultural reform, suggesting that for some of these communities, a Shakespearean education could offer a weapon with which to combat racism, sexism, or class oppression.

"To prove that we are men"

In the 1789 letter to the *American Museum,* the former slave who quotes *The Merchant of Venice* also specifically addresses the question of his education. He says that he learned to read in slavery and that as soon as he became free, he began to read those European authors "venerated" by whites in order to better understand white Atlantic culture, and that those authors obviously included Shakespeare. As the writer notes, "The first thing which seems necessary in order to remove those prejudices which are so justly entertained against us is to prove that we are men . . . I learn from writers who Europeans hold in highest esteem . . . that to deliver oneself and one's countrymen from tyranny is an act of sublimest heroism."[5] Here, the author synthesizes Shakespeare's rhetoric with the very sentiments that had fueled the American Revolution. The author also describes the white legal system as something alien to enslaved Africans: "We have written laws composed in a language we do not understand and never promulgated."[6] Yet he suggests that the works of men like Shakespeare provide a bridge between blacks and whites *and* that they demonstrate the ways in which Africans *can* engage with European culture—that they are educable and thus, ultimately, worthy of citizenship.

How might a slave or a free black have acquired a Shakespearean education in early America? Both schools and theaters played a role in that process, particularly in cities with strong antislavery factions such as Philadelphia, New York, and Boston. For example, in 1740 Philadelphia's former dancing master inaugurated a school for black children that might well have included lessons in deportment and elocution (and during the eighteenth century, elocution lessons frequently included passages of Shakespeare).[7] By 1789, the city had also established an Association for the Free Instruction of Adult Colored Persons. However, heavy work demands meant that the focus of the education these pupils received necessarily shifted from daily schooling in reading, writing, and arithmetic to the kind of informal education that slaves and free blacks might get independently, in small groups, or through their churches.[8] For those deprived of formal schooling, the city's active theater companies (the Chestnut Street Theatre, Ricketts Circus, and later the Walnut Street Theatre) also offered ample opportunities for slaves and free blacks to *see* and *hear* Shakespeare and thus to acquire their Shakespearean education "extratextually" (much like they would acquire Bible knowledge through a sermon).[9]

New York City established a formal system through which African Americans might imbibe a Shakespearean education. In 1787, New York's Manumission Society (whose secretary, William Dunlap, was also the manager of the Park Street Theatre) launched the New York African Free School. The school's emphasis on oral interpretation challenged black students to assimilate white elocutionary conventions through regular performances of poems, essays, and famous speeches. As Anna Mae Duane notes, the students in the African Free School used two main sources for their study of English and elocution: Lindley Murray's *The English Reader* and Caleb Bingham's incredibly popular and widely used *American Preceptor*.[10] Although neither of these works incorporates Shakespearean passages, they might still have led young African American students to Shakespeare; for example, Ira Aldridge, the best-known black Shakespearean actor of the nineteenth century, attributed his love of performance to his experience in the African Free Schools in the early 1810s.[11] Charles Andrews asserts in his 1830 history of the school, "The African Free Schools helped to create a Negro intelligentsia which later participated actively in the leadership of the Abolitionist movement . . . and proved by its own example that, given the same opportunities, the potentialities of the Negro and the whites are the same."[12]

Within forty years, black New Yorkers had acquired sufficient familiarity with Shakespeare (either in school or in the "classroom" of the theater) that the nation's first black newspaper, *Freedom's Journal*, could run a story in 1828 in which the author used the word "changeling" and observed to his readers, "It may be considered impertinent were I to explain what is meant by a changeling; both Shakespeare and Spenser have already done so, and who is there unacquainted with the *Midsummer Night's Dream* and the *Fairy Queen?*"[13] A year later, the paper ran another essay on the subject of slander in which it quoted Shakespeare's famous passage from *Othello*, "who steals my purse, steals trash."[14] In 1837, the *Weekly Advocate* cited Shakespeare in an essay encouraging young men to avoid the dangers of alcohol.[15] Interestingly, not every black citizen automatically embraced Shakespeare as the key to citizenship and moral behavior. On February 16, 1839, the *Colored American* reprinted an essay from the *New York Observer* entitled "Selection of Books," which warned readers of the potential danger of studying Shakespeare's works. On the subject of Shakespeare, the author (Dr. Humphrey) wrote, "I admire his genius exceedingly, and can easily conceive how he might have been, as Milton will be, I have no doubt, one of the favorite poets in the millennium. But if I must speak frankly, under the pains and penalties of the highest literary tribunals in the world, I am sorry the most of his plays were ever written." Humphrey argued that Shakespeare's plays would ultimately do "more harm than good" to young readers, noting that "Shakespeare as he is, is not a fit book for family reading. What Christian father, or virtuous mother, would allow him, if he were now alive, to come into a blooming circle of sons and daughters and write his plays, just as they stand in the best editions? It is scarcely possible they should pass through the youthful mind and imagination without leaving a stain behind them." Humphrey advocated the zealous pruning of Shakespeare's texts, recommending that "[i]f they must be read by our sons and daughters in their homage, let us have a carefully expurgated edition."[16]

The warning by a (presumably) white minister that Shakespeare might be harmful to "our sons and daughters" might have steered African Americans towards carefully edited versions of Shakespeare's plays, rather than his complete works. Yet the trajectory from 1827 to 1839 is an interesting one, since the article in the 1827 *Freedom's Journal* assumes a widespread knowledge of Shakespeare's plays, while the 1839 essay in the *Colored American* advocates a censored and carefully monitored exposure to Shakespeare. It is tempting to draw parallels between the explosion of African American print culture in the late 1820s and the seeming popularity of Shakespeare as a cultural touchstone in African American life, and the subsequent restricted access to Shakespeare in the late 1830s during the time of the infamous "gag rule." The gag rule, imposed by Congress in 1836, forbade *any* government debates over slavery (and was particularly aimed at those groups that had deluged Congress with antislavery petitions). As Ezra Tawil has argued, the gag rule doomed the "dangerous eloquence" of the abolitionists to a "discursive death."[17] The *Colored American's* choice to reprint Humphrey's essay appears striking, precisely because of the extraordinary opposition that black Americans encountered in their struggle for education and advancement, and the "discursive death" they faced in a government that had just voted to deny them the right to present public petitions.

The process of African American education was complex and contentious—members of the black community struggled against prejudice from white Americans who derided their efforts and abilities or who tried to exclude them from white cultural activities. How, why, or where African Americans then encountered Shakespeare in early American culture is not always clear. Aside from the free schools in various northern cities or in the playhouses that flourished up and down the coast and that were gradually making their way onto the frontier, one alternate venue may have been the African American literary clubs that developed throughout the early part of the nineteenth century. By the 1850s, more than fifty African American literary clubs and reading societies had sprung up in cities including Albany, Boston, Baltimore, Buffalo, Cincinnati, Detroit, Hartford, New York, Poughkeepsie, Providence, Rochester, Schenectady, and Washington, DC. Members of these societies (which might include freeborn blacks and former slaves) passed their time in reading aloud from both popular and classical texts and in learning to create their own pieces of fiction, poetry, or oratory modeled on their readings. As historian Dorothy Porter notes, these literary institutions served a primarily educational function rather than a recreational or social one.[18]

By the 1850s, knowledge of Shakespeare had become an important part of the black educational experience in America—whether it was in the playhouse, the classroom, or the privacy of a select reading club.[19] The experience of one African American in particular helps to illustrate this phenomenon.

William Cooper Nell, a free black living in Boston in the mid-nineteenth century, fought a passionate battle for the civic and cultural education of his people. In 1853 he was part of a successful lawsuit against the Howard Athenaeum for discrimination against black theatergoers.[20] In 1855, he helped sue the city of Boston to end segregation in the city's school system. In the 1840s, he had founded a Literary Society for the city's adult black population, and in the 1850s he established Boston's first amateur black theater company, known as the Histrionic Club. For Nell, both a formal education and access to cultural opportunities (such as theatergoing and performing) seemed equally important for the elevation of blacks in American culture.

Nell's passion for Shakespeare is evident in many areas of his life—including his personal correspondence. Throughout his letters, he makes frequent references to Shakespeare, citing lines of text from plays such as *Romeo and Juliet* and *Hamlet*. In some instances, he simply cites the lines in passing: they are not the focus of his letters, but are rather the popular phrases culled from Shakespeare that one might hear in everyday conversation. However, in other instances, his letters reveal a closer study of Shakespeare's text, including one letter in which he compares himself to the apothecary in *Romeo and Juliet*.[21] Upon his return to Boston after several years spent living in New York, Nell wrote to a friend with instructions for sending his luggage. In his letter, he specifically requested that his collection of Shakespeare's works be sent on immediately, as he did not like to be without it.[22]

While very few records of Nell's literary society and the Histrionic Club survive, it seems likely that these organizations he helped to organize—which involved an intriguing cross-section of the city's black population from recently escaped slaves to the wealthy black middle class[23]—would have included at least passages from Shakespeare in their readings, performances, and tableaux.[24] For Nell and his compatriots, proof of a Shakespearean education, however acquired, also offered proof of ability to participate as equals in white society.[25]

RUDE MECHANICALS

In 1803, the *Philadelphia Repository and Weekly Register* asked readers if there were such a thing as "original genius." In an essay that occupied two and a half columns of print, the author concluded that many great artists considered "geniuses" had actually come to their art by accident from much more humble backgrounds. The essayist particularly remarked that Shakespeare had been destined for the wool trade, before his "imprudence" led him to the theater.[26] The paper's claim that Shakespeare had begun life as an ordinary working man who discovered his genius by accident made him more accessible to the young nation's working-class population. By linking Shakespeare to labor, the *Philadelphia Repository and Weekly Register* opened a rhetorical and intellectual space for considering Shakespeare's plays in the context of America's working-class culture.[27]

The 1803 effort to cast Shakespeare as a working man echoed attempts of only a few years before to claim Shakespeare as a spokesman for the nation's first working-class theater. In 1798 a production of *King John* at Boston's elite Federal Street Theatre drew the ire of working-class audiences for its supposedly anti-Jacobin message. The *King John* incident helped to launch a fierce rivalry between the city's elite theatergoers and their working-class counterparts over who controlled Boston's culture. Newspapers warned the public against the danger of using familiar plays like Shakespeare's to deliver veiled political messages. Yet such messages would only be effective if one could be sure that a large segment of Boston's approximately 17,000 eligible theatergoers were sufficiently well versed in Shakespeare that they would be able to interpret the play's subtler meaning.[28]

New England's seven-year public school system catered to middle- and upper-class boys and focused primarily on arithmetic and Greek and Latin translation. But schools that taught Greek and Latin translation were obviously not geared toward boys destined to be carpenters or bricklayers. How might an audience of mechanics and artisans become sufficiently familiar with *King John* that they could protest its performance on the grounds that it was not educational, but propagandistic?

Boston had two theaters in the late 1790s—the Federal Street Theatre and the Haymarket Theatre. The former had been founded by the city's wealthy elite, and it featured extremely undemocratic seating arrangements (working-class patrons were excluded from the boxes and relegated to the pit and galleries). The Haymarket had been founded in protest by the city's mechanic (or artisan) population in 1796. Their shows included Thomas Abthorpe Cooper's famous *Hamlet* and numerous other Shakespearean productions. Their playhouse allowed them to enjoy Shakespeare in an environment in which they felt more comfortable, away from the censure of their upper-class rivals.

The short-lived Haymarket playhouse assiduously copied the repertoire of its competition. Boston's mechanics, having declared their independence from the upper classes, struggled to emulate the elite theater's offerings. Thus to some extent, they took their cues about what constituted a "good" text from the city's upper class. But they had additional sources from which they might have drawn their Shakespearean education besides the theater. Indeed, their playhouse was only part of the mechanics' larger effort to affect the intellectual, cultural, and economic mobility of their group, as the formation of the Massachusetts Charitable Mechanics Association in 1795 suggests. Claiming a mission both educational and cultural, Boston's mechanics positioned themselves as the aesthetic and intellectual arbiters of the city's working-class population.

Excerpts of Shakespearean texts appear in numerous schoolbooks and general pocket literature circulating in New England in the 1780s and 1790s. These books suggest how Shakespeare's work might have been integrated into white, working-class culture. For example, the 1790s Boston edition of *Woods Mentor (American Teacher's Assistant)*, created specifically for Massachusetts students, contains references to Shakespeare, the lyrics to the patriotic tune "Hail Columbia" (often performed in the theater), extracts from speeches made during and after the Revolution, pieces of classical literature, *and* a discussion of the Massachusetts State Constitution. As the editor writes, "The greatest attention has been paid to the Choice of such pieces as would afford most Entertainment and Instruction."[29] The intriguing juxtaposition of Shakespeare with the Massachusetts Constitution suggests that the campaign to claim him as an integral part of American (and even "local") education was already well underway by the 1790s.

The text I have mentioned (which represents only one of the numerous examples from the period) fits neatly with the other part of the Mechanics' educational mission, aimed at raising a younger generation of mechanics equipped with the necessary cultural, as well as practical, knowledge to compete in Massachusetts society. By 1819, the Mechanics had formed their own library, consisting of over 1,480 volumes that included works on astronomy, physics, farming, and popular literature, such as plays. By 1828, they had founded their own school to teach apprentices the fundamentals of reading, writing, and accounting. By 1838, that school had expanded to include a series of monthly lectures for those who had left the classroom but who still wished to continue their education. But even if a mechanic avoided the school, the lectures, the libraries, and playgoing, by 1824 newspapers such as the *Masonic Mirror and Mechanics' Intelligencer* frequently printed short works of fiction that featured Shakespearean quotations in the introduction or in the conclusion. Artisan readers might thus acquire at least a small, regular exposure to Shakespeare in their newspapers, if nowhere else.

Nor was this simply an urban working-class phenomenon. As William Gilmore-Lehne notes in his study of material and cultural life in New England from 1780 to 1835, even the most rural artisan family was likely to have a modest library (ranging from one to sixty books) that included some selection of popular literature and plays. Moreover, Gilmore argues that the increased emphasis on reading in late eighteenth-century New England helped to fuel enthusiasm for cultural/intellectual organizations where members of the artisan class could share or show off their knowledge. If, by the early 1820s, mechanics across New England were gathering regularly (either informally at the houses of family and friends or more ceremoniously at the Mechanics' annual festivals or lyceum events), it seems possible that their early interest in Shakespeare was part of their larger effort to integrate the nation's most popular playwright into their own educational experience, and to demonstrate that they too had a right to comment on his work.[30]

Unfortunately, by the mid-nineteenth century, artisan interest in literature and culture shifted as American society drew sharp distinctions between the intellectual and manual components of labor. By that time, the Boston mechanics' school had been absorbed by other local institutions; only twenty years later, their library, once the country's largest such institution for working-class citizens, was dissolved as well. By that point too, Shakespeare had (seemingly) become the province of the middle and upper classes and the hallmark of a different kind of education. While the working classes might still evince some familiarity with his works (as Lawrence W. Levine's and Eric Lott's research suggests),[31] the connotation of cultural and educational uplift had diminished, as emphasis shifted towards more "functional" education. After all, if knowledge could not be directly translated into dollars, was it part of a "useful" education? Some regretted the change, as a letter from the mid-nineteenth century suggests: "These men, as they have the ability, should have some stimulus to improve their tastes, to enlarge their intellectual operations, to enjoy the works of genius which are adapted to the capacities and tastes of all men."[32] This comment draws a sharp contrast between the wish to use Shakespeare as a tool to engage *all* men with the intellectual life of their nation, and the bloody Astor

Place Riots of 1849 that pitted a white urban working-class population against the city's wealthiest residents. That showdown, ostensibly over who had a better right to perform *Macbeth*—the working-class hero, Edwin Forrest, or the darling of the elite, William Macready—indicated how far Shakespeare's work had moved away from its role as a leveling force in American culture.

AN INVASION OF MAN'S PREROGATIVE

This essay has briefly explored the ways in which working-class white men and African Americans might have encountered Shakespeare in their formal and informal education. One critical group remains. How did women's education in the late eighteenth and early nineteenth centuries intersect with Shakespeare as playwright, moralist, or historical figure? I suggest that Shakespearean education for women assumed two distinct forms: one oblique, as morsels of Shakespeare (or allusions to his works) were discreetly inserted into everyday readings and lessons; and one direct, as Shakespeare's heroines were explicitly invoked as a model for female behavior.

The oblique insertions of Shakespearean text into women's educational manuals appear particularly intriguing. For example, the 1799 text *The New Pleasing Instructor, or Young Lady's Guide to Virtue and Happiness* contains no actual selections from Shakespeare. Instead, it features poems about his characters, including sonnets entitled "Ophelia's Urn" and "A Prayer for Indifference to Oberon."[33] This work is suggestive for several reasons. First, the poetry it contains presupposes a prior acquaintance with Shakespeare's plays or characters (but does not specify how one is to have acquired that knowledge). Second, the editor makes a direct comparison between Shakespeare and the Bible, attributing to both the same "sweet simplicity" (and appropriateness for women's reading). Third, it contains a number of poems and essays written by women, including playwright and performer Susannah Rowson, who was one of the most popular theatrical figures and novelists of the late eighteenth century (and who opened a girls' school after her retirement from the stage). Fourth, the preface explicitly disclaims any intention to teach young women to step outside their proper sphere, "[a]s it is the opinion of the most judicious of both sexes, that public exhibitions and speaking, are not only unnecessary but highly improper for Misses." The author claims the dramatic dialogues in the text are "designed only to assist them in learning to read this kind of composition with propriety." Dramatic texts are thus situated in a

specifically educational, rather than performative, context. But the
author also assumes that her female readers will have sufficient
knowledge of Shakespeare's works in a *private* context that they will
be able to engage with her arguments. Nor was this an unreasonable
expectation. As the work of scholars such as Mary Kelley and Margaret Nash shows, eighteenth- and nineteenth-century women regularly read Shakespeare in the privacy of their own homes. Some
recall reading his works with their fathers, while others recount stories of sneaking into the family libraries to devour plays like *Romeo
and Juliet*.[34] Why, then, the stigma against performance?

The preface to the *New Pleasing Instructor* suggests that performance of Shakespeare's texts may have been considered indelicate (at
least for women). Yet women of all social classes and races attended
productions of Shakespeare's plays. Extracts from letters and dia-
ries, as well as newspaper advertisements specifically targeting
female audiences, testify to women's active presence in the playhouse. Female actresses embodied the major Shakespearean heroines to general acclaim, as the popularity of Nancy Hallam, Anne
Merry, Susannah Rowson, Fanny Kemble, and Charlotte Cushman
demonstrate. These actresses' performances offered concrete (and
very popular) examples of women using the power and passion of
Shakespeare's language. Moreover, even male audience members
considered these actresses as "authorities" on Shakespeare's texts.
For example, Fanny Kemble, a member of the famous Siddons acting family, became a successful performer and personality in
America. She also sustained a voluminous correspondence with several well-known American political and cultural icons. In letters
from figures as diverse as Henry Greville to Cassius Clay, Kemble
debated topics ranging from the current state of American politics
to the respective merits of various Shakespearean tragedies. Moreover, Kemble encountered these men on equal ground. As a letter
from Greville observes, "I was interested in what you say of Othello,
but if I had time, wd. argue with you on what you say of Desdemona."[35]

Given the recognized intellectual achievements of actresses like
Kemble, why was it considered permissible for young ladies to memorize passages of Shakespeare for private consumption, but not to
recite them as their male colleagues did?[36] As Faye Dudden has suggested in her history, *Women in the American Theatre*, the profession
of actress was a perilous one during the eighteenth and nineteenth
centuries; even the most refined female performers (like Susannah
Rowson or Fanny Kemble) had to struggle to assert their respectabil-

ity.[37] Thus for "ordinary" women to actually perform Shakespeare, rather than just reading him in the privacy of the home or the classroom, would be a doubly suspect activity, and one that could not be imagined to serve any kind of useful educational function.

Although there seem to be greater limitations placed on how women could glean or use their Shakespearean education in the late eighteenth century and antebellum period, one might argue that Shakespeare is actually being used in a more subtle way in women's educational texts and literary journals. As historian Mary Kelley suggests, female authors and educators such as Rowson and Judith Sargent Murray frequently appropriated classical history in order to reconfigure it around the achievements of women, thus emphasizing women's roles in creating the classical republics of the past.[38] By appropriating Shakespeare's texts in the same way—writing around his characters and stories—but with a message specifically directed toward women, female educators could give their young pupils unique ownership of Shakespeare's texts (but still within the "respectable" confines of a female education).

In addition to the excerpts and allusions in schoolbooks, a survey of several popular journals from the 1820s and 1830s, including *The Ladies' Literary Cabinet, The Ladies' Museum, The Ladies' Port Folio, The Ladies' Magazine, The Diana, and Ladies' Spectator,* and *The Intellectual Regale, or the Ladies' Tea Tray,* reveals regular references to Shakespeare's work—and to his specific usefulness for women. For example, in *The Ladies' Literary Cabinet,* the editor points out the ways in which Shakespeare's unique female characters may serve as moral education for American women: "A difficulty seldom surmounted by dramatic writers is a successful delineation of female characters: here Shakespeare seems to have even outrivalled himself. Where can we find so much modest simplicity as in the gentle Desdemona? Where so much faithfulness and constancy as in the romantic Imogen? Or where is there so much ferocity as in the darkened character of Lady Macbeth?"[39] It may be worth noting that some *men,* such as John Quincy Adams, characterized Desdemona as the very worst of women—immodest and indecent for her choice to marry the Moor. The fact that *The Ladies' Literary Cabinet* hails her as a paragon of modesty and decorum hints that at least some women identified Desdemona as a potential role model (an intriguing choice for a female character who makes a direct address to the Venetian Senate and who challenges her father's authority).

The Ladies' Port Folio used reviews of female actresses in great Shakespearean roles to educate its female readership about proper conduct. For example, in describing Mrs. Barnes's performance as

Juliet in 1820, the author commented on "the delicacy and sweetness of her intonations," and "the exquisite grace of her deportment."[40] As Juliet, Barnes embodied everything gentle and feminine, and thus offered an ideal role model for her feminine spectators and the paper's readers. Yet the journal reacted with horror when Barnes donned breeches to play the role of Hamlet that same season: "This being the first, and we earnestly hope the last, attempt of the kind within our observation. In truth, we protest against such an invasion of man's prerogative. We do not think in this instance that a female ought to have worn the breeches and have attempted to counterfeit 'man's fair proportion.' . . . It may perhaps pass off for a night or so as a *gag* upon the multitude."[41]

Perhaps the most striking contrast between women's versus men's Shakespearean educations appears in the notion that Shakespeare could teach men how to *act* and women how to *be*. As the passages above suggest, women might learn proper deportment from Shakespeare when he was performed "as intended," but the lesson would be a negative one when a woman stepped outside her proper sphere and into the realm of action. Women might co-opt Shakespeare's texts for their own uses, as long as they did not carry him into the arena of public performance, or into the realm of action or activism.

CONCLUSION

Returning to the question of what constituted a Shakespearean education in early America—to whom did he give the all important access to cultural, political, and social agency, and *how?* Numerous traditionally marginalized groups in early America used his works to understand and improve their own experience, and to try to create a common language that would let them transcend the boundaries of race, class, and gender.

NOTES

The quotation in the title is from *The Taming of the Shrew*, 1.1.9. Quotations from Shakespeare's works are taken from *The Riverside Shakespeare*, 2nd ed., G. Blakemore Evans, gen. ed. (Boston: Houghton Mifflin, 1997).

1. Quoted in Peter P. Hinks, *To Awaken My Afflicted Brethren: David Walker and the Problem of Antebellum Slave Resistance* (University Park: Pennsylvania State University Press, 1997), 176–77. The "Othello" letter is an often-cited piece of early American rhetoric on the evils of slavery.

2. *American Museum*, July 1789, vol. 6, 77. It is worth noting that the essay

appeared at a time of great antislavery agitation in the Atlantic circuit, as Great Britain revitalized its antislavery movement and as interested Americans contemplated how or whether the young nation should follow suit. More than half a century later, Frederick Douglass would invoke the same passage to stir pity for the plight of the slave.

3. Heather S. Nathans, *Early American Theatre from the Revolution to Thomas Jefferson: Into the Hands of the People* (Cambridge: Cambridge University Press, 2003).

4. *The New Pleasing Instructor, or Young Lady's Guide to Virtue and Happiness, consisting of essays, relations, descriptions, epistles, dialogues, and poetry, carefully extracted from the best Modern Authors, designed principally for the use of Female Schools but calculated for General Instruction and Amusement By a Lady* (Boston: I. Thomas and E. T. Andrews, 1799). Property of Louisa Curtis in Beverly (noted on flyleaf—later Mrs. Louisa C. Nichols of Beverly). Collection of the Massachusetts Historical Society.

5. *American Museum,* July 1789, vol. 6, 77.

6. *American Museum,* July 1789, vol. 6, 77. Also see Heather S. Nathans, *Slavery and Sentiment on the American Stage, 1787–1861: Lifting the Veil of Black* (Cambridge: Cambridge University Press, 2009). In chapter 1, I discuss the legal debate over slavery in the colonial and early national periods.

7. Gary Nash, *Forging Freedom: The Formation of Philadelphia's Black Community, 1720–1840* (Cambridge: Harvard University Press, 1988), 18–19. Nash suggests that the dancing master underwent a conversion experience that encouraged him to turn his attention to teaching the city's African population.

8. Philadelphia's A. M. E. Mother Bethel Church served as both a refuge for runaways and a site for the education of the city's black citizens. Thus, newly escaped slaves from the South would also have had the opportunity to engage with elocution manuals and other materials that might have included passages from Shakespeare. Additionally, the city's two most prominent black preachers, Absalom Jones and Richard Allen, were men of letters whose names appear on subscription lists for major new publications in the city and who also published their own works and sermons.

9. Theater historians know that blacks were present both as audience members and as laborers backstage. Scholar Jeffrey H. Richards has developed an exciting new project that traces the history of black labor behind the scenes in the early American playhouse, and his research suggests that black stagehands would have had repeated exposure to Shakespearean texts in performance. I am grateful to Professor Richards for discussing his ongoing research with me.

10. Anna Mae Duane, "Performing Freedom in Antebellum New York: The New York African Free School," unpublished paper delivered at Luce Hall, Yale University, November 13, 2006. I am very grateful to Professor Duane for sharing this paper with me.

11. Aldridge won prizes for declamation while he was in the African Free School. Although we do not have evidence that the students at the African Free Schools performed Shakespeare, Charles Andrews's history of the African Free Schools *does* describe a few of the plays that children read from, including Mathew Lewis's *Castle Spectre* and James Cobb's *Paul and Virginia*. These two works are particularly significant because of their comments on slavery. The former features a slave named Hassan who has numerous monologues about his capture from Africa; the latter includes an escaped slave named Alambra. Both describe scenes of the Middle Passage. See Charles C. Andrews, *The History of the New-York African Free-Schools* (New York: M. Day, 1830). Aldridge was a celebrity in nineteenth-century black culture as well. For example, in 1852, *Frederick Douglass's Paper* published an essay entitled

"An African Roscius," tracing the path of Aldridge's career. While much of the story printed in the paper had been fictionalized (Aldridge's father was *not* the son of an African prince, nor had Aldridge been born in Africa), it remains useful for what it reveals about the construction of Aldridge's persona. For more on Aldridge, see Errol Hill, *Shakespeare in Sable: A History of Black Shakespearean Actors* (Amherst: University of Massachusetts Press, 1984).

12. Andrews, *The History of the New-York African Free-Schools*, 27.

13. *Freedom's Journal*, September 26, 1828. *Freedom's Journal* was founded in 1827.

14. *Freedom's Journal*, March 21, 1829.

15. *Weekly Advocate*, January 28, 1837.

16. *Colored American*, February 16, 1839.

17. Ezra Tawil, *The Making of Racial Sentiment* (Cambridge: Cambridge University Press, 2006), 33.

18. Dorothy B. Porter, "The Organized Educational Activities of Negro Literary Societies, 1828–1846," *Journal of Negro Education* 5 (1936): 556–66.

19. See *The National Era*, February 12, 1852. The paper contains a long letter from a woman who signs herself "Grace Greenwood" and describes all the social and cultural gaieties of the capitol city. She offers a lengthy description of a production of *Othello*, which she describes as "painfully unsatisfactory." Black newspapers seldom printed dramatic reviews, but responses to *Othello* seem to appear on a more regular basis than other plays—perhaps because the authors were interested in claiming the character as their own.

20. See *The Liberator*, May–June 1853. The June 10, 1853, issue carries a particularly extensive account of the incident that prompted the lawsuit.

21. Dorothy Porter Wesley and Constance Porter Uzelac, eds., *William Cooper Nell: Nineteenth-Century African American Abolitionist, Historian, Integrationist; Selected Writings 1832–1874* (New York: Black Classic Press, 2002), 355.

22. Ibid.

23. The surviving cast list for the Club offers a collection of names that I have cross-referenced with Boston census records from the 1850s. I have been able to identify many of the members of the club, as well as their professions and places of residence. Some names have proved more elusive. For example, the name "Elizabeth Smith" appears on the Histrionic Club's cast list, and there are twelve black Elizabeth Smiths listed in Boston for the period in question. I have tentatively identified some of the members of the club as former slaves, based on their places of birth, and on the fact that Nell and many of his fellow club members were active in the Underground Railroad. For more on the Histrionic Club, see Nathans, *Slavery and Sentiment on the American Stage*.

24. The following notice appeared in *The Liberator*, April 2, 1858: "The Histrionic Club will celebrate its first anniversary on Wednesday evening, April 7. The following exercises will take place at the Twelfth Baptist Vestry, Southac Street; —An address by William C. Nell and an original poem by George L. Ruffin will be delivered. Appropriate music will be furnished by members of the club. An admission fee of ten cents (to defray expenses) will be taken at the door. Exercises to commence at half-past 7 o'clock. Jacob R. Andrews, Secretary." Some historians have dated the origins of the Club to more than a decade earlier; however, this advertisement seems to suggest that the Club had its official beginning in 1857.

25. Given Nell's love of Shakespeare and his fond recollections of occasions in which he and his white colleagues spent evenings reading the plays aloud, it is interesting that so little information about the Histrionic Club's potential performances / readings of Shakespeare has come to light. However, while Nell was

certainly aware of Ira Aldridge's success as a Shakespearean performer, he was likely aware of the ridicule and persecution that had faced the African Grove Theatre in New York City in the 1820s. That company had "presumed" to perform Shakespeare, and white critics and audiences had attacked the players both in the press and in the playhouse. The memory of that company lingered in American culture through the 1830s and 1840s as a popular cartoon series satirizing blacks in Philadelphia makes clear. The "Life in Philadelphia" series (widely imitated and replicated on both sides of the Atlantic until well after the Civil War) poked malicious fun at the efforts of black Americans to participate in "highbrow" white culture, including dancing lessons and performing Shakespeare. One of the cartoons features a black man dressed as Romeo positioned beneath Juliet's balcony, declaiming Romeo's famous lines in very broken English. For more on the history of the African Grove Theatre, see Marvin McAllister, *White People Do Not Know How to Behave at Entertainments Designed for Ladies and Gentlemen of Colour: William Brown's African and American Theatre* (Chapel Hill: University of North Carolina Press, 2003).

26. *Philadelphia Repository and Weekly Register,* August 27, 1803.

27. The terms "mechanic" and "artisan" were often used interchangeably during the early national period and encompass a range of professions from carpenter to hairdresser. A "mechanic" or an "artisan" is one who practices a skill (often on an individual basis). Paul Revere, for example, was considered a mechanic and was a prominent member of the Massachusetts Charitable Mechanics Association. By the mid-nineteenth century, "working class" takes on the connotation of factory labor. However, many mechanics' societies persisted even after the advent of the factory system.

28. For a discussion of the mechanics' theater, see Nathans, *Early American Theatre,* chapter 3.

29. Preface, *Woods Mentor (American Teacher's Assistant),* Massachusetts Historical Society. This copy bears the inscription "Thomas Roberts Bromfield presented to him by George Ronald, 1799."

30. William J. Gilmore-Lehne, *Reading Becomes a Necessity of Life: Material and Cultural Life in Rural New England, 1780–1835* (Knoxville: University of Tennessee Press, 1989).

31. See Eric Lott, *Love and Theft: Blackface Minstrelsy and the American Working Class* (New York: Oxford University Press, 1993); and Lawrence W. Levine, *Highbrow / Lowbrow: The Emergence of a Cultural Hierarchy in America* (Cambridge: Harvard University Press, 1988).

32. Undated letter, believed to be from Martha Stevenson to Mr. Curtis. The letter was found in her desk in 1879. Curtis-Stevenson Family Papers Collection, Massachusetts Historical Society.

33. *The New Pleasing Instructor: or, Young Lady's Guide to Virtue and happiness* (Boston: I. Thomas and E. T. Andrews, 1799).

34. For numerous anecdotes of nineteenth-century women's encounters with Shakespeare see Mary Kelley, *Learning to Stand & Speak: Women, Education, and Public Life in America's Republic* (Chapel Hill: University of North Carolina Press, 2006), and Margaret A. Nash, *Women's Education in the United States, 1780–1840* (New York: Palgrave Macmillan, 2005).

35. Henry Greville to Fanny Kemble, 1861 (?); Kemble Letters, Folger Shakespeare Library, Washington, DC.

36. City newspapers often carried descriptions of end-of-year public recitations by male students. For example, see *The Boston Weekly Magazine,* May 13, 1818. The paper describes a performance at the Boston Latin School, noting in particular one

young man's performance as Hotspur, which the reviewer claimed, "was characteristic and eloquent, approaching a maturity of excellence far beyond his years."

37. Faye E. Dudden, *Women in the American Theatre: Actresses and Audiences, 1790–
1870* (New Haven: Yale University Press, 1994).

38. Kelley, *Learning to Stand & Speak.*

39. *The Ladies' Literary Cabinet,* June 1, 1822.

40. *The Ladies' Port Folio,* January 15, 1820.

41. *The Ladies' Port Folio,* January 29, 1820.

Eloquent Shakespeare

Sandra M. Gustafson

Henry clay folger, the founder of the folger shakespeare Library, was converted to Shakespeare in 1879. Like the religious conversions that had become a characteristic feature of American religious experience, Folger's cultural conversion came by hearing when he attended a lecture that Ralph Waldo Emerson delivered at Amherst College and was inspired to read more of Emerson's works, including his essay on Shakespeare. In Stanley King's account, Emerson "fired him with a love of Shakespeare to which he decided to devote his life."[1]

That Folger's conversion to Shakespeare began with a lecture aptly reflects an important aspect of his attraction to the Bard. Folger shared the interest in eloquent speech that powerfully shaped American society in the nineteenth century. Emerson, who developed his printed essays from his oral presentations on the lecture circuit, once described the prose writer as an "orator manqué."[2] Folger's parents named him after Henry Clay, the Kentucky orator and politician who, along with Daniel Webster and John Calhoun, formed the Great Triumvirate that led the antebellum U.S. Senate.[3] For almost thirty years, these men used eloquence to achieve and maintain political power. Folger was a product of the culture that celebrated oratory as the preeminent republican verbal art. At Amherst College, the future chairman of Standard Oil won a prize for an essay on "Dickens as Preacher" and was elected Ivy Orator in his senior year, when he gave the Ivy address on "The Sovereignty of Sentiment." Folger's wife, Emily, shared her husband's appreciation for eloquent speech. The initial leadership of the library, appointed after Henry's death in 1930, included two directors, one for the scholarly staff and the other responsible for the operating staff. Emily Folger wanted to appoint a director of speech as well, whose task it would be to improve the oral expression of the American people. The Amherst faculty was asked to evaluate the candidate for this position, but he was rejected as "a representative of an older

school of elocution" and "a good example of 'ham' acting."[4] Emily
Folger dropped the idea, but the connection between Shakespeare
and eloquent speech lived on.

In *Representative Men*, Emerson described Shakespeare as essentially a talker. "He was a full man, who liked to talk," Emerson wrote,
with "a brain exhaling thoughts and images, which, seeking vent,
found the drama next at hand." Dramatic form was incidental to
Shakespeare, Emerson insisted. What mattered was the substance of
his insight, beside which his use or abuse of dramatic conventions
meant little: "Had he been less, we should have had to consider how
well he filled his place, how good a dramatist he was,—and he is the
best in the world. But it turns out that what he has to say is of that
weight as to withdraw some attention from the vehicle." In the face
of such genius, "the importance of this wisdom of life sinks the
form, as of Drama or Epic, out of notice. 'Tis like making a question
concerning the paper on which a king's message is written."[5]

"Did the bard speak with authority?" Emerson asked, and proceeded to compare Shakespeare's use of his sources and his ability
to absorb and articulate broadly shared views to the work of great
statesmen: "The learned member of the legislature, at Westminster
or at Washington, speaks and votes for thousands. Show us the constituency, and the now invisible channels by which the senator is
made aware of their wishes; the crowd of practical and knowing
men, who, by correspondence or conversation, are feeding him with
evidence, anecdotes and estimates, and it will bereave his fine attitude and resistance of something of their impressiveness. As Sir Robert Peel and Mr. Webster vote, so Locke and Rousseau think, for
thousands."[6]

Emerson's central points in these passages—that Shakespeare's
art transcends genre, making his abilities as a dramatist insignificant; and that his ability to "channel" public will and popular meaning make him "representative" in a manner akin to the political
representative—were not unique to him. They derive from an
approach to Shakespeare popularized by the eighteenth-century
Irish dramatist and pedagogue Thomas Sheridan. Sheridan originated the elocutionary movement that profoundly shaped American
education for more than a century. In 1756, he published *British
Education: Or, The Source of the Disorders of Great Britain*, his first major
statement on educational reform in what became an extended campaign to establish vernacular education and speech training at the
center of the British system.[7] Sheridan found much to criticize in
British society, lamenting that "irreligion, immorality, and corrup-
tion are visibly increased, and daily gather new strength." The "vir-

tuous few" are powerless before the "numerous wicked," he complained, and the law is rendered useless by the prevailing mores. The title page of *British Education* summed up Sheridan's argument, which he pursued over nearly 400 pages, promising to correct "Immorality, Ignorance, and false Taste" with "a Revival of the Art of Speaking." Turning to the examples of ancient Athens and Rome, Sheridan concluded that "a Revival of the Art of Speaking, and the Study of our own Language, might contribute, in a great measure, to the Cure of those Evils." Eloquence is essential to good governance in a constitutional republic, he argued. It should be a cultivated quality, not left to chance but incorporated into general education. Only then would British society benefit from the talents of its best minds. "If in the multitude of counselors there be safety," he asked quoting Proverbs, "will not the state be in danger, in proportion as their number is reduced" by the lack of training in oratory?" He claimed that Christian religion suffered as well, as the lack of well trained preachers had undermined the Anglican church and fostered an outbreak of enthusiasm characterized by wild and unseemly preaching. Pulpit eloquence would help restore order to a chaotic religious scene and improve public morality. And Sheridan thought that training in eloquence promised still more. Arguing that speech was the first and most important art influencing all others, he speculated that "Poetry, Music, Painting, and Sculpture, might arrive at as high a Pitch of Perfection in England, as ever they did in Athens or Rome."[8]

Sheridan quickly followed up the general defense of pedagogical reform presented in *British Education* with two works that provided inspiration and means to achieve those reforms: *A Discourse delivered in the Theatre at Oxford, in the Senate-House at Cambridge, and At Spring-Garden in London* (1759) and *A Course of Lectures on Elocution* (1762). Sheridan's later works, including *A Plan of Education* (1769), *Lectures on the Art of Reading* (1775), and *A General Dictionary of the English Language* (1780), continued to elaborate and build upon the arguments laid out in *British Education*. In Britain's former American colonies, *Lectures on Elocution* was reprinted twice between 1796 and 1803.[9]

Sheridan's influence was not limited to his lectures and printed works on pedagogy and language. He also sparked a vogue for dramatic readings with the "Attic Mornings" that he began at Bath in 1763 and later staged in London.[10] Such readings spread throughout the English-speaking Atlantic world. In the colonies and early republic, the readings supplemented and sometimes substituted for full-scale theatrical fare. Dramatic readings became popular events in the late eighteenth century and continued to draw audiences for over a century. The variety, popularity, and endurance of such performances are suggested by a broadside from 1855 that advertises a series of readings presented by Mrs. Webb. Many other dramatists, including African-American performer James Hewlett, had done solo readings of Shakespeare before Webb took the stage. The timing of the tour—five years after the Compromise Measures of 1850 and six years before the outbreak of the Civil War—make this broadside a particularly interesting testament to the ways that Shakespeare shaped American popular culture and political discourse at a volatile moment. The advertisement positions Webb in a line of Shakespeare performers, calling her the "black Siddons," a reference to the British Shakespearean actress Sarah Siddons who trained with Sheridan and later held her own "Attic Mornings" in London in the late eighteenth century. Webb's selections included excerpts from *Twelfth Night* and *Romeo and Juliet*. The broadside excerpts reviews of her performances from Boston, Worcester, Philadelphia, and Maine, and compares her favorably to other dramatic readers then performing. According to the Philadelphia review Webb was surpassed as a reader only by Fanny Kemble, a member of the famous acting family (she was Siddons's niece). During the 1850s, Kemble supported herself as a dramatic reader of Shakespeare after her sensational divorce from Georgia slave owner Pierce Butler, a public marital failure linked partly to Kemble's abolitionism.

Shakespeare is the connecting thread between Sheridan, Emerson, Webb, Kemble, and the Folgers. His works figure significantly in *British Education*, where he represents an untutored vernacular style that provides the ideal model for English training. Here we see Shakespeare described, not as a great dramatist, but as a master of spoken English. His plays are disparaged as dramatic works but valued for their passages of oratorical excellence.[11] Like Emerson after him, Sheridan thought of Shakespeare as principally a talker: "It might be easily shewn, that the great success of his pieces at this day, and the effects which they produce in the representation, have been chiefly owing to his skill in the art of speaking." He "had acquired from the very profession in which he was engaged, an habitual and practical knowledge of the oratorical art, far superior to all theory." It is this mastery of eloquent speech and his ability to reproduce it that "form a true dramatick style, that happy arrangement and disposition of his words, so perfectly adapted to his subjects, which throw such a luster on his sentiments, and are so admirably suited to the mouth of the speaker." Sheridan argued that the speeches in

Shakespeare's plays provide their dramatic structure and "sufficiently make amends for all the irregularities of his drama." The best evidence that Shakespeare was attentive to the arts of speech comes from the plays themselves. Sheridan singled out Hamlet's speech to the players as an especially insightful account of eloquence. "We can not but wonder how it was possible, that so just and comprehensive a system of rules both for action, and speaking, could have been comprised in so narrow a compass," he observed.[12]

It is this eloquent Shakespeare who entered English language education through the ubiquitous courses in elocution and the elocutionary manuals that were standard fare in American schools and universities beginning around 1800. The impact of Shakespeare's plays on American education operated at two levels: as a source of model speech texts such as appeared in the elocution handbooks and as a set of culturally authoritative texts that were incorporated into the growing body of American oratory and used to contest major ethical and political issues such as slavery. In the public life of the United States, debates over the legacy left by the Founders were conducted as debates over the meaning of a culture founder, William Shakespeare.

A variety of elocutionary handbooks that prominently included speeches from Shakespeare demonstrate the pedagogical purposes to which his works were put. Moral and political lessons were inculcated through the choice and labeling of texts. The books demonstrate some of the techniques for "sampling" Shakespeare's plays, which included brief excerpts, full speeches or scenes, and speeches marked for delivery. They also reveal some of the debates about Shakespeare's aesthetic and pedagogical value that accompanied the practice of elocutionary instruction.

William Scott's popular *Lessons in Elocution: Or, a Selection of Pieces in Prose and Verse, or the Improvement of Youth in Reading and Speaking* (1779) originated in England and went through several American editions. Scott noted that "elocution has, for some years past, been an object of attention in the most respectable schools in this country. A laudable ambition of instructing youth in the pronunciation and delivery of their native language, has made English speeches a very conspicuous part of those exhibitions of oratory, which do our seminaries of learning so much credit." Scott rejected schoolroom performance of complete plays, observing that the practice raises issues of morality, practicality, and the worthwhile use of time. He concluded that "it is speaking, rather than acting, which school boys should be taught"; more specifically, boys should "be accustomed to speak such speeches, as require a full, open, animated pronunciation; for which purpose they should be confined, chiefly, to orations, odes and such single speeches of plays, as are in the declamatory and vehement style." He provided a substantial number of excerpts from Shakespeare, including speeches from *Macbeth, Henry VIII,* and *Julius Caesar.* The largest number appears in the section "Speeches and Soliloquies," where sixteen out of twenty-five selections are from Shakespeare's plays, including extracts from *Hamlet, 1* and *2 Henry IV, Othello, Henry V, Julius Caesar, Richard III,* and *As You Like It.* The first selection in this section is "Hamlet's advice to the players," which was one of the most commonly cited works in elocutionary texts, and elsewhere Scott paraphrases Hamlet, noting that "the exact adaptation of the action to the word, and the word to the action, as Shakespeare calls it, is the most difficult part of delivery" and thus is beyond the capacities of children. Instead they are trained in "a general style of action" that "is not expressive of any particular passion" but rather "shall not be inconsistent with the expression of any passion."[13] Scott's goal was to train students in graceful movement, with the passions treated only in a general way.

Increase Cooke's *American Orator* series was perhaps the first set of elocution manuals originating in the United States to use Shakespeare as a marketing device. Imports and American editions of Scott and other influential elocutionists had already made Shakespeare a common figure in elocutionary education. What distinguished Cooke's series was his prominent linking of the idea of the American orator with the guiding presence of Shakespeare. The books may have been modeled on the immensely influential *Columbian Orator* compiled by Caleb Bingham, which first appeared in 1797 and was issued in twenty-three editions over the next half-century. Bingham's early editions included no Shakespeare.[14] Cooke's other main American competitor was Noah Webster, who had begun publishing his *Grammatical Institutes* in 1783, and who included a relatively small number of selections from Shakespeare's works, explaining in a preface that he preferred to focus on American authors and topics.[15] Cooke soon made his inclusion of the Bard into the signal mark of his series. *The American Orator* was first published in New Haven in 1811 and reissued several times before 1820. In 1813 Cooke published a *Sequel to the American Orator,* which portrays a bust of Shakespeare opposite the title page (Figure 1).[16] These decisions to highlight the Shakespearean content of the volumes may have been a strategy to distinguish the series from Bingham's and Webster's books. They may also have reflected the presence, beginning in the late 1790s, of star English Shakespearean

WM SHAKSPEARE.
Born Apr. 23. 1564.
Died Apr. 23. 1616.

Figure 1. Increase Cooke, *Sequel to the American Orator, or, Dialogues for Schools: To Which Are Prefixed Elements of Elocution.* . . . New Haven: Increase Cooke and Sidney's Press, 1813. Frontispiece. By permission of the Folger Shakespeare Library.

actors on the American stage. Thomas A. Cooper, George Cooke, and later Edmund Kean made Shakespearean heroes newly exciting to American audiences and contributed to the Americanization of Shakespeare.[17]

The American Orator includes unattributed brief extracts from a variety of works, including several by Shakespeare, with instructions for reading them well. "Hamlet's Directions to the players" is included in the section titled "Didactic Pieces," where it is identified as Shakespeare's work. The *Sequel* includes a number of additional Shakespeare extracts. In contrast to the earlier volume these are all clearly labeled. They include "humorous scenes" from *A Midsummer Night's Dream* and *Henry VI;* "serious pieces" including "King John's Conference with Hubert," "Orlando and Adam," an excerpt from *Henry IV, Part I,* and two excerpts from *Henry IV, Part II;* and scenes from *Richard II, Henry V,* and *Henry IV, Part I, The Tempest, The Merchant of Venice,* and *As You Like It* in "promiscuous pieces," a designation referring to the fact that they were varied and lacked thematic unity. A number of additional Shakespeare selections are included in the reading texts of the appendix.[18]

Cooke's *Sequel* went beyond his earlier volume, which simply includes some extracts from the plays, in that it offered a substantive pedagogical rationale for emphasizing Shakespeare. He argued that training in the recognition and the representation of the passions was central to learning the orator's art. Cooke observed that he had included many selections from the plays because Shakespeare portrayed the passions "in a clearer and more affecting way than in any other Poet" and provided "the best description that could be given of the passions in any language."[19] Shakespeare offered authoritative support for the art of elocution, which for Cooke prominently included the ability to represent, evoke, and manage the passions, both the student's own passions and those of others.

The republican goals of civic rhetoric are strongly visible in an 1822 compilation by E. G. Welles, published in Philadelphia and called *The Orator's Guide; Or Rules for Speaking and Composing; from the Best Authorities.* Welles included an impassioned defense of the civic value of oratory, including its capacity to emancipate "millions from slavery" and redeem "innumerable captives." He chose speeches that thematized the relationship between oratory and liberty. This relatively brief, 100-page manual includes just a dozen selections, among them a speech by "Grenville Sharpe, the negro's advocate" along with two thematically appropriate speeches from Shakespeare. "Othello's Apology" is Othello's speech to the Venetian court vindicating himself and describing how he wooed Desdemona with a "round unvarnish'd tale." "Brutus and Cassius" from *Julius Caesar* includes Cassius's announcement that "I had as lief not be, as live to be / In awe of such a thing as I myself." Welles also included Cassius's mocking depiction of the supposedly godlike Caesar during an illness when "that tongue of his, that bade the Romans / Mark him, and write his speeches in their books, / Alas it cry'd—Give me some drink, Titinius—/ As a sick girl."[20] Welles's choice of this dialogue, with its relatively sympathetic portrait of the conspirators and its account of Caesar's diminished speech, is in keeping with the overall pro-republican tone of his volume.

A similarly sympathetic portrait of the defenders of the Roman republic is displayed in Jonathan Barber's 1831 adaptation of Gilbert Austin's *Chironomia*, which Barber prepared for his classes on gesture at Harvard University.[21] Austin's gestures were designed for public speaking and dramatic declamation. Barber, who identified himself on the title page as a member of the Royal College of Surgeons in London, explained that he liked Austin's work on gesture but found it included matter on voice that he did not need for his Harvard classes, so he cut the text down to reduce the cost for his readers. Barber followed Austin when he included Brutus's funeral speech for Caesar as one of his three exemplary texts (the others are Gray's *Elegy* and Young's *Night Thoughts*), rather than the more commonly cited speech by Marc Antony. A preference for Brutus's less compelling oration reflected republican sympathies. The texts are marked for gesture, with extensive accompanying notes describing just how the body should be positioned in delivery. The volume also includes illustrations taken from Austin of oratorical postures, with some of the figures clad in togas (Figure 2).

Increasingly in the 1820s, elocution manuals included modern exemplars alongside extracts from Cicero, Shakespeare, and other historical figures. Like Barber, Dickinson College professor C. D. Cleveland included Brutus's funeral oration in his compilation *The National Orator* (1832), along with Hamlet's instructions to the players, Othello's address to the Senate, and roughly a dozen other Shakespeare extracts. The bulk of Cleveland's volume consists of excerpts from speeches by contemporary American and British orators, with Daniel Webster's works especially well represented, including short samples from his Plymouth oration, his Greek speech, the reply to Hayne, and an antislavery address. Webster was also a major figure in William B. Fowle's *The New Speaker, or Exercises in Rhetoric*, which appeared in Boston in 1829. Fowle, who was a teacher at the Monitorial School in Boston, included nine Webster selections, more than any other single figure including Edmund Burke (who

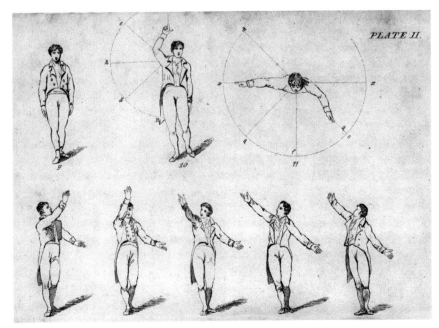

Figure 2. Jonathan Barber, *A Practical Treatise on Gesture: Chiefly Abstracted from Austin's Chironomia; Adapted to the Use of Students, and Arranged According to the Method of Instruction in Harvard University.* Cambridge: Hilliard & Brown, 1831. Plate 2. By permission of the Folger Shakespeare Library.

was represented with seven selections) and Edward Everett (who had eight extracts). In his comparatively small set of Shakespeare passages, Fowle chose to include Antony's funeral oration for Caesar rather than that of the republican Brutus, along with three "dramatic pieces" from *Othello, Henry IV,* and *Henry VI.*

The elocutionary movement created an eloquent Shakespeare who could be used to teach young people the value of speaking standard English well. One thinks here of the scene in *My Fair Lady* where Henry Higgins reforms Eliza Doolittle's Cockney accent: "The rain in Spain falls mainly on the plain." From their earliest years, elocution lessons offered the means to reduce the signs of class and regional identities. Lord Wedderburn, Benjamin Franklin's opponent in the "Cockpit," studied with Sheridan to tame his Scottish brogue.[22] He was just one of many aspiring individuals from the British periphery who took speech lessons in order to soften an uncouth accent. In the United States, the enforcement of standard spoken English was important to the continued flourishing of elocution lessons well into the twentieth century. The contributions of elocution to white hegemony are evident, for example, in the broadside description of the dramatic reader Mrs. Webb as "living proof of the capacity of the race for culture." Beyond the emphasis on standardized speech, the focus on Shakespeare contributed to a reassessment and reinterpretation of republican values and not simply their passive reproduction. From at least the early nineteenth-century African-American theater troupes, dramatic readers, educational institutions, and orators drew on Shakespeare's plays to educate citizens and entertain audiences. These interpreters of Shakespeare's legacy did not simply embrace what Leonard Tennenhouse has described as "a pervasively normative and yet curiously elastic definition of Englishness."[23] Rather, as we shall see, they actively contested the meaning of America's distinctive version of Englishness in their efforts to redefine modern republicanism.

Joseph Quincy Adams, the first director of scholarship at the Folger Library, celebrated the hegemonic power of Shakespearean eloquence in the dedication speech for the library that he delivered on April 23, 1932. Insisting that Shakespeare "is the common possession of both branches of the Anglo-Saxon race," Adams identified three important periods in the formation of American culture when Shakespeare helped forge "bonds of a common Anglo-Saxon culture": the era of British settlement, the period of territorial expansion in the early nineteenth century, and the era of foreign immigration after the Civil War.[24] Adams observed that Increase Mather and William Byrd both owned the First Folio, that copies of the 1709 Rowe *Works* were in the Harvard library and owned by the Washington family, and that Jefferson owned a complete copy of the 1619 quartos. Shakespeare's plays were produced in America as early as the middle of the eighteenth century, he noted, and an American edition of Shakespeare appeared by century's end. In a passage worth quoting at length, Adams describes how early in the next century Shakespeare accompanied settlers to the frontier:

> Copies of his works were purchased and set in homes by the side of the family Bible; children studied him at school, men and women read him in the evenings by the light of the open fire; itinerant elocutionists gave recitals from his more famous plays; traveling troupes of actors, seedy in worn costumes, yet trailing the glory of the Eastern theatre, came to present the ever-popular "Hamlet," "Othello," and "Richard III"; public lectures, flaunting the weeds of scholarship, delivered orations on his mind and art; preachers quoted him in their sermons, lawyers and politicians in their speeches; even manufacturers of patent medicines, of which there seemed to be no end, issued what they called "Shakespearean Almanacs," adorned with elegant extracts from his works.[25]

Adams celebrated the fact that Shakespeare provided a common cultural legacy, preserving "the elements of British culture . . . in the hearts of a far-flung people who in race were still essentially English" and lending to "American civilization something like homogeneity."[26]

That homogeneity came under threat in the later nineteenth century, Adams observed, as waves of immigrants arrived and "America seemed destined to become a babel of tongues and cultures." The "menace" that this immigration posed to what Adams called "our long-established English civilization" was countered by compulsory education, with Shakespeare playing a central role in training immigrants in Anglo-Saxon values: "Everywhere pupils were set to the memorizing of his lines, of reciting on platforms his more eloquent passages, of composing innumerable essays on his art, his technique, his ideals of life, his conceptions of character, of presenting his plays in American theatricals. What American child, during the last half-century, could not repeat Portia's speech on the quality of mercy, or Mark Antony's orations over the dead body of Caesar?" Adams celebrated the fact that training in Shakespearean eloquence helped weld "a homogeneous nation, with a culture that is still essentially English" out of diverse immigrant communities.[27]

Elocution embodied more egalitarian ideals, as well as these troubling ones proposed by Adams. Sheridan had imagined no less than the wholesale reformation of British politics and religious life to make it both more participatory and more creative through the power of widely shared eloquence, and Shakespeare played a crucial role in that process. These sometimes conflicting applications of Shakespearean elocution reflect Sheridan's double goal: bringing more people into active political life by teaching them how to speak well in public settings, and creating an orderly and morally disciplined society, which could be interpreted as Adams did to mean a more homogeneous one. In the newly independent United States, educators embraced Sheridan's vision of vernacular speech training as the soul of republican governance without necessarily adopting an emphasis on uniformity. Shakespeare's speeches provided a set of core texts that were increasingly taught to young people and that the great orators used to hone their skills. Several generations of civic leaders with varied political agendas, from Fisher Ames in the 1790s, to Daniel Webster from around 1800 until his death in 1852, to Abraham Lincoln and Frederick Douglass in the 1840s and 1850s and beyond, took Shakespeare as a model and a source text second only to the Bible. And like the Bible, Shakespeare was an authority to be invoked in political debates over fundamental ethical issues such as racial slavery. Speeches by Daniel Webster and Frederick Douglass demonstrate that Shakespeare's speeches provided a cultural touchstone that could be used to explore the nation's republican inheritance and contest its legacy of slavery.

In his justly famous 1852 antislavery speech "What to the Slave Is the Fourth of July?" Frederick Douglass appropriated Shakespeare's cultural authority in defense of the abolitionist cause. Douglass asserted his stake in a cultural heritage when he regularly quoted Shakespeare in his editorials and included an epigram from Shakespeare for his single work of fiction, *The Heroic Slave.*[28] His choice of passages from *Julius Caesar* and *Macbeth* in his 1852 speech reinforced the "scorching irony" that he identified as his central and necessary trope, for both passages concern a gap between perception and reality that Douglass identified as a profound failing of the early American republic.[29] Both of the passages occur in discussions of ideas about paternity and American political traditions, amplifying Douglass's urgent question: what did the Founding Fathers bequeath to their descendants? No one claimed greater authority over the meaning of the Constitution and the significance of the founding than Daniel Webster, the Massachusetts Senator whose support for the Compromise of 1850, including the poisonous Fugitive Slave Act, was based on the kind of Constitutional interpretation that Douglass mocked with his "scorching irony." Webster was an implied interlocutor and a central object of Douglass's ire in his speech. At the time Webster was serving as Secretary of State, a position that required him to enforce the Fugitive Slave Act despite his earlier abolitionist convictions and the profound hostility of a large part of his Massachusetts constituency. Although Douglass did not directly name Webster, he referred to him by his title, describing how "your President, your Secretary of State, your *lords, nobles,* and ecclesiastics enforce, as a duty you owe to your free and glorious country, and to your God, that you" accept "the most foul and fiendish of all human decrees" and make "your broad republican domain" into a "hunting ground for *men.*"[30]

Douglass posed a further challenge to Webster when he alluded to a prominent passage from "The Constitution and the Union," Webster's speech in favor of the Compromise Measures of 1850. Webster opened his speech with an image of the ship of state in peril: "The imprisoned winds are let loose. The East, the North, and the stormy South combine to throw the whole sea into commotion, to toss its billows to the skies, and disclose its profoundest depths." In this dire situation, Webster insisted, "I am looking out for no fragment upon which to float away from the wreck, if wreck there must

be, but for the good of the whole, and the preservation of all." "I
speak today for the preservation of the Union," Webster continued;
then, quoting Brutus's funeral oration for Caesar, he pleaded with
the assembled Senators to " 'Hear me for my cause.' "[31] Where Webster understood the Union as the nation's salvation, Douglass in his
response argued that "the principles contained in [the Constitu-
tion] are saving principles." Directly revising Webster's image of the
impending storm threatening the United States, Douglass urged his
audience to prefer principled disunion to unprincipled union:
"From the round top of your ship of state, dark and threatening
clouds may be seen. Heavy billows, like mountains in the distance,
disclose to the leeward huge forms of flinty rocks! That bolt drawn,
that chain broken, and all is lost. Cling to this day—cling to it, and
to its principles, with the grasp of a storm-tossed mariner to a spar
at midnight."[32] Better to grasp the spar of principle and float away
from the shattered Union, Douglass suggested, than seek "the preservation of the Union" with Webster.

Both Webster and Douglass quoted *Julius Caesar* in order to take
opposing sides in the perennial debate over the meaning of the historic Caesar, who brought the Roman Republic to an end while
promising greater economic equality, and the equally contentious
question of Shakespeare's attitudes toward the historic events that
he portrayed. As several of the elocution manuals that I discussed
earlier illustrate, modern republicans such as Webster identified
with Brutus and Cassius, who murdered Caesar in an effort to pre-
serve the Republic. Webster's decision to quote Brutus at the beginning of his speech suggests the deep ambivalence that runs through
the address: he has to kill something he loves (abolition and his
commitment to human rights) in order to save something that he
loves more (republican self-rule as embodied in the union). His listeners may well have recalled the end of Brutus's speech, where he
urges his audience to value their own liberty: "Had you rather Caesar were living, and die all slaves, than that Caesar were dead, to live
all freemen? . . . Who is here so base, that would be a bondman?"
(3.2.22–24, 29). Brutus characterizes submission to a tyrant as a
form of political slavery; the problem of chattel slavery lies outside
his frame of reference. In much the same way Webster elevated the
survival of the republic above the interests of those enslaved within
it.

Douglass responded to this framing of the debate by presenting
"the slave's point of view." He noted the ironic fact that "Washington could not die till he had broken the chains of his slaves," and
yet in Douglass's day "his monument is built up by the price of

human blood, and the traders in the bodies and souls of men shout—'We have Washington to *our father.*'" At this moment Douglass quoted Mark Antony's funeral oration for Caesar: "The evil that men do, lives after them, / The good is oft interred with their bones" (3.2.76). These lines, coming at the very beginning of Antony's speech, set the stage for Antony's eventual revelation that in his will Caesar has left a "rich legacy" (3.2.137) of money and property to the common people of Rome. Like Caesar, Washington intended to leave a "rich legacy" of freedom to enslaved people, but that legacy had been diverted so that "the rich inheritance of justice, liberty, prosperity, and independence, bequeathed by your fathers, is shared by you, not by me." After quoting Antony, Douglass mimicked his expressions of reluctance to continue addressing his audience. Antony tells the plebeians gathered by Caesar's coffin what he will not do in his speech: "If I were disposed to stir / Your hearts and minds to mutiny and rage, / I should do Brutus wrong, and Cassius wrong, / Who (you all know) are honourable men" (3.2.122–25). Douglass claimed a similar (and similarly ephemeral) reluctance to speak. "Why," he asked, "am I called upon to speak here to-day? What have I, or those I represent, to do with your national independence?"[33] The question hinged, as Douglass went on to show, on how the Constitution—Washington's "will" or legacy—was interpreted.

Douglass impersonated Brutus's opponent Mark Antony in order to emphasize the deeply flawed nature of a republicanism used to cover personal ambition, which Antony suggests was Brutus's true motive. For decades, similar accusations had been made against Webster, who associated with wealthy business interests and repeatedly sought the presidency. As Antony's speech unfolds, he denies Brutus's accusations that Caesar was himself ambitious and stresses his generosity to the plebeians, transforming him from a power-hungry demagogue into a warm-hearted man of the people. Douglass traded on this transformation when he reinvented Washington and the other Founding Fathers as abolitionists who intended the values espoused in the founding documents to extend the freedom envisioned there to enslaved people.

To a certain extent, Webster concurred with Douglass's point. In the "Seventh of March" speech, he argued that the political compromise behind the Constitution was founded on the assumption that slavery would be abolished within a few decades, not extended across new territories and developed into an increasingly integral part of the nation's economy. But Webster's primary commitment was to the republican ideals that he found embodied in the Union and in peril elsewhere around the Atlantic world. By 1850, the repeated failure of republican experiments in the Caribbean, Spanish America, and Europe had elevated the significance of U.S. republicanism in his mind. Like Shakespeare's Brutus, he valued republican self-governance even in the limited, exclusive form that it took in both ancient Rome and the modern United States. Like Shakespeare's Mark Antony, although presumably less cynically, Douglass stressed the demands of equality and social justice over the continued existence of the flawed American republic.

Douglass's second Shakespearean reference, the passage from *Macbeth*, likewise echoed and revised Webster. In 1830, Webster had made an interpretation of *Macbeth* central to his argument about the Constitution, the Union, and slavery in his "Second Reply" to Senator Robert Hayne of South Carolina. Webster's Second Reply was arguably the best-known speech of the era. There were well over 100,000 copies of the printed separate circulated, it was widely anthologized, and it was used in schools as an elocutionary text well into the twentieth century. Douglass almost certainly knew the speech and the famous aphorism extracted from it, "Liberty *and* Union, now and forever, one and inseparable!" This phrase became Webster's slogan and laid the groundwork for his position on the compromise measures twenty years later.[34]

The ability to justly interpret foundational texts—whether Shakespeare or the Constitution—was at the heart of the Senate dispute between Webster and Hayne.[35] Both sides of the debate claimed to be perpetuating the values of the nation's political and cultural founders. Webster's eloquence on this occasion both mimicked and interpreted Shakespeare, reproducing and interpreting a culture founder in much the same way that he sought to reproduce and interpret the Constitution. One observer claimed that in this much anticipated and widely attended speech, the Massachusetts Senator spoke with the vigor, clarity, and effect of Shakespeare.[36] Shakespeare provided Webster with a central model of legitimate descent that he appropriated to nineteenth century debates about the meaning of American republicanism.

In the Senate debate, Webster cleverly used an inept reference by Hayne to a passage from *Macbeth* to establish his interpretive authority and to assert the moral superiority of his unionist ideology. The reproduction of political authority is central to Shakespeare's play, and the ability to interpret foundational texts—whether Shakespeare or the Constitution—was at the heart of the Senate dispute. Shakespeare provided Webster with a central image of legitimate political descent that he appropriated to nineteenth century debates about the meaning of American republicanism. Challenging Hayne's political and literary competence, he launched into a long and mocking rebuttal focused on Hayne's misinterpretation of a passage from *Macbeth:* "The gentleman asks, if I were led or frighted into this debate by the spectre of the Coalition. 'Was it the ghost of the murdered Coalition,' he exclaims, 'which haunted the member from Massachusetts; and which, like the ghost of Banquo, would never down?'" Webster at first attacked Hayne for dragging up the "cast-off slough of a polluted and shameless press" with this reference to the controversial alliance between John Quincy Adams and Henry Clay in the election of 1824. This alliance between representatives of the East and West was thought to take place at the expense of the South, an exclusion that Hayne hoped to reverse by allying himself with Westerner Thomas Hart Benton. Webster reproached Hayne for the slur and went on to impugn Hayne's literary judgment by revealing his mistaken application of the Shakespeare passage: "It was not, I think, the friends, but the enemies of the murdered Banquo, at whose bidding his spirit would not *down.*"[37]

Webster then played out the scene in substantial and vivid detail, incorporating additional passages from the play: "The ghost of Banquo, like that of Hamlet, was an honest ghost. It disturbed no innocent man. It knew where its appearance would strike terror, and who would cry out, A ghost! It made itself visible in the right quarter, and compelled the guilty and the conscience-smitten, and none others, to start, with, 'Pry'thee, see there! Behold!—look! Lo / If I stand here, I saw him!'" Webster conjured up this famous scene to suggest that it was Hayne who was guilty of anti-unionist thought, since he was the one who perceived the "ghost" of "the murdered Coalition." This section concludes with a further application to Hayne: "Those who murdered Banquo, what did they win by it?"—followed by Macbeth's paraphrase of the witches's prophetic words regarding his own fate, but substituting a plural pronoun for the first person singular of the original: "a barren scepter in their gripe, / *Thence to be wrenched with an unlineal hand, / No son of theirs succeeding.*"[38] By aligning Hayne and his associates with the childless and soon deposed Macbeth, Webster suggested that the Southern states' rights and nullification movement had no future. Yet the movement could still wreak considerable havoc as Macbeth had done. Asserting interpretive authority over Shakespeare's play and linking it to authority over the United States Constitution, Webster turned Hayne's allusion against him, recasting *Macbeth* in a manner that made nullification a regicidal threat to the sovereignty of the union.

In "What to the Slave Is the Fourth of July?" Douglass incorporated a passage from *Macbeth* to make an argument similar to Webster's, though by this time Webster had shifted his ground to accept slavery as a necessary evil. Presenting the contested question of whether the U.S. Constitution protected slavery or mandated its elimination, Douglass summed up the argument of his opposition thus: "the right to hold, and to hunt slaves is a part of that Constitution framed by the illustrious Fathers of the Republic." If this was true, he asserted, then one must admit that "your fathers stooped, basely stooped" to "palter with us in a double sense: / And keep the word of promise to the ear, / But break it to the heart." These are the words that Macbeth speaks to Macduff upon learning that he was "ripped untimely from his mother's womb" and thus poses a peculiar threat to Macbeth, for he can fulfill the witches' prophecy that Macbeth cannot be killed "by one of woman born."[39] Encouraged by the witches' doublespeak, Macbeth has undertaken the murder of Duncan for which he is now to suffer retribution. Douglass argued that those who espoused a proslavery reading of the Constitution likened its authors to the deceptive witches, whose words led Macbeth on the violent and ultimately self-destructive course that, he suggested, mirrored that of the proslavery forces. Similarly, Douglass implied a presumably unwelcome identification between Macbeth, the self-promoting regicide, and those who supported a proslavery interpretation of the Constitution. In the remainder of his speech, Douglass went on to deny this interpretation and the identification it made between those who offer this reading of the Constitution and Macbeth, arguing instead for an abolitionist understanding of the founders' intentions for their Constitution grounded in Washington's deathbed abolition of his slaves.

The eloquent Shakespeare fashioned by the elocutionary movement continues to influence the ways that political leaders think about and discuss power and civic leadership, and as in the Webster and Douglass speeches *Macbeth* still provides an especially resonant text for the contemplation of these subjects. The eminent Shakespeare scholar Stephen Greenblatt related an encounter with President Bill Clinton that suggests the ongoing presence of Shakespearean eloquence in the corridors of national power. At a 1998 black-tie event at the White House, Greenblatt had an opportunity to shake the President's hand. During his speech earlier in the evening, Clinton had described memorizing Shakespeare passages for his junior high school English teacher. When Greenblatt later asked him about it, Clinton recited part of Macbeth's soliloquy: "If it were done when 'tis done, / then 'twere well / It were done quickly." The President offered an interpretation of Shakespeare's tragedy: "'I think *Macbeth* is a great play about someone whose immense ambition has an ethically inadequate object.'"[40] Earlier presidents, notably including Abraham Lincoln and Ronald Reagan, turned to *Macbeth* in public performances and private reflections.[41] In their uses of Shakespeare we see that the legacy of Thomas Sheridan, Ralph Waldo Emerson, Daniel Webster, Frederick Douglass, Henry Clay Folger, and the countless others who turned to Shakespeare for poetic inspiration and political ammunition lives on.

From the national founding until Henry Clay Folger's day and beyond, it was Shakespeare's eloquence that made his words central to American English education and the civic rhetoric that it promoted. Shakespeare could be used to establish white hegemony and instill Anglo-Saxonist conformity; his works also played a central part in the modern republican tradition of inclusive civic debate and could be used to foster political movements such as abolitionism. It is this dual quality that makes Shakespeare such a central and complex figure in American literary and political traditions.[42]

NOTES

1. See Romans 10:17: "Faith comes from what is heard"; *The New Oxford Annotated Bible*, ed. Bruce M. Metzger and Roland E. Murphy, (New York: Oxford University Press, 1991). See also Stanley King, *Recollections of the Folger Shakespeare Library* (n.p.: Cornell University Press, 1950), 1. Esther Ferington notes that the lecture Folger heard Emerson deliver was on "superlative mental temperance" in Ferington, ed., *Infinite Variety: Exploring the Folger Shakespeare Library* (Washington, DC: Folger Shakespeare Library, 2002), 12. There is some ambiguity about which of Emerson's Shakespeare essays Folger read. Ferington claims that it was Emerson's 1864 speech on the anniversary of Shakespeare's birth, but this appears not to have been published until 1904. See Emerson, "Shakespeare," *Atlantic Monthly* 94 (1904): 365–67. The more likely candidate is "Shakespeare," which appeared in *Representative Men* (1849). The Folger collection includes two printed separates of this essay which appeared in 1899 and 1904.

2. Emerson is quoted without attribution in F. O. Matthiessen, *American Renaissance: Art and Expression in the Age of Emerson and Whitman* (New York: Oxford University Press, 1941), 22.

3. Merrill D. Peterson, *The Great Triumvirate: Webster, Clay, and Calhoun* (New York: Oxford University Press, 1987).

4. King, *Recollections*, 17.

5. Ralph Waldo Emerson, "Shakespeare: Or, The Poet," *Essays and Lectures* (New York: Library of America, 1983), 710–26, esp. 721–22.

6. Ibid., 715.

7. Thomas Sheridan, *British Education: Or, the Source of the Disorders of Great Britain* (1756; fasc. repr., New York: Garland, 1970).

8. Ibid. 1, 2, 129, title page.

9. Before 1800, the *Course of Lectures on Elocution* had been reprinted three times in Dublin and four times in London. There were two American imprints of this text, the first of which appeared in Providence in 1796/97; a second edition was published in Troy, New York, in 1803. This was the final reprinting of the lectures until they were brought out in a facsimile edition from the Scolar Press in 1968.

10. W. Benzie, *The Dublin Orator: Thomas Sheridan's Influence on Eighteenth–Century Rhetoric and Belles Lettres* (Menston, UK: University of Leeds Press, 1972), 56–63.

11. Marvin Carlson described the literary context that led to controversies over Shakespeare's skills as a dramatist in *Theories of the Theatre: A Historical and Critical Survey, from the Greeks to the Present* (Ithaca: Cornell University Press, 1984), chapter 9. In his preface to *All for Love* (1674), John Dryden offered an influential account of his attempt to unite French-derived neoclassical principles with traditional English dramatic practice in his adaptation of *Antony and Cleopatra*. The preface is available online at http://www.bibliomania.com/0/6/192/1089/frameset.html.

12. Sheridan, *British Education*, 351–52.

13. William Scott, *Lessons in Elocution: Or, A Selection of Pieces in Prose and Verse, For the Improvement of Youth in Reading and Speaking*, 4th ed. (Boston: Isaiah Thomas, Jun., 1814), 9, 21, 10.

14. I have spot-checked several editions of Bingham without finding any Shakespeare passages.

15. Noah Webster, *An American Selection of Lessons in Reading and Speaking* (Philadelphia: Young and M'Culloch, 1787), 5–6. This was a reprinting of the third volume of Webster's *Grammatical Institute*, repackaged and with a new preface to emphasize its American contents.

16. Increase Cooke, *Sequel to the American Orator, or, Dialogues for Schools* (New Haven: Increase Cooke, and Sidney's Press 1813). The Folger Library's copy of the 1818 edition of *The American Orator* includes this image as well. Increase Cooke, *The American Orator; or, Elegant Extracts in Prose and Poetry* (New Haven: Sidney's Press, 1818). The same edition in the American Antiquarian Society's collection has a portrait of George Washington in the same place. Other editions have no illustration there.

17. Don B. Wilmeth and Tice Miller, *Cambridge Guide to American Theatre* (Cambridge: Cambridge University Press, 1996), 346. On Shakespeare as a popular icon in the early nineteenth century United States, see Lawrence W. Levine, *Highbrow/Lowbrow: The Emergence of Cultural Hierarchy in America* (Cambridge: Harvard University Press, 1988); Kim C. Sturgess, *Shakespeare and the American Nation* (Cambridge: Cambridge University Press, 2004); and Marvin McAllister, *White People Do Not Know How to Behave at Entertainments Designed for Ladies and Gentlemen of Color: William Brown's African and American Theater* (Chapel Hill: University of North Carolina Press, 2003).

18. Cooke, *The American Orator*, esp. 119.

19. Cooke, *Sequel to the American Orator*, iv.

20. E. G. Welles, comp., *The Orator's Guide; Or Rules for Speaking and Composing; From the Best Authorities* (Philadelphia: G. L. Austin, 1822), 3–4, 80–82.

21. Jonathan Barber, *A Practical Treatise on Gesture, Chiefly Abstracted from Austin's Chironomia; Adapted to the Use of Students, and Arranged According to the Method of Instruction in Harvard University* (Cambridge: Hilliard and Brown, Booksellers to the University, 1831).

22. Benzie, *Dublin Orator*, 24.

23. Leonard Tennenhouse, *The Importance of Feeling English: American Literature and the British Diaspora, 1750–1850* (Princeton: Princeton University Press, 2007), 8.

Tennenhouse rightly stresses the importance of education and eloquence in the diasporic adaptation of English culture that shaped the early American republic.

24. Joseph Quincy Adams, "Shakespeare and American Culture," *The Spinning Wheel* 12 (June–July 1932), 212–15, 229–31, esp. 213–14.

25. Ibid., 215.

26. Ibid., 229.

27. Ibid., 230–231.

28. On Douglass's uses of Shakespeare, see Sturgess, *Shakespeare and the American Nation*, 154.

29. Frederick Douglass, "The Meaning of July Fourth for the Negro," *The Life and Writings of Frederick Douglass,* ed. Philip S. Foner (New York: International Publishers, 1950), 2.181–204, esp. 2.192. I have used the more familiar title of Douglass's speech, "What to the Slave Is the Fourth of July?"

30. Douglass, "The Meaning of July Fourth for the Negro," 195.

31. Webster quotes *Julius Caesar,* 3.2.13. See "The Constitution and the Union," *The Works of Daniel Webster* (Boston: C. C. Little and J. Brown, 1851), 5.325–66, esp. 5.325–26.

32. Douglass, "The Meaning of July Fourth for the Negro," 185.

33. Ibid., 188–89.

34. "Second Speech on Foot's Resolution," *The Works of Daniel Webster* (Boston: Little, Brown, 1851), 3.270–342, esp. 3.342. I have used the familiar title "The Second Reply to Hayne." Publication statistics are provided by Craig R. Smith in *Daniel Webster and the Oratory of Civil Religion* (Columbia: University of Missouri Press, 2005), 118. Historian Daniel Walker Howe remembered memorizing the Second Reply to Hayne at East Denver High School in the 1950s in *What Hath God Wrought: The Transformation of America, 1815–1848* (New York: Oxford University Press, 2007), 371.

35. The best accounts of the debate are in Maurice G. Baxter, *One and Inseparable: Daniel Webster and the Union* (Cambridge: Belknap Press of Harvard University Press, 1984), chapter 11; and Peterson, *Great Triumvirate,* chapter 4.

36. Peterson, *Great Triumvirate,* 175.

37. Webster, "Second Speech on Foot's Resolution," 3.275–76.

38. Ibid., 3.275–77.

39. Douglass, "The Meaning of July Fourth for the Negro," 201; cf. *Macbeth* 5.8.20–22.

40. Stephen Greenblatt, "Shakespeare and the Uses of Power," *New York Review of Books* (April 12, 2007), 75–77, 81–82, esp. 75.

41. Barry Edelstein, "To Get Out of Those Damned Spots," *New York Times,* April 26, 2009, 5.

42. I discuss the place of Shakespeare and the elocution movement in *Imagining Deliberative Democracy: Politics and Letters in the Early American Republic,* forthcoming.

II
Moral and Practical Educations

Lay On, McGuffey: Excerpting Shakespeare in Nineteenth-Century Schoolbooks

Jonathan Burton

Most americans have a story to tell about their first exposure to Shakespeare. While a few recall a particularly affecting experience in the theater, most anecdotes have to do with an English class and particularly the rote memorization of a particular soliloquy or speech. In most cases, the speech derives from one of Shakespeare's tragedies, which became a mainstay of twentieth-century high school curricula. In many cases, those adults asked to do so can still recite a passage or at least recall its most stirring phrases. My own aunt, for example, recalls her seventh-grade classmates in the Crown Heights section of Brooklyn mock-upbraiding one another, "You blocks, you stones, you less than senseless things" (1.1.34).[1] This introduction to Shakespeare via the preliminary name-calling of *Julius Caesar* reminds us that, for many Americans, Shakespearean education endows us with a stockpile of memorable phrases or rousing, half-remembered fragments rather than complex, gripping narratives.

This essay too will tell a story about Shakespeare in American education, one that also features Shakespeare recalled in fragments. It was in fragments, after all, that Shakespeare first entered into American education, in schoolbooks that extracted two- or three-line excerpts from his plays and poetry exemplifying rhetorical modes and principles of elocution. In early America, it is often argued, it could not have been otherwise: Puritan antitheatricality in certain parts of the country meant that Shakespeare's works would only be taught if presented as a means of acquiring the rhetorical tools requisite to republican citizenship. Thus, many accounts of Shakespeare in American life endorse Lawrence Levine's claim in the first chapter of *Highbrow/Lowbrow* that through the nineteenth century Shakespeare was taught "as declamation or rhetoric, not literature."[2] In fact, Levine has little to say about schooling. His particular interest lies in a performance history that testifies to the movement of Shakespeare from popular to elite culture. This essay will interrogate that shift by turning to a distinctly different history, the history of Shakespeare in American education, and particularly in the most popular of all nineteenth-century schoolbooks, the *McGuffey Reader.*

Highbrow / Lowbrow remains the most significant account of Shakespeare's changing place in nineteenth-century American culture. Brimming with fascinating anecdotes of performances from New York stages to California mining camps, Levine's book argues that for Americans, "Shakespeare was popular, first and foremost, because he was integrated into the culture and presented within its context . . . because so many of his values and tastes were, or at least appeared to be, close to *their own.*"[3] The thrust of the argument has to do with the eventual sacralization of Shakespeare that occurred over the course of the nineteenth century, so that by the 1880s and '90s, "Shakespeare was being divorced from the broader world of everyday culture."[4] The story of Shakespeare's move from "lowbrow" to "highbrow" in American culture is also an argument for a shift from a single culture ("their own") to one that is bifurcated ("highbrow / lowbrow"). It tends to paper over difference in early nineteenth-century American culture while highlighting it at the century's close. Levine's argument dovetails neatly with Henry Simon's account of a narrowing canon of plays determined by the implementation, at the close of the nineteenth century, of admissions exams for the elite few admitted to American colleges and universities. Both trace a kind of depopularization of Shakespeare as his works are moved increasingly into the realm of the elite and away from everyday culture.

Schoolbooks like the *McGuffey Readers* tell a different story. These suggest instead that Shakespeare's integration into American culture was not entirely uniform, natural, or trouble free. His values and tastes did not simply fit into American culture, particularly because that culture was, even in the first half of the nineteenth century, variegated with diverse constituencies. American attitudes were shaped by racial, religious, and class identities; gender; sexuality; and a host of regional affiliations. Consequently, Shakespeare's works were, from the beginning, culled and expurgated to shape a citizenry. To the extent that schooling—in or out of the formal classroom—was a component of quotidian life, schoolbooks like the *McGuffeys* suggest that Shakespeare actually *remained* a part of everyday culture through the nineteenth century not so much because his works reflected *an* American culture but because they could be used consistently to form and hierarchize American *cultures.*

Of course, the *McGuffey Readers* are not a skeleton key that we can use to unlock all the questions concerning Shakespeare's place in nineteenth-century education or the emergence, in the twentieth century, of a high school canon of Shakespearean tragedies. Yet the *McGuffeys* may help us to consider new ways of approaching the questions, ways that recognize continuities across the centuries, as well as the impact of seemingly extracurricular forces such as immigration, slavery, sentimentalism, and the movement for women's suffrage. I turn to the *McGuffey Readers* in order to suggest that, long before the culture wars, the standards movement, and conservative calls to teach Shakespeare "in defense of civilization," Shakespeare was extracted for school readers and thereby enlisted in moral education and the formation of a citizenry.[5] Finally, I will suggest that a renewed focus on Shakespeare's place in nineteenth-century moral education may help us to better understand the later shaping of a Shakespearean canon for American high schools.

With sales upwards of 120 million between 1836 and 1920, the *McGuffey Readers* were arguably the most important set of school-books in the history of American education and second in sales only to the King James Bible.[6] Instrumental to the growing common school movement of the mid-nineteenth century, they were being used in thirty-seven states by the century's end.[7] Initially a series of three elementary readers assembled by William Holmes McGuffey, the series grew to include six levels, with the last three intended for advanced students in the equivalent of what we might designate middle and high school.[8] McGuffey assigned the later books in the series to his brother Alexander, who was provided by the publishers with "a great load of old school readers from which, as from other and higher sources, [he] was to make the selections."[9]

Like most advanced elocutionary readers of the time, the *McGuffeys* began with a set of themes on declamation and oratory, derived in large part from Thomas Sheridan's *Course of Lectures on Elocution* (1762) as filtered through Hugh Blair's *Lectures* (1783) and Lindley Murray's *English Reader* (1799). The remainder and bulk of the *McGuffey Readers* was devoted to an "eclectic" selection of short, easily digestible readings, culled from various genres and periods, both English and American, and organized into a sequence of lessons. Here, students could expect to come across poetry and biblical passages; speeches by Patrick Henry, William Pitt, and Daniel Webster; and excerpts from Shakespeare, Washington Irving, Nathaniel Hawthorne, Samuel Johnson, Maria Edgeworth, Oliver Goldsmith, Lydia Sigourney, and Lyman Beecher, among others. Across this range, there appears a clear discourse of Protestant morality, most evident in selections such as "The Bible, the Best of the Classics," "Religion, the Only Basis for a Society," and "Death—Life—Heaven." In these and other selections, readers encounter an idealized, homogeneous society where threats come only in the form of decaying morals and tenuous self-control. Furthermore, students "learned to associate men with productive labor, especially labor outside the home, and women with nurturing, child-rearing, and household tasks."[10]

Passages from Shakespeare were used more than any other author in the advanced *McGuffey Readers,* both to illustrate modes of elocution in the first part and as longer readings in the second.[11] Twenty pieces for reading were drawn from ten of Shakespeare's plays: four from *Hamlet;* three from *King John* and *Othello;* two from *Julius Caesar, The Merchant of Venice,* and *Henry VIII, or All is True;* and one each from *All's Well That Ends Well, Henry V,* and *Richard II.* As was the case with other authors, selections changed over the numerous editions, reflecting shifts in taste, cultural attitudes, and pedagogical strategies. Thus, the selections from *Merchant, All's Well,* and *King John* were dropped after 1867, while every edition from 1844 through 1896 included the funeral orations of *Julius Caesar, Hamlet*'s "To be or not to be," *Henry V*'s "Once more unto the breach," and Cardinal Wolsey's renunciation of the world's "vain pomp and glory" in *Henry VIII.*[12]

The *McGuffey Readers* were not particularly novel in their selections. Of the twenty Shakespearean passages to appear in the *McGuffeys,* seventeen had been used in earlier schoolbooks. Most influential among these were English readers such as John Walker's *Elements of Elocution* (1781) and William Enfield's *The Speaker* (1799), both of which were later published in the United States. Until the end of the nineteenth century, it was rare for students to read Shakespeare in anything other than excerpts. Even when adults formed reading groups, they typically made use of the more advanced readers, rather than graduating to complete texts.[13] Thus, most Americans did not experience Shakespeare's plays as complete works outside of the theater. For that matter, theatrical productions, as well as most available editions of Shakespeare's plays, were often drastically excised.

Where the *McGuffey Readers* are exceptional in their treatment of Shakespeare is in the ways in which their selections might be expurgated, rewritten, and/or presented entirely out of context in accordance with the social and moral directives of the series. Take the three selections from *Othello.* The first, a lesson entitled "The Folly of Intoxication" (which appeared in the *Fourth Readers* of 1844, 1853, and 1857 before being moved to the *Sixth Reader* for the 1866, 1867, 1879, and 1896 editions), excerpts Cassio's lamentation over

a night of drunken carousing. Taken out of context, students learn
the consequences of insobriety but nothing of how Cassio's lapse
comes only through Iago's trickery.[14] Likewise, a seven-line extract
entitled "A Good Name" (*The Sixth Reader*, 1879 and 1896 editions)
renders Iago's insincere and destructive advice to Cassio as earnest
direction.[15] The last selection, "Othello's Apology" (appearing in
the *Fifth Readers* of 1844 and 1853), draws on Act 1, scene 3, where
Othello defends his marriage to Desdemona before the Venetian
senate. McGuffey found this selection in both Walker and Enfield,
and he reproduced the cuts he found in these earlier readers. Thus
removed from the scene are Othello's description of Desdemona's
coming to him with a "greedy ear [to] devour up my discourse" or
his suggestion to "let her speak of me before her father" and the
assembled dignitaries. Indeed, the scene is cut off just at the
moment of Desdemona's entrance, as if in fear of admitting a woman's speech. Desdemona's lines were often drastically cut for the
nineteenth-century stage, perhaps in response to the comments of
figures like John Quincy Adams, who described her as "unnatural"
and deserving of her fate not only because she "violates her duties
to her father, her family, her sex, and her country, but she makes
the first advances" in her relationship with Othello.[16]

Agitated responses to Desdemona's forcefulness were emblematic
of a broader concern with vocal women. In 1852 correspondence
with his half-sister Nancy, who was attending school in New Wilming-
ton, Pennsylvania, Alexander McGuffey made explicit his own concerns with women's speech: "I hope you succeeded satisfactorily in
your declamation. I do not, however, think public declamation a
proper or profitable exercise for females. It is well enough for boys
and young men, who may in after life be called on to address *public*
assemblies. But public speaking can never be any part of woman's
duty, unless she is willing to unsex herself."[17]

McGuffey's allusion to Lady Macbeth ("unsex me here") gestures
toward a broad discomfort that is palpable in the *Readers* with
women assuming public roles. In a particularly sentimental lesson
entitled "The Good Reader," a young girl, the daughter of a laborer
employed by the royal gardener, is enlisted to read a petition to the
King when two boys fail to read the document with proper feeling
and articulation. In reward for her service, "Ernestine had the satisfaction of aiding her father to rise in the world, so that he became
the King's chief gardener. . . . As for the two pages, she was indirectly
the means of doing them good, also; for, ashamed of their bad reading, they commenced studying in earnest. . . . Both finally rose to
distinction, one as a lawyer, the other as a statesman; and they owed

their advancement in life chiefly to their good elocution."[18] For her part, Ernestine must rejoice in the accomplishments of the men around her and selflessly "use [her] literacy to serve the community."[19] Of course, the "community" comprises only young men of the professional class, and Ernestine's service models what Barbara Welter called "the cult of true womanhood," consigning women to the domestic sphere while men pursued public life.[20] If, as critics since Welter have argued, the "separate spheres" paradigm suffers from a myopic focus on white, middle-class women, it was nonetheless presented as an ideal in America's most popular schoolbooks, where it also seems to have informed editorial practices.[21]

Of the twenty prolonged extracts from Shakespeare selected for *McGuffey Readers* between 1843 and 1901, just one includes a woman, and she appears only to praise a man.[22] This brings me to my title, which styles McGuffey as a MacDuff figure. Although the *McGuffey Readers* include no prolonged passages from Shakespeare's *Macbeth,* the allusion to MacDuff, the Scottish thane distinguished for being "not of woman born" is quite fitting. For the *McGuffey Readers,* in their treatment of Shakespeare, likewise deny the feminine. Thus, in an example I will treat at some length, we find Portia and her maidservant Nerissa "untimely ripped" from the climactic scene of Shakespeare's *Merchant of Venice.*

"Shylock, or A Pound of Flesh" was not one of the three Shakespearean excerpts that were entirely unique to the *McGuffey* upon their publication.[23] Yet when it first appeared in the 1844 *Fourth Reader,* cut, expurgated, and even rewritten in places, this profoundly mangled extract was like no previous version of *Merchant's* famous trial scene.[24] Earlier readers had included the trial scene uncut or very minimally cut.[25] On stage, it was the climax of every production and remained wholly intact, with the exception of Portia's bristling at her husband's offer to sacrifice her for Antonio's sake, which was removed from most performances. "The whole of the trial-scene, both before and after the entrance of Portia," had been praised by Hazlitt in the first quarter of the century as "a master-piece of dramatic skill."[26] Likewise, the noted mid-century scholar and editor of Shakespeare, Henry Norman Hudson cited the trial scene for its "tugging vicissitudes of passion" while emphasizing that Portia "shows no unwomanly craving to be in the scene of her triumph: as she goes there prompted by the feelings and duties of a wife, for the saving of her husband's honour and peace of mind, so she gladly leaves when these causes no longer bear in that direction."[27] McGuffey, it seems, did not agree.

Of the 452 lines in Shakespeare's original scene, McGuffey cut

312, or nearly seventy percent. Stanley Lindberg in *The Annotated McGuffey* assures us that "most of the line deletions . . . appear to have been motivated by a desire to reduce the scene to its basic plot line and to eliminate passages that might confuse with archaic words or images"[28] Although excerpting was common for readers, McGuffey's addition and reassignment of lines and his cutting of six of eight characters accomplish far more than a simple streamlining of the scene.[29] And what remains suggests that Shakespeare was not so much included in the curriculum as he was enlisted in a project of inculcating values, particularly with regard to women and minorities, both ethnic and sexual.

Gone from the scene are Bassanio, Gratiano, Salerio, the Duke, Nerissa, and (most significantly) Portia. Since this is, in Shakespeare's original, a trial scene presided over first by the Duke and then by a disguised Portia, these are not insignificant edits. Where Shakespeare's Duke is powerless to sway Shylock to mercy, the cross-dressed Portia infiltrates and redirects the legal proceedings, redeeming a seemingly doomed Antonio while stripping the usurer Jew of his assets and religion. Removing Portia from this scene is akin to removing Lady Macbeth from the scene of Duncan's murder. To fill this void, McGuffey compounds Portia and the Duke into a nameless "Judge," whose gender is clarified in the lesson's single footnote, glossing the term "doctor," used by Shylock to address the judge: "This word here means a learned *man*" (emphasis mine). Thus, at a time when American women were fighting for property rights and suffragists were meeting at Seneca Falls, McGuffey replaced Shakespeare's feeble Duke with a nameless, but definitively male "Judge" who deftly moves Shylock into self-incrimination without the presence, let alone aid, of a woman.

To see in the record of nineteenth-century performances of *The Merchant of Venice* the qualities stripped from Portia—her irreverence, self-interest, and loquaciousness—is to better understand what Alexander McGuffey found objectionable in her. Yet performance histories typically pay scant attention to Portia, tracing instead the evolving approaches to Shylock as embodied by theatrical titans such as Edmund Kean, William Charles Macready, and Henry Irving.[30] While Portia was never excised or replaced as she was in the *McGuffey Readers,* productions did tend to cut her scenes in Belmont in order to focus interest on Shylock's Venice. Most performances followed John Philip Kemble's 1810 revision of the play, dropping Portia's first two suitors, Morocco and Aragon, as well as her lengthy speeches first detaining Bassanio, and later detailing her plans to impersonate a young doctor of law by speaking "between the charge

of man and boy" and offering "a thousand raw tricks of these bragging jacks." For more than half a century, promptbooks for American productions followed suit by suppressing and sanitizing Portia.
The "bragging jacks" remained unscathed by Portia's criticism and
several performances even went so far as to cut the play's fifth act,
where Portia outmaneuvers a cowed Bassanio into repledging his
devotion while threatening to deny the young doctor "not my body,
nor my husband's bed."[31] Thus, instead of tricking Bassanio into giving up his wedding ring, only to later chastise him for his negli-
gence, an unassuming Portia is instead made to throw off her
disguise after waving off her husband's gratitude: "He is well paid
that is well satisfied, / And I delivering you am satisfied, and therein
do account myself well paid."

Other performance practices seem to inform, or at least resonate
with, McGuffey's version of the trial scene. The elimination of
Morocco and Aragon from most stagings of the play, a practice dat-
ing back as far as George Granville's 1701 adaptation *The Jew of Venice,* finds its equivalent in McGuffey's efforts to muffle instances of
blatant prejudice in the scene. With Gratiano, the play's most strident anti-Semite, removed from the *Reader* and Antonio's lines
about Jewish obduracy excised, McGuffey transforms the biased and
xenophobic aggression of Venetian society into a moral lesson and
a celebration of Christian values. There is no mockery of Shylock,
none of the play's dehumanizing of Jews, indeed no Christian ill-will
at all. And of course, no mention of slavery. Shakespeare's Shylock
draws attention to the hypocrisy of the Christians who demand
mercy while

> You have among you many a purchased slave
> Which, like your asses and your dogs and mules,
> You use in abject and slavish parts,
> Because you bought them. Shall I say to you,
> "Let them be free, marry them to your heirs!
> Why sweat they under burdens?"
>
> (4.1.89–94)

Like Increase Cooke before him, McGuffey must have seen these
lines as too inflammatory in the context of American slavery.[32] They
appear nowhere in the reader.

Of course, slaves were not the only ethnic outsiders in mid-nine-
teenth-century America. Census data indicate that between 1830
and 1850, the foreign-born population in the United States
increased from roughly 200,000 to 2,244,000, a rise of more than

1,000 percent.[33] According to the website for "Shakespeare in American Communities," a National Endowment for the Arts project cochaired by Laura Bush, "Shakespeare served as a unifying force throughout the [nineteenth] century: his works were one of the only things that were constant while the country and its people were expanding."[34] Nigel Cliff's recent account of the Astor Place Riot of 1849 tells a less sanguine story. Cliff locates the riot in a series of "Shakespeare Riots," where performances of Shakespeare actually contributed to the division of urban Americans along economic and ethnic lines.[35] In keeping with this history, we should not confuse McGuffey's muting or even elimination of the scene's most blatant anti-Semitism, or his refusal to engage with debates over slavery, as an effort to draw outsiders into the fold. On the contrary, by titling the selection "Shylock, or A Pound of Flesh," the *Reader* narrows its focus to the Jew and his grisly desire for revenge. Severed from the rest of the play, this scene reduces Shylock's motives to a "lodged hate and certain loathing I bear Antonio." Thus when asked in the appended questions at the end of the lesson, "Why did Shylock choose the pound of flesh rather than the payment of his debt?" a student is left only with the outsider's inscrutable malice. Gone is Shylock's humanizing speech that emphasizes his suffering at the hands of Antonio and others, and asks, "Hath not a Jew eyes?" (3.1.49–50). Gone are any explanations on Shylock's behalf, the ostracism, ridicule, and personal animosity that we witness. Gone, too, is the loss of his daughter Jessica, for whom Shylock, at least in Shakespeare's version, continues to wish a faithful husband. If, as Hazlitt had argued, Shylock had by 1817 "ceased to be a popular bugbear" and become instead "a half favourite [with whom] we can hardly help sympathising," this cannot be the case in the *McGuffey Readers,* where we find nary a trace of the sympathetic Shylock.[36]

If Antonio's railing on Jewish obduracy is removed, it is only because the whole episode, reduced as it is, zeroes in on precisely that quality. There is no confusing Shylock and Antonio, and it is therefore unsurprising that McGuffey cuts Portia's opening query, "Which is the merchant here, and which the Jew?" (4.1.169). The Jew cannot be mistaken for the Christian, and accordingly, he cannot be incorporated, either through conversion or the possibility of an amiable settlement—which is at least considered in Shakespeare's play in Bassanio's proposal to return Shylock's principal and the Duke's suspicion that Shylock merely "lead'st this fashion of thy malice/To the last hour" when he will surprise all with great "mercy and remorse" (4.1.17–18, 19). Shylock is an outsider, an immigrant, and McGuffey ensures that his readers understand the consequences of this by defining the term in a brief lexicon that begins the lesson: "AL-IEN, n. one who is not entitled to the privilege of a citizen."

Shakespeare's Venetian citizens certainly enjoy their privilege, but by the end of the play we are by no means convinced of their entitlement. Antonio, in particular, is a dubious figure in his committed anti-Semitism, summed up in a promise to spit upon Shylock again even after accepting his ostensible generosity. McGuffey clarifies and justifies Antonio's questionable moral standing. His railing on Jewish obduracy and comparison of Shylock to a wolf are meticulously expunged. More importantly, the homoerotic elements of Shakespeare's play are erased so that Antonio is no longer the "tainted wether of the flock" (4.1.113) who repeatedly emphasizes his willingness to die for Bassanio and insists that Portia learn "whether Bassanio had not once a love" (4.1.272) in Antonio.[37] (Likewise, Bassanio's stated willingness to sacrifice his wife to deliver Antonio is cut.) Where in Shakespeare's play Antonio seems to wish himself a martyr for a relationship that could never be socially acceptable, in the *McGuffey Reader* he is instead Christ-like and "armed to suffer with a quietness of spirit."

McGuffey's version of the scene is cut short with a seven-line exchange that appears nowhere in Shakespeare's play. Shylock asks leave "to go where I may die in peace: since *what I hold dearer than my life, is taken from me*" (emphasis added). Shylock's request corrupts an earlier explanation in Shakespeare's text where the Jew explains that the court takes from him the means by which he may "sustain [his] house" (4.1.371). That is, where Shakespeare's Shylock merely seeks the means to live, McGuffey's Shylock values money above life. In response, the Judge pronounces, "The court has mercy on your life; / Go, repent, and live, And with a softer heart, remember mercy too." Lindberg's *Annotated McGuffey* explains that the changes to the end of the scene "helped . . . to point out the moral more clearly than Shakespeare had been able to manage in the original" (238). But where Lindberg argues that Shakespeare failed to achieve moral clarity, it strikes me as more reasonable to argue that McGuffey imposes a didacticism that Shakespeare withholds.

The *McGuffeys* were innovative for the study questions appended to each selection. In the questions following "Shylock, or A Pound of Flesh," McGuffey calls specific attention to the lines he added, as well as passages that take on new meaning in light of his excisions. I have already indicated how McGuffey narrows the range of possible responses to his first question concerning Shylock's choice of the pound of flesh rather than payment of his debt. In his next question, McGuffey reinforces student responses to the first by slyly calling attention to Shylock's Jewishness. "What does he mean," McGuffey asks, "by saying 'my deeds upon my head?'" With its famous echo of Matthew 27:25, where the Jewish mob at Christ's crucifixion proclaims, "His blood be upon us and upon our children," Shylock's words are here enlisted in his own condemnation: Shylock chooses the pound of flesh because he is a bloodthirsty Jew, descended from the murderers of Christ.[38]

After three fairly straightforward reading comprehension questions, McGuffey returns to his interpretive questions asking, "Was [Shylock's] punishment just? Why?" This question, as well as the six grammatical questions that follow, focus the reader's attention squarely on the judge and particularly the interpolated ending to the trial scene. If Shakespeare's play makes a mockery of justice, McGuffey's judge is a divinely inclined and seemingly impartial symbol of transcendent justice. Speaking just four lines of Portia's twenty-two-line encomium to "the quality of mercy," McGuffey's judge instead emphasizes the letter of the law. No one dares suggest to the judge, as Bassanio urges Shakespeare's Duke, to "wrest once the law to your authority" to free Antonio. That he forces no conversion (as the Duke does in Shakespeare's play), renders him even more authoritative, and more impartial, refusing to violate the American right to freedom of religion. Consequently, in regard to the question of justice, a student is left only with the possibility of echoing the sentiments expressed in the court's judgment: "The court has mercy."

The judge's closing statement is not merely a neat ending to the excerpt; it works to erase formally and technically the ambiguities of Shakespeare's scene. McGuffey asks students to identify the verbs in the last three lines and then to distinguish between those in the indicative and imperative moods. Of the five verbs—"has," "go," "repent," "live," and "remember"—only the first is in the indicative mood. But what is the point of this exercise in language rules? McGuffey asks, "What does the word indicative mean?" and "Why is this mode so called?" Those students inadequately trained in grammar are directed to Thomas Pinneo's *Analytical Grammar* (1850), where they would learn that the indicative is used in statements of fact. By turning their direction to grammatical analysis, the *Reader* provides students with a more systematic method of substantiating their conclusions concerning Shylock's fate. "The court *has* mercy." This is a statement of fact.

Following the publication of the 1866 edition, "Shylock, or A

Pound of Flesh" was removed from the *McGuffey* series. Jean Carr explains that by the 1870s, "textual accuracy became a literary expectation and a selling point, a way of distinguishing a series from its competitors, and readers like McGuffey's . . . [now] denounced adaptation."[39] Yet the turn to accuracy can only account in part for the removal of the trial scene, for no excerpts from *any* Shakespearean comedies appeared after 1867.[40] Something else was happening in readers like the *McGuffeys*, something apparent in the educational apparatus that encrusts "Shylock . . ." and the other selections. For the questions that I have been discussing supplement a time-honored approach to the plays as texts for recitation and stylistic analysis, with an understanding of the plays as objects of interpretation for sociomoral development.[41]

Certainly, from the time in which they were first produced, Shakespeare's works had been recognized for their didactic capacity. We can trace this tradition from the early modern debates featuring the likes of Stephen Gosson and Philip Sidney, through Hugh Blair's eighteenth-century assertion that the "intention of tragedy" is "to improve our virtuous sensibility."[42] But it was not until the middle of the nineteenth century that American schoolbooks began to harness *explicitly* the moral force of plays that had been long treated as repositories of stirring oratory. Indeed, by the end of the century there were those, like Henry Norman Hudson, who argued against attempting to incorporate into the study of Shakespeare "any thing of grammar or rhetoric or philology . . . the end should be to make the pupil understand and relish what the author delivers."[43] Most often, what the author was understood to deliver was "sympathies and inspirations" with "pleasant surprises of truth and good."[44] Of course for *female* pupils, Hudson explained, literary study "should, first of all, be . . . attuned to the honest and ennobling delectations of the fireside; their heads furnished and disposed to be prudent, skillful, dutiful wives and mothers and housekeepers . . . and the best thing that the school can do is to cooperate with the home to that end."[45]

Perhaps then the eventual purging of Shakespearean comedy (such as *Merchant*) from the high school canon has to do with those qualities that made it incompatible with prevailing didacticism. With comedy, Blair explained, "there is a hazard of doing mischief, instead of good, to society."[46] Although Blair went on to praise Shakespearean comedy, perhaps McGuffey noticed how it tends to end in rather inconclusive or even unsettling fashion—with Malvolio promising revenge in *Twelfth Night*, Demetrius still drugged in *Midsummer*, Rosalind speaking as both man and woman in *As You*

Like It, and of course Shylock, shuffling offstage sickened by his treatment and fate while his daughter, Jessica, endures an increasingly unhappy marriage. Certainly he noticed how the women of the comedies—Portia, Rosalind, and Helena, for example—readily impersonate, excel, and even correct the failings of men.

If my suspicion is correct, and the eventual formation of a canon of tragedies for high school study may be traced in part to sentimentalism and the rise of sociomoral reading, how then can we explain the intense popularity of *The Merchant of Venice* at the close of the nineteenth century? *The Merchant of Venice* that many readers knew by the end of the nineteenth century was not *Merchant* as we know it. In spite of the turn to textual accuracy, many editors (and theaters, for that matter) continued to produce expurgated versions of the play.[47] John Hows's *Shakspearian Reader* (1849) featured "severe revision[s]," retaining Portia's masquerade and even Shylock's condemnation of Christian slave-holding but cutting almost all of the scenes featuring Launcelot, Jessica, and Lorenzo and ending the play after the trial scene in order to appease "the most fastidious Teacher" and "the most refined and pure-minded Family, or Social Circle."[48] Scenes featuring Launcelot, Jessica, and Lorenzo were also missing from Hudson's *Plays of Shakespeare Selected and Prepared for Schools* (1877) and his *Merchant of Venice Classics for Children Edition* (1883). This excision meant that Portia's rejection of the dark-skinned Prince of Morocco was not unsettled by Launcelot's "getting up of the Negro's belly" (3.5.32), nor was Shylock's authority as a father unsettled by Jessica's disobedience. Along with Hudson, the most popular school edition of *Merchant* was William Rolfe's series, which also cut any reference to Launcelot's affair with a Moor. While these editions may not include the text of *Merchant* as we have come to know it, they were certainly adequate to prepare students for college entrance exams like Columbia's, which required students in 1889 to produce just "250 words on The Story of Shylock," or in 1892 to recount "The Story of the caskets in *The Merchant of Venice.*"[49]

So what are we to make of this history that suggests that Shakespeare's place in nineteenth-century education went far beyond providing paradigms for public speaking? Perhaps it is too early in the project of examining Shakespeare in American education to draw extensive conclusions. Thus, I will end here not with answers but rather with a set of questions raised by this essay and demanding our further pursuit: To what extent does the history of Shakespeare in nineteenth-century American education offer a counter-narrative to the predominant story of American cultural bifurcation? Were canons for secondary education necessarily handed down from elite universities, or might they also have percolated upward from school readers that encouraged, far earlier than the colleges, a broader, less philological approach to literary analysis?[50] If nineteenth-century readers after McGuffey were innovative in explicitly harnessing the moral force of Shakespeare's plays, to what extent were high school canons informed by those same concerns? And thus finally, to what extent can we attribute the dominance of Shakespearean tragedy in American high schools today to a residual, or worse, a continuing sense that unexpurgated Shakespearean comedy is hazardous to American values?[51]

NOTES

1. Stephen Greenblatt, gen. ed., *The Norton Shakespeare, Based on the Oxford Edition* (New York: W. W. Norton, 1997). Unless otherwise indicated, all citations from Shakespeare's plays are from the Norton edition.

2. Lawrence W. Levine, *Highbrow / Lowbrow: The Emergence of Cultural Hierarchy in America* (Cambridge: Harvard University Press, 1988), 37.

3. Ibid., 36 (emphasis added).

4. Ibid., 33.

5. The publications of the American Council of Trustees and Alumni have been particularly strident in continuing to make a case for Shakespeare's moral force. In *The Shakespeare File: What English Majors Are Really Studying* (1996), Shakespeare is made responsible for providing Americans with "a common frame of reference that helps unite us into a single community of discourse." See also *Defending Civilization: How Our Universities Are Failing America and What Can Be Done about It* (2001), and *Becoming an Educated Person: Toward a Core Curriculum for College Students* (2003).

6. D. A. Saunders, "Social Ideas in the McGuffey Readers," *Public Opinion Quarterly* 5.4 (1941): 579–89, esp. 579.

7. The *McGuffeys'* greatest popularity was in the Midwest and South and in rural and small-town schools, rather than in major cities. They never did particularly well in the Northeast.

8. Formal grade-level divisions were only very slowly replacing the district school with its single classroom in the mid-nineteenth century, so it is only possible to make rough correlations between nineteenth- and twentieth-century schooling. Furthermore, it is important to keep in mind that the number of students attending public secondary schools in the nineteenth century was miniscule. See David Tyack, *The One Best System: A History of American Urban Education* (Cambridge: Harvard University Press, 1974) indicates that "in 1870 only about 16,000 students graduated from public and private high schools, only 2 percent of the population aged seventeen" (57).

9. Dolores P. Sullivan, *William Holmes McGuffey, Schoolmaster to the Nation* (Rutherford, NJ: Fairleigh Dickinson University Press, 1999), 105. Although later editions were overseen by teams of editors, the editions I discuss here were supervised solely by Alexander McGuffey.

10. Elliot J. Gorn, introduction, *The McGuffey Readers: Selections from the 1879 Edi-*

tion (New York: Bedford / St. Martin's, 1998), 13. In a Fourth Reader excerpt entitled "The Wife," Washington Irving figures women as "the mere dependent and ornament of man in his happier hours, [she] should be his stay and solace when smitten with sudden calamity."

11. In *Henry Ford and the Jews: The Mass Production of Hate* (New York: Public Affairs, 2001), Neil Baldwin notes that the Pulitzer Prize-winning author Hamlin Garland, who grew up with the Readers, recalled with particular fondness his first exposure to Shakespeare: "From the pages of [McGuffey's] readers . . . I got my first introduction to Shakespeare . . . Shylock and his pound of flesh . . . became part of our thinking" (228).

12. An interesting project beyond the scope of this argument might consider if and how these shifts are related to the popularity of the actors who toured in these roles. I will have more to say below concerning performances of *Merchant* concurrent with and joining in the sociomoral project of the *McGuffey Readers*.

13. Jean Ferguson Carr, Stephen L. Carr, and Lucille M. Schultz, *Archives of Instruction: Nineteenth Century Rhetorics, Readers, and Composition Books in the United States* (Carbondale: Southern Illinois University Press, 2005), 133.

14. After five editions from 1844 to 1867 with no indication of context, the 1879 Sixth Reader included a note appended to the selection explaining Iago's motives.

15. Fuller versions of these two selections had appeared in *The Reader, or Reciter* of 1799.

16. James Henry Hackett, *Notes, Criticisms, and Correspondence upon Certain Plays and Actors of Shakespeare* (New York: Carleton, 1863), 224. Edward Kahn, "Desdemona and the Role of Women in the Antebellum North," traces attitudes toward Desdemona in the North "from idealization of her virtue, to disapproval of her passivity, and finally to condemnation of her independence" (235).

17. Sullivan, 111.

18. Alexander McGuffey, *McGuffey's Fifth Eclectic Reader: Selected and Original Exercises for Schools* (Cincinnati,OH: Sargent, Wilson & Hinkle, 1857), 42.

19. Carr et al., 90.

20. Barbara Welter, "The Cult of True Womanhood, 1820–1860," *American Quarterly* 18 (Summer 1966): 151–74.

21. For a useful account of the "separate spheres" debate, see Cathy N. Davidson and Jessamyn Hatcher, *No More Separate Spheres!* (Durham, NC: Duke University Press, 2002).

22. In *All is True*, 4.2, Queen Katherine is taught to recognize the good in her deceased nemesis, Cardinal Wolsey. This extract had a short run in the *Fifth Readers* of 1844 and 1853 but was removed prior to the 1857 edition.

23. The three Shakespearean selections in the *McGuffeys* that had appeared nowhere previously include another scene from *Merchant* (1.3.103–25) simply entitled "Shylock," as well as two heavily excised composite scenes entitled "Rosencrantz and Guildenstern" (drawn from *Hamlet* 2.2 and 3.2) and "The Knave Unmasked" (drawn from *All's Well That Ends Well* 3.6, 4.1, and 4.3).

24. The same version appeared again in 1848 and 1853 editions before being moved to the *Fifth Reader* in 1857 and 1866.

25. William Enfield, *The Speaker* (1799), left the scene fully intact. Increase Cooke, *The Sequel to the American Orator* (1813), named the scene "Intercession—Obstinacy—Cruelty, etc.," excised Shylock's lines regarding slavery, but otherwise left the scene intact.

26. William Hazlitt, *Characters of Shakespeare's Plays* (1817) available online via Project Gutenberg at http://www.gutenberg.org/dirs/etext04/chrsh10.txt.

27. Rev. Henry Norman Hudson, *The Works of Shakespeare: The Text Carefully Restored according to the First Editions (Boston: J. Munroe and Co., 1851), 20, 18.*

28. Stanley Lindberg, *The Annotated McGuffey* (New York: Van Nostrand Reinhold, 1976), 237.

29. In his *Shakspearian Reader* (New York: D. Appleton & Co., 1849), John Hows, a professor of elocution at Columbia, prepared a "severe revision" (ix) of sixteen of Shakespeare's plays "expressly for the use of classes, and the family reading circle" (title page). Hows's version of *The Merchant of Venice* ends the play at the conclusion of the trial scene but leaves Portia's role wholly intact.

30. In particular, see James Bulman, *"The Merchant of Venice": Shakespeare in Performance* (New York: Manchester University Press, 1991); and John Gross, *Shylock, A Legend and Its Legacy* (New York: Simon and Schuster, 1992).

31. The final act was dropped for Charles Kean's 1845–47 American tour, as well as in New York performances by Henry Betty in 1845 and Edwin Booth in 1857 and 1867. Act 5 was cut from American performances as late as Henry Irving's tours of the United States in the 1880s.

32. In a section of the 1837 *Fifth Reader* entitled "The Miseries of Imprisonment," excerpted from Laurence Sterne's *A Sentimental Journey,* McGuffey replaces the term "slavery" with "oppression or misery." This selection was never reproduced in later editions.

33. The groups immigrating to the United States in greatest numbers during this period were Irish, German, British, and French.

34. During the production of this volume, the particular passage quoted here was removed from the website for Shakespeare in American Communities (http://www.shakespeareinamerican communities.org/). A slightly altered form appears at http://www.nosweatshakespeare.com/resources/shakespeare-and-america.htm.

35. Nigel Cliff, *The Shakespeare Riots: Revenge, Drama, and Death in Nineteenth-Century America* (New York: Random House, 2007).

36. Henry Norman Hudson in *The Works of Shakespeare* (1851) expresses great sympathy for Shylock, described as "a type of national sufferings, sympathies, and antipathies" (18). Sympathy for Shylock may have developed in the wake of Edmund Kean's transformative performance of 1814, which figured Shylock as a tormented Jew driven to cruelty by his Christian oppressors. (Kean brought this Shylock to America in 1819.) Yet while Kean's performance ushered in an era of less monstrous Shylocks, McGuffey's Jew is perhaps more like the Shylock of Granville's *Jew of Venice,* where the bulk of Shylock's suffering is omitted.

37. The criticism on Antonio's sexuality is too lengthy to rehearse here. One particularly helpful essay addressing Antonio's self-characterization as a castrated ram is Alan Sinfield, "How to Read *The Merchant of Venice* without being Heterosexist," in Terence Hawkes, ed., *Alternative Shakespeares 2* (London: Routledge, 1996), 122–39.

38. Lindberg claims that in the McGuffey Readers, "the Jews receive fairly unbiased treatment . . . in the very few lessons where they appear" (237). Yet Neil Baldwin points out that "elsewhere in the *Fifth Reader,* students read of 'Paul's Defense before King Agrippa,' in which the apostle laments the fact that despite his wide-ranging efforts to spread the gospel of repentance at Damascus, Jerusalem, and along the coasts of Judea, 'the Jews caught me in the temple, and went about to kill me.'" Furthermore, in the *Fourth Reader* students were warned that "Jewish authors were incapable of the diction and strangers to the morality contained in the gospel . . . [and] misguidedly failed to heed [even the Old Testament]" (3).

39. Carr et al., 114.

40. The only other excerpt from a comedy selected for the *McGuffeys* was "The Knave Unmasked," which patched together three scenes from *All's Well that Ends Well*. This excerpt, which appeared in the *Fifth Readers* of 1844 and 1853, and the *Sixth Readers* of 1857, 1866, and 1867, was also mysteriously transformed. In this case, Parolles was renamed Delgrado, while Bertram Rousillon was called Bertram Rosencrantz.

41. Carr et al. argue that over the course of the nineteenth century, school readers "turn from recitation to analytic study" and "prepared the way for literary instruction, by transmitting valued selections, by developing a language about authors and genres, by prefiguring the procedures for stylistic analysis and interpretation" (147).

42. Hugh Blair, *Lectures on Rhetoric and Belles Lettres,* 2 vols., ed. Harold F. Harding (Carbondale: Southern Illinois University Press, 1965), 479.

43. Henry Norman Hudson, ed., *The Merchant of Venice* (1879; repr., Boston: Ginn & Co., 1903), 30.

44. Ibid., 29.

45. Ibid., 9.

46. Blair, 528–29.

47. There were, of course, some readers that continued to produce only excerpts of the plays. William Swinton's *Studies in English Literature Being Typical Selections of British and American Authorship, from Shakespeare to the Present.* (New York : Harper & Brothers, 1881) included the trial scene as one of only two Shakespearean excerpts but cut Shylock's lines about slavery. Richard Edwards's *Analytical Sixth Reader* (New York, Mason Brothers, 1866) includes the first three scenes of *Merchant* nearly in their entirety, thus featuring a Portia who abides by her father's wishes and never usurps a man's public role.

48. Hows's *Othello* omits the opening scene of Othello with its sexually charged racism, while his *Measure for Measure* cuts the entire culture of whorehouses so central to the play.

49. See Henry W. Simon, *The Reading of Shakespeare in American Schools and Colleges, An Historical Survey* (New York: Simon and Schuster, 1932). As Simon points out, the knowledge of Shakespeare necessary for these exams "could have been perfectly well obtained from reading one or two of Lambs's tales" (125).

50. In a related argument entitled "Teaching Shakespeare in America," *Shakespeare Quarterly* 35 (1984): 541–59, Charles Frey credits the work of late nineteenth-century Shakespeare editors such as Henry Norman Hudson and William J. Rolfe "for insertions of Shakespeare into secondary school curricula before pressure to include Shakespeare came from the colleges' entrance examinations" (544). My argument draws attention instead to the earlier influence of popular school readers.

51. I am grateful for the suggestions made by my colleagues in the West Virginia University English Department faculty research group, as well as for a meticulous reading by my good friend and colleague Jennifer Waldron. I am especially grateful to Heather S. Nathans, whose support for and close reading of this essay led me to see the connected histories of pedagogy and performance that I have only begun to develop here.

Shakespeare in American Rhetorical Education, 1870–1920

Nan Johnson

Shakespeare with sympathies as wide as creation, sensibility as deep as old ocean, and susceptible to all objects of universal nature becomes its painter and its dramatist and reveals the heart of man for all time to its fellows. As we turn his pages we seem not to be conversing with an individual mind or to come in contact with an individual character. The works of a god seem to be before us, but they are so varied and all so perfect that they seem to give us no trace of their parent. The creator of this rich and boundless world of literature is lost in his works; we cannot trace him—we cannot detect the personality of him who "holds the glass up to nature's face" and reveals her as she is. Mimic and painter of universal nature, he paints all character with equal truth and seemingly with equal relish.[1]

IN THESE LAUDATORY REMARKS ON SHAKESPEARE, FRANCES P. HOYLE, author of a popular rhetoric manual, *The Complete Speaker and Reciter for Home, School, Church and Platform* (1905), outlines a portrait of Shakespeare as the exemplary author of English literature and the writer whose works have the most to offer the general reader in terms of wisdom, human drama, and examples of formal rhetorical power. Texts like *The Complete Speaker and Reciter* had a high profile in American popular culture between 1870 and 1920 and formed the keystone of the popular self-help movement that swept America after the Civil War. Deployed in rhetoric manuals, letter-writing books, encyclopedias, and conduct manuals, self-help texts offered a parlor education for all literate Americans in subjects ranging from math and English to bookkeeping and housekeeping. The common use of rhetoric anthologies in the home, community organizations, and church groups provided instruction in rhetorical performance such as public speaking and reciting aloud and extended an education in Shakespeare in the process. Shakespeare is the only literary author typically awarded an entire "department" in such anthologies, and certainly, the only author singled out for *godlike* rhetorical powers and superior insight into human nature. "The Shakespearean Department" in *The Complete Speaker* provides scenes for reading and performance from the plays under titles such as "Othello's Apology," "Lost Reputation, Iago and Cassius," "Trial Scene from Merchant of Venice," "Mark Antony to the People, on Caesar's Death," and the "poem" "Seven Ages of Man."[2]

The excerpts collected in *The Complete Speaker* were typical but by no means inclusive of the canon of Shakespeare's works highlighted and analyzed across the scope of nineteenth-century rhetorical education. As rhetoric manuals offering training in public speaking and oral recitation spread across the parlor tables of America after the Civil War, the academic study of rhetoric in colleges, universities, and professional schools promoted rhetorical expertise in oratory, writing, critical appreciation, and platform reading to a public eager for liberal education and curriculums of self-improvement. Enshrined in this vast educational enterprise as a foremost rhetorical exemplar, Shakespeare was a favored choice within a curriculum that stressed the study of model texts. Shakespeare's plays were studied critically as prose models, orations, and eloquent dramas under the assumption that such habits of study would encourage students to emulate the rhetorical powers of composition and oratory, as well as the intellectual habits of mind that graced the work of the great Shakespeare.

Nineteenth-century rhetorical education in America, both academic and popular, was dedicated to fostering eloquence in speaking and writing and to developing critical standards of taste in the American public. Within the rhetorical curriculum of both classroom and parlor, "taste" implied intellectual and moral virtues that could be obtained by any serious student of rhetorical theory and careful reader of the exemplars of English literature and oratorical performance. The nineteenth-century rhetorical curriculum stressed *imitatio,* the classical principle that to study the great works was to become closer to the profound level of thought of great minds and to be instructed by the example of their rhetorical skill. This pedagogical philosophy is fundamental to rhetorical education in the American academy and also underwrites popular venues of rhetorical education.[3] The configuration of Shakespeare as a masterful rhetorician focused on Shakespeare's command of form, his ability to portray and to appeal to human emotion and motive, and the general perception that his commentary on the human condition was instructive and persuasive. For nineteenth-century rhetoricians, these were the qualities of a great speaker and writer, one whose works could be studied both for insight into how to compose and deliver a powerful speech or essay but also for the example of a wise and moral heart.

The study of Shakespeare as a model rhetorician was promoted by four major forms of rhetorical education throughout the nineteenth century and into the early decades of the twentieth: 1) the academic tradition supported by rhetorical treatises studied in college classrooms that outlined the theory and genres of effective discourse and also stressed the rhetorical principles of invention, arrangement, and style; 2) the elocutionary tradition, which provided instruction in the canon of delivery the use of the voice and body in public speaking and public reading for the classroom and an audience of "private learners"; 3) the circulation and immense popularity of the speaker-reciter genre (*The Complete Speaker* is an example of this kind of parlor rhetoric, which offered basic guidelines in both oratory and public readings along with numerous selections for practice); and 4) professional schools of oratory, which began to develop after the Civil War and enjoyed success into the twentieth century. Academic rhetoric treatises and elocution manuals were used in the preparation of students and those who aspired to professional and public life. The speaker-reciter genre had the broadest audience of all; authors of these texts set their sights on individual readers, families, community organizations, literary societies, social groups, churches, and school recitals. Schools of oratory appealed to professional men and women, such as teachers, entertainers, ministers, lecturers, and public speakers, and promised the best education in oratory and self-presentation. Into these settings, rhetorical educators carried their message of the relationship between the study of rhetoric and the development of the powers of expression, skills that had socioeconomic benefits and intellectual and moral consequences.[4]

As an exemplary rhetorician and wise scholar of the human heart, Shakespeare's presence is marked in American rhetorical education in its every facet. In *The Practical Elements of Rhetoric* (1886), an influential academic rhetoric treatise used in the American academy between 1880 and 1920, John Franklin Genung praises Shakespeare as an exemplary rhetorician in his discussion of how to address the feelings in persuasive discourse:

We have seen that argument and exposition predominate in presenting the thought to the intellect; to rouse the emotions, however, the particularizing forms, description and narration, are mostly depended on. In order to be felt, a situation must be vividly realized in imagination; therefore the portrayal must be concrete, picturesque, impassioned; while special skill is to be devoted to putting in strong relief the moving points of the scene, those points which are especially adapted to close home to the hearer. No better exemplification of consummate skill in working on men's emotions could be found than Mark Antony's speech over Caesar's dead body, as given by Shakespeare. Familiar though it is, let us quote a part of it and note the concrete, vivid, amplified portrayal:—

"If you have tears, prepare to shed them now.
You all do know this mantle: I remember
The first time ever Caesar put it on;
'Twas on a Summer's evening, in his tent,
That day he overcame the Nervii.
See what a rent the envious Casca made;
Through this the well-beloved Brutus stabbed;
And, as he plucked his cursed steel away,
Mark how the blood of Caesar follow'd it,
As rushing out of doors, to be resolved
If Brutus so unkindly knock'd or no;
For Brutus, as you know was Caesar's angel:
Judge, O you gods; how dearly Caesar loved him!
This was the unkindest cut of all;
For, when the noble Caesar saw him stab,
Ingratitude, more strong than traitors' arms,
Quite vanquish'd him: then burst his mighty heart;
And, in his mantle muffling up his face,
Even at the base of Pompey's statua,
Which all the while ran blood, great Caesar fell."[5]

In citing this speech from *Julius Caesar* to illustrate and praise Shakespeare's rhetorical poetics, Genung continues a pedagogical approach in academic rhetoric of citing Shakespeare (among other authors) as a rhetorician from whom students can learn. The most frequently cited plays in Genung are *Hamlet, Henry IV, Julius Caesar, King Lear, Macbeth, Measure for Measure, The Merchant of Venice,* and *Richard II.* Genung presents excerpts from these plays to illustrate economy and power in diction, sentence structure, the use of the figures of speech, descriptive and narrative style, persuasive language, adaptation to audience, and insight into human motivation. In *Working Principles of Rhetoric* (1900), used in American colleges into the 1920s, John Franklin Genung reviews the high standards for rhetorical skill and performance that rhetorical educators have urged upon the American public over the previous century: "The highest reach of good art is repose, that self-justifying quality wherein everything is obviously right, in place, coloring, and degree. If in any point the work is violent or unfit, there is a lack of wise

temperament somewhere, some [formal] element is forced at
expense of others. And the only adequate adjuster of the qualities is
something deeper than skill; in the last analysis it is a sound, balanced, masterful character." Genung cites the authority of Shakespeare to put the force behind this principle about the crucial
interdependence of rhetorical form and authorial character. Genung reminds his readers that "Hamlet's advice to the players (Hamlet, Act. iii, Scene 2) is as full of good sense for writers as for
speakers: 'Nor do not saw the air too much with your hand, thus;
but use all gently: for in the very torrent, tempest, and as I may say,
whirlwind of your passion, you must acquire and beget a temperance that may give it smoothness.'"[6]

The range of plays treated as rhetorical examples varies to some
degree in other influential college-level rhetoric treatises but the
process of citing Shakespeare's works as rhetorical exemplum is consistent. David J. Hill's *Science of Rhetoric* (1877) and Adams Sherman
Hill's *The Principles of Rhetoric* (1878) augment Genung's coverage of
model plays by adding *Henry VIII, The Tempest, As You Like It,* and *A
Midsummer Night's Dream.* Offering advice on how to capture the
quality of the beautiful in composition, David J. Hill cites this
excerpt from *Merchant of Venice* in *The Elements of Rhetoric* (1878) as
an example of how

> the poet's soul transforms into rhythmical language the beauty when he
> sees in nature. Shakespeare thus describes a night scene:
>
> > How sweet the moonlight sleeps upon this bank?
> > Here will we sit, and let the sounds of music
> > Creep in our ears: soft stillness and the night
> > Becomes the touches of sweet harmony
> > Sit, Jessica. Look how the floor of heaven
> > Is thick inlaid with patines of bright gold.[7]

Hill also cites "Wolsey's Soliloquy" (*Henry VIII*) as an example of
how to depict pathos, "one of the most powerful elements of both
literature and oratory."[8] Similarly, Barrett Wendell discusses ele-
gance in style as the "exquisite" adaptation of language to the
expression of thought and emotion in *English Composition* (1891)
and praises Shakespeare for this achievement in *Hamlet:* "Again,
take, almost at random, one of Shakespeare's descriptions: the
beginning of the speech that tells how Ophelia died: 'There is a *wil-
low* grows *aslant* a *brook/* that shows his hoar leaves in glassy
stream. . . .' Read the passage through; and when you have finished,

see for yourselves how this simple picture that begins it sets the whole in a background of just such gentle, homely nature as should best make us feel the loveliness of the dying girl, and the mournfulness of her end."[9]

The praise Wendell offers of Shakespeare's descriptive style is typical of how academic rhetoricians use Shakespeare's texts to illustrate the effectiveness of rhetorical skills such as description and narration, the use of the figures, pathos, diction, and energetic syntax. In addition to directing readers to the critical reading of a range of plays, academic rhetoricians also enhance Shakespeare's rhetorical reputation by citing the opinions of well-known literary critics on Shakespeare's rhetorical powers. This approach not only affirms Shakespeare's stature but also offers students an education in critical opinion. For example, in *A Practical System of Rhetoric* (1835), Samuel P. Newman, one of the most influential American rhetorical educators before the Civil War, honors Shakespeare's quality of mind and heart by quoting from Dryden's *Essay on Dramatic Poetry:* "'To begin with Shakespeare. He is the man, who of all modern, and perhaps ancient poets, had the largest and most comprehensive soul. All images of nature were still present to him, and he drew the not laboriously, but luckily: when he describes any thing, you more than see it—you feel it.'"[10] Similarly, Adams Sherman Hill quotes James Russell Lowell's essay, "Shakespeare Once More" on the rhetorical importance of diction and word choice: "'When I say,'" writes Lowell, 'that Shakespeare used the current language of his day, I mean only that he habitually employed such language as was universally comprehensible,—that he was not run away with it by the hobby of any theory as to the fitness of this or that component of English for expressing certain thoughts or feelings. That the artistic value of a choice and noble diction was quite as well understood in his day as in ours.'"[11]

After the Civil War, essential components of the academic curriculum were extended to the general public through a fleet of elocution treatises and speaker anthologies designed to promote a rhetorical education in rhetoric, composition, and public reading taste to any American who could read and had the price of a handbook. As we have seen by the homage paid to Shakespeare in Hoyle's *Complete Speaker,* Shakespeare's popularity as an icon of tasteful eloquence was affirmed in popular rhetoric manuals that continued to promote Shakespearean plays as subjects for public recitations and community events, and Shakespeare himself as an icon of rhetorical skill and persuasive power. This marked preference for Shakespeare is even more pronounced in the popular elocutionary and parlor rhetoric movements than in academic instruction.

The title of Robert I. Fulton and Thomas C. Trueblood's widely circulated elocution manual, *Choice Readings from Standard and Popular Authors Embracing Complete Classification of Selections, a Comprehensive Diagraph of the Principles of Vocal Expression, and Indexes to the Choicest Readings from Shakespeare, the Bible, and the Hymn-Book* (1884), reveals that Shakespeare's rhetorical stature in the realm of elocution instruction is rivaled only by the Bible and religious hymns. As is often the case in elocution manuals, Shakespeare is the author that takes up the most space in *Choice Readings*. Fulton and Trueblood provide an elaborate fifteen-page index of scenes in Shakespeare's plays that is "best suited for public readings, and which will give the clearest idea of the dominant characters and dramatic situations of the plays." This index, covering thirty-seven plays in all, identifies a range of four to twelve scenes in each play (for example, four scenes in *As You Like It* but ten in *Hamlet*). The detail of this index makes clear that a close reading of the plays was a prerequisite to an understanding of Shakespeare's work from a rhetorical perspective as the authors confirm in their preface to the index: "For the sake of convenience in the class-room and the social circle, and also because a standard edition with expurgated text is highly desirable for such use, the references here made are to the Rev. H. N. Hudson's series of "Annotated English Classics," as far as that series extends, and to his *Harvard Edition of Shakespeare* for the rest of the plays." Fulton and Trueblood's claims for the reputable quality of their Shakespeare index and their emphasis on "standard" editions, tell us more about the kinds of readers a manual like *Choice Readings* was trying to reach.[12]

The dual educational focus of *Choice Readings* on the classroom and the social circle reflects the audiences of an entire segment of rhetorical education that appealed to academic and popular audiences simultaneously. Fulton and Trueblood have the same expectations for their classroom readers and their readers from social circles: close reading of a complete text in a standard edition is the best preparation for understanding the "cast and spirit" of each scene. In Fulton and Trueblood's stance on authoritative editions and the extensive course in Shakespeare that their fifteen-page index outlines, we can observe a significant effort on the part of elocutionists to craft not only a rhetorical reputation for Shakespeare but also a canonical one. The reputations of literary authors are also enhanced by the inclusion of their works in elocution manuals, most notably Byron, Dickens, Irving, Longfellow, Tennyson, Scott, and

Wordsworth; however, none of these authors garner a complete rhetorical index of their works.

Dozens of examples of American elocution manuals from the post-bellum period could be cited to confirm the stature of Shakespeare in the elocutionary arm of rhetorical education. Less ambitious theoretically but just as widely circulated is Robert Kidd's *New Elocution and Vocal Culture*, first published in 1858, which includes more selections from Shakespeare in its section on texts to study and practice than any other author, offering scenes from *Othello, Romeo and Juliet, Hamlet, Henry VIII, Henry V, Richard III, and Julius Caesar*. In *New Elocution and Vocal Culture*, Kidd uses a generic categorization rubric based on type of rhetorical appeal. Selections from Shakespeare appear in this text, as these excerpts typically do in elocution manuals and speaker-reciters, under generic categories such as "Dramatic and Rhetorical" readings.[13] In other influential elocution texts published after the Civil War such as S. S. Curry's *Classical Selections from the Best Authors adapted to the Study of Vocal Expression* (1888), the study of Shakespeare edges out Wordsworth and Sir Walter Scott with several selections taken once again from what seem to be mainstay of the Shakespearean elocutionary canon by the 1880s: *Hamlet, Romeo and Juliet, Macbeth, Othello, Merchant of Venice, and Julius Caesar*.[14]

In elocution texts directed to the education of students and home-learners alike, Shakespeare is treated primarily as master of spoken rhetoric: his plays are cited as examples of the eloquent renderings of characters and the powerful dramatization of emotion. In the speaker-reciter textbook tradition that popularizes the parlor rhetoric movement, Shakespeare is confirmed as a master of oratory and also as a great writer. Hoyle's *Complete Speaker* presents Shakespeare as a master of great oratory but also includes attention to Shakespeare's powers of rhetorical composition. This focus on both the spoken and written word reflects the more inclusive treatment of Shakespeare as a master of all rhetorical forms promoted by academic treatises. In Henry Allyn Frink's well-circulated text, *The New Century Speaker and Writer with Etiquette for All Occasions for Home, School and Platform* (1898), excerpts from Shakespeare's plays dominate the section titled "Specimens of Elegant Composition" featuring eight scenes from *Julius Caesar* and *Hamlet:* "Marullus to the Roman Mob," "Mark Antony over the Body of Caesar," "Cassius Instigating Brutus," "Brutus on the Death of Caesar," "Hamlet on His Mother's Marriage," "Hamlet on the Emotion of the Player," and "Polonius to His Son Laertes." These passages are presented as model prose selections.[15]

Speaker-reciters consistently fuse instruction in public speaking with elocutionary techniques focusing on the use of the voice and gesture. Selections from Shakespeare frequently are keyed to the use of particular gestures or management of the voice. *The New Select Speaker* (1902) incorporates a special section entitled "Shakespearean Department" to assist in general oratorical training and offers this rationale: "We are all interested in oratory, eloquence, public school and all other entertainments. Every person holding a public position is expected to be a speaker, one who is able to address an audience on popular questions and furnish information in convincing and pleasing manner such as will enlighten the people and form the basis of action."[16] Readers of the "Shakespearean Department" are offered scenes featuring great orators: from *The Merchant of Venice,* "'Shylock and Antonio' [Act. I, Scene 3]," the "Trial Scene" and "The Quality of Mercy" speech; "Cardinal Wolsey on Being Cast Off by King Henry III"; "The Murder Scene" and "The Incantation" from *Macbeth;* "Hotspur's Defense"; the "Balcony Scene" from *Romeo and Juliet;* "The Barge she sat in, like a burnished throne" description from *Antony and Cleopatra;* and "Othello's Farewell" with the opening line, "Now for ever / Farewell the tranquil mind!"[17]

In *The Ideal Orator and Manual of Elocution* (1895), editors John Wesley Hanson and Lillian Woodward Gunckel underscore the oratorical aspect of Shakespeare by including a gesture key that performers should consult in dramatic readings of "Marc Antony's Address to the Romans." This selection is annotated and cross-referenced to a "Key to Gestures."[18] For example, in the first two lines of Antony's speech: "Friends, [#29] Romans, countryman! Lend me your ears; I come to bury Caeser, not to praise him [#56], the numbers *29* and *56* correspond to photographs in the text in which a performer strikes poses of "Announcement" and "Meditation."[19] The performance and critical reading of Shakespearean passages is cross-referenced in elocution-based readers to the emotional state of mind that best captures the Bard's meaning. Despite what may seem like an artificial apparatus to us, editors of popular speakers are quite clear about the general application of elocution to public speaking and the development of effective expression in general. In this arena, once again, Shakespeare is the master of all rhetorical trades and the best teacher.[20]

Speaker-reciters in the 1890s and the early twentieth century typically included photographs of performers or actors in powerful oratorical and dramatic poses. *The Peerless Reciter or Popular Program* (1894) compiled by Henry Davenport Northrop includes several photographs of Shakespearean players often depicted as models of oratorical delivery, including Mary Anderson as Juliet, Edwin Booth as Julius Caesar, Ellen Terry as Viola, Henry Irving as Shylock, and Helena Modjeska as Ophelia (Figure 3).[21] *The Peerless Reciter* connects training in gesture and voice to public reading, drama, and public speaking. Certainly, one of the consequences of the use of photographs of Shakespearean actors in costume delivering lines of dialogue from the plays is to further canonize Shakespeare's plays to a vast popular readership and to advance the profile of notable Shakespearean actors. The enterprise of Shakespeare study in this context, close reading of scenes, reading the plays aloud, and performing scenes in public or the parlor is promoted by manuals like *The Peerless Reciter* as preparation for the general rhetorical literacy needed in public speaking and self-presentation, not as training for the professional stage.

Despite the variations in approach or emphasis among types of rhetorical instruction, (academic, elocution instruction, and oratory), by the end of the nineteenth century, Shakespeare emerged as the undisputed "must read" in American rhetorical education and its program of self-improvement. Shakespeare's stature in rhetorical education was confirmed by one more significant site of rhetorical education: the rise to popularity and influence between 1870 and 1920 of schools of oratory. An understudied development in American rhetorical education, the School of Oratory movement consisted of the development in major cities and smaller towns across the east of professional schools specializing in training in oratory, elocution, and literary study. Well-known schools included Boston University School of Oratory (1872), the National School of Elocution and Oratory (Philadelphia, 1873–1943), the Emerson College of Oratory (Boston, 1880–1919), and the Columbia School of Oratory (Chicago, 1890–1927).[22] The school of oratory curriculum conflated the study of public speaker and elocution with oral interpretation under the assumption that "the art of oral interpretation was the art of embodying the spirit and essence of literature."[23] The president of Newcomer's School of Expression, W. W. Newcomer, explains the general goal of Schools of Oratory in the 1902–3 school catalog: "The School was organized to meet the demands of progressive education. It aims to give . . . a thorough training of the voice, body and mind and the harmonious development of all the powers of the individual. . . . Our training gives [the pupil] command of all his powers when before an audience."[24]

At the Newcomer School of Expression and at the many similar schools it typified, "Shakespeare Study" was a required part of the curriculum along with elocution and criticism to which literary study

Figure 3. "And here's some for me; we may call it herb of Grace o' Sundays."
Helena Modjeska as Ophelia. From *The Peerless Reciter or Popular Program*,
compiled by Henry Davenport Northrop. Chicago: Monarch, 1894. Page 217.

was closely aligned. "Shakespeare Study" is described as the study of "Criticism and Dramatic Art": "In the class in Criticism short selections will be given for practical development of the expressive qualities of the voice. The student will be trained to bring into unity the mind, voice and body. The Class in Dramatic art will study the different forms of the drama and also work upon short scenes from various [Shakespearean] classic plays for a stage presentation."[25] The Detroit Training School of Elocution and English Literature regularly published class materials on "Questions on the Plays of Shakespeare," which outlined detailed readings of plot, characters, key speeches, and themes of plays. For example, study questions on *The Merchant of Venice* from an 1880 Shakespeare course at the Detroit Training School cite Henry N. Hudson's edition of the play ("Rev. Henry N. Hudson's Text-books used") and set over eighty questions on the play that stress familiarity with characters, scenes, and speeches: "Arrange in diagram the characters in Scenes 1 and 2;" "Was [Portia] a wit? Quote to prove;" "Quote the first words of Portia and Antonio. In what respect do these speeches show the two to be alike?"[26]

The curriculum at larger institutions such as the National School of Elocution and Oratory (founded in Philadelphia by J. W. Shoemaker) also included lectures on Shakespeare. The *Catalog* for 1875–76 notes the importance of attending the lecture series that complements the regular course of instruction, including lectures on Shakespeare.[27] Similarly, catalogs of the Boston School of Oratory describe courses in the "Analysis for Expression of Shakespeare and Dickens, incidentally as a means of literary culture" (1889).[28] Individual plays were studied at Emerson College using William J. Rolfe's widely circulated editions of *Macbeth*, *The Merchant of Venice*, *Lear*, *Julius Caesar*, and *Hamlet*. Of considerable interest is Rolfe's position as faculty member at the Monroe College of Oratory in Boston (later renamed the Emerson College of Oratory in 1891). At Monroe, courses in "Shakespeare with Prof. Rolfe" are listed as required in both the junior and senior years (*Monroe College of Oratory Catalogue*, 1888–90).[29]

In addition to rhetorical study of Shakespeare, students at schools of oratory enjoyed a regular course of Shakespearean performances and readings by faculty members, visiting lecturers, and Shakespeare players. Students at Detroit Training regularly put on performances of plays. Leland Todd Powers, who taught oral interpretation at Emerson and Columbia and was regarded as one of the most popular dramatic readers on the Redpath Lyceum circuit, made regular appearances at Emerson and Columbia performing several Shakespeare plays in a style described as "monoacting," Power's term for playing all the characters in a given play. This approach to instruction in Shakespeare influenced the curriculum at other schools: for example, students at the Newcomer School are encouraged not to miss W. W. Newcomer's performance of "Julius Caesar, as a Monologue—The entire play given from memory. An Interpretive reading of this great masterpiece."[30]

Presidents and faculty members of various Schools of Oratory often produced elocution manuals and speaker-reciters intended to extend the curriculum of their schools to a broader public. J. W. Shoemaker, founder of the National School of Elocution and Oratory in Philadelphia, authored the influential textbook *Practical Elocution for Use in Colleges and Schools and by Private Students* (1878). Outlining a course of study directly tied to the school curriculum, Shoemaker gives Shakespeare a high profile as he cites dozens and dozens of excerpts from the plays to illustrate elocutionary force. Similarly, Robert I. Fulton, coauthor of *Choice Readings* and compiler of the "Index to Scenes from Shakespeare" was also director of the School of Oratory at Kansas City, Missouri. If Fulton followed the popular practice in rhetorical education of producing a textbook based on classroom practices, the Shakespeare "Index" could be an indication of the "Shakespeare Course of Study" at the Kansas City School of Oratory. Emma Griffith Lumm, compiler of *The Twentieth Century Speaker* (1899) and faculty member at the American Conservatory of Music and Oratory, includes "Scenes from Shakespeare" in her speaker that she describes as designed "to give one and all the skill of powerful expression."[31] Like Fulton and Trueblood, Lumm includes an index to scenes rather than excerpts from *As You Like It, Henry VIII, Henry V, The Merchant of Venice, Julius Caesar, Much Ado about Nothing,* and *Romeo and Juliet.* Mrs. Lumm explains: "These selections are appropriate for plays, readings or recitations. It is not necessary to reproduce them here, as Shakespeare's complete works are already in many homes and can also be found at the various city libraries."[32]

Lumm assumes that Shakespeare's plays in their complete form are readily available to her readers and that she is relying on that as she outlines Shakespearean selections for close reading and performance. This reinforces the rationale within academic and elocutionary education guiding the practice of excerpting Shakespeare's plays; whether highlighted as examples of elegant composition, oratorical power, or elocutionary force, excerpts are intended to be read within a more general context of a complete understanding of the play. Lumm's perspective on the conspicuous placement of Shakespeare in American reading habits also explains more clearly why elocutionists like Fulton and Trueblood can provide an "Index to Scenes in Shakespeare" covering over thirty plays and be able to assume, from both a critical and pedagogical perspective, that complete and authoritative editions of Shakespeare were available to their readers if not already in their hands.

Schools like the Emerson College of Oratory enjoyed a long life in American education from 1870 into the 1920s. Notable schools of oratory evolved into institutions with broader curriculums, such as the Boston College of Oratory, which became Emerson College in 1939. The Chicago Conservatory of Oratory became the School of Speech at Northwestern in 1921. The Philadelphia School of Elocution and Oratory only closed down in 1943. (One of the unexplored connections about education in Shakespeare would be the curricular influence of the Schools of Oratory movement on how Shakespeare was taught in the early decades of the twentieth century at the institutions that originated as Schools of Oratory or were influenced by their example.)

The historical narrative about the place of Shakespeare in American rhetorical education is one of consistency and complexity. As this enterprise asserted the educational value of rhetorical training to professional and everyday Americans in the late nineteenth and early twentieth centuries, Shakespeare is omnipresent as a touchstone of excellence. Shakespeare's example is both an inspiration to master the English language as powerfully as possible and a model of the persuasive impact on mind and heart when one does. In his general preface to an 1879 edition of Shakespeare's *Merchant of Venice*, Henry N. Hudson, editor of the *Shakespearean Classics* series used widely in high schools, schools of oratory, and colleges (and upon whose editions Fulton and Trueblood rely), reiterates conventional wisdom regarding the value of rhetorical models in this advice heeded by generations of readers: "As for the matter of rhetoric, [it] is best learned in the concrete, and by familiarizing the mind with standard models of excellence. . . . by those authors as have been tested and approved by a large collective judgment . . . if you would learn to speak and write the English tongue correctly, tastefully, persuasively, . . . give your days and nights to the mastery of English style."[33] Hudson and a legion of nineteenth-century educators unanimously urged generations of American students and readers to regard the study of Shakespeare as fundamental training in excellent speaking and correct writing in the English tongue.

NOTES

1. Frances P. Hoyle, "The Shakespearean Department," *The Complete Speaker and Reciter for Home, School, Church and Platform* (Philadelphia: World Bible House, 1905), 362.

2. "The Shakespearean Department," in *Complete Speaker and Reciter*, 362–76. The book was also published under the title *The World's Speaker, Reciter and Entertainer for Home, School, Church, and Platform* (1905). This edition includes "Quarrel of Brutus and Cassius" and "Antony and Ventidius."

3. Nan Johnson, *Nineteenth-Century Rhetoric in North America* (Carbondale: Southern Illinois University Press, 1991), chapters 3–5.

4. Nan Johnson, "The Popularization of Nineteenth-Century Rhetoric" in *Oratorical Culture in Nineteenth-Century America*, ed. Gregory Clark and S. Michael Halloran, (Carbondale: Southern Illinois University Press, 1993), 139; and Jean Ferguson Carr et al., *Archives of Instruction: Nineteenth-Century Rhetorics, Readers, and Composition Books* (Carbondale: Southern Illinois University Press, 2005), chapter 1.

5. John Franklin Genung, *The Practical Elements of Rhetoric* (Boston: Ginn, 1886), 460.

6. John Franklin Genung, *The Working Principles of Rhetoric* (Boston: Ginn, 1900), 43.

7. David J. Hill, *The Elements of Rhetoric* (New York: Shelton, 1878), 149.

8. Ibid., *Elements*, 158.

9. Barrett Wendell, *English Composition* (New York: Scribner's, 1891), 285–86.

10. Samuel P. Newman, *A Practical System of Rhetoric* (New York: Dayton, 1842), 303.

11. Adams Sherman Hill, *The Principles of Rhetoric* (New York: American, 1895), 100.

12. Robert I. Fulton and Thomas C. Trueblood, *Choice Readings from Standard and Popular Authors Embracing Complete Classification of Selections, a Comprehensive Diagraph of the Principles of Vocal Expression, and Indexes to the Choicest Readings from Shakespeare, the Bible, and the Hymn-Book* (Boston: Ginn, 1898), 681. The authoritative claims of Fulton and Trueblood's rhetorical analysis of the plays is further corroborated in the "Preface" to *Choice Readings* in which the authors remark: "We here acknowledge our indebtedness for the valuable criticisms and suggestions of the Rev. Henry N. Hudson, the well-known Shakespearian, who has revised and approved the selections, and has himself furnished some of them, and has superintended and corrected the printing throughout; which of itself should be endorsement enough to satisfy the most critical" (vi). Fulton and Trueblood's index covers the following plays: *Antony and Cleopatra, As You Like It, Coriolanus, Cymbeline, Hamlet, 1* and *2 Henry IV, Henry V, Henry VIII, Julius Caesar, King John, King Lear, Macbeth, The Merchant of Venice, A Midsummer Night's Dream, Much Ado about Nothing, Othello, Richard II, Richard III, Romeo and Juliet, The Tempest, The Winter's Tale, Twelfth Night, All's Well that Ends Well, The Comedy of Errors, 1–3 Henry VI, Love's Labor's Lost, Measure for Measure, The Merry Wives of Windsor, Pericles, The Taming of the Shrew, Timon of Athens, Titus Andronicus, Troilus and Cressida,* and *The Two Gentlemen of Verona.*

13. Robert Kidd, *New Elocution and Vocal Culture* (New York: American Book Company, 1883), xi–xii, xi.

14. S. S. Curry, *Classical Selections from the Best Authors Adapted to the Study of Vocal Expression* (Boston: Expression Company, 1888), 199–253.

15. Henry Allyn Frink, *The New Century Speaker* (New York: Books for Libraries, 1971), 319–46.

16. Ibid., iv.

17. Ibid., 392–97.

18. John Wesley Hanson and Lillian Woodward Gunckel, *The Ideal Orator and Manual of Elocution* (n.p., 1895), 85, 41.

19. Hanson and Woodward, 29, 56.

20. Delsarte training in gesture and dramatic action had a pronounced influence on parlor rhetoric as well as nineteenth-century acting. I want to locate this particular crossover in popular rhetoric manuals as directly embracing elocution pedagogy and critical reading instruction directed to a general readership. This pedagogical motive locates *The Peerless Reciter* and texts like it squarely within the enterprise of rhetorical education with Shakespeare as its champion. For a brief summary of how Delsarte affected elocution instruction see Renshaw, "Five Private Schools of Speech," and Claude L. Shaver, "Steele MacKaye and the Delsartian Tradition," in Wallace, ed., *History of Speech Education*, 308–9, 202–18.

21. Henry Davenport Northrop, *The Peerless Reciter or Popular Program* (Chicago: Monarch, 1894), 24, 184, 217.

22. See Edyth Renshaw, "Five Private Schools of Speech" and Francis Hodge, "The Private Theatre Schools in the Late Nineteenth Century," in *History of Speech Education in America*, ed. Karl Wallace, 301–25, 553–71 (New York: Appleton-Century-Crofts, 1954).

23. Renshaw, 318.

24. *Annual Catalog of Newcomer's* (n.p., 1902), 3.

25. Ibid., 3–4.

26. *Detroit Training School of Elocution* (n.p., 1888), 2–3.

27. *Catalogue of the National School* (Philadelphia, 1875), 26.29.

28. Jerome Tarver, Notes from private collection (March 6, 2007), 10.

29. Ibid., 7.

30. Ibid., 9. A particularly revealing artifact about the curricular stature of Shakespeare at schools of oratory is a performance program tucked into the pages of a Rolfe edition of *Macbeth*—a surviving text from the library of Elizabeth Smalley, a student at Emerson College of Oratory. Among the heavily annotated pages of Elizabeth's copy, we find a program for a performance of *Macbeth* by Helena Modjeska and Joseph Haworth in Boston on March 7, 1888. While more suggestive than definitive, Elizabeth Smalley's theater program invites us to imagine that students at Emerson College of Oratory were encouraged to attend the performances of such notable Shakespearean actors as Madame Modjeska and the versatile Haworth. I am indebted to Jerome Tarver for bringing this artifact to my attention.

31. Emma Griffith Lumm, *The Twentieth Century Speaker* (New York: Boland, 1899), 376.

32. Ibid., 376.

33. Henry N. Hudson, *Shakespeare's Merchant of Venice* (Boston: Ginn, 1893), 32–34.

III
Ivy-Covered Shakespeare

Shakespeare in the College Curriculum, 1870–1920

Elizabeth Renker

By 1870, SHAKESPEARE HAD HAD A LONG LIFE IN MANY SPHERES OF AMERI-can culture, as Michael D. Bristol, Esther Cloudman Dunn, Law-rence W. Levine, Peter Rawlings, Kim C. Sturgess, and others have documented. Yet his cultural status was about to shift. American higher education was on the brink of a massive structural transfor-mation, and the college curriculum would become a new and cen-tral institutional location producing the meaning of "Shakespeare." Thomas Dabbs argues that the single most important event in the long history of Shakespeare's reception was his transformation into an academic product during the mid- to late-nineteenth century; Levine traces a shift in Shakespeare's image in the United States from lowbrow to highbrow during the same period. Although Lev-ine does not include the American school system in his analysis, the academic sphere, as Dabbs stresses, is a major force in this reception history. The present study is not concerned with textual analysis of Shakespeare, but with his changing sociological status, specifically in the institutional sites of higher education. Here I follow Bristol, who argues that "it is precisely the sociological and thus the epistemolog-ical status of textual analysis that is in question."[1]

"English," which we think of today as the home of Shakespeare studies, emerged as a trendy field of higher education during this time, indeed, as one of its signal innovations. Consolidations in the higher study of English in the 1880s, such as the founding of the Modern Language Association of America in 1883, led to the stan-dardization of English "departments" across the landscape of higher education in the 1890s.[2] Since English as a higher field was new, it was not immediately clear what it would include or how it would be internally classified, categorized, or stratified by sub-subject. Indeed, the decades in question present a fascinating moment in both the history of the canon and in the social history of knowledge, a time when subjects within English emerged, rose, and

131

fell in level as the new higher curriculum defined a first hierarchy of knowledge areas. It was of course not immediately clear what place, level, or role Shakespeare would occupy in this new institutional sphere. His former place in American education had been in lower-level schools, where he served as a basis for elocutionary exercises.[3] If he were to enter the higher curriculum, the new culture of English would have to reinvent him as a higher-level subject.

This essay presents selected empirical cases of the early formation of Shakespeare's new curricular identity as a college "English" subject in America. Methodologically, I have sampled institutions representing differences of region, educational ethos, institutional status, and student population, including local and lesser-known, as well as more prestigious, schools. The history of colleges and universities in the United States is in fact notable for a tremendous range of institutions, and any history that aims to represent the extent and diversity of Shakespearean educations must attend to a broad array of settings, not only to the most famous institutions or those hiring the best-known scholars. By definition, every college and university in operation from 1870 to 1920 is part of the larger history I have here begun to compile. All of them were teaching students, regardless of how small or poorly funded they might be. While my space is limited, this study invites expansion; each new case will aid fuller comprehension of the larger sociological formations under investigation here. My cases include a small, sectarian southern institution that aspired (and failed) to become a large state university (Kentucky University); a large, coeducational, public, Midwestern university, one of the first to teach Shakespeare as "literature" (the University of Michigan); and the elite, East Coast, male institution that invented the American Ph.D. and professionalized the job class of the professor (the Johns Hopkins University).

These cases show the development of a rough consensus that placed rhetoric and composition at the most elementary level of college study, while Old and Middle English and history of the language rose to the most advanced level.[4] Indeed, in a fascinating moment in this history of the curricular canon, at roughly 1890 "English literature" drops in level from the senior year of study, to be replaced by classes in historical English as the new pinnacle. Within this emergent dynamic of distinction, to borrow Pierre Bourdieu's term, Shakespeare plays a revealing role.[5] While Levine traces how Shakespeare moved from a lowbrow to a highbrow cultural position during this era, and Dabbs stresses that Shakespeare's transformation into an academic product specifically meant to redefine him as a difficult author rather than one associated "with recreation or leisure"[6] whom people could understand on their own, the curricular data adds an additional layer of nuance to both Levine's and Dabbs's accounts. Perhaps Shakespeare was becoming highbrow and difficult, but the higher curriculum initially placed him at its lower to middle range, not its most rarefied position. In this respect, Shakespeare had not simply become difficult. Rather, he played a transitional role that mediated between lower and higher schools and, in turn, between the newly defined elementary and advanced forms of study within the English higher curriculum. While the old-school subject called "rhetoric," in which Shakespeare had once belonged, acquired an updated place in the freshman college curriculum, Shakespeare acquired an additional and new curricular identity as a "literature" class, distinct from rhetoric, which in turn necessitated redefining Shakespeare's meaning.

"English" and the New Higher Education

Shakespeare's fortunes as a college subject must be placed in the broader context of the postwar revolution in American higher education. The classical curriculum that had largely organized study in the antebellum college toppled after 1870. Three institutions in particular best emblematize the growing cultural pressures that forced its demise. First, the new Cornell University opened in 1868 as, in benefactor Ezra Cornell's famous words, "an institution where any person can find instruction in any study." Second, President Charles William Eliot became president of Harvard University in 1869 and inaugurated the elective system there. Cornell and Harvard embodied the distinction between vocational and liberal higher education, yet these otherwise competing institutions nevertheless united in legitimizing the idea of a broader curriculum. In so doing, they challenged and in fact demolished the curricular criteria of the traditional classical colleges. Third, the Johns Hopkins University opened in 1876, redefining higher education as a form of advanced scientific expertise. With its ideological and material focus on hiring faculty who were expert scholars, on producing published research, and on training Ph.D. students, Hopkins operated in a manner wholly independent of the antebellum collegiate model. Its educational philosophy functioned as what Frederick Rudolph aptly calls a "successful assault on the undergraduate course of study."[7]

It was amid these larger changes that the new subject tentatively called "English" emerged in the higher curriculum, at first uneasily and then with increasing strength and institutional stability by the mid- to late-1880s. But prior to this time, the idea of English was completely different from what it became in the new higher education. Developed first in lower schools, the "English" curriculum did not necessarily have anything to do with the English language or English literature; "English" was specifically defined as the modern, practical alternative to the classical curriculum. English trained both male and female students for practical pursuits such as business or homemaking, whereas the classical curriculum prepared boys in Greek and Latin for admission to the classical colleges (from which female students were barred) and eventually for the learned professions of law, medicine, and the ministry. While the classical curriculum centered in Latin and Greek, it typically also included subjects like logic, rhetoric, natural philosophy (later to become physics), and mathematics. By contrast, the English curriculum included what were called "modern subjects": usually a "modern" (as opposed to classical) foreign language, especially French, German, and Spanish; mathematics; sciences, such as natural philosophy, physiology, chemistry, botany, geology, and/or zoology; history (American, English, and "modern," rather than ancient); geography; moral philosophy; an array of subjects conceived to be "practical," like mensuration and astronomy; and the individual subject that was itself called "English," which at this time included grammar, orthography, etymology, syntax, prosody, reading, literature, rhetoric, and occasional classes in elocution.[8] The 1868 Trustees' Report of the Frankfort Public Schools in Kentucky nicely distills the broader social meaning of "English" at that time: "It is the intention of this course to provide a substantial English education. . . . It is designed to be *perfectly practical,* and of a character that will fit each pupil for the duties and business of an active and useful citizen."[9]

The institutional changes in the new university culture also entailed a radical shift in the nature of academic labor. A growing new job class of college English professors looked more and more different from the college teachers of the past. Spurred largely by the increasingly powerful credential of the Ph.D. and the ideology of advanced research cultivated at Johns Hopkins, these new professionals fought to overcome the lower-school, antischolarly (that is, "perfectly practical") image attached to English. Rather than an easier alternative to the classics for nonscholarly students headed for practical pursuits, English became a serious, professional subject fit for experts. The philological method in particular carved out an alternative, rigorous, scientific identity for English that would become increasingly hegemonic.[10] The history of curricular Shakespeare is part of this larger story of the social meaning of English.

KENTUCKY UNIVERSITY

The history of higher education in Kentucky is complex and laby-rinthine, characterized by vigorous sectarian battles among an array of small denominational colleges that frequently combined, split, and recombined. Kentucky University, a Christian Church institu-tion, incorporated a range of other schools after the Civil War in order to try to build a large, unified state university out of compo-nent parts. Through the tireless efforts of benefactor John Bryan Bowman, Kentucky either established, or incorporated through affiliation, a College of Arts, a College of the Bible, a College of Law, a Commercial College, a preparatory Academy, and the brand new state-controlled Agricultural and Mechanical College established by the Morrill Federal Land Grant Act of 1862. It was not uncommon in the nineteenth century for reality to belie such grand educational plans, and Bowman's vision of a total university would indeed fail, victim not only to meager budgets and inadequate facilities but (pri-marily) to firestorms between church factions. Despite its larger goals, Kentucky University remained essentially a small, conserva-tive, sectarian undergraduate institution.[11]

Here, I assess three of the divisions of Kentucky University, each serving a different curricular mission: the liberal arts college, the College of the Bible, and the Agricultural and Mechanical College. Separating in 1878 because of divisive church battles, all were located in Lexington and remained unofficially tied, positively or negatively, by thick church and local politics.[12] The liberal arts col-lege retained the name "Kentucky University" after the other parts split off; it shared a single building with the newly independent Col-lege of the Bible. The president of the latter, Robert Graham, was simultaneously Professor of the English Language and Literature at the former; he had also been the first teacher of English at the Agricultural and Mechanical College. According to university histo-rian John D. Wright, as other states moved into a period of growth and prosperity in higher education in the latter nineteenth century, Kentucky was left far behind and would not catch up for a century.[13] Yet amid these institutional problems and instabilities, Kentucky University and its various offshoots, like many other troubled small colleges in the nineteenth century, conducted their classes and taught their students.

In the 1860s, the curriculum at Kentucky was not yet organized into "departments," since that bureaucratic structure would only become standard in higher education in the 1890s. Instead, we find the curriculum organized by class year, routine practice at this time, with all students in each year taking the same prescribed classes. The freshman through senior courses simply announced the textbooks to be used. In the era before the professor-expert had become a primary commodity of higher education, the textbook *was* the class.[14] In English language and literature, freshmen studied the structure of the English language, composition, and elocution; sophomores, rhetoric; and juniors, logic and rhetoric. Seniors studied a handbook of English literature. Handbooks, a standard kind of textbook in this period, typically included excerpts from a vast number of writers along with general assessments of historical periods; they were the generic predecessors (albeit slimmer) of today's classroom anthologies.[15]

This curriculum remained relatively stable for decades until the 1890s, a contrast that exemplifies just how revolutionary the nineties indeed were. Colleges and universities across the nation reorganized at breakneck pace during this decade to keep up with modern trends. As Laurence R. Veysey observes, the 1890s represented a formative decade in higher education. Institutions entered a stage of significant bureaucratic growth, fostered and shaped by a national focus on standardizing education. These related developments produced a surge of new organizational behaviors at a rapid pace, including new titles and stratifications of academic rank and a proliferation of academic departments.[16] English departments were a particularly stylish addition. Many schools proudly reported expanding English offerings at this time to keep current. For example, Ellen J. Chamberlin, Head of English Literature at the University of Washington, noted in 1896, "Until the last quarter of a century, little attention was paid in our colleges and universities to the English classics, those of Greek and Latin occupying the most important place, but at the present time, a strong English department is the pride of every well-regulated American institution."[17]

The changes at Kentucky University in the 1890s are legible in this broader context. In 1891–92, English literature moved down from its former position in the senior curriculum to the junior year. It was replaced at the senior level by "Historical English Grammar," Chaucer, and Spenser, which, as subsequent cases will show, was a broader pattern at this time. In addition, this is the first year in which the word "Anglo-Saxon" appears in the Kentucky curriculum.[18] By the nineties, the philological method had become the core of English as a profession for specialized experts.[19] Both the class in historical grammar and the term "Anglo-Saxon" were hallmarks of the philological approach, and they start appearing in departmental rhetoric across the country at this time. Their sudden appearance at

Kentucky was a clear sign that the university was attempting to adopt the philological method and thus to claim currency in English studies.[20] From the standpoint of curricular hierarchy, the demotion of "literature" in favor of historical linguistics was also typical of broader trends, and we will see it repeated in the cases to come.

But change is sloppy. New models do not uniformly replace old ones overnight. 1891 was a transitional year at Kentucky, as indeed it was across the country. While English was reorganizing in the liberal arts college to adapt to modern trends, across the hall in the College of the Bible, the English course still defined itself as for "pious young men who have neither the time nor the means to obtain a classical education, but yet have a desire and the ability to be very useful in the ministry." The conception of English as a practical alternative to the classical curriculum hearkened back to a prior educational model, one by now long outdated, rather than to the new and increasingly hegemonic vision of English as an advanced scholarly subject. These visions of English coexisted in two schools that literally occupied the same building. The old-time College of the Bible justification for English study was indeed a relic. Across the country, English was winning in the battle against classics, in both lower and higher schools. While the two kinds of curricula were roughly equivalent in popularity in the high schools at midcentury, as of the 1860s the English curriculum increasingly overtook the classical.[21] It was no longer simply the lower-school alternative curriculum for students who did not have the time, means, or ability to prepare for classical colleges. At Kentucky, for example, English drew large numbers of students in 1892, 296 that year compared to 110 in Greek.[22]

The definition of English in the College of the Bible indeed changed the very next year, 1892, with the addition of a new senior-year historical linguistics class. Previously, the school had offered a three-year course that began with English grammar in the first year, followed by rhetoric and composition, and culminating in the senior year studying "English and American authors from Chaucer to the present."[23] In 1892, the College added a fourth year of study. The freshman grammar class and sophomore rhetoric and composition classes remained intact; the literature class moved downward in level to become the junior class, and historical linguistics moved into the top slot. This is also the first year in which the curriculum mentions Shakespeare. The junior literature class spent the second term on "the drama of Shakespeare," with "every effort made to cultivate a taste for good literature." The new senior class was a "comprehensive study of English philology" focused on Old and Middle English.[24]

The college of liberal arts named Shakespeare in its course offerings for the first time five years later, in 1897. That year, Shakespeare was taught in the middle (junior) year of a three-year curriculum. The reading list included "selected plays of Shakespeare," a handbook of American literature, a handbook of English literature from Milton to Tennyson, and selections from *Paradise Lost*. The catalog classified its courses in an ascending trajectory from rhetoric in the freshman year to the history and development of the language in the senior year, with Shakespeare and other literary topics falling in between.[25] This bifurcation of the curriculum, from rhetoric and composition at the most elementary level, to historical linguistics at the most advanced level, remained in place in the following years. Professor of English Clarence C. Freeman explained in 1899, "The course in Rhetoric and composition is practical" while "The courses in literature are both historical and critical."[26] His justification for the rhetoric and composition classes retained its rhetorical ties to practical justifications for English study in an earlier era, ones specifically tied to lower schools, a link that helped to sustain rhetoric and composition's elementary place in the new higher curriculum. Meanwhile, his rhetoric about the emergent courses in "literature" ("historical," "critical") is tied to the emergent discourse that justified the development of English as a higher field.

In 1899, the college of liberal arts began to offer a four- rather than three-year curriculum. Now both the junior and senior classes focused on Old and Middle English and the history and development of the English language. Rhetoric and composition once again fell in the first year. The second year of study was the one most in flux; indeed, what is most fascinating about this middle range in the curriculum more generally is that it is here that we find the uncertain terrain in which new "literary" subjects—those which were *neither* rhetoric and composition *nor* historical linguistics—began to define themselves. It was the new "literature" classes whose level in the hierarchy of knowledge had not yet been determined, particularly as literary study moved away from equating English literature classes with a handbook and instead began focusing on increasingly specialized individual authors, texts, and periods. At Kentucky at this time, all the literature classes went into the second year as a kind of curricular grab bag, a space that allowed for a new array of classes, including a new "Elizabethan Drama" class covering "the life, times, and dramatic art of Shakespeare and his contemporaries" (covering three unnamed Shakespeare plays); the first dedicated

American literature class in this curriculum; a class on Dryden and his contemporaries ("Literature of the Classical Period"); and a nineteenth-century British poetry class on Wordsworth, Tennyson, and Browning.[27] This was an important shift from the previous year, when all the literature topics that fell outside Old and Middle English were covered together in the second year via handbook-based surveys covering long time periods of time. Thus we see that, in 1899, the curriculum shifted in the direction of specialized topics covering discrete historical period as areas worth a course each, a radical change indeed. The second-year class that in 1898 had used a handbook to cover material from "Milton to Tennyson" was replaced with specialized courses like "Poetry of the Nineteenth Century."[28] Departments carved out the relation not only between "English language" and "English literature," but also among new "literature" subtopics. Elsewhere, I coin the term "curricular canonicity" to denote the canonical status of subject areas within the curriculum, a matter distinct from the canonicity of individual authors and texts. These are discrete registers of the canonical and must be disentangled if the historical process of canon formation is to be fully understood.[29]

By 1908, the hierarchy of these specialized literature classes from the early nineties shakes out further. Only two of them—the Elizabethan Drama class and the American literature class—became required sophomore classes to follow the two required freshman classes, rhetoric and composition and the basic English literature survey.[30] The other literature classes, by contrast, became electives. In one sense, they had been dressed up and taken uptown, along with the Old and Middle English electives. Yet they simultaneously remained in a different administrative category than the latter, a bureaucratic residue of the previous hierarchy. All the new literature electives appeared in the catalog under "Course C (Electives)," while Old and Middle English appeared as "Course D (Electives)." Previously, the individual classes now in Courses C and D would have been distinguished from one another not only by historical period, but also by the additional status marker of level. Now they were moving more closely into the same curricular category. The incipient bureaucratic order we see here is the early form of the "field-coverage principle" articulated by Gerald Graff, which, in Graff's analysis, would eventually lead to diversity without coherence. At the same time, the descriptions for the literature classes that have achieved this newly elevated level now promise to pursue "minute study," a phrase that was standard philological shorthand in the period for rigorous methodology. Whether or not the teachers of these courses

actually engaged in such a methodology is unclear from the record;
but their claim to do so is certainly a rhetorical bid to advanced
status.[31] At the top of the undergraduate elective curriculum, we
find Advanced Old English and English Language and "Research
Work," "Open only to graduate students for specialized investigation in English Philology."[32] Shakespeare remained a sophomore
requirement alongside American literature, whose connotations in
the higher curriculum at this time were lower-school and antiprofes-
sional, so its placement here alongside Shakespeare is historically
legible.[33] We find no "minute study" in the course description for
either of these more elementary subjects.

Yet Shakespeare's midrange placement not only signified that
Shakespeare classes were neither the least nor the most prestigious
in the English curriculum. Notably, it meant that Shakespeare had
been redefined as a "literature" class, to be radically distinguished
from the rhetoric classes in which he had prominently figured as a
model of excellence in the old-time classroom. The school textbooks of the 1850s and 1860s called "readers," like McGuffey's, took
their greatest number of quotations from Shakespeare.[34] While the
old-school subject called "rhetoric" did acquire an updated place in
the college curriculum, albeit at the elementary level, Shakespeare
took on an additional and new curricular identity as a "literature"
class, distinct from rhetoric, and typically higher up. In this sense,
we can place Shakespeare as an instance of the more general curricular trend Henry W. Simon has noted at the close of the nineteenth
century, away from elocution and toward literary criticism, history
of English literature, and biography.[35] Indeed, in 1900 the Normal
College at Kentucky, which trained teachers to work in schools
below the college in level, offered training in grammar and rhetoric
but not in "literature" as such.[36]

The Agricultural and Mechanical College of Kentucky was
founded in 1865 under the terms of the Morrill Federal Land Grant
Act of 1862, through which the federal government provided funds
to the various states for agricultural and mechanical education for
all classes of society. The Morrill Act would democratize higher education.[37] Although the Agricultural and Mechanical College was initially a part of Kentucky University, the idea of a state-supported
land-grant school clashed with Kentucky's denominational foundation; church squabbles hastened a split.[38] A newly independent institution in 1878, the Agricultural and Mechanical College of Kentucky
offered English language and literature classes that included grammar and composition for freshmen, rhetoric and composition for
sophomores, rhetoric and logic for juniors, and "English literature"

at the pinnacle of the curriculum, in senior year, taught by hand-book.[39] In 1881–82, Anglo-Saxon was added to senior class studies, and the "English Literature" classes moved downward from their former place in the senior year, a pinnacle now unsurprisingly given over instead to "Early English," while the English literature classes dropped to the first and second year.[40] As at Kentucky University, "literature" was demoted in level, as philological courses in histori-cal English replaced them at the top tier.

Shakespeare's name first appeared in this curriculum in 1886 in the sophomore, junior, and senior classes; the freshman class in rhetoric and composition was the only one whose description did not mention him. In the second-year English class, "Studies in English Literature," each pupil was "required to commit to memory and recite in class selections from the great English poets and prose writers, including parts of Shakespeare's *Julius Caesar* and the *Merchant of Venice*," as well as selections from Milton, Gray, Goldsmith, Lowell, Wordsworth, Coleridge, Tennyson, Webster, and other selec-tions common on college entrance exams in this era.[41] The juniors studied logic in the first term and, in the second, rhetoric and "History of English Literature." Here the "Class Readings from . . . great English writers" included Bacon, Burke, Milton, and Shakespeare, although the particular play or plays went unnoted. The senior cur-riculum still included Shakespeare, but changed the terms in which he was contextualized: "Selections from Chaucer's Canterbury Tales and Spenser's Faerie Queene; Studies of Early English words and idioms; Critical study of a selected play of Shakespeare." Here we find the key term "critical study" which, like "minute study," signi-fied an advanced approach distinct from the memorization and reci-tation model associated with the antebellum college and with lower-level schooling; this old approach was still legible in the sophomore class's premise that Shakespeare was to be memorized and recited. The methodological rubric of "critical study" placed this senior-level Shakespeare in company with historical linguistics and thus dif-ferentiated senior Shakespeare from sophomore Shakespeare. This process of elevation lasted only temporarily. By 1894, Shakespeare dropped out of this senior class, but remained in the second- and third-year classes.[42]

The next big change came in 1900, due, as is commonly the case in curricular history, to a change in faculty. In these early years of the English profession, it was common for a subject to appear or disappear with a particular faculty member. Professor John Shackle-ford, who had been teaching at the Agricultural and Mechanical College since 1878, resigned and Alexander St. Clair MacKenzie replaced him.[43] When MacKenzie took over, he undertook a reorganization like that occurring in English departments around the nation in the 1890s: "The intention is to make the course in English as thorough and comprehensive as that of any college in the United States."[44] A new freshman course consisted of "American literature, its genesis and genius"—the first time an entire class in American literature appeared in this curriculum—and a single Shakespeare play (initially, *Hamlet*), followed by surveys of English literature in the sophomore and junior years that included Shakespeare, and concluding in senior year with Anglo-Saxon and comparative philology. Notably, the sophomore through senior curriculum moved backward chronologically, emblematic of the semiotic of prestige in the field at this time that construed historically remote eras, with their difficult language, as more serious and advanced. Thus, the sophomore survey from "the Elizabethan to the Victorian period" began with Shakespeare, while the junior survey "English literature from Chaucer to Shakespeare" ended with him. The senior class moved further back in time, to focus on Anglo-Saxon.[45]

There were no rhetoric and composition classes in this curriculum at this point; instead, both the American literature and the Shakespeare class were used to teach "the writing and criticism of essays" and thus operated at the lowest level of the curriculum as the equivalent of the composition class.[46] As these instances have shown, up through 1900, Shakespeare and American literature in particular occupied a transitional curricular space, typically following freshman rhetoric and composition but preceding the upper-division classes centered in historically remote works "critically" studied via "minute" linguistic methods. American literature and Shakespeare were common high school subjects at this time, and placed as they were at the low- to mid-range of the college curriculum, they served a transitional purpose, particularly in an era of growing frustration among educators about the relation between secondary schools and colleges.[47]

The most particular historical circumstance driving Shakespeare's ambiguous position between levels of the school was his regular appearance on college entrance exams.[48] When in 1874 Harvard announced that it would require a composition on the work of "standard authors as shall be announced from time to time," the high schools took note. As Charles Van Cleve points out, the fact that the subjects first required were *The Tempest, Julius Caesar,* and *The Merchant of Venice,* as well as Goldsmith's *Vicar of Wakefield* and Scott's *Ivanhoe* and *Lay of the Last Minstrel,* produced a formal movement to teach Shakespeare's plays in high schools.[49] Simon points out that the texts being taught in the high schools probably also influenced the college entrance requirements, so that influence moved both ways; but it remains difficult to determine the exact circulation of reciprocal effects.[50] Of course, any branch of English could have suited the role of transitional work between levels of schooling, so we see here nothing inherently lower-level about Shakespeare and American literature in particular. Indeed, the later curricular history of both areas as advanced undergraduate and graduate subjects belies the conceptions animating late nineteenth-century curricular history.

The sorting of subjects by curricular level during these transitional years was determined not only by the nominal content of subjects, but also by hierarchies within the shifting academic labor pool. In the post-1880 era through about 1910 in particular, the academic labor model was in transition. Ph.D.-certified English professors gradually displaced and replaced a prior job class of college teachers, whom, for ease of reference, I call "preprofessionals." A quick sketch of the largest contrasts between the two classes of teachers is instructive. The new professors were valued for their Ph.D. credentials; the old teachers, by contrast, had been valued for their moral character or "culture."[51] The new professors were certified in their capacity for original research in an area of specialization; the old teachers typically taught a variety of subjects, indeed, they were not defined as specialists to begin with. The new professors could ostensibly reproduce research skills in their students, pedagogically symbolized by their signature classroom model called the "seminary" (shortened in today's parlance to "seminar"); the old teachers transmitted standard forms of handbook knowledge to their students, pedagogically symbolized by their signature classroom model of the "recitation," which required daily memorization of the handbook. The preprofessional teacher often ranged among a variety of subjects from year to year, a range required by the nature of the job of teaching in the old-time college, indeed, by the concept of *knowledge* itself as it functioned in the old-time college. President Daniel Coit Gilman of Hopkins described the nonspecialist as "willing to teach anything or to take any chair." For Gilman, this portrait was derogatory; it was this preprofessional model of teaching labor that the Hopkins Ph.D. credential sought to overturn.[52] Returning to the Agricultural and Mechanical College of Kentucky, while we don't know exactly why Shackelford resigned and was replaced by MacKenzie, we do know that Shackelford, a minister with a degree of A.M., had classic preprofessional credentials, whereas MacKenzie was a transitional hire typical of these years, particularly at more marginal institutions: he did not have the Ph.D., but had done "post-graduate work" in comparative philology.[53]

In 1908, Shakespeare vanished from curricular records entirely; if he was taught under the rubric of another more general topic such as "Modern Drama," it is impossible to tell from the course descriptions.[54] When he returned by name to the curriculum in 1913–14, he did so in the first class ever offered under the title "Shakespeare." Its teacher, Anna J. Hamilton, A.M., was Dean of Women and Associate Professor of English.[55] Hamilton, like many preprofessional teachers of this era, had previously worked in a secondary school.[56] The ambiguous status of preprofessional teachers in the new knowledge economy often fostered disrespect for them from the English specialists, a disrespect that extended to the subjects and classes they taught. Indeed, the preprofessional teachers were often compartmentalized into particular subject areas, leaving more highly respected subjects for the real experts.[57] Professional disdain for kinds of teachers transferred to the subjects they taught, both teacher and subject construed as less scholarly and less serious, easy enough for anyone to teach (and learn). It is thus unsurprising that when Hamilton, one of a vast number of female preprofessional college teachers who would be expunged from higher education during these transitional years, stopped teaching Shakespeare the next year, it passed to another preprofessional.[58] At this point the class was called "Pre-Shaksperean and Shaksperean Drama," offered by Edward Franklin Farquhar, who in 1916 also began teaching the American literature class. Both classes were junior and senior electives at this time, so they had moved up.[59] A later departmental history in 1964 described Farquhar as "not a publishing scholar in the modern sense." Although the author of the report, English professor William S. Ward, listed the degrees other faculty possessed, he did not bother to note Farquhar's. Farquhar had an A.B. and M.A. from Lafayette College (1905, 1908) and, like other professors during this professionally transitional era, had studied toward his doctorate during two summers in an effort to keep up with the expectations for advanced credentials that were leaving him behind.[60] Both of Kentucky's Shakespeare teachers in the nineteen-teens thus fell into the transitional labor category of the preprofessional increasingly outmoded and replaced by the Ph.D. "publishing scholars" Ward cited. Just as we saw earlier that the level at which Shakespeare was taught was imbricated in a broader semiotic of distinction, so too was the labor status of his teachers.

The University of Michigan

The University of Michigan, a state university, began operating in 1841 and was the only university in the Midwest to achieve an eminent reputation before 1890.[61] Here again, we find that Shakespeare and American literature classes are linked in the 1890s. In 1898–99, among a total faculty of five teachers, Professor Isaac Newton Demmon taught both of these subjects.[62] Like Farquhar at the Agricultural and Mechanical College of Kentucky, Demmon was a preprofessional. He moved to Rhetoric, Anglo-Saxon, and finally English from an initial place in Mathematics, before which he taught Greek and ancient languages at other colleges. Prior to that, like Anna Hamilton at Kentucky, he was a high school principal.[63] Moving in this way from one subject area to another and even from high school to college was common among preprofessionals, who coexisted with Ph.D.'s while institutions retooled their hiring.[64] A 1950 department history—similar to Ward's on Farquhar—described Demmon as a teacher whose "interest in his subject is broad and general, rather than highly specialized" and who "deprecated and resisted the latter day [sic] tendency to import into literary criticism and history the implications and methods of modern science."[65] Further, although he had A.B. and A.M. degrees from Michigan (1868, 1871), he tellingly returned to school in midcareer for an LL.D. (Doctor of Laws) from the University of Nashville (1896). As with Farquhar, returning to school for an advanced degree was a common practice for preprofessional teachers attempting to keep up with the new demands of Ph.D. culture. Demmon remained behind, however; although the LL.D. was common for the nonspecialist in the antebellum college, it was not a professional degree for an English professor at this time.[66]

Demmon taught both Shakespeare and American literature as "seminaries," terminology for the most advanced undergraduate research courses, which had trickled out and down from the The Johns Hopkins University, whose "seminary" (based on the German model) was its signature method of graduate instruction in advanced research.[67] Demmon's "English Literature Seminary," which included "Shakespeare's Sonnets," and his "American Literature Seminary" were the only seminaries in this curriculum at this time. He also taught a graduate course called "Studies in the text of Shakespeare."[68] As department head at a Midwestern institution, Demmon, although a preprofessional, was in a position to place these subjects at an advanced level of the curriculum. Simon shows

that Shakespeare appeared first in college curricula that were less
tradition-bound, citing Michigan among them as perhaps the first
university to teach Shakespeare as literature, in 1858. Notably, the
assistant professor who taught the first Shakespeare class there,
Datus C. Brooks, did so in the university's "scientific course." Just as
"English" in the lower schools had meant "modern," the scientific
schools that began to open in the colleges in the 1850s, like the Sheffield Scientific School at Yale, were typically less prestigious divisions
of traditional colleges. They offered classes, including but not limited to technological subjects, as a practical alternative to conventional classical training. They often provided a more open curricular
space in which new subjects like English first crept into the college
curriculum.[69]

Shakespeare's ties to old school models persisted even as English
carved out its new identity. For example, in 1898–99, Michigan also
offered a Shakespeare course in the "Elocution and Oratory"
Department. Amid six classes in "Elocution" and the "Study of
Great Orators," only one class listed a particular author by name
and indeed spent an entire class on him: "Shakespearean Reading"
covered "Critical study and reading of two of Shakespeare's plays."[70]
This was the college-level version of the old-time lower-school Shakespeare. J. V. Denney, who took an A.B. at Michigan in 1885 and was
both a graduate student and instructor there in 1890–91 (roughly
contemporary to this history), later described the "'Elocution and
Oratory'" teachers of this era as "pseudo-scientific entertainers."
When he made this assessment in 1929, Denney, a scholar of rhetoric, reported favorably that now "a new race of teachers is appearing."[71] Henry D. Sheldon similarly wrote in 1901 that the last quarter
of the nineteenth century saw "oratory as a fine art" on the decline,
still effective with the "vast mass of the population" but inducing
"irony" among "the critical portion of the professional classes."[72]
Levine concurs that there was a "surprisingly rapid decline in oratory" at this time.[73] Sheldon also observes that oratory endured in
particular as a subject in "the West"—a term that, at that time,
included the Midwest—well after it had lost caste in the East.[74] The
New York Times reported in 1909 that Shakespeare had lost his appeal
with theatergoers because of his associations with oratory and elocution.[75]

At Michigan, this curricular moment at the cusp of a new century
shows the increasingly outmoded oratorical and elocutionary Shakespeare lingering alongside the English departments that were carv-
ing out his new identity. Indeed, English needed to reinvent the
oratorical and elocutionary Shakespeare if he were to thrive in the

new knowledge economy. Simon reports that the period after 1870 saw Shakespeare separating from elocution and achieving a "new dignity" as "literature," a process reinforced by a shift from reading excerpts for declamation to reading whole plays. A former Yale College student recalled of the era before Shakespeare became "literature," "In those days nobody knew what to do with a play of Shakespeare's." When two good teachers of Shakespeare finally joined the Yale College faculty, neither, he noted pointedly, "could make a speech."[76]

THE JOHNS HOPKINS UNIVERSITY

The Johns Hopkins University was more responsible than any other single institution for inventing the research model in American higher education. Hopkins transformed the pursuit of an advanced degree from a marginal academic exercise into a necessary, competitive credential for a new profession: the scholar-expert. These new professors would increasingly staff faculty positions, displacing the preprofessional teachers who lacked this programmatic training. From 1876 to1900, Hopkins stood as the national model in doctoral education, surpassing all other institutions in the number of degrees granted, with only Harvard a close second. By 1910, the Ph.D. had become a job requirement for many faculty positions.[77]

The higher study of English at Hopkins defined the field in a way that would suit these new professionals and their advanced methods. They envisioned their work as "scientific" inquiry, in pointed contrast to belletristic approaches. When in his 1926 history of the English Department philologist Kemp Malone wrote, "Literature is indeed not in any proper sense a science (or branch of learning)," he summed up the attitude toward "literature" that had animated English at Hopkins since its founding.[78] The department's hierarchies of "proper" subjects of advanced research are legible in the ways that it stratified its curriculum. In the 1880s, it organized work into four programmatic spaces. First, the "Seminary" served as the intensive research space for original investigation, pursued by graduate students under the direction of a professor. The Hopkins Seminary was infamously cutting-edge in curricular developments of its day, operating at the ideological pinnacle of the curriculum.[79] As noted in the case of Michigan, undergraduate courses called "seminaries" at other schools were aping the Hopkins model of advanced research, attempting to keep current. Moving downward in level and prestige, we find the "advanced" or other graduate courses; the

English major courses; the English minor courses; and finally the courses required of all undergraduates.[80]

Shakespeare comes up obliquely in the most advanced courses, as a kind of reference point who marks a time and stage in the history of the language. Despite the routine invocation of his name in class titles as a period marker, he does not receive concerted attention in class content. His primary curricular location was the less serious and less prestigious "English minor class," whose teachers and methods were distinct from those of the rarefied Seminary. Here, classes engaged him with energy. John Hampton Lauck points out that, more generally, Shakespeare found a place within both philological and belles-lettres courses at this time;[81] at Hopkins, Shakespeare played a minor role in the advanced classes with their philological work and a much larger curricular role at the lower and more belletristic end of the curriculum. This is particularly interesting for the way it illuminates a resistance at the most advanced level to fully incorporate him. Hopkins had showed such resistance to other subjects with lower-school connotations; external factors, as we will see, would eventually force the department's hand.[82]

In 1884, the undergraduate course bulletin justified English offerings in philology by noting that "Anglo-Saxon, Early and Middle English are only earlier stages of Shakespearian English," using the name of Shakespeare to ground the kind of work the department construed as most prestigious.[83] By the late 1880s, the English curriculum at its higher levels circled around and defined itself with respect to Shakespeare, without teaching much Shakespeare as such. In 1887, for example, philologist James W. Bright taught an advanced half-year class on the legend of Troilus and Cressida, concluding with Shakespeare "as the last significant product in a long line of traditions."[84] Outside the classroom, graduate students and professors gathered to deliver papers and discuss recent scholarship, including Shakespeare topics in 1889 and 1890.[85] In 1891, the Seminary used Shakespeare's name in its title, "The English Drama from the Morality Plays to Shakespeare," but the course description, written retrospectively and so presumably summarizing the work actually done, does not include him. Meanwhile, the Seminary bestowed its telltale method of "minute study" upon an array of other topics such as liturgical drama and the four great cycles of miracle plays, while the "advanced courses" included phonetics, Middle English grammar, and the Anglo-Saxon version of Bede's *Ecclesiastical History*.[86]

Despite his tepid presence higher up, Shakespeare's role grew livelier and more focused at the lower levels of the curriculum. In

1887, the English minor class studied the Elizabethan period, including *Twelfth Night,* and, at the bottom of the curriculum, the survey required of undergraduates read aloud "under the guidance of the instructor, Shakespeare's *Julius Caesar,* and selections from Chaucer and Milton." Its teacher, William Hand Browne, was not a faculty member to whom the Seminary was ever assigned (at Hopkins, a clear sign of scholarly rank), and he was using an old oratorical model of pedagogy.[87] In 1891, "A few members of the [English major] class who did not take the Anglo-Saxon of the major course read Shakespeare's historical plays under the guidance of the instructor." Shakespeare served as a curricular alternative to the dominance of Anglo-Saxon philology at the core of the department.

This packaging of curricular Shakespeare as a subject suited to college classes, but not the most advanced ones and not the graduate Seminary, continued to obtain at Hopkins for years. These curricular locations were very much tied to labor stratifications. Herbert Eveleth Greene, notably titled the "Collegiate Professor of English," who was "specially responsible for the undergraduate work in the dept" and thus who did not teach the graduate students, offered a survey of English literature in 1893 that included "Chaucer, Spenser, Milton, and Shakespeare."[88] Outside class, he offered in 1901 "four readings from the poems of Chaucer and twelve lectures upon the dramas of Shakespeare . . . for the benefit of those members of the class who desired to attend them."[89] As of 1906, we still find no Shakespeare in "Advanced Courses." The American literature and the Shakespeare courses are located primarily at the bottom of the curriculum. Bright's seminary did not extend past "the period following immediately after Chaucer."[90] Greene's optional Shakespeare class is an instance of how the extracurriculum allowed space for new or marginal subjects not taught in the classroom proper. (Indeed, English literature itself had initially had a lively life in the extracurriculum of classical colleges, where the debating and literary societies and their libraries provided a place for students to explore the subject before it was admitted to the curriculum.[91] In 1888, Hiram Corson of Cornell, a well-known professor famously opposed to the research model in the study of literature in favor of humanistic culture, gave twenty lectures at Hopkins on Shakespeare "to present the plays on the human side rather than on the scholastic," and the students formed a Shakespeare Circle in conjunction with them. The lectures were optional and students received no credit for attendance, yet they were so popular that the University needed to find a larger space in which to hold them.[92] This "human side" of the approach to Shakespeare, with its popular appeal, was markedly not the kind of advanced research in which the English Department took pride.

External forces would change the curricular meaning of Shakespeare at Hopkins. A Shakespeare boom in 1919 included the first Seminary devoted to Shakespeare alone and as such, called "Plays of Shakespeare," in addition to a surge in undergraduate offerings.[93] The immediate context here is the aftermath of World War I, which gave a forceful ideological boost to school subjects construed to serve democracy. As Arthur N. Applebee notes, the Declaration of War in April 1917 "crystallized definitions of 'needs and interests' in terms of national aims, and English teachers across the nation responded with enthusiasm." Literature became a means to instill an awareness of national heritage and to foster patriotism.[94] The war repositioned the British literary legacy as the wellspring of democracy and thus as freshly valuable in those terms.[95] For example, Edwin Greenlaw, the Hopkins Spenserian, published secondary-level and college textbooks at this time that lauded America's achievements in self-government, which he placed in a continuous tradition with prior such achievements by the Anglo-Saxon race in Britain. The introduction to his *The Great Tradition: A Book of Selections from English and American Prose and Poetry, Illustrating the National Ideals of Freedom, Faith, and Conduct* (1919) concludes:

> The faith of the martyr, the courage of the pioneer, the steadfastness of the hero, the love of the emancipator, the vision of the poet,—and the virtue of plain and inarticulate men and women everywhere, gain their power from this great tradition of the race. It was this idealism, sleeping but not dead, that swept America like a divine fire in the months following April of 1917. In the great war this heredity met and conquered the heredity of brute power. Other crises remain to be met, for the warfare never ends. It is the task of school and college to guard the flame.[96]

Assessing curricular history in the ascendant era of the English profession reminds us that the placement of English subjects, including Shakespeare, was historically contingent upon factors that had little to do with the content of texts and more to do with institutional phenomena such as professionalization, hierarchy, prestige, and image. Although in the old-time curriculum the teaching of Shakespeare had been attached to rhetorical and oratorical training, between 1870 and 1920 rhetoric and composition settled to the bottom of the college curriculum, and Shakespeare was moving outside that sole location. Yet his curricular identity remained in flux. Discussions among educators from grade school through college level during the years of my study about how to teach Shakespeare typically share one large assumption: that "Shakespeare" was, and ought to be, a curricular given, and that the only active question was that of pedagogy. The right method would communicate Shakespeare's inherent qualities and lead to classroom success.[97] But as Bristol has noted, Shakespeare is a complex institutional reality. The apparatus of reproduction that disseminates his work also in part constitutes its meaning, since there is no "really real" Shakespeare outside the historical processes through which he is circulated, read, and taught.[98] The new institutional culture of higher education in America after 1880 redefined Shakespeare to accommodate an array of institutional pressures in the complex new world of English studies.

NOTES

I thank B. J. Gooch, Special Collections and Archives, Transylvania University, Lexington, KY, and Silas Adkins, student assistant there; Deirdre Scaggs, University of Kentucky Libraries, Lexington, KY; Brenda J. Smith, the Kentucky Historical Society Special Collections, Frankfort, KY; Karen L. Jania, Bentley Historical Library, University of Michigan, Ann Arbor, MI; and James Stimpert, The Ferdinand Hamburger Jr. Archives, The Johns Hopkins University, Baltimore, MD.

Abbreviations

JHU: The Ferdinand Hamburger Jr. Archives, The Johns Hopkins University, Baltimore, MD.
KHS: Kentucky Historical Society, Special Collections, Frankfort, KY.
MHC: The Mount Holyoke College Archives and Special Collections, South Hadley, MA.
TU: Special Collections & Archives, Transylvania University, Lexington, KY.
UK: University Archives, University of Kentucky Libraries, Lexington, KY.
UM: Bentley Historical Library, University of Michigan, Ann Arbor, MI.

1. For overviews, see Michael D. Bristol, *Shakespeare's America, America's Shakespeare* (London and New York: Routledge, 1990); Esther Cloudman Dunn, *Shakespeare in America* (New York: Macmillan, 1939); Lawrence W. Levine, *Highbrow / Lowbrow: The Emergence of Cultural Hierarchy in America* (Cambridge: Harvard University Press, 1988); Kim C. Sturgess, *Shakespeare and the American Nation* (Cambridge: Cambridge University Press, 2004); and Thomas Dabbs, "Shakespeare and the Department of English," in *English as a Discipline Or, Is There a Plot in This Play?* ed. James C. Raymond (Tuscaloosa: University of Alabama Press, 1996) 82–98, esp. 82. Although Dabbs primarily focuses on England, he notes the similarity of the process he describes to the one Levine traces in America during the same half-century (85–86). Gary Taylor points out that, beginning in 1870, Parliament created the state school system and that Shakespeare became the "dominant component of the new subject of English Literature, itself an expanding part of an expanding educa-

tional system"; see *Reinventing Shakespeare: A Cultural History from the Restoration to the Present* (New York: Weidenfeld & Nicholson, 1989), 194. For Bristol's comment, see 8.

2. The emergence and standardization of English departments is, of course, a story of development and transition rather than instant change. See Arthur N. Applebee, *Tradition and Reform in the Teaching of English: A History* (Urbana, IL: National Council of Teachers of English, 1974). Applebee places the establishment of English departments between the founding of the Modern Language Association of America in 1883, and 1900, when graduate degrees in the subject were available across the United States (27–28); see also Elizabeth Renker, *The Origins of American Literature Studies: An Institutional History* (Cambridge: Cambridge University Press, 2007), esp. 150n33.

3. Henry W. Simon, "Why Shakespeare?" *English Journal* 23.5 (1934): 363–68, esp. 365.

4. Scholars of the history of composition as a field have long noted its curricular construction as fundamentally elementary and unserious. See John C. Brereton, ed, *The Origins of Composition Studies in the American College, 1875–1925: A Documentary History* (Pittsburgh: University of Pittsburgh Press, 1995); and Robert J. Connors, *Composition-Rhetoric: Backgrounds, Theory, and Pedagogy* (Pittsburgh: University of Pittsburgh Press, 1997), and "Crisis and Panacea in Composition Studies: A History." In *Composition in Context: Essays in Honor of Donald C. Stewart*, ed. W. Ross Winterowd and Vincent Gillespie (Carbondale: Southern Illinois University Press, 1994), 86–105.

5. Pierre Bourdieu, *Distinction: A Social Critique of the Judgement of Taste*, trans. Richard Nice (1979; repr., London: Routledge and Kegan Paul, 1984).

6. Dabbs, 86.

7. Renker, *Origins*, 2; Frederick Rudolph, *The American College and University: A History*. (1962; repr., Athens: University of Georgia Press, 1990), 266–68, esp. 294, 266 (quoting Cornell); and Frederick Rudolph, *Curriculum: A History of the American Undergraduate Course of Study Since 1636* (San Francisco, CA: Jossey-Bass, 1978), 116–38, 131.

8. Renker, *Origins*, 16; William J. Reese, *The Origins of the American High School* (New Haven: Yale University Press, 1995), 65, 2, 95, 107–8, 115–16; personal correspondence with William J. Reese, December 10, 2002; Rudolph, *Curriculum*, 159, 31–32, 34–36. Some schools were exclusively English schools or classical schools; the increasingly popular new institution called the high school often offered both curricula and allowed students to select (Reese, *Origins*, 95).

9. *Annual Report of the Board of Trustees of the Frankfort Public Schools, 1868–1869*, 23 (370, p.v.4, No. 4), KHS.

10. Renker, *Origins*, 19–22; Gerald Graff, *Professing Literature: An Institutional History* (Chicago: University of Chicago Press, 1987); Allen J. Frantzen, *Desire for Origins: New Language, Old English, and Teaching the Tradition* (New Brunswick: Rutgers University Press, 1990); Phyllis Franklin, "English Studies: The World of Scholarship in 1883," *PMLA* 99 (1984): 346–70; and Michael Warner, "Professionalization and the Rewards of Literature: 1875–1900," *Criticism* 27 (1985): 1–28.

11. John D. Wright, *Transylvania: Tutor to the West* (Lexington: University Press of Kentucky, 1975), 215, 238, 241.

12. ibid., 231–32. The liberal arts division changed its name over the years. For ease of reference, I refer to it generically as the liberal arts college. While the complex history of higher education in Kentucky makes it hard to trace direct lines of descent to today's institutions, the school in Lexington, Kentucky known today as

Transylvania University is one descendant of the liberal arts college at the Kentucky University I discuss here; the Agricultural and Mechanical College would go on to become the University of Kentucky. The best source on the complex history of Kentucky University and Transylvania University is Wright.

13. ibid., 214, 234.

14. Warner; "Professionalization," Graff, *Professing.*.

15. *Catalogue of Kentucky University*, 1865, 24; 1866, 24; 1867, 35–36; 1869, 41; 1870, 44; TU.

16. Veysey, *Emergence*, 305–24.

17. Report by Ellen J. Chamberlin to President Harrington, October 9, 1896, University of Washington President Records, Accession 70–028, Special Collections, University of Washington Libraries, Seattle, Washington. Such statements are routine in administrative announcements of the period at many institutions.

18. *Catalogue of Kentucky University, 1891/92*, 30; TU.

19. Warner, "Professionalization"; Renker, *Origins.*

20. Renker, *Origins*, 19–22.

21. Reese, *Origins*, 95.

22. *Catalogue of Kentucky University, 1892/93*, 59, TU.

23. *Annual Catalogue of the College of the Bible, 1891–92*, 8; TU.

24. Ibid., 36; TU.

25. *Catalogue of Kentucky University, 1898/99*, 23, TU. The curriculum fluctuated between a three- and four-year program.

26. *Catalogue of Kentucky University, 1899/1900*, 25–26, TU.

27. Ibid., 25–27, TU.

28. *Catalogue of Kentucky University, 1898/99*, 23; *Catalogue of Kentucky University, 1899/1900*, 26; *Catalogue of Kentucky University, 1900/01*, 29, TU.

29. Renker, *Origins*, 4.

30. *Catalogue of Kentucky University, 1908/09*, 87–91; TU.

31. Ibid.

32. Ibid., 91; TU.

33. Renker, *Origins*, 23–39.

34. Henry W. Simon, *The Reading of Shakespeare in American Schools and Colleges: An Historical Survey* (New York: Simon and Schuster, 1932), 44. On McGuffey's readers, see the essay by Jonathan Burton in this volume; on the history of teaching Shakespeare in lower and secondary schools, see Simon; and Charles Van Cleve, "The Teaching of Shakespeare in American Secondary Schools," *Peabody Journal of Education* 15.6 (1938): 333–50. On the history of rhetorical education, see Nan Johnson, *Nineteenth-Century Rhetoric in North America* (Carbondale: Southern Illinois University Press, 1991); on Shakespeare in particular as a model of excellence, see Johnson's essay in this volume.

35. Simon, *Reading*, 42, 100.

36. *Catalogue of Kentucky University, 1900/1901*, 53; TU.

37. Rudolph, *American*, 247, 252; and James F. Hopkins, *The University of Kentucky: Origins and Early Years* (Lexington: University of Kentucky Press, 1951), vii.

38. Wright, *Transylvania*, 219.

39. This institution underwent an array of name changes as well as affiliations and combinations with other institutions over the years, from the Agricultural and Mechanical College of Kentucky to the State College of Kentucky in 1908 and the University of Kentucky in 1916. See *Catalogue, 1908/09*, 11, UK; Hopkins, *The University of Kentucky*, 250; personal correspondence with Deirdre Scaggs, UK, April 29, 2009; *Annual Register of the Agricultural and Mechanical College of Kentucky, 1878/79*, 18, UK.

40. *Annual Register of the State College of Kentucky, 1881/82,* 18; and *Annual Register of the State College of Kentucky, 1883/84,* 17, UK.

41. *Annual Register of the State College of Kentucky, 1886/87,* 28, UK; and Applebee, *Tradition,* 275–277.

42. *Annual Register of the State College of Kentucky, 1894/95,* 14–15, UK.

43. *Lexington Daily Press* clipping, May 5, 1894, 1, Departmental File to 1956, Box 15, Folder: English Language and Literature, 1 of 2; and Faculty/Staff Biography File: MacKenzie, Alexander St. Clair, 1865–2002, Box 114; both at UK.

44. *Catalogue of the State College of Kentucky, 1899/1900,* 18, UK.

45. Ibid., 18–20, UK.

46. Ibid., 19, UK.

47. These growing tensions led to the formation of the Committee of Ten in 1892 and the College Entrance Examination Board (CEEB) in 1900, with the first CEEB exam administered in 1901. See Rudolph, *The American College and University,* 437–38; and Claude M. Fuess, *The College Board: Its First Fifty Years* (New York: Columbia University Press, 1950), 38. On American literature in secondary education, see Renker; and Donald E. Stahl, *A History of the English Curriculum in American High Schools* (Chicago: Lyceum Press, 1965), 19, 20; on Shakespeare in secondary education, see Simon, *Reading;* and Renker, *Origins.*

48. For an extended analysis of Shakespeare and the college entrance exams, see Denise Albanese's essay in this volume.

49. Van Cleve, "Teaching," 334.

50. Simon, *Reading,* 120–21.

51. Veysey, *Emergence,* 45.

52. Francesco Cordasco, *The Shaping of American Graduate Education: Daniel Coit Gilman and the Protean Ph.D.* (Totowa, NJ: Rowman and Littlefield, 1973), esp. 73 (quoting Gilman); John Guillory, "Preprofessionalism: What Graduate Students Want," *ADE Bulletin* 113 (1996): 4–8. Guillory uses the term "preprofessional" to describe the labor position of graduate students. I use the term, of course, in a different historical period in a different sense, but also calling attention to stratifications of academic labor.

53. *Annual Report, Agricultural and Mechanical College of Kentucky, 1878–9,* 18; typescript from the *Lexington Leader,* November 15, 1901, Departmental File to 1956, Box 15, Folder: English Language and Literature, 1 of 2; William S. Ward, *The English Department University of Kentucky. An Informal History, with Personal Recollections: The First Hundred Years, 1865–1964* (Department of English, Lexington, KY), 4; all at UK.

54. See the catalogs between 1908 and 1913 to trace this record. The first inkling by way of a course title that "Shakespeare" is coming back is the class "Pre-Shakespearean English Drama," which appears for the first time in 1913 (*Catalogue 1913/1914,* 81–84, UK).

55. *Catalogue, 1914,* 83, 18, UK.

56. Hamilton received her M.A. from the University of Kentucky in 1912; previously, she was principal of the Semple School of Louisville (personal correspondence with Deirdre Scaggs, UK, January 2, 2007; Minutes of the University of Kentucky Board of Trustees, June 4, 1912, UK).

57. Renker, *Origins,* 23–36, 47–50.

58. For a record of the transitions in female academic labor in this period, see Renker, *Origins,* 40–63.

59. *Catalogue, 1914/15,* 108; *Catalogue, 1915/16,* 122; and *Catalogue, 1916/17,* 127–129, UK.

60. Ward, "English," 79; Edwin Franklin Farquhar, Faculty / Staff Biographical Files, UK.

61. Peckham, *Making*, 22; Veysey, *Emergence*, 6. Michigan opened its doors to women in 1870 (Peckham, 65).

62. *Calendar of the University of Michigan, 1898–1899*, 75–77, UM.

63. Wilfred B. Shaw, ed., "The Department of English Language and Literature," in *The University of Michigan: An Encyclopedic Survey In Four Volumes* (Ann Arbor: University of Michigan Press, 1951), UM, 2:545–57, esp. 2:549.

64. For a thorough treatment of preprofessional labor, see Renker, *Origins*.

65. Shaw, ed., 2:552, UM.

66. Shaw, "Department," 2:549, UM; personal correspondence with Karen L. Jania, UM, February 26, 2007.

67. Renker, *Origins*, 29.

68. *Calendar of the University of Michigan, 1898–1899*, 74–76, UM.

69. Simon, *Reading*, 119, 97, 77; Rudolph, *American*, 232–33; Rudolph, *Curriculum*, 103–4.

70. *Calendar of the University of Michigan, 1898–1899*, 76–77, UM.

71. *The Ohio State University Catalogue, 1896–1897*, 9; *Annual Report of the Board of Trustees of The Ohio State University, 1891*, 20; To Pres. Geo W. Rightmire, November 21, 1929, Col of A&S, RG 24/a/5, "English Dept 1924–1931"; all at The Ohio State University Archives, Columbus, OH.

72. Henry D. Sheldon, *Student Life and Customs* (New York: Appleton, 1901), 203.

73. Levine, *Highbrow*, 46.

74. Sheldon, *Student*, 212–14.

75. Levine, *Highbrow*, 46.

76. Simon, *Reading*, 42–43; for the quotation, see 86.

77. Cordasco, *Shaping*, 2, 110; Rudolph, *American*, 396; and Renker, *Origins* 13–14.

78. Kemp Malone, "Historical Sketch of the English Department of The Johns Hopkins University," *Johns Hopkins Alumni Magazine* 15 (1926–27): 116–28, esp. 127.

79. Renker, *Origins*, 23–36, 47–50.

80. The "major" courses were two-year courses, of which students had to take two; "minor" courses were one-year courses, of which students had to take three. See *Annual Report, 1882*, 51, JHU.

81. John Hampton Lauck, "The Reception and Teaching of Shakespeare in Nineteenth and Early Twentieth Century America," Ph.D. diss., University of Illinois at Urbana-Champaign, 1991, 222.

82. Hopkins programmatically marginalized American literature; see Renker, *Origins*, 13–39.

83. *The Johns Hopkins University Register, 1884–85*, 90–91, JHU.

84. *Annual Report, 1888*, 63–64, JHU.

85. *Annual Report, 1889*, 50; and *Annual Report, 1890*, 47; JHU.

86. *Annual Report, 1891/92*, 51, JHU.

87. *Annual Report, 1888*, 63–64, JHU.

88. *Annual Report, 1893/94*, 63–65; *Annual Report, 1924/25*, 5; JHU.

89. *Annual Report, 1901–02*, 46–47, *Annual Report, 1924/25*, 5, JHU. Greene himself was not a preprofessional, having received a B.A. in 1881, an M.A. in 1884, and a Ph.D. in 1888, all from Harvard. His dissertation was entitled "Allegory as Employed by Spenser, Bunyan, and Swift." He published a 1913 Tudor Shakespeare edition of *The Tempest*. At Hopkins, he was compartmentalized into undergraduate

teaching, for reasons the record does not indicate, whether personal preference or institutional politics; see *Johns Hopkins Half-Century Directory,* comp. W. Norman Brown (Baltimore, Md), 138.

90. *Annual Report, 1906/1907,* 44–47, JHU.

91. Rudolph, *American,* 138, 143.

92. *Annual Report, 1888,* 14–15, JHU; on Corson, see Veysey, 185–86.

93. *University Register, 1919/20,* 238, JHU.

94. Applebee, *Tradition,* 67, 68.

95. Ibid., 68. See also Kahn's essay in this volume on Charles Mills Gayley.

96. Edwin Greenlaw and James Holly Hanford, *The Great Tradition: A Book of Selections from English and American Prose and Poetry, Illustrating the National Ideals of Freedom, Faith and Conduct* (Chicago: Scott, Foresman, 1919), xxii.

97. See, for example, Carol Maxcy, "Teaching Shakespeare," *School Review* 1.2 (1893): 105–8; Charles Washburn Nichols, "Teaching Shakespeare to Engineers," *English Journal* 2.6 (1913): 366–69; Percival Chubb, "What the Shakespeare Tercentenary Celebration Might Mean for the Schools," *English Journal* 5.4 (1916): 237–40; Ellen Fitz Gerald, "Shakespeare in the Elementary School," *English Journal* 3.6 (1914): 345–53; Winifred Smith, "Teaching Shakespeare in School," *English Journal* 11.6 (1922): 361–64; and Julia E. Booth, "The Teaching of Shakespeare," *English Journal* 9.4 (1920): 219–23.

98. Bristol, *Shakespeare's,* 2, 4.

Canons before Canons: College Entrance Requirements and the Making of a National-Educational Shakespeare

Denise Albanese

In his essay parodically entitled "Give an account of Shakespeare and Education, Showing Why You Think They Are Effective and What You Have Appreciated about Them. Support Your Comments with Precise References," Alan Sinfield describes how examination questions for admission to elite universities in England demand that students provide a representation of Shakespeare that is at once celebratory and anodyne, deprived of any complicating subtexts, ambiguities, or counterplots that might interfere with understanding Shakespeare as a poet of national values.[1] Although different universities administered different tests, the family resemblances among the questions they asked and the particular Shakespeare plays they presumed the students had read allowed Sinfield to describe a class-based consensus on how Shakespeare was to be presented in elite English public schools that send students for admission to well-established and well-celebrated universities. Even more fundamentally, for Sinfield such examinations reveal that Shakespeare functions as cultural capital in the British educational apparatus, a metonym for the privileges of class. To "have" Shakespeare in the sense elicited by the entrance examinations is, it would seem, to be marked out as a once or future member of a comparatively rarefied and privileged category of student. At base, then, Shakespeare's presence on a college entrance examination in Great Britain brings together plays, privilege, and precollegiate pedagogy in a union as much naturalized as it is revelatory.

While it is commonplace to consider Shakespeare symbolic of class privilege in the United States no less than in the United Kingdom, one cannot use Shakespeare's name to track how access to higher education in America is connected to highly restrictive admissions practices. Granted, Shakespeare is included among the

157

authors recommended for study in an advanced placement (AP) course in English literature, and the ability to present evidence of high competence in literary analysis and interpretation is presumed to be quite helpful in the admission process.[2] And there is evidence that more elite college-preparatory institutions offer greater variety and sophistication than public secondary schools when it comes to which Shakespeare plays are studied and which editions used. I am, therefore, not suggesting that there is no correlation between how, where, and by whom Shakespeare is studied and the chances of gaining admission to a selective college. Although Shakespeare no longer seems to possess broad currency as a form of cultural capital, in very delimited educational contexts his is still a name to conjure with.

Even so, there is no formal test of admission from high schools to colleges of any caliber that *demands* applicants demonstrate knowledge of Shakespeare. Since about the second third of the twentieth century until very, very recently, the most dominant form of educational testing, that administered under the authority of the Educational Testing Service (ETS), has sought the imprimatur of objectivity and exactitude, preferring the multiple choice test over the essay as a way to measure "aptitude," an ability supposed to be innate, rather than, strictly speaking, a knowledge base that approximates the English examinations Sinfield described in 1986. How, then, to explain the fact that apart from AP courses, Shakespeare is nevertheless taught in an overwhelming percentage of secondary schools in the United States, and has been for most of this century? Or the apparent consensus about *which* Shakespeare plays precollege students should know: witness, for example, the durability and pervasiveness of *Julius Caesar* and *Macbeth?* Is the convergence coincidental, merely one suggestive element in a curriculum otherwise unconstrained by national or governmental standards?

In education as in the market, things are seldom as free as they seem. Certainly the development and transformation of secondary school curricula follow a complicated trajectory, within which issues peculiar to the specific institution and the particular state cannot but play a large role. However, the apparent disjuncture in present-day America between what college admissions tests test for on the one hand, and the presence of Shakespeare in current high school curricula on the other, can nevertheless be explained. The curriculum is a matter of historical sedimentation: if there is no longer a test for college admission as such in the United States that demands a selective knowledge of Shakespeare, there once was, thanks to the efforts of the College Entrance Examination Board (CEEB), which was founded around the turn of the twentieth century and which published reading lists for college entrance examinations from 1901 until 1931. No other institution, I would argue, is as directly responsible for the pervasiveness of Shakespeare in American secondary education.

The College Board was set up to bring together college professors and masters and instructors in academies and secondary schools, the better to participate in the movement to standardize pretertiary education nationwide in line with institutional expectations about appropriate college-level knowledge, even as the consensus around the value of a classical education—an education, that is, largely steeped in the study of Latin and Greek—was breaking down. Under various other influences, such as the American adoption of the German research university model and the appearance of the land-grant institution, college education was slowly being refocused to reflect competence in technical and scientific subjects, designed to educate a new type of man (or, less frequently, woman) to play a significant part in the creation and reproduction of wealth during the emergence of industrialized capital. University bulletins and registers, the chief source of my data, began to publish annual lists of texts and textbooks in a variety of disciplines, from history to mathematics and usually including German, French, and Latin or Greek, which had to be mastered in order to sit for qualifying examinations. In some universities, a category of English vernacular texts was simply added to an already-extant body of readings; in others, the new appearance of such lists signaled institutional participation in the burgeoning project of standardization. In either case, Shakespeare seems to have been brought into curricular prominence by the same shifts, as well as by a related discourse with the aim to articulate (and in some cases inculcate) the British, indeed Anglo-Saxon, basis of American culture against shifts in immigration bringing more and more non-Anglophone speakers to the country.[3] (Hence publicly funded lectures in Italian and Yiddish on Shakespeare in New York City shortly after the turn of the century, which were offered alongside lectures on the history of U.S. democracy, the evils of socialism, and on proper sanitation techniques in the household as a matter of public health.)[4]

Just as at the elite institutions with whose examinations Sinfield is concerned, the materials I have examined suggest a top-down discourse, if an unevenly emerging one, about both texts and reading strategies. The College Board was thus not only an important institution in the dissemination of whole-text Shakespeare via the college entrance requirements, passed on to secondary institutions, that it helped develop and promote. Because of the particular Shakespeare plays privileged by those standards, the Board was also responsible for the development of what might be called a protocanon—a small selection of Shakespeare plays that were read in their entirety for college admission and that replaced the broader but more fragmentary reading knowledge of Shakespeare that had been the province of the wider public who might have studied primers. That canon was initially aimed at the small proportion of the American populace then destined for college; indeed, the ability to write well-crafted paragraphs on selected plays seems to have been all but identical with college-level literacy in English at the turn of the twentieth century.[5] The work thus inaugurated of putting Shakespeare in the secondary schools was the first step of many that have turned Shakespeare above all into an ineluctable part of American education, particularly in the high school.

Such ineluctability took some time to accomplish. While the College Board reading lists were influential, they were not uniformly and immediately adopted even in the Northeast, among the institutions that generally supported the Board's aims (or, as in the case of Harvard, helped spur the innovation). Especially in the initial years that are my focus, the College Board's drive to standardize both the requirements for college admission and the school form (i.e., the high school) that brought students to the threshold of college competed with regional and status-based practices outside its immediate and elite purview. Educational standardization proceeded unevenly: if the archive at the University of Virginia is any indication, some portions of the South came to College Board-inflected rigor comparatively later. In New York, where the Board's reading lists were most readily implemented at the turn of the twentieth century, there remained a notable gap between what obtained at private institutions like Columbia and public ones like City College.

As those facts suggest, if there was emerging unanimity about the importance of Shakespeare by the end of the first decade of the twentieth century, it also took some time for opinion to coalesce around certain plays as opposed to others. A great deal of emphasis was placed on *Macbeth* in and around New York City, where College Board member and president of Columbia University, Nicholas Murray Butler, worked to have Board texts set the examinations not just at Columbia and Barnard but at New York University as well. *The Merchant of Venice* and *Julius Caesar* were also frequently to be found on entrance examination reading lists, and it is these three texts that seem to have had a particularly durable career in the high school curriculum of the twentieth century; today, many high school stu-

dents will read two of the three. However, in the late 1890s and for
at least ten to twenty years thereafter, variation elsewhere among the
plays chosen revealed at times some lingering affinity with the collection of Shakespearean set-pieces for oratorical and rhetorical
analysis that appeared in handbooks of oratory and rhetoric and in
readers such as McGuffey's, which were drawn from a wider range
of plays than the College Board embraced.[6] This variation also
revealed that at times institutions that were either geographically or
culturally distant from universities like Columbia, Harvard, Yale, the
University of Pennsylvania, and the other founding members of the
College Board seemed to have had differing ideas about what Shakespeare texts ought to be known.

Any straightforward or definitive answer concerning why an individual play came to prominence is difficult to extrapolate from the
welter of archival materials I have been able to examine, materials
that represent a very small selection from a wide range of possibilities. Nevertheless, a few threads emerge about the nature of this protocanon, which place Shakespeare in the middle of formations
around race and ethnicity in the wake of the Civil War.[7] Sinfield's
point about Shakespeare's role in the British national imaginary
might be applied retroactively to Shakespeare in American education some one hundred years ago: even as the plays were increasingly being read as aesthetic documents, they were still understood
to refer to a world beyond themselves, a world in which distinctions
of class were defined by access, and distinctions of race were naturalized not only by a discourse of Anglo-Saxon patrimony but by a
eugenicist "race knowledge" endemic to educational discourse at
the time and that abutted upon what specific Shakespeare plays *represented,* what they put on offer as interpretive and hence as subjective possibilities.

Hence the importance of noting an apparently contradictory fact:
Shakespeare was undoubtedly prominent in the College Board's
view of education—but he was not necessarily more prominent than
other Anglophone authors appearing on College Board reading
lists. Among the other titles suggested for either "Reading" (to be
discussed generally in an examination essay) or "For Study and Practice" (to be discussed in greater detail and with greater nuance)
were Milton's *Comus, L'Allegro,* and *Il Penseroso,* with books 1 and 2
of *Paradise Lost,* choices that may seem natural to us. Less so, surely,
are such texts as Webster's *First Bunker Hill Oration,* Longfellow's
Evangeline, Sir Walter Scott's *Ivanhoe,* or William Macaulay's writing,
whether his *Life of Johnson* or his *Essays* on Addison, Milton, or Dryden.[8] My focus here on Shakespeare is motivated, of course, by the

fact of this volume—but also by the fact that Shakespeare alone retains educational, indeed public, consequence to this day: very few of the readings listed alongside his plays have any sort of currency in the modern pretertiary curriculum or, for that matter, in public debate. In tracing the College Board's initial decisions about admissions standards, it is possible to see how the writings of Shakespeare, already familiar to the late nineteenth century, were refunctioned to suit new exigencies. But the pre-collegiate canon that then emerges—a canon, that is, of Shakespeare plays known via reading and analysis to a growing public—has proved capable of yet further modulation, as the intervening years suggest. It is in this exceptional flexibility that we might begin to locate Shakespeare's continuing effect on our national cultural life.

I

In order to appreciate the influence of the College Board in enshrining Shakespeare's plays in the secondary school curriculum, it is necessary to trace Shakespeare's place in colleges during the period leading up to the first examination of 1901. As I have suggested, New York City is central to the College Board's endeavors, so that is where I begin. During the period just prior to the turn of the century, mentions of Shakespeare in the curriculum are very scarce: in the 1880s, Columbia's entrance requirements were heavily influenced by Latin and Greek texts, which led into a related college curriculum. The first appearance of a Shakespeare play in Columbia College's handbook seems to have been in the degree requirements for the "classical course of study" during that period, which stipulated *Macbeth* as the central reading in a sophomore requirement. When women were first admitted to Columbia as special certificate students in 1887–88, however, they were given *Love's Labor's Lost* to study "with analysis of plot, language, figures and allusions," rather than the *Macbeth* typically assigned to male students. The following year, while the men persisted with *Macbeth,* the women were assigned *The Tempest.* (The year after that, Barnard was officially established.) It is hard not to see in this brief divergence a certain horror at the prospect of educated women being asked to contemplate the ambitious virago that is Lady Macbeth. If horror, there was, however, it was comparatively short lived: by 1898 Barnard women are reading *Macbeth*—but the men have moved on to *Othello.* This shift might have been influenced by the fact that a Columbia faculty member, Thomas Price, published a study on prosody in *Othello* in 1888: as

befits an increasing concern with linking the study of English with a
discourse of Anglo-Saxon origins via Germanic philology, Price's
study resembles nothing so much as an approach to prosody like
that dedicated to Anglo-Saxon verse forms.[9]

But Shakespeare does not yet appear as part of the Columbia
entrance requirements. It is not until the handbook for 1892–93
appears that students are asked to present knowledge of Shakespeare for admission, when *Julius Caesar* and *The Merchant of Venice*
are specified—and continue to be until the formal adoption of College Entrance examinations in 1901.[10] At that point, entrance examinations in English are divided into two parts, reflecting the divisions
between "Study" and "Reading" to which I have referred: students
are asked to present *Merchant* for part 1, "Reading" and *Macbeth* for
part 2, "Study." In 1903–5, *Merchant* and *Julius Caesar* were assigned
for part 1, while *Macbeth* persists through at least 1905 for part 2.
Indeed, the Board of Education archives suggest a remarkable
municipal convergence around this play, since the qualifying examinations for those aspiring to become school teachers and principals
that were published in the Superintendent's Annual Report also
demanded a knowledge of this play above all.[11]

But the case is different when it comes to the city's public college.
Macbeth had far less institutional presence at the City College of New
York, which served a population that was both more ethnically
diverse (unlike Columbia, it had no quota on the number of Jewish
students it enrolled) and far less rarefied in terms of its preparation.
Indeed, having originally begun as the "Free Academy," City College combined the functions of the high schools New York City was a
historical laggard in setting up with the functions of a college. When
Shakespeare makes an appearance in this less elite environment,
therefore, it is, strictly speaking, neither at the collegiate level nor at
the level of entrance requirement; rather, it is as part of a five-year
degree designed to meld preparatory study with college, and so represents an institutional form that diverges from the College Board's
proposition that there should be a clear separation between secondary school and university. In 1895–96, we find the first mention of a
Shakespeare text, *Julius Caesar,* designated for the third year of
study, a state of affairs that appears to persist at least until 1897–88
(the archives are spotty here). By 1901–2, third-year students were
asked to read an extensive number of Shakespeare plays: *A Midsummer's Night's Dream, As You Like It, Hamlet, King Lear,* and *The Tempest.*
If *Julius Caesar* is likely introduced to the curriculum as a vernacular
substitute for the classical texts demanded at more elite institutions,
the 1901–2 course of study looks far more like comparable univer-

sity-level courses being offered at Columbia. Notable, however, is the apparent idiosyncrasy of most of the selections, plays that did not loom large in the early years of College Board entrance requirements. And offering a tantalizing possibility for speculation is the fact that, in the years I have considered, *The Merchant of Venice* is being read in other universities in the city, but it is not being studied at City College of New York, whose registers of students and alumni attest to the large number of Jews it admitted and graduated.

If City College seems to reflect the way Shakespearean selections were indices of status differences registered in the same geographical location, Howard University and the University of Virginia suggest that geography too might play a role, given their remoteness from New York and New England as centers of educational influence. This is not to say, however, that questions of institutional prestige are irrelevant: although both Howard and Virginia are now counted among the ranks of elite institutions, during the period with which I am concerned they look a great deal more like the case of New York's City College than of those colleges and universities participating in the College Board—and for comparable, although historically distinct, reasons. And as one might therefore expect with universities that also offered a precollegiate program, the place of Shakespeare in both curriculum and entrance requirements does not precisely mirror what is going on farther north. For instance, Howard, founded in 1867, insisted on the rigorousness of its course of study as it included a Preparatory Department (later renamed Academy) in acknowledgment of the practical difficulties involved in preparing emancipated slaves as well as freemen and -women for college-level work. In its 1894–95 catalog, Shakespeare first appears outside of a "Rhetoricals" requirement in the Preparatory Department, under the heading of "Collateral Exercises," which appear to be a list of ancillary readings: texts specified include *Julius Caesar* and *Henry VIII*. The collateral exercises of 1896–97 ask for *The Merchant of Venice* and *As You Like It*. Thereafter, Shakespeare disappears from mention, although collateral exercises are specified and in 1900–01 the catalog proclaims that Howard's "requirements for admission are higher than in most Southern Institutions."

Howard's aim, however, seems to have been to invite comparison with Northern institutions or at least to emulate their adoption of College Board protocols, an aim indicated by several larger-scale institutional transformations that appear to culminate with the publication of examination reading lists for admissions. Around the turn of the twentieth century, a formal English Department apart from the certificate-based general training began to emerge; by

1903–4, Howard developed a College of Arts and Sciences and entrance requirements began to be specified more fully, as its Teachers College asks students to take a course in Shakespeare, with half a year on *Romeo and Juliet* and selected comedies, and half a year on *Macbeth, Hamlet, King Lear, The Tempest,* and *Richard II.* In 1904–5, "Shakespearean drama" is indicated as the object of English Composition; in 1905–6, *Macbeth* is assigned to the middle year of the preparatory school. By 1908–9, the College of Arts and Sciences merges with the Teachers College to become the School of Liberal Arts. It is at this comparatively later moment that Howard's entrance requirements come to resemble those of universities officially affiliated with the College Board, an affiliation signaled rhetorically by its division of preparation into "Study and Practice" on the one hand and "Reading" on the other. Notably, the selection of Shakespeare plays published for admission at Howard is broader than those generally found on College Board lists. Just as in College Board examinations, *Macbeth* is designed "for study and practice"; however, for reading a longer list of Shakespeare plays, including *As You Like It, Henry V, Julius Caesar, Merchant of Venice,* and *Twelfth Night,* appears.

As Howard's telling comparison of itself to "most Southern institutions" might imply, white Southern schooling historically lagged behind practices in the Northeast and the Midwest. Rather like Howard, the University of Virginia had by charter long combined the functions of a college and a preparatory school; moreover, the state charge to admit any (white male) student who presented the appropriate credentials meant that, in this period at least, the university necessarily had less restrictive entrance requirements, which are partly demonstrated by the fact that little mention of Shakespeare occurs in them. And in the period after the Civil War, Virginia's educational institutions were in a precarious state: the registers note the university properties that were destroyed in the war and the large number of instructors who were its casualties.

The matter of curricular reform, therefore, necessarily assumes different contours in such an environment. While in the Northeast, Shakespeare is being introduced as a way to reform the curriculum and make it less overtly "elitist" than the study of the classics, during approximately the same time period at the University of Virginia the increasing presence of Shakespeare seems to have been the sign of *greater* curricular and hence greater preparatory rigor, as is the case for Howard. In a 1905 Virginia entrance examination students were asked to write only about "An English author of the 19th century," "Any period of American Lit," and "An English dramatist of the

Elizabethan period"; in 1901, they were asked to write "a good paragraph on Lady Macbeth" and to discuss the role of the witches in the play. And by 1908, under the influence of the Association of Colleges and Preparatory Schools of the Southern States, a regional institution set up to parallel the aims of the College Board, Virginia was announcing standard exams with reading lists at least as extensive as those that obtained up North. In fact, the list of Shakespeare plays from which students were to choose two for study was particularly comprehensive: *A Midsummer Night's Dream, The Merchant of Venice, As You Like It, Twelfth Night, The Tempest, Romeo and Juliet, King John, Richard II, Richard III, Henry V, Coriolanus, Julius Caesar, Macbeth,* and *Hamlet*. It is easier to say what was left out rather than what was included: while perhaps no one would expect *Henry VI, Timon of Athens,* or *Titus Andronicus,* one might well wonder about the exclusion of *Antony and Cleopatra*—and *Othello*.

II

In an age before standardized testing, and equally before the post–World War II emergence of university bureaucracies, much educational policy seems to have been driven by university presidents; indeed, testing policy led by "great men" seemed to be in homology with the Gilded Age robber barons to whose needs for an educated workforce reform and regularization of the schools were sometimes overtly addressed. It was Charles William Eliot, president of Harvard from 1869 to 1909 (and before that Professor of Analytical Chemistry at the Massachusetts Institute of Technology) who first gave impetus in the 1870s to the educational reform that would allow for vernacular literature—notably, literature in English—to come to prominence alongside classical languages in entrance requirements.[12] It was the president of Columbia, Nicholas Murray Butler, whose influence in New York City educational circles first set the College Board exams as entrance requirements for several New York universities in 1901. It was not until the University of Virginia appointed its first president in 1904, Edwin Alderman, that it began to specify examinations resembling those being required at the other institutions considered here. And it was the first president of Stanford, David Starr Jordan, who designed the content of the entrance examinations for students interested in enrolling: his somewhat idiosyncratic deployment of Shakespeare was reflected in the content and makeup of the exams he seems to have personally administered as part of his efforts to recruit students for the new institution.

Like Howard and the University of Virginia, Stanford was not a part of the College Board, nor would it become one for many years. Jordan was influenced by Eliot's New Education model, as well as the proximate example of the University of California, Berkeley, and his prior experience at Midwestern land grant institutions. Jordan's sense of the ends to which education might be put was instrumental; as befits someone chosen by the Stanfords to found a new university, he was frankly open to pleasing the representatives of industry. Given his sense that one had, in effect, to be "Greek-minded" to derive knowledge from Greek classics, and that modern men were not necessarily nor advantageously so, it is not wholly clear that knowledge of Shakespeare was, for him, indeed coterminous with a vernacularized form of cultural capital.[13] I do not mean, of course, that it did not matter if students did not know Shakespeare's texts, nor that knowing the right ones did not give one a better chance at entrance to Stanford and other universities: the moment when particular texts would be replaced by any texts, specific knowledge by a test of skills to be applied to any texts, was in the Board's future. Rather, I mean to suggest that as Jordan was examining students' comprehension of a given passage it appears he was also, at times at least, using Shakespeare as a kind of proving ground for ideas about race.

Witness the examination question for May 1893, designed to admit the second year's students. Part A of the opening examination, which tests for English, introduces the following exchange:

> First Speaker: Mislike me not for my complexion,
> The *shadow'd livery* of the burnish'd sun,
> To whom I am a neighbor and near bred.
> Bring me the fairest creature *northward* born,
> Where *Phoebus'* fire scarce thaws the icicles,
> And let us *make incision* for your love,
> To prove whose blood is reddest, his or mine.
> I tell thee, lady, this *aspect* of mine
> Hath *fear'd* the valiant: by my love I swear
> The *best-regarded* virgins of our clime
> Have loved it too: I would not change this hue,
> Except to steal your thoughts, gentle queen.
>
> Second Speaker: In *terms of choice* I am not solely led
> By *nice* direction of a maiden's eyes:
> Besides the lottery of my destiny

Bars me the right of voluntary choosing:
But if my father had not *scanted* me
And hedged me by his *wit,* to yield myself
His wife who wins me by what means I told you,
Yourself, renowned prince, *then stood* as fair
As any comer I have look'd on yet
For my affection.

Students were asked to identify the exchange, naming the speakers, the situation, and the play, as well as to gloss the italicized words and phrases. While *Merchant of Venice* was, as we have seen, already a familiar text, I hope I am not alone in finding Jordan's choice of Morocco's courtly speech to Portia remarkable. Despite the rhetorical interest of the passage, its subject matter, marked as it is by a declaration of Morocco's exceptional identity, seems unlikely to lend itself to a broad audience that might be interested in the management of the passions, the usual purpose of extracts found in McGuffey's and elsewhere in the primer tradition, on which preparation many incoming college students might be supposed to draw. Jordan showed a notable interest in this minor character; in the 1897 entrance examination, students are asked: "By what line of argument does the Prince of Morocco persuade himself to choose the golden casket?"

Similarly, in the examination question for May 1895, applicants were presented with Shylock's speech denouncing Antonio as a Christian, referring to both his tribe and his "sacred nation" (a phrase that students were particularly asked to gloss, along with "usance" and the phrase "there where merchants most do congregate"). In 1898, students were asked: "Was Shylock treated unjustly? Give the reasons for your answer." This question appeared in the same examination where students were also asked to explain the following passage from *Merchant*, again paying particular attention to italicized words: "The Duke cannot *deny* the *course of law.* For the commodity that *strangers have With us in Venice,* if it be denied, *Will much impeach the justice of the state.*"

Let me be less oblique here. Jordan was a noted ichthyologist; he was also well-known as a eugenicist, a field of pseudoscientific study that had a great deal more legitimacy in the first part of the twentieth century, particularly in educational discourse, than is sometimes remembered. Jordan was no crude racist: he hoped that evolution would cause human society to develop past the point where slavery was anything but repellent, and he seems to have engaged directly, amicably, and more than once with San Francisco's large assimilated

Jewish population. At the same time, Jordan was the author of such studies as a 1902 volume entitled *The Blood of the Nation: A Study of the Decay of Races through the Survival of the Unfit.* "Blood" was for him "while technically incorrect," nevertheless a potent metaphor for the work of heredity and a "symbol for race unity." In this treatise he proclaimed "the superiority of the Anglo-Saxon" and averred that "wherever an Englishman goes, he carries with him the elements of English history. It is a British deed he does, British history he makes. Thus, too, a Jew is a Jew in all ages and climes, and his deeds everywhere bear the stamp of Jewish individuality."[14]

Although Jordan never specifies a positive content for his tautological statement "A Jew is a Jew," it requires no great stretch of the imagination to read his focus on Shylock's utterances as eliciting from applicants an engagement with eugenicist premises concerning raced, Jewish identity. By the same logic, the emphasis on Morocco's "shadow'd livery" in the 1893 examination lends itself at once to affirming the reality of racial difference, of the matter of "blood," and to the possibility of revaluing it, at least insofar as Morocco's emphasis on his worth and Portia's response to him are concerned. (In the absence of students' responses to these prompts, I can only hazard contextualized guesses, and it must be underscored that they are but guesses.) In the wake of Delia Bacon's and Ignatius Donnelly's autodidactic efforts to recast Shakespeare as Francis Bacon, the "father of English Science"—that is, to place the texts of Shakespeare's plays in the ambit of the scientific knowledge in the late nineteenth century—it seems we have a less tendentious enlisting of the texts for similar purposes.[15] The possibility that at Stanford Shakespeare was used to explore the doctrines of "race knowledge" recalls my initial claim about Shakespeare's centrality and the way his texts have lent themselves to new ends. If my surmises prove accurate, the plays become vehicles for historically congruent discourses about race and national identity as they are worked out in educational practices—practices that are themselves shifting away from reflecting the preparation of traditional Anglo-Saxon elites and toward standards potentially broad enough to admit of the raising up of selected members of "lesser" races.

III

As might be suggested by the case of Jordan's questions about *Merchant of Venice* and the play's absence from the curriculum of the City College of New York, there cannot but be myriad factors at work in the new privileging of some Shakespearean plays over others in this period of formation for the pretertiary, public canon. It may be speculated that some Shakespearean texts, once central to the rhetorical and indeed forensic tradition when introduced as fragments in primers, are deemed less able to accommodate questions that ask for critical reflection or aesthetic assessment. As Mary Trachsel has argued, the College Board became more and more concerned with students' ability to demonstrate a specifically literary (and institutionally congruent) form of knowledge, a demonstration that, in turn, necessitated the reading of whole plays rather than selected speeches aimed at performance.[16] Hence, plays like *King John* and *Henry VIII*, extracts from which once had regular currency in McGuffey's and other versions of the nineteenth-century educational-oratorical tradition, began to drop out of currency, in favor of *Macbeth* above all. *Julius Caesar,* deployed in primers as an occasion for lessons on civic duty, patriotism, and sacrifice of self-interest for a greater good, is a notable exception; perhaps because of its latent content, it remains a staple of the high school curriculum to this day.

However, some plays must have been dropped for reasons that had less to do with the analytical priorities of formalized literary study and the emerging profession of English than with the role Shakespeare was to play in producing and policing the imaginative and ideological space of the republic. Witness the all-but-total absence of *Othello,* now generally regarded as one of Shakespeare's most exquisite constructions in language, from the turn-of-the-twentieth-century college examination and curriculum materials I have studied. As with *King John* and *Henry VIII*, selections from *Othello* had been a staple of schoolhouse oratory, and McGuffey students had studied the expressive capabilities encoded in, among other selections, Othello's final speech, apparently without regard to the race of the speaker. Yet when it comes to the initial college selections with which I have been concerned, interest in the play is scarce—all but nonexistent. This might seem the more surprising given that Elaine Brousseau has described *Othello* as "Shakespeare's American Play," a staple of the nineteenth-century stage.[17] Or, more precisely, the minstrel theater, where, as Alexander Saxton has argued, the burlesquing of racial difference is part of the construction of white nationhood.[18]

It is naturally hard to account with certainty for the omission of *Othello* from the limited collegiate examinations and curricula I have surveyed. The College Board's lists were influential, but hardly all determining: witness the appearance of the play in the texts set for

Harvard's own examinations in 1882, as well as in the Columbia curriculum of 1898.[19] And if the absence is motivated, Howard University may well have bypassed the play for reasons wholly different from those that obtained at, say, the University of Virginia. Given the interest in race identity and race knowledge—the knowledge, that is, naturalized by racial identity, by birthright—that appears intermittently in contemporary educational materials, and the growing unease in the wake of the Civil War about interracial desire and its consequences, it seems that the movement from oratorical selections to whole plays might have rendered *Othello* a peculiarly volatile text. The word "miscegenation" emerged in American legal discourse starting in 1863, replacing the older and less legalistic term "amalgamation"; in juridical opinions of the time, *Othello* became a touchstone for, as William Lamartine Snyder termed it in the title of his 1889 study, the "legal perplexities of wedlock in the United States."[20] Debate also focused on whether Shakespeare could possibly have meant to endorse a union so contrary to sense—a sense exquisitely, paranoically calibrated to the affective possibilities of a nation in which slaves were no longer chattel. And such erotic paranoia was by no means a purely Southern phenomenon: the 1863 U.S. District Court entry that introduced "miscegenation" to the realm of legal discourse in America occurred in the Southern District of New York, that is, in the New York City that was so significant when it came to institutionalizing College Board protocols some thirty-five years later.[21]

The burgeoning discourse concerning the criminalization of "mongrel marriages" coincided with the fact that *Othello,* publicly unobjectionable to white educators when previously encountered in decontextualized oratorical extract or to white citizens in parodic minstrelsy, was not featured in the College Board's initial efforts to modernize—and homogenize?—admissions requirements. It must also be remembered that the Board's emphasis on Shakespeare reinforced the enshrining of the playwright as the bearer of highbrow, because Anglo-Saxon, values being given motive force at this same historical moment, as Levine has suggested. In this regard, it is tantalizing to wonder about the almost fetishistic prominence of Shakespeare's less obviously problematic Scottish play, especially given the parallel emphasis given to Sir Walter Scott's novels in College Board reading lists. A New York University dissertation, published in 1913, notes that Scott's writings and *Macbeth* are useful texts for teaching "race heritage" in the public schools.[22] Absent a significant amount of further information, caution must be used in pushing this suggestion too far: why, for instance, did no *English*

history of Shakespeare's serve the purpose of inculcating a racialized
consciousness? Did *Macbeth* constitute a text peculiarly useful both
to the inculcation of literary quality and to the representation of
"race" within an educational discourse interested in the subject?

IV

In his influential study *Shakespeare's America, America's Shakespeare,*
Michael Bristol designated Shakespeare a "tutelary deity," the
object of "cultic veneration" whose authority is at once mystical and
benign.[23] In the period with which I am concerned, however, it does
not appear that Shakespeare yet possesses such potency, nor yet perhaps such innocuousness. Due in large part to the efforts of the College Board, Shakespeare began his rise to educational prominence,
and there is reason to believe that the capacity of some of his plays
to stand as literary exemplars may well have traveled alongside other
capacities as well. Such capacities cannot explain his durability, his
persistence in the precollegiate curriculum to this very day. But, as
the example of Mozart might suggest, exceptional "greatness," once
established, seems capable of ready perpetuation. All it takes is a sufficient body of work and a precipitating event or series of events: the
Mostly Mozart festivals that began in 1970s New York quickly spread
elsewhere and helped establish Mozart as a composer not just of
eminence, but of preeminence.

Quality is not the only issue in either case. Enabling conditions
include a body of work sufficiently large to admit of variety, but not
so large that no one could really be said to comprehend its scope.
Equally, the number would need to be large enough for some texts
to rise to prominence and others to fall by the wayside, to suit changing taste or cultural agendas. Moreover, demand should not be too
great in terms of novelty of form: the classical style wears its innovation lightly, and it is generally only musicologists who can denatural-
ize the Mozartean tonalities we take for granted as the grammar of
the classical. Might a comparable statement be made of Shakespeare?

In that case, it may be that if a single determining event, like the
formation of the College Board, first raises Shakespeare's profile in
twentieth-century American culture, other factors must contribute
to maintaining the texts there. A series of iterations and points of
difference, from rhetorical treatises to stage productions, from
schoolroom editions to summer programs, may well constitute the
material support for an act of assessment that follows, "naturally,"

as it were, upon them—and that brings us to the ineluctable literary presence whose very pervasiveness in American education this volume documents.

Notes

1. Alan Sinfield, "Give an Account of Shakespeare and Education, showing why you think they are effective and what you have appreciated about them. Support your comments with precise references," in *Political Shakespeare: New Essays in Cultural Materialism,* ed. Jonathan Dollimore and Alan Sinfield (Manchester: Manchester University Press, 1985), 134–57.

2. For information about the AP English Literature curriculum, see "AP Subjects: English Literature," College Board. Online at http://www.collegeboard.com/student/testing/ap/sub_englit.html. It should be noted that the course of study for language and composition, which often stands in for freshman composition, stresses nonfiction such as biography, criticism, and science writing and excludes fiction, poetry, and drama.

3. Lawrence W. Levine, *Highbrow / Lowbrow: The Emergence of Cultural Hierarchy in America* (Cambridge: Harvard University Press, 1988), 169–77; William Uricchio and Roberta E. Pearson, *Reframing Culture: The Case of the Vitagraph Films* (Princeton: Princeton University Press, 1993), 17–40; and in this volume, see Coppélia Kahn's essay.

4. Henry Leipziger, *Annual Report of the Supervisor of Lectures to the Board of Education, 1911–1912* (New York: Department of Education, 1912), 11–30.

5. For a demonstration of this point, see Elizabeth Renker's essay in this volume.

6. See Jonathan M. Burton's essay in this volume.

7. To this extent, the tests stand in broad support of Levine's argument that Shakespeare became increasingly associated with the "highbrow," with the Anglo-Saxon elites whose interests most elite colleges were overwhelmingly dedicated to serve, in the years under discussion (221–24).

8. For a more complete listing, see Arthur N. Applebee, *Tradition and Reform in the Teaching of English: A History* (Urbana, IL: National Council of Teachers of English, 1974), appendix 3, 275–77. I acknowledge my general indebtedness to Applebee, both for this invaluable study and for suggestions he made for future research on the occasion of the March 2007 conference at the Folger, out of which this essay emerged.

9. Thomas R. Price, *The Construction and Types of Shakespeare's Verse as Seen in Othello* (New York: Press of the New York Shakespeare Society, 1888).

10. According to Applebee, the following year, 1893–94, is when a precursor to the College Board, the Committee of Ten, meets at Vassar to establish entrance requirements in English literature apart from composition; see *Tradition and Reform,* appendix 1, 271.

11. For the first two years (1898–99 and 1899–1900) after the five boroughs were constituted into a single administrative unit and put under the supervision of the New York City Board of Education, a report was produced for the Superintendent of Schools that reproduced qualifying examinations for school principals and teachers that yields some insight into the centrality of *Macbeth* at all levels of teacher training. An 1899–1900 examination for a high school teacher, for example, asked

the applicant to interpret passages, explain metaphors, and "Describe [his] method of treating the play of 'Macbeth' in a literature class, stating aims and collateral work." See New York City Superintendent of Schools, *Annual Report, 1899– 1900* (New York: Board of Education, 1899), 156–57. However, the Board of Education archives for this period contain no information about how this Shakespeare play or any other was actually taught.

12. Charles William Eliot, "The New Education: Its Organization, Part 1," *Atlantic Monthly* 23 (February 1869): 202–20, and "The New Education: Its Organization, Part 2," *Atlantic Monthly* 23 (March 1869): 358–67. His concern in "The New Education" was not merely curricular but pragmatic, insofar as it concerned the utility of education in an industrialized world.

13. "We find that Greek-mindedness is necessary to receive from the Greek all that this noblest of languages is competent to give. We find for the average men better educational substance in English than in Latin, in the Physical or Natural Sciences than in the Calculus." See David Starr Jordan, "The Building of the University," in *The Voice of the Scholar: With Other Addresses on the Problems in Higher Education* (San Francisco: Paul Elder and Company, 1903), 28.

14. David Starr Jordan, *The Blood of the Nation: A Study of the Decay of Races through the Survival of the Unfit* (Boston: American Unitarian Association, 1902), 9, 29.

15. Delia Bacon is famous for having inaugurated the phenomenon of anti-Stratfordianism (which still persists) with her volume, *The Philosophy of Shakespeare's Plays Unfolded* (Boston: Ticknor and Fields, 1857); in it, she names Francis Bacon as the true author of the plays. Her cause was taken up by, among others, Ignatius Donnelly in *The Great Cryptogram: Francis Bacon's Cipher in the So-Called Shakespeare Plays* (Chicago: R. S. Peale, 1888).

16. Mary Trachsel, *Institutionalizing Literacy: The Historical Role of College Entrance Examinations in English* (Carbondale: Southern Illinois University Press, 1992), 70– 103.

17. Elaine Brousseau, "'Now, Literature, Philosophy, and Thought, Are Shakspearized'": American Culture and Nineteenth Century Shakespearean Performance, 1835–1875 (Ph.D. diss., University of Massachusetts–Amherst, 2005).

18. Alexander Saxton, *The Rise and Fall of the White Republic: Class Politics and Class Culture in Nineteenth-Century America*, with a new forward by David Roediger (1990; repr., London: Verso, 2003), 165–182.

19. Applebee, appendix 3, 275.

20. William Lamartine Snyder, *The Geography of Marriage: Or, Legal Perplexities of Wedlock in the United States* (New York: G. P. Putnam's Sons, 1889). A passage from *Othello*, in which Brabantio wonders whether Desdemona can be "half the wooer," serves as an epigraph on page 64 and introduces an argument asserting that mixed race marriage is disgusting and against popular taste, but that it ought nevertheless not be subject to legal prosecution.

21. This historical information may be found in the *Oxford English Dictionary*.

22. Frank Forest Bunker, *The Functional Reorganization of the American Public School System*, Ph.D. dissertation, New York University, 1913 (Washington: Government Printing Office, 1916).

23. Michael Bristol, *Shakespeare's America, America's Shakespeare* (London: Routledge, 1990), 19.

The Works of Wm Shakespeare as They Have Been Sundry Times Professed in Harvard College

Dayton Haskin

When academic departments called "English" began to appear in North American colleges, for the first time in history adolescents were able to make formal courses on modern vernacular literary works, including Shakespeare, the respectable object of their sustained attention. At the oldest college in the United States, this radical change began slowly and accelerated dramatically. During the four decades of Charles W. Eliot's presidency (1869–1909), the creation of new disciplines and a variety of elective courses coincided with a sharp increase in the student body and the hiring of a much larger and more specialized faculty. At the outset of this development, in order to make room for the installation of the system of free electives, the amount of English study traditionally prescribed for undergraduates was greatly reduced. In the early 1870s, "English" was drawing only about three percent of the total enrollments. When Francis Child introduced a Shakespeare elective in 1876, his new department was offering fewer electives than almost any other.[1]

Over the next two decades, an astonishing transformation of English studies took place. Child's Shakespeare course was at once foundational to the growth of Harvard's English Department and increasingly influential in American higher education. By 1887, the Dean proudly announced that "the most noteworthy" development in the college's new curriculum would be "the enlargement of the instruction offered in English literature."[2] Less than a decade later, a writer in *The Harvard Monthly* proclaimed that "[t]he English department enlists a larger corps of instructors, and offers a greater number of courses, than any other academic department"; and "[i]n its elective courses the English department enrolls . . . a larger number of students than other departments." He also observed,

175

"Following Harvard's lead, other colleges are beginning to give more attention to the subject; but at none of these is provision yet made for the study of English on a scale commensurate with that made for the study of Latin or Greek. Even at the colleges which are most penitently alive to their long neglect of it, the English department is far from being regarded, as it is at Harvard, as of at least equal importance with other leading departments."[3] By the end of the nineteenth century, English at Harvard had replaced the classics as the principal bearer of the liberal arts tradition.

The teaching of Shakespeare became distinctive in a number of ways. The University was unusual in its early creation of a year-long Shakespeare course and in offering it precisely as an elective. English 2, as it was designated, became a model for inventing other English electives. It also enjoyed an astonishing stability: while in other colleges, courses devoted exclusively to Shakespeare appeared by stops and starts, English 2 was given every year all through and long after the Eliot era. The course retained virtually the same format, took up the same dozen or so plays, and was never given by anyone except Child or George Lyman Kittredge. When, in 1892, Barrett Wendell introduced an alternative course called "The Works of Shakspere," he acknowledged the priority of the "orthodox" course and made having taken it a prerequisite for enrollment in his English 23. Elsewhere, there were many attempts by Harvard graduates and other imitators to extend the orthodoxy associated with the teaching of Shakespeare by Child and Kittredge. Yet no institution was able fully to reproduce it, and the most powerful witness to its influence may well be the strength with which some faculties resisted it.[4] That is another story, however.

What follows is an attempt to describe various ways, some typical, some distinctive, in which Shakespeare was taught at Harvard during Eliot's presidency. The description has been written with as full an awareness as I have been able to develop by working in the archives of several other colleges about what was going on elsewhere.[5] The number and type of collegiate institutions that one might study could of course be profitably expanded. I have been able to broaden the base for comparison by attending also to the remarkable collection of essays from twenty English departments first published in *The Dial* in 1894 and then reprinted, with additions, in *English in American Universities*, edited by William Morton Payne. Although the report on Harvard in this collection, written by Wendell, is less informative than any other, the Harvard Archives contain an incomparably rich cache of materials with which to reconstruct the early teaching of English literature. These materials also enable us to explore a fundamental tension between what emerged at Harvard as orthodoxy in the teaching of Shakespeare and what, following Wendell's lead, may be deemed a "heretical" approach. It was at the so-called Harvard Annex (officially, the Collegiate Society for the Instruction of Women, which was to become Radcliffe College in 1894) that Wendell first taught Shakespeare, and while teaching women that he developed his alternative to English 2. Wendell's experience with women students led to his publishing, notoriously, his objections to coeducation at Harvard, including his view that having women in class was deleterious to professors and likely to "diminish their scholarly vigor."[6] By exploring what constituted orthodoxy, and by examining when and how and under what conditions "unorthodox" approaches developed, we can appreciate something of Harvard's distinctive contribution to the academic study of Shakespeare. We can also catch glimpses of how the early teaching of Shakespeare there was embroiled in controversies about pedagogy and coeducation that have continued to reverberate into our own time.

ORTHODOX SHAKESPEARE

In the report on "English at Lafayette College" written at the earliest of American English departments by its founder, it was proposed that a good way to begin the study of Shakespeare is with a consideration of the spelling of his surname. This "opens," F. A. March observed, questions "about the nature of evidence, the history and rules of naming, the literary orthography of proper names, and the like."[7] At Harvard, the spelling of the Bard's surname was also considered important, although not because it opened questions. From the mid-1870s, even before Child began assigning Edward Dowden's *Shakspere Primer* as outside reading, until the 1930s, when Kittredge retired, English 2 was called "Shakspere." For more than half a century in official Harvard publications, as the spelling espoused by the New Shakspere Society remained in use, it increasingly marked the distinctive conception of a subject that remained under the control of two esteemed professors.

For Child, who had been exposed during studies in Berlin and Göttingen to the leading German methods for teaching literature, the way to begin the study of Shakespeare—and the way to keep studying his works—was to attend to his language. Not long after the new academic disciplines began to take rudimentary shape, Child introduced the study of Anglo-Saxon as Harvard's first English elective. Two years later, he added another in which "Abbot's Shakespearian Grammar" was a textbook, and the students read three (unspecified) plays. In these years the college also began requiring candidates for admission to write on particular works of English literature, which therefore became integral to the high school curriculum in its feeder schools. Shakespeare was given pride of place among the set texts, with *The Tempest, Julius Caesar,* and *The Merchant of Venice* required.[8] Soon, Child could begin counting on incoming students having had experience with at least one whole play and on some more mature students having studied older stages of the language. In 1876–77, he offered a new Shakespeare elective that would long remain Harvard's only year-long English course devoted to a single author. In the mid-1880s he put a rotation into place, so that a student could take the course for two years running. Typically, in one year he taught *King Lear,* both parts of *Henry IV, Julius Caesar, All's Well That Ends Well, Macbeth,* and *The Tempest;* in the next, *Hamlet, Romeo and Juliet, Henry V, The Winter's Tale, Antony and Cleopatra,* and *Othello.*

The slow growth of English courses before the mid-1880s must have depended in part on Child's insistence that, on the model by which classical languages had been taught, an "English" curriculum begin with the study of old English and then of older English literature. Child's vision of the new discipline went against the grain of what Payne, introducing *English in American Universities,* referred to as the practice of "progressive modern teachers," whereby the curriculum proceeded "from the near and the familiar to the strange and remote."[9] Nonetheless, with only a few English electives available, his Shakespeare course quickly became popular. It took about three decades of curricular expansion before an array of choices reduced the *relative* proportion of English students who enrolled in Shakespeare. By 1898, two years after Child's death, there were still 103 students in English 2. At the same time, there were more than 1,100 students taking three large composition courses, to say nothing of several smaller writing courses. In 1901, when 96 students took Kittredge's Shakespeare, the course on early nineteenth century literature enrolled 326 students and the course on English Literature of the later nineteenth century enrolled 349.[10] In the free elective system, students voted with their feet.

Since Child and Kittredge were committed to teaching the plays by concentrating squarely on language that seemed far away and unfamiliar, the grounds of their considerable pedagogical success remain something of a mystery. This is not for lack of enthusiastic testimonies, many by former students whom they inspired to enter the teaching profession. "Stubby" Child was by all accounts genial and learned, a wonderfully entertaining reader and an endearing personality. He upheld high standards, which is after all one of the most effective means of successful teaching. Kittredge, Child's protégé, was rather more eccentric. Dozens of students have left behind recollections of his teaching, the great majority of them remarks about his quirks of personality, his odd behaviors, or his irascible temper. A few have described, concretely, his methods of teaching. We will return to their descriptions in due course.

First, it makes sense to consider the pedagogical practices employed by Child and Kittredge by examining the mass of data lodged in notes taken by their students. At least nine sets of such notes for English 2 are extant from the era of Eliot's presidency, four from Child's classes, five from Kittredge's. The earliest set, kept by F. J. Ranlett, belong to 1879–80.[11] Five of the seven plays that Child taught that year were to become part of the standard two-year rotation. The other two—*As You Like It* and *Twelfth Night*—received only scant attention. (*Antony and Cleopatra* was substituted for these plays; the absence from the syllabus of what Dowden referred to as the mirthful and joyous comedies is conspicuous.) The sixty-some students used newly created school editions, in particular those of William J. Rolfe.[12] Ranlett's notes from the classes are unusual among the nine sets in that they are written into a notebook rather than on interleaved blank pages, which became a standard feature of the Rolfe texts. The great majority of Ranlett's notes are otherwise typical. All nine sets show what students copied down as the principal objects of their learning: glosses on unfamiliar words and phrases and on familiar words used in unfamiliar senses; notes providing historical background or, occasionally, calling attention to a textual variant; remarks on characters, not in general, but to make sense of what they said, or of what was said to or about them, in a particular dramatic context. The centrality of line by line and scene by scene glossing in the classroom procedure is surprising, inasmuch as the Rolfe editions already contained extensive materials of this kind. Apparently, both the lecturer and the students ignored Rolfe's apparatus. In extant copies annotated by sundry students, while both the interleaved pages and the pages on which the text is printed are generally dense with annotation, the pages where Rolfe provides notes and glosses have been left almost wholly untouched.

Clearly, Child and Kittredge's practice differed markedly from the love of generalization that was common in other colleges, where early English courses often consisted of lectures on the history of writing in English. At Brown during the 1870s, for instance, Timothy Bancroft taught Shakespeare within a course called "Outlines of English Literature" in which he paired the Bard with Marlowe. He said little about Kit Marlowe's life and spoke in detail about *Tamburlaine, Dr. Faustus,* and *Edward the Second.* Then, curiously, when he took up Will Shakespeare, he moved in the opposite direction: he discussed not at all, and perhaps did not even mention by name, any particular play. Instead, he rehearsed a sustained biographical narrative that climaxed in a celebration of Shakespeare's ultimately triumphant public success.[13] Something similar may be said about the very earliest teaching of Shakespeare at Smith College. Founded in the 1870s at Northampton, Massachusetts, to offer higher education to young women, Smith sought to provide a curriculum that would be as extensive in Greek and Latin as what was available at Yale and Harvard, Brown and Amherst, and would also afford "more attention . . . than in other colleges to the English language and literature, [and] to criticism on the standard English authors."[14] The first president of the college lectured on English literature and also seems to have taught Shakespeare without reference to any particular works; this is the distinct impression created in some twenty-five pages of undated lecture notes on Shakespeare in his personal papers.[15] English studies at Smith changed quickly, however, as new faculty were hired. Pedagogy headed in the direction set by Child. By 1879, students could elect "Critical Study of Shakespeare" for one hour a week. In the following year some juniors spent one hour a week during two (of the three) terms taking an elective in which they read *Macbeth* and *Hamlet* in Rolfe's editions; some seniors elected, also for one hour a week, "English of Shakespeare," in which they read *Julius Caesar.*

In these years Child's course met for three hours per week through the year and took up five to seven plays in their entirety. While the instructor's concentration on the language was unusual, it was not unique, as the example of Smith suggests. At Lafayette, where there were fewer than three hundred students and the offering of numerous electives would have been impractical, a required English literature curriculum was devised earlier than elsewhere, by March, who followed an imperative according to which "English should be studied like Greek." March taught a one-term Shakespeare course for juniors in which four hours per week were devoted to a single play. Typically, as would be the case at Harvard, a class hour was given to considering a short scene or part of a scene, with most of the time lavished on only a few lines. While the instructor explained obsolete language and unusual constructions, he knew quite well that "the secret of Shakespeare's power is not to be found in these" but rather in the ways in which the Bard deployed familiar words. For this reason he required students to enlist a concordance and to extract information from a historical dictionary (this was before the *Oxford English Dictionary*, for which March became American editor, was published) so that they could trace the associations that had accrued around words that Shakespeare had made to do a good deal of work. The idea was to get the students to rivet their attention on words and speeches that, with a gradual unfolding of their perceptions of what Shakespeare had made the words do, would remain lastingly memorable.[16]

Like March, Child had been trained to read the classics. He gave examinations in English 2 that show he expected students above all to be able to gloss many short quotations from the plays. He also required outside reading from Dowden's *Primer*, and expected a knowledge of key dates from Shakespeare's life and from the history of the plays' publication.[17] Despite the prestige that had accrued around the idea that a biography could be constructed out of a sequential reading of the whole oeuvre,[18] Child had no truck with Dowden's arrangement of the plays into biographical periods, such as the ones during which, for instance, he was supposed to have written his tragedies "out of the depths" of some personal suffering or composed the late "Romances" with "a grave tenderness," having "learned the secret of life."[19] The surviving data in the notebooks kept by Child's students might, in fact, give the impression that his classes were so thoroughly trained on linguistic minutiae as to have been insufferably boring. Taken collectively, the materials offer no evidence that Child ever devoted a sustained patch of lecturing to anything like a theme, a character, or a plot. Yet his course remained popular through his whole career and proved, as one ex-student remarked when he entrusted his English 2 notes to the archives, "the chief undergraduate course of one of the great scholars of the nineteenth century."[20] Its unparalleled success owed a good deal to the general popularity of Shakespeare in nineteenth-century American culture, which gave his works a value that warranted expert scrutiny. As the late Lawrence Levine has documented,[21] Shakespeare's presence in American life was far livelier and more thoroughgoing than that of, say, Virgil or Horace. Students were aware that the study of vernacular literature in the college curriculum was a mark of a new dispensation that they had been fortunate enough to enter. This meant that, by contrast with what was still going on in courses on classical literature, when Child or March provided philological commentary, their students could feel a certain excitement that a virtually living, vernacular writer was being treated on a par with the ancient classics. It is important to realize, then, that the eventual appropriation of Shakespeare for "high culture," to which Child's course contributed, was to a great extent at cross purposes with the instructor's own designs. For Child, Shakespeare was above all popular entertainment. He took it for granted that the plays belonged squarely within the broad spectrum of American culture in which oral performances of Shakespearean materials were pervasive and pseudo-Shakespearean language (of the sort evoked in the title of this essay) was likely to seem playful.

Other aspects of Child's classroom practice added urgency to the project of understanding Shakespeare's language. In continuity with the traditional rhetorical education received by their fathers, for part of each class some students were expected to recite passages and the rest became the audience. Child worked hard to teach students how to handle the meter and assigned them to get by heart several passages of every work they studied, running to, say, something like six hundred lines per year. There was always a measure of drama in the recitations that students were required to give before the class, if only because failure would prove embarrassing. Beyond this, the instructor created another, less anxious, and more pleasing sort of drama himself.

In the 1860s, when as Boylston Professor of Rhetoric and Oratory Child had been giving rhetoric courses, like teachers elsewhere he mined the plays for great speeches and required his students to memorize rhetorically rich excerpts. His own reading aloud modeled his preference "for low-key and expressive reading" rather than oratorical declamation.[22] Soon after President Eliot empowered him to offer English electives, Child proposed to give optional readings from English literature, notably from Shakespeare, for an hour one day a week. The first time that he appeared at the appointed classroom, even the adjoining hall and stairway were filled with students; as one of them recalled, "like another Moses, he had to lead his flock about the building until he got habitation in a [much larger] room," to which "a gentle mob" continued to repair weekly until the end of the course.[23] Once Child was able to turn an offer from the new Johns Hopkins University into a bargaining chip to make his way out of teaching composition (and marking hundreds of essays every week!), as Harvard's first Professor of English he developed English 2 out of the public readings he had been giving.

More than his mentor Child and differently from his friendly rival at Yale, William Lyon Phelps, Kittredge contributed to the elevation of Shakespeare to "high" cultural status. Kittredge's Shakespeare course was precisely the legacy of Child, and however much he made it his own, it was "traditional." He retained the established rotation, and he employed the same classroom protocols that directed attention squarely to the language. "The object of the course," Kittredge wrote, "was to give students a thorough acquaintance with the language and matter of the plays read. Much attention was given to interpretation and no hard passage was passed over without at least an attempt to ascertain its meaning."[24] There was little difference between what students wrote down in the two professors' classes.

Kittredge's thorough appropriation of his mentor's method may be discerned as well in the notes that he himself began compiling early in his career, and which he refined and augmented through the years. These notes show that the two teachers, although they did not comment on exactly the same points and often did not say the same thing about the points that they both glossed, practiced virtually the same method.[25] Kittredge's notes on *Othello* are more copious than for any other play, and as it happens Walter Naumburg studied the play with Child the year before he took Kittredge's version of the course. Close examination of Naumburg's annotations points up the fact that Kittredge's personal notes include many examples of parallel uses of words and phrases, either in other Shakespearean texts or in works by other authors, which he rarely drew upon for teaching undergraduates.[26] Conversely, Kittredge's notes evince little interest in another aspect of Shakespearean language, the bawdry that led Rolfe to omit, for example, Iago's animalistic descriptions of sexual desire and activity. This suggests that the choice of bowdlerized editions first made by Child was ratified by his successor, who continued to operate under a pedagogical imperative long allied with the idea that teachers acted *in loco parentis*. The canon that teachers ought to take care not to lead astray the youth in their care may seem to make the inclusion of *All's Well That Ends Well* in the rotation rather odd; for (as we will have occasion to consider in more detail when we take up Wendell's conspicuous exclusion of *All's Well* from the plays that he taught to young women), Kittredge seems to have been made uncomfortable by the fact that the female lead takes some extraordinary sexual initiatives.[27] On the second title-page of a copy of *All's Well*, Howard Savage quotes him as having told the students, "The situation is impossible. G.L.K. says 'I never saw anything like it in all my life.' "[28]

In teaching young men, both Child and Kittredge acknowledged that they were puzzled about what Helena could have seen in so loathsome a young man as Bertram. Kittredge remarked that he is "the poorest person one ever tried to make a hero out of" and that "[w]e want to kick" him. Helena's love for him "rather lowers her." While Savage reports that Kittredge promised that "every page is full of interest," he also quotes him as having acknowledged that "'it is certainly a rancid plot.'" Such remarks reveal a surprising ambivalence and provoke the question—on what grounds the play continued to be included in the rotation. The retention of the play at Harvard suggests that there may have been something set in stone in Kittredge's allegiance to Child's syllabus.

At Radcliffe, as at Harvard, Kittredge was both feared and beloved, often by the same person. Helen Keller, who took Shakespeare in 1903–4, recalled being especially happy to be in his company. "[W]hen a great scholar like Professor Kittredge interprets what the master said," she wrote in her autobiography, "it is 'as if new sight were given the blind.' He brings back Shakespeare, the poet."[29] Another student recalled a related pleasure: "Helen Keller sat in the row behind me with her teacher Miss Sullivan. It was an interesting thing to see Helen's face light up with mirth just a few seconds after a joke of some kind had broken upon the class."[30] Others were less sanguine, of course. A student who took the course about ten years later wrote to her parents:

> The first class in the morning is English 2, and it is enough to keep my mind busy all the rest of the day, for we do a lot of rapid fire work. To tell you the truth, we are all "scared blue" of Professor Kittredge. He is so dogmatic and so abrupt in all his questioning, that he awes us all. He fires questions around the room regardless, and then pounces on you so unmercifully if you don't know or don't answer correctly, that you never want to open your mouth again. I feel quite grown up. . . . I shall make the course one of my biggest efforts . . . , as I want to . . . get a lot out of it. If one is willing to work all the time and just memorize and memorize he will get along all right.[31]

Similar descriptions and conclusions appear elsewhere in the record. Stuart Sherman, in his trenchant essay, "Professor Kittredge and the Teaching of English," noted that his teacher acknowledged, "There are many ways of studying Shakespeare," but insisted that "the object of this course is to ascertain what Shakespeare said and what he meant when he said it." To this end, Sherman noted, he taught in a way that while it seemed dictatorial actually left the students a great deal of room to make a synthesis for themselves. Here is Sherman's description of a typical class:

> The session ordinarily began with five or ten minutes during which we called out questions on difficult points in the previous day's reading.

These he answered instantly, always without consulting the book, and succinctly or copiously as the case required. For the next ten or fifteen minutes he subjected us in our turn to a grilling examination on whatever we had prepared for the day. For the rest of the hour he commented with racy phrase and startling illustration, and left the room at the last minute, talking all the way down the aisle and halfway down the stairs.[32]

Another student, who took a version of English 2 at Radcliffe shortly after 1900, remarked that Kittredge was always coming "into class looking as if he had been up all night. Often he ran his hand through his hair," she remembered, "and closed his eyes. He had one deficiency I never like[d] and apparently it lasted. He never looked his students in the eye. He used a card system. He would call a name, put a question, and then look into space just over one's head. . . . I never felt he knew me or, for that matter, any one else. There was no personal relationship." Still, she observed, "I did not find a single minute of it boring," and "I liked even the examinations given when they came."[33] She shared many others' sense that Kittredge was about the business of making people competent—and eager—to read Shakespeare on their own.

The examinations given by Kittredge go a good distance in explaining, in fact, the almost complete absence of any record in his students' notebooks of sustained lecturing. This absence, which makes the notebooks appear dull to us, shows that students did not consider large generalizations the stuff for their record-keeping, which they tied closely to their being "held . . . responsible for every word." Sherman paid tribute to his instructor's purity of focus:

> Now and then Professor Kittredge paused to give an interesting glimpse of an episode in the biography of a word; but all these bits of word history bore directly on his main purpose. He gave much time to the discussion and interpretation of the characters, with occasional praise or pungent criticism of famous performers. The course left with the student a sense of intimate acquaintance with the characters and the plays, and an understanding of Elizabethan English which enabled him to go on reading Shakespeare and his contemporaries intelligently.[34]

Elsewhere, Sherman wrote that Kittredge "threw the full strength of soul and body into the discovery and apprehension of the objective fact and inspired that passion in his pupils." He "brought," Sherman continued, "no tendency to philosophical generalization to his work; his ideas had no tendency to form a system. His ardour was towards the collection of isolated facts, towards the annotation of texts, the establishment of readings, the ascertainment of dates, the understanding of separate literary phenomena. He feared general ideas and destroyed them."[35]

Eventually, when on the occasion of the Shakespeare tercentenary in 1916 Kittredge was persuaded to sum up his most cherished views in a lecture, which he then consented to publish and later assigned to his students to read, he insisted that the "irresistible" temptation to read the man from the works was thoroughly misguided. Looking back on the nineteenth-century quest to trace the development of a genius—"Arrange the plays in order of time, and infer from them the biography of Shakspere's soul; and, from the biography of his soul, infer events and experiences that (in the usual course of human life) may account for moods that the several dramas seem to designate or illustrate or portray"—he expressed as much disdain as frustration when he reflected on the distorting effects created when anachronistic frameworks are imposed upon the plays in order to generate a life narrative that determines their meaning.[36]

Kittredge's conviction that the nineteenth-century quest to tell the true story of Shakespeare's development had produced nothing more than "novel-writing" issued into what must be the largest, most thoroughgoing, and perhaps also the most deeply held, generalization that he offered about Shakespeare: "We are dealing with the supreme dramatist—with that extraordinary man who—more than any other of whom the world holds record—could put himself in the place of any human being (male or female) in any imaginable situation and any imaginable mood—and then could make that person utter his or her thoughts and feelings and emotions and passions as he or she would utter them if endowed with superhuman power of expressions" (2).

Convinced as he was of the limits of his own method, Kittredge firmly disallowed the presumptions of those who turned to the sonnets to find the unlocked heart of Shakespeare. The sonnet, Kittredge insisted, is highly conventional; and by convention "a good sonnet appears to be a confession." "Nothing can prove" Shakespeare's sonnets "autobiographical except the discovery of outside evidence that they accord with the facts of the poet's life; and no such evidence is forthcoming" (3). Above all, the assumption of their "sincerity" is naïve. Hamlet's soliloquies and "Iago's cynical revelations of his code" and "Macbeth's poetic imaginings" are all "sincere." To suppose that there's anything "other than a dramatic sincerity in the sonnets" requires us to enter into "the most vicious of circles" (4).

Still, Kittredge's reluctance to go beyond what he judged the text to warrant did not preclude his entering unobtrusively into famous interpretative debates. He was not about to spend precious class time summarizing the history, say, of discussions of Hamlet's alleged delay. Yet the sum of his remarks about particular moments in the play shows that he saw Hamlet as a man caught between "mighty opposites"—the stuff of tragedy—not as a "weak-willed delayer" or the "chronically indecisive procrastinator envisaged by Coleridge" and others.[37] It was not Kittredge's way to write a lecture that would bring forward a thesis and illustrate its validity. Rather, he left his students to assemble, evaluate, and digest for themselves his pronouncements on individual words and phrases. On examinations, even more than had been the case with Child, he asked for many glosses on short passages. Each student's sustained interpretation of larger wholes was his or her own business, too subjective a matter to be scrutinized by the examiner's abstracted eye, but nonetheless the personal goal that the instructor's method respected and that his repeated focus on salient details prepared each student to achieve with a measure of independence.

Supplementary Shakespeare

To observe that Harvard was unusual in isolating the plays into a full-year elective and to point out that the course was unique in its stability over more than sixty years is not to deny that Shakespeare's writings made their way into other courses at Harvard or that study of his plays entered the curriculum early in other colleges as well. In ways different from Harvard, other institutions of higher learning prepared many students to teach Shakespeare in secondary schools and in college. At Yale, for instance, where English literature became an increasingly significant part of the curriculum in the mid-1880s and there was a decided emphasis on the early Stuart and Commonwealth periods, Shakespeare was just one of several authors whose works were studied. Before 1900 his plays had a larger place in the curriculum of Yale's Sheffield Scientific School than they did in Yale College. Shakespeare also had some part in the Elizabethan Drama course taught by Phelps, who had taken while at Harvard, in addition to English 2, George Pierce Baker's drama course.[38]

At Harvard, while Shakespeare occupied a conspicuous place in the newly created English Department, the work of the Bard also served as a focal point in relation to which the curriculum grew. When in the late 1880s new courses were added, each being assigned a higher number than the last, the central place occupied

by Shakespeare was evinced by the presence of his name in the titles
of new half-courses, even ones from which his works were excluded.
(A "half-course" typically met either for only one term or for one
hour per week through the year.) In 1887–88, for instance, English
14, "The Drama (excluding Shakspere) from the Miracle Plays to
the Restoration" was offered for the first time. In this course Shakespeare's absence was repeatedly made conspicuous: the Bard's work
was the principal reference point in relation to which the whole history of his predecessors, contemporaries, and successors was
unfolded. In the hands of Wendell who invented it, the course drew
heavily upon J. A. Symonds's *Predecessors of Shakespeare* and built cli-
mactically to a sustained study of Marlowe.[39] In the hands of Baker,
who took it over and eventually integrated the study of Shakespeare
into it, the Bard was the constant reference point in relation to
which all the materials were considered.[40]

In another half-course that he first devised, Wendell directed sustained attention to Shakespeare's poems. While teaching English 17
("English Literature of the Elizabethan Period, exclusive of Drama
and Bacon"), he kept a personal notebook in which he outlined his
lectures. His notes show that he conceived the course chiefly in reference to Shakespeare's achievement. He began with the claim that
the goal is "to acquaint ourselves with the literature surrounding the
Elizabethan drama." "This drama," he announced, "with Shakspere as its central figure is so far & away superior to any other literary expression of the period that any view of the subject which
should not always recognize that to the drama belongs chief place
would be hopelessly distorted."[41] As he proceeded to lecture on six-
teenth-century poetry from Wyatt and Surrey onward, he lingered
for several lectures over Spenser, only to build to the destination of
his whole endeavor: the two consummate dramatists. Wendell presented their narrative poems as the "acme of the period" and discerned in them evidence of what writers in the English Renaissance
had found in the pagan classics, viz., not objects for academic study
but sources for "romantic" imaginings. *Hero and Leander,* he proposed, is "a superb revel of purely pagan fantasy," as innocent in its
decadence and immorality as it is frank, worthy of comparison with
the "exuberant sensuousness" found in paintings by Titian, and
utterly unlike the "puritanical & delicately restrained" style of *The
Faerie Queene.* By contrast, the "motive" for *Venus and Adonis,* in
which a young man is wooed by an utterly forward goddess, was
"monstrous" and the poem "indecent." According to William T.
Brewster's notes on this lecture (March 30, 1892), Wendell went on
to propose that Shakespeare displaces the "fantastic" strain created

by Marlowe with something far more "realistic" and portrays a degenerate and "lascivious love of woman for man." In short, "the mistress becomes the whore."[42] The charge of indecent sexuality prepared for Wendell's next lecture, in which he would present the sonnets as both the climactic achievement of Elizabethan poetry and as uniquely revealing about their author's life.

Brewster's notes also record an abbreviated version of what Wendell would develop more extensively in a book that he was to publish on Shakespeare: the claim that in the sonnets we find "the most perfect fusion of fact and imagination, of thought and phrase," so that in them, "more than anywhere else," Shakespeare "shows himself . . . the perfect artist" (51). Neither in Wendell's notebook, nor in Brewster's, is there evidence that the lecturer made an attempt to articulate criteria by which readers might recognize this "perfect fusion" or that he presented grounds for the superiority of the sonnets to the plays. There is plenty of evidence, however, that Wendell's lecture opened questions about Shakespeare's biography that had not been explored in other Harvard courses.

Wendell's praise for the sonnets was tinged with ambivalence about their implications, as suggested in a series of questions that he articulated and sought uneasily to answer: "What do the sonnets express? Are they autobiographic in a sense other than that in which any work of art—which at the utmost can express nothing that the artist has not known—must be autobiographic? Do they tell anything of the actual events in the life of the man Shakspere?"[43] Such responses as Wendell offered moved in opposite directions. On the one hand, he treated matter of factly the idea that Shakespeare had a mistress who also became sexually involved with the young friend to whom he had addressed many of the sonnets. He also sought to dismiss interest in whatever events may have been behind the writing of the sonnets as "a question of gossip and of scandal" unworthy of readers who appreciate their poetry for its consummate artistry. On the other hand, Wendell allowed credit to the "plausible" conjecture of Thomas Tyler that the young man and the dark lady of the sonnets were, respectively, William Herbert, the Earl of Pembroke, and Mary Fitton, a former maid of honor to Queen Elizabeth.[44] In the lecture that Brewster heard, Wendell concluded that the sonnets in any event prove that Shakespeare experienced a "real succession of moods" and went through a period of deep depression that is also reflected in his "great tragedies." He then urged that the sonnets "really do express with amazing excellence the moods of one who lives as he ought not to live." The sonnets were finally to be understood therefore not as the "spontaneous expression of evanescent mood," but as deliberate, conscious, highly artistic abstractions from firsthand experiences with evil. These experiences meant that, as a playwright, Shakespeare would leave behind the romantic idealism that had marked his joyous comedies. Whatever his experiences concretely entailed, they enabled him to infuse into his writing an unprecedented spiritual depth. In his book of 1894, *William Shakspere: A Study in Elizabethan Literature,* Wendell would elaborate on his claim that the sonnets reveal the "deep depression, the acute suffering, the fierce passion" experienced by a writer who then, in his great tragedies and in certain peculiar comedies, would give "vent" to "such emotional disturbance as unexpressed would have been intolerable."[45] At least in the short term, these biographical claims had a surprising impact upon Kittredge, Child's heir apparent and yet only in the early stages of his career.

The year 1894 witnessed the inauguration of an important new course for Harvard freshmen, English 28, "History and Development of English Literature in Outline." Child and his colleagues designed this survey to provide orientation to the burgeoning literature curriculum, and they decided to cover the history in about fifty classes. The teaching was divided among four charismatic lecturers, Child and Kittredge on older literature, Briggs on the seventeenth century, and Wendell on the eighteenth and nineteenth. A half-course that met over the whole year, it offered a previously unavailable context for the teaching of Shakespeare: it placed the Bard's work within a chronology that extended from medieval times to the present and required programmatic decisions about the specific contexts in which his work would be represented, about how much scope should be accorded him, and about the texts that the students would be expected to read. As a course for young men starting out in college, it identified for them who the significant writers of English had been and offered brief glimpses of the lives and careers of men who had made a mark by writing. We know a good deal about how these matters were first handled because the notes compiled by James Duncan Phillips (class of 1897) were meticulously taken, thoughtfully organized, carefully indexed, and preserved with what must have been a recognition that they might someday prove valuable for reconstructing the early history of English studies in the university.[46]

Child himself gave five full lectures on traditional ballads and other popular forms, the materials on which he was he was expert and the grounds for his conviction that Shakespeare's appeal lay in the fact that his plays tapped common folk themes. When the course moved into the sixteenth century, there was brief mention of More's

Utopia and then relatively sustained concentration on two works, the Bible and the *Book of Common Prayer,* studied for their language. At the end of the first term there followed a climactic segment devoted to drama, taught by Kittredge, on whom Child had bestowed the honor of teaching Shakespeare. It was assumed that every student was familiar with some of the plays; no particular play was assigned or taught. Kittredge simply asked each student to submit a list of all the Shakespeare plays he had previously read and then to read three more. Students were also told, for the purposes of the examination, to learn the playwright's life out of Dowden's *Primer.* The actual examination asked for a short essay on the style of Shakespeare's predecessors. Just as there had been no lecture on any individual play, students were not expected to write on any particular work.

Surprisingly, in lecturing on Shakespeare, Kittredge's approach was utterly discontinuous with the typical work done in English 2. He recommended Wendell's new book, and he followed its lead by dwelling on the playwright's biography. Kittredge not only acknowledged the existence of the sonnets, but remarked that there was a "scandal about a dark woman" connected with them. He seems not to have gone into detail, although he did give her name as Mary Fitton. Instead, making the story of Marlowe's short and dissolute life a foil, he told how Shakespeare eventually achieved fame and financial success; and he brought his treatment of English drama to a climax by asserting that it was Shakespeare who at last made playwriting respectable.[47]

In subsequent versions of the course, after Child died in 1896, either Wendell or Baker usually lectured on English drama, and the center of gravity in the course changed subtly and profoundly. Coverage of the medieval period and of language remained in Kittredge's hands but was curtailed, and the scope accorded to both Marlowe and Shakespeare was expanded. In 1899, Wendell talked at length about Shakespeare's life and treated his writing as the epitome of English literature. As he had done in his book, he presented the oeuvre as falling into various periods, attention to which would show the Bard's maturation, which climaxed in the tragedies, above all in *Antony and Cleopatra.* Wendell also urged the excellence and importance of the sonnets, and remarked that no one knows whether the situations referred to in them were based on actual fact. A tutor then followed up in a Saturday conference class by asking students to compare Shakespeare's work with Marlowe's up to 1593, the year of Marlowe's death, and to rehearse the main facts known about Shakespeare's life.[48] In 1905–6, the year before a young student from St. Louis named Tom Eliot enrolled in the course, Baker apparently did the lecturing on Shakespeare. Like his mentor, Baker spelled out the idea that the tragedies reveal Shakespeare's personal despondency, and he presented the final period as a falling off into a prevailing decadence.[49] We can conclude therefore that over the first decade of its existence Harvard's first survey of English literature moved in the direction of placing greater emphasis on Shakespeare's place at the very pinnacle of English literature. While the lecturers made large claims for his achievement, increasingly the discussion of his writing was put at the service of a narrative about his life.

Meanwhile, in 1903–4, William Allan Neilson, Kittredge's former student and his friend, took the lead in creating an alternative survey, "English 41: History of English Literature from the Anglo-Saxon Period to the Present Time."[50] Three years later, Wendell took over leadership of this course, and the tendencies that we have seen in the early history of English 28, to reduce the lecture time initially given to the history of the English language and to magnify the place of Shakespeare, led to a radical revision of the scope of the new survey. This was summed up in its revised title, "History of English Literature from Elizabethan Times to the Present." In lecturing on the Elizabethan period in English 28, Wendell contrasted its vitality with what he deemed the stagnancy of the medieval period. He celebrated the arrival of the Renaissance in England and proposed to let "Shakespeare stand for the moment as perfection," in relation to which all the writing previously covered "may be called the raw material, the imperfect preparation for later perfection." Focusing squarely on "the first period of lasting English literature," Wendell was already on his way to the remaking of English 41, which would simply do away with all that "imperfect raw material" and get right to what he considered the good stuff.[51] The revised survey readily attracted a larger enrollment than English 28. A few years later, when President Eliot's successor, A. Lawrence Lowell, asked the faculty for advice on how to revamp an increasingly unwieldy curriculum, Wendell singled out several English courses that were "secondary" (Spenser, the English Bible, Milton, the novel) or "superfluous" (King Arthur, English letter writers, Dryden) and recommended the suppression of English 28, which he said merely duplicated English 41.[52]

HERETICAL SHAKESPEARE

The career of the first Harvard "literature" teacher to publish a book on the Bard offers an unusual perspective from which to understand what was distinctive in the early teaching of Shakespeare within his institution. Wendell liked to begin his courses by insisting on the amateur and dilettante nature of the enterprise, and he warned that he had an impatience of detail.[53] Like many other remarks that he made, these served to shock and disarm students, some of whom developed a genuine affection for him. It quickly became evident that he loved making sweeping assertions as if their truth were beyond all argument and that, as one former assistant put it, he felt an "antipathy to all that German scholarship holds dear."[54] Nonetheless, for most of the courses that he taught, during the first two or three times that he gave them Wendell worked hard to perfect his lectures until he was ready to publish them. He did this influentially with *English Composition* (1891) and *A Literary History of America* (1900).

Wendell preserved in rich detail many traces of the path that he took to completing his *William Shakspere*. The earliest may be seen in a notebook that he kept while teaching, as he later wrote into it, "the first [course] in which I have tried my hand as a teacher of literature."[55] He gave this course not in Harvard College but at the Annex, which was staffed chiefly by Harvard faculty members who repeated their lectures there in order to augment their salaries. As chairman of the department, Child did not participate in this work; and in 1884–85, before Kittredge joined the faculty, teaching Shakespeare to the young women was entrusted to Wendell, at that time an Instructor in composition. Wendell proceeded to create a wholly new model for the course, lecturing throughout the year on a different play for one hour each week in an attempt to cover the whole oeuvre. He repeated the course three years later, when the institution's *Annual Report* summarized it as follows: "All the plays except Measure for Measure, All's well that ends well, Troilus and Cressida and Pericles have been read rapidly. . . . The object has been to gain an acquaintance with Shakspere as a whole."[56] The absence here of reference to any play actually taught, and the explicit enumeration of those not taught, is peculiar. Inevitably, it raises a question about the grounds on which these plays were omitted.

What Wendell considered offensive, or (as we might now say) inappropriate, about the four plays becomes somewhat clearer when we look to the alternative Shakespeare course that he went on to develop. The syllabus for English 23 organized the plays according to chronology, in order to illustrate the periods of Shakespeare's career—but with a sharp difference from Dowden's construction of a narrative about Shakespeare's maturity. The plays that had been omitted in the women's version of the course were important for the

detective work on which Wendell reported somewhat cryptically in
his lectures for the young men, the dark secrets of the Bard's inte-
rior life. Wendell was more forthcoming in his book, where three of
the omitted plays are considered along with the sonnets and with
Hamlet in a section devoted to a major rewriting of Dowden's narrative. In his chapter on the sonnets, Wendell rehearses in greater
detail and with explicit quotation from the sonnet on "lust in
action" his discovery of the precise ground of Shakespeare's acute
spiritual suffering. Having pronounced that "the first series of *Sonnets* [1–126] expresses a noble fascination," Wendell avers that "the
second" (127–54) involves "a base one, of which the baseness grows
with contemplation."[57] He promotes further contemplation of what
he calls, rather vaguely, "the lasting tragedy of earthly love" (230)
when he remarks that *All's Well* treats "the fact of love with a cynical
irony almost worthy of a modern Frenchman" (249). This play is
said to convey "a mood not hitherto found in [Shakespeare's]
plays" (249), an "unsettled, unserene, unbeautiful" mood (250)
familiar from the dark lady sonnets and tied to "the mysterious mis-
chiefs which must flourish in this world as long as men are men and
women are women" (249). (This last phrase, repeated with knowing
and unspecified implication, becomes Wendell's refrain through
this whole section of the book.) As the author moves next into his
discussion of *Hamlet,* it turns out that this play, puzzling as it has
been to the critics, reveals "the knowledge of what evil comes from
the fact of sex so cynically set forth in *All's Well*" (262). As in the
sonnets, in both these plays and in *Measure for Measure* and *Troilus
and Cressida,* Shakespeare "faces the fact of sexual passion, which is
"at once mysterious and evil. In *Hamlet* Shakspere expressed his
sense of the mystery; in *Measure for Measure* he expresses his sense of
the evil. Here his dominant mood is grimly contemplative, almost
consciously philosophic. No more than in *Hamlet* can he offer any
solution to the dreadful mystery" (269). If this sounds more than a
little like the language of Calvinism, it should come as no surprise
that Wendell crowns his discussion with a sustained comparison
between the moral climate of Shakespeare's Vienna and "a potent
contemporary mood" that has left its record in the Puritans.

> As with them, life is a positively evil thing, made up of sin, of weakness,
> of whatever else should deserve damnation. Fate is overpowering; pure
> ideals are bent and broken in conflict with fact; and, above all, sexual
> love is a vast, evil mystery. Even though, here and there, a gleam of per-
> sistent purity suggest the possibility of rare, capricious election, most
> men are bound by the very law of their being to whirl headlong toward

merited damnation. In *Measure for Measure*—so strangely named a comedy—one may constantly find this unwitting exposition of Calvinism, with no gleam of hopeful solution. (270)

From these assertions it is but a short way to Wendell's pronouncement that *Troilus and Cressida* is another "bad play," where "what breeds trouble is the wantonness of woman" (273). There are no "free agents" in this play, and the feminine lead is virtually equivalent to a backsliding reprobate: "in Cressida we have a full-length portrait of a fascinating wanton all the more fatal because of her momentary, volatile sincerity" (273). The playwright is said to have expressed his "sense both of the irony of fate, and of the evil inherent in the fact that women are women" (277).

In the last section of his book, as he takes up the plays that were increasingly being read as "Romances," Wendell aims for another striking revision of Dowden's biographical surmises, in particular, the claim that the last plays evince Shakespeare's spiritual recovery. Far from showing that in old age Shakespeare dramatized the theme of reconciliation because he had emerged from his spiritual depths, the plays of this period are said by Wendell to be indicative of the playwright's declining power. Wendell presents the late plays as characteristic of Shakespeare's implication in a general decay of the drama, which was predictable on the basis of an inevitable cycle of growth, development, and decay that all genres necessarily go through. (Wendell draws on this cyclical theory of literary history in several of his books.[58]) In his consideration of *Antony and Cleopatra*, "in some respects the most masterly of Shakspere's plays," Wendell had already discerned in the title characters "the greatest picture in English Literature of decadent virtue" and found a summary of the playwright's "sense of all the harm which woman can do" (340–41). Yet the last plays are said, by virtue of their merely experimental character, to amply demonstrate the decay both of the artist's personal powers and of the genre itself. Shakespeare's willingness to deal with father-daughter incest in *Pericles* and the threat of miscegenation in *The Tempest*—a "horror" almost as great as "the massacre of lower-races" and equally forbidden "to the noble instinct" of the truly supreme races (373)—is reminiscent of his failures in *Measure for Measure, All's Well,* and *Troilus,* where he had displayed "a profound sense of the evil which must always spring from the mysterious fact of sex" (418).

There were of course many other things in Wendell's book, including handy gatherings of information about the publication history of each play, discussions of how the playwright recycled

themes that appeared in the work of his predecessors or in his earlier plays, and a celebration—amid the treatment of *A Midsummer
Night's Dream, Much Ado about Nothing, As You Like It,* and *Twelfth
Night*—of the fact that once Shakespeare had learned his trade, he
first excelled in the writing of comedy. (For anyone around Harvard
who was paying attention, this must have called to mind a salient
lacuna in the English 2 rotation.) Still, the most original facet of the
book was its twofold revision of Dowden's narrative: the insistence
that Shakespeare's mid-life despondency was the product of a firsthand encounter with sexual evil, and the denial that the material
success and respectability that the Bard enjoyed in old age was
underwritten by a spiritual recovery that also inspired his last plays.
At the risk of dignifying a book that a Stephen Dedalus could have
titled "Aesthetic Mastery Abounding to the Chief of Sinners," we
might say that this feature of Wendell's book marks it as epitomizing
the idea of originality that T. S. Eliot caricatured in "Tradition and
the Individual Talent." (Eliot was a student at Harvard through the
very years when Wendell's ideas about the course of literary history
had their greatest impact upon the English curriculum.) The "contribution" of Wendell's Shakespeare book lay in its conspicuous difference from Dowden's narrative of spiritual maturation, that is, in
its mere eccentricity, what Kittredge came to refer to as "novel-
writing."

Finally, it is ironic that English 2 should have been called "Shakspere" and English 23 "The Works of Shakspere." For, while Child
and Kittredge held steadfastly to the text of the plays, Wendell's concern was ultimately with the man as imagined through a chronological reading of his writings. As a lecturer who taught his students
"nothing except what to think about what you [already] happened
to know,"[59] Wendell proceeded in the classroom not by pinpointing
difficulties or working through problems but chiefly by a knowing
urging of opinion. "This is the way things will always be as long as
men are men and women are women." There seems to have been
scarcely any activity that involved genuine inquiry: there was little
puzzling over data that admit of potentially contradictory explanations, very little testing of hypotheses or weighing of evidence, and
no attempt to show how responsible conclusions may be drawn or
an illuminating thesis may be convincingly argued. There were, however, many incontestable pronouncements.

To be fair, Child and especially Kittredge, who was often said to
be dogmatic, did little to show how to produce an interpretative
argument either. Nor did they encourage, when glossing words and
phrases, the discernment of what we would now call Empsonian

ambiguities. They did attempt to ensure, however, that "no hard passage was passed over without at least an attempt to ascertain its meaning." When they held a magnifying glass close to some small detail in the text, it was with a view to making Shakespeare's meaning clear. They did this with hundreds of small components in each play. From time to time, the instructor pulled the magnifying glass gradually back, allowing a general understanding to develop in the students' minds. He did not intrude an explicit formulation of some large point that he expected the students to copy down, because he trusted that a more abstract understanding would come on its own, as it were, to all who encountered the myriad details with care.[60]

NOTES

1. Unless otherwise indicated, statistical data and assertions about course offerings, their dates, and their enrollments are based on the *Annual Reports of the President and Treasurer of Harvard University,* available online on the website of Harvard University Archives at http://hul.harvard.edu/huarc (cited below as *AR,* by year and page[s]).

2. *AR,* 1886–87, 73.

3. Frederic Atherton, "A Suggestion to the English Department," *Harvard Monthly* 22 (March 1896): 10–14, esp. 10–11.

4. Stuart Sherman, "Professor Kittredge and the Teaching of English," in *Shaping Men and Women: Essays on Literature and Life,* ed. Jacob Zeitlin (Garden City, NY: Doubleday, Doran, 1928), 84–85.

5. I have made fairly extensive studies of the early English curriculum in the archives at Yale, Columbia, Princeton, Brown, Case Western Reserve, and the Johns Hopkins Universities; at the University of Pennsylvania, Boston University, and Boston College; and at Oberlin, Smith, and Radcliffe Colleges.

6. See Barrett Wendell, "The Relations of Radcliffe College with Harvard," *Harvard Monthly* (October 1899): 8.

7. F. A. March, "English at Lafayette College," in *English in American Universities, by Professors in the English Departments of Twenty Representative Institutions,* ed. William Morton Payne (Boston: D. C. Heath, 1895), 74–85, esp. 78.

8. *AR,* 1872–73, 48.

9. Payne, "The Teaching of English" (Introduction), in *English in American Universities,* 7–28, esp. 8.

10. *AR,* 1898–99, 62–63; 1901–2, 69–70.

11. F. J. Ranlett, Notes on English 2, 1879–80, Harvard University Archives, HUC 8879.324.2. Besides the sets of notes from Child's English 2 identified in this and subsequent endnotes, a set made by F. N. Robinson in 1889–90 may also be found in the Harvard Archives, at HUC 8889.324.2, and a set made by Edward Kirby Putnam in 1898–99, at HUC 8898.324.1.

12. Rolfe had been headmaster of schools in several towns in Massachusetts, including Cambridge. His "Friendly" edition of Shakespeare was published in New York by Harper and Brothers in the 1870s and early 1880s.

13. Notes taken by Charles Evans Hughes on Bancroft's "Outlines of English Literature" are in the Brown University Library Archives, MS 1M-2. See 61–66.

14. Smith College *Annual Circulars* no. 1 (1873), 4–5, Smith College Archives.

15. L. Clark Seelye Papers, Smith College Archives, Box 14, Folder 18.

16. March, "English at Lafayette," 75–77.

17. Printed copies of two hour examinations have been preserved among the papers of William Lyon Phelps in the Yale University Archives; see Notes on Shakspere with Professor Child, 1890–91, MS Group 578, Series III, Box 17, Folder 202.

18. On the prestige of Dowden's attempt to uncover Shakespeare's spiritual biography by following through the plays chronologically, see Gary Taylor, *Reinventing Shakespeare: A Cultural History from the Restoration to the Present* (New York: Oxford University Press, 1989), 173–82.

19. Edward Dowden, *Shakspere*, Literature Primers (1875; New York: D. Appleton, 1882), 59–60.

20. W[illiam] T. Brewster, Notes on Shakespeare [English 2], 1890–91, Harvard University Archives, HUC 8890.324.2.9. Brewster's remarks are pasted into his copy of *Macbeth*.

21. Lawrence W. Levine, *Highbrow / Lowbrow: The Emergence of Cultural Hierarchy in America* (Cambridge: Harvard University Press, 1988), 11–81.

22. Jo McMurtry, *English Language, English Literature: The Creation of an Academic Discipline* (Hamden, CT: Archon, 1985), 77.

23. Francis Gummere, "A Day with Professor Child," *Atlantic Monthly*, 103.3 (March, 1909): 421–25, esp. 423; see also *AR*, 1875–76, 22–23.

24. After Kittredge gave the course to women for the first time, this description appeared in the *Reports of the Treasurer and Secretary*, Society for the Collegiate Instruction of Women, 1888–89, 12. See *Annual Reports of the President and Treasurer of Radcliffe College*, Harvard University Archives; online at http://hul.harvard.edu/huarc/ (cited below as Radcliffe's *AR*, by year and page[s]).

25. Five boxes of George Lyman Kittredge's notes on Shakespeare are in the Harvard University Archives, HUG 4486.30. Notes on *Othello* are most extensive in Boxes 1 and 2.

26. Two sets of Rolfe editions that belonged to Walter W. Naumburg, who annotated them in English 2, are in the Harvard University Archives: for 1887–88, when one rotation was taught by Child, at HUC 8887.325.2; and for 1888–89, when the other was taught by Kittredge, at HUC 8888.324.2.

27. In "Planned Parenthood: Minding the Quick Woman in *All's Well*," Caroline Bicks emphasizes aspects of the play that have often made men uncomfortable; see *Modern Philology* 103 (February 2006): 299–331.

28. Howard Savage, Annotated classroom texts in Professor Kittredge's English 2, Harvard University Archives, HUC 8908.324.2. The notes quoted here are written on a sheet found between pages 34 and 35 of *All's Well*.

29. Helen Keller, *The Story of My Life with Her Letters (1887–1901)*, ed. John Albert Macy (New York: Doubleday, Page, & Co., 1903), chapter 20.

30. Ethel Winward Howland, autobiography transcript, Radcliffe College Archives, SC113, Box 1, Folder 5, 37–38.

31. Madeline Ware Cobb, letter of Oct. 6, 1914 to her parents, Radcliffe College Archives, SC69, Box 2, Folder 9.

32. Stuart Sherman, "Professor Kittredge and the Teaching of English," 74.

33. Howland, autobiography, 36–37.

34. Jacob Zeitlin and Homer Woodbridge, eds., summarizing Sherman's view of Kittredge, in *Life and Letters of Stuart P. Sherman*, 1.106; quoted by Clyde Kenneth

Hyder, *George Lyman Kittredge: Teacher and Scholar* (Lawrence: University of Kansas Press, 1962), 62.

35. Stuart Sherman, quoted by Jacob Zeitlin, Introduction, *Shaping Men and Women*, xxiii.

36. Kittredge, "Shakespeare's Birthday—Address," 2, Notes on Shakespeare, Harvard University Archives, HUG 4486.30, Box 1. Subsequent references to the typescript preserved under this title are cited parenthetically within the text.

37. Hyder, *George Lyman Kittredge*, 183.

38. In addition to information found in the Yale catalogues for the relevant years, see Albert S. Cook, "English at Yale University," in *English in American Universities*, 29–39.

39. See Wendell's Lecture Notes for English 14, 1887–89, Harvard University Archives, HUC 8887.224.14.

40. Baker's notes on English dramatists are part of the George Pierce Baker Papers in the Special Collections of the Harvard Theatre Collection, currently uncatalogued, formerly shelf number P2.09.06.06, and more recently kept at P2.35.07.03. A clearer idea of his version of English 14 may be had from any number of student notebooks in the Harvard University Archives. An early example is that of William Tenney Brewster, Notes for English 14, 1893–94: HUC 8893.324.14.9. The notebook of Walter Morris Hart shows that at least by 1900–1 Baker had incorporated Shakespeare into the course, which was offered primarily for graduate students; see Harvard University Archives, HUC. 8900.314.5.

41. Barrett Wendell, Lecture Notes for English 17, 1889–90, Harvard University Archives, HUC 8889.224.17, opening lecture, 2 October 1889. This notebook was begun when Wendell taught the course in 1889–90; he augmented it when he taught it again in 1891–92.

42. Wendell, English 17, Lecture 19, March 23, 1892. See also William T. Brewster, Notes on English 17, 1891–92, 49–50, Harvard University Archives, HUC 8891.324.17.9. Subsequent citations of Brewster's notes are made parenthetically within the text.

43. Wendell, English 17, Lecture 20, March 30, 1892.

44. See Thomas Tyler, *Shakespeare's Sonnets* (London, 1890); quoted by Barrett Wendell, *William Shakspere: A Study in Elizabethan Literature* (London: Dent; New York: Charles Scribner's Sons, 1894), 224.

45. Wendell, *William Shakspere*, 236, 239.

46. James Duncan Phillips, [Notes on] English 28 "English Literature 500–1895" for 1894–95, Harvard University Archives, HUC 8894.324.28. In addition to Phillips's class notes and essays for the course, this folder contains copies of examinations.

47. See Phillips's notes on Lecture 23, 60.

48. Anonymous, Notes on English 28, 1899–1900, 26–29, Harvard University Archives, HUC 8899.324.28.

49. Francis M. Rackemann, Notes on English 28, Lecture 18, 1905–6, Harvard University Archives, HUC 8905.325.28. Baker later published his own book, *The Development of Shakespeare as a Dramatist* (New York: Macmillan, 1907).

50. A Scotsman who had studied with David Masson at Edinburgh, Neilson would edit school editions and teach Shakespeare at Columbia and at Smith, where he served as President of the College.

51. Anonymous, Notes on English 28, 19.

52. See Wendell's annotations for President Lowell in the *Official Register of Harvard University* 19 (September 21, 1912), no. 7, in particular in the "Announcement

of the Courses of Instruction Offered by the Faculty of Arts and Sciences 1912–13," 2d edn., published by Harvard University; Harvard University Archives, HUG 1876.4.

53. See, for example, Wendell's notes for his opening lecture in his Shakespeare course, English 23, as given in 1892–93, Harvard University Archives, HUC 8892.224.23.

54. See the remarks by Professor [C. N.] Greenhough, in *Proceedings of the Massachusetts Historical Society*, October 1920–June 1921, 54 (1922): 201.

55. Wendell, Shakespeare Course at Radcliffe, 1886–88, Harvard University Archives, HUG 1876.54.14. The designation "Radcliffe College" here is anachronistic, and the dates given in the heading of this item are incorrect. Wendell himself erred when he wrote into the back of the notebook in May 1893 that he had made the notes in 1886–87. He actually began this notebook, as the dates he wrote on many pages show, in the fall of 1884; he added notes to it the second time that he taught his Shakespeare course for young women in 1887–88.

56. Radcliffe's *AR*, 1887–88, 16–17. Some grounds for the exclusion of *Pericles* may be well discerned in Caroline Bicks's emphasis on women's roles in the play; see *Midwiving Subjects in Shakespeare's England* (Burlington, VT: Ashgate, 2003), 175–86.

57. Wendell, *William Shakspere*, 225. Further citations are made parenthetically within the text.

58. See, for example, *The Temper of the Seventeenth Century in English Literature* (New York: Charles Scribner's Sons, 1904), 46–73, 97–100, 125–27; see also *A Literary History of America* (New York: Charles Scribner's Sons, 1900), 4–5.

59. This observation was made by Wendell's long-time colleague, George Santayana, in *The Middle Span*, vol. 2: *Persons and Places* (New York: Charles Scribner's Sons, 1945), 172.

60. For the analogy of the magnifying glass, I am grateful to Colin Ryan.

Poet of America: Charles Mills Gayley's Anglo-Saxon Shakespeare

Coppélia Kahn

"CHARLES MILLS GAYLEY" WAS ONCE A NAME TO CONJURE WITH. CHAIR of the English Department at the first campus of the University of California in Berkeley from 1889 to 1919, Gayley made his department a leader in the nascent academic study of English in the United States and helped put Berkeley on the map as a great university. His career spanned the era in which the universities that we know today first took shape, in which English literature changed from a belletristic pastime to a scholarly discipline. Gayley's life as teacher and literary scholar was full of accomplishment, and his extracurricular activities were myriad. As a spellbinding teacher, he was legendary: his Shakespeare course was held in the university's outdoor Greek Theater, the only place big enough to accommodate the several hundred students enrolled plus hundreds more visitors. According to the Berkeley yearbook of 1897, Gayley's teaching methods were "peculiarly his own" in their combination of "recitation, lecture, and free discussion on the part of the class," in which he followed the Socratic method, "drawing out the student to help him unfold the best that is in him." His lectures, the yearbook declares, were characterized by "ease, naturalness, lucidity, but pervaded by a fire, an aggressive, magnetic, exhilarating force . . . . enhanced in charm by frequent readings, in which he has a rare faculty of bringing out the hidden light and beauty of rhythm and thought."[1]

Outside the classroom, he composed school songs—"The Golden Bear," "The Blue and Gold"—still sung at football games, founded a chapter of Psi Upsilon and the campus debating union, and at his fireside, read Kipling's poetry aloud to enraptured students. He was also a teacher of teachers, writing textbooks, anthologies, and manuals for systematic instruction in English literature. A productive scholar, he wrote books on medieval drama, the dramatist Francis Beaumont, and Shakespeare. Many, if not most, of these volumes

201

can still be found on college library shelves today. Finally, like other professors at newly established state universities, he performed as a one-man speaker's bureau on behalf of the often-embattled, financially needy institution. When he died in 1932, flags on the Berkeley campus were flown at half-mast, and President Robert Gordon Sproul called him "a truly great teacher," who had placed his gifts "at the service of the community, the faculty, and particularly the students of the university."[2]

Gayley was what historian Henry F. May calls, in his study of pre–World War I America, "a custodian of culture." This is the role on which this essay will focus, placing Gayley in the context of his academic generation, his place at Berkeley, and his moment in the history of the American university. May defines the culture guarded by its custodians as "a particular part of the heritage from the European past, including polite manners, respect for traditional learning, appreciation of the arts, and above all an informed and devoted love of standard literature, [which] usually meant British."[3] Gayley would have applauded those words. His position as college professor gave him a podium from which he could bring that kind of culture to a wide public: lecturing to women's clubs, churches, and posh groups of California's businessmen and civic leaders, publishing poems and articles in newspapers and magazines. In the last decade of his career, during the agonized period from August 1914 to March 1917, Gayley joined the heated national debate over whether America should remain neutral or join the fight in support of Great Britain and France against the Allies. His ticket of entry, so to speak, was Shakespeare.

Gayley's book *Shakespeare and the Founders of Liberty in America,* written for the general reader and published by Macmillan in 1917, positioned the poet at the center of a complex circuitry that linked him as the noblest practitioner of the English language to the foundations of American democracy located, Gayley claimed, in the Jamestown colony of 1607. Through Shakespeare, Gayley made the case for this country to fight on behalf of Great Britain in defense of their common "Anglo-Saxon heritage." By invoking the term "Anglo-Saxon," moreover, Gayley signaled his position in a related controversy that predated the war, a controversy over American identity impelled by the arrival of huge numbers of immigrants, many of whom, unlike earlier ones from the British Isles, didn't speak English. By 1907, the annual total of immigrants entering the United States came to one million. From that year to the beginning of World War I in 1914, about 650,000 immigrants per year arrived at Ellis Island.[4] The 1920 census reported that 13 percent of America's population were foreign born, and another 21.5 percent were children of foreign-born parents.[5] In the eyes of the founding fathers, "To be or become an American. . . . all [a person] had to do was commit himself to the political ideology centered on the abstract ideals of liberty, equality, and republicanism," regardless of his or her national origins and native language. But in 1790, roughly eight out of ten white Americans were of British derivation, so there was little if any conflict between national identity and ethnic origin.[6]

In 1917, the situation was strikingly different. The fact that many if not most of the newly arrived immigrants didn't speak English revived the long-established prejudices of a faction called nativists, who made a distinction between former immigrants who, like themselves, had become citizens, and newly arrived prospective citizens, whom nativists dubbed foreigners. Between 1906 and 1914, nativists also began to distinguish between "old" immigrants from northern and western Europe who belonged to the same racial stock that had founded America, and "new" immigrants from southern and eastern Europe whom nativists considered unassimilable. Moreover, nativism was becoming racialized. Such intellectuals as Madison Grant, founder and chair of the New York Zoological Society, Henry Cabot Lodge, senator from Massachusetts, and Francis A. Walker, president of the Massachusetts Institute of Technology, drew on pseudoscientific classifications developed in physical anthropology to argue that immigrants from the Mediterranean, the Balkans, and eastern Europe were genetically inferior to those born into "Anglo-Saxon" societies allegedly possessing a native love of liberty. This culture, passed down by the founding fathers, they held to be fundamental to Americanness, and still dominant.[7]

In engaging with these questions as a Shakespeare scholar, Gayley bears out Michael Bristol's claim that "[i]nterpretation of Shakespeare and interpretation of American political culture are mutually determining practices."[8] I would add that they are also educational practices. For Gayley as an educator, there was little difference if any between giving a lecture to his Shakespeare students in the Greek Theater, and writing *Shakespeare and the Founders of Liberty in America* for a wide audience—and not because the book follows the conventions of scholarly argument, or because it is based on exhaustive research in primary sources, or because almost half of it interprets Shakespearean texts, from the sonnets to the history plays to *The Tempest*. Rather, as a university professor, he saw himself as a custodian of culture who mediated it not just to students but to the public at large.

Gayley's generation was, simply, the first generation of professional academics in the United States; the first one to embrace college teaching as a career rather than a genteel calling, to seek specialized training for it, and to rely on salary alone for livelihood, without recourse to private income. Gayley was born in 1858 in Shanghai where his father, a naturalized American citizen born in Ireland, was serving as a Presbyterian missionary. When the Reverend Gayley died of cholera in 1862, the family moved to Ireland, where Gayley was educated at the Blackheath School for Sons of Missionaries. In 1875, at the invitation of and supported by his great-uncle, he entered the University of Michigan, taking his B.A. in classics in 1878. After a stint as high school principal, for most of the eighties he was an instructor, then an assistant professor of Latin at Michigan. Endowed with what his biographer calls "a musical baritone of great range and richness" and a charismatic enthusiasm for literature as "the vital center of life-at-its-best," Gayley was soon commandeered by Michigan to chair its English department and to resuscitate the teaching of its freshman and sophomore English curriculum.[9]

Word of his success at the job spread to the president of Cornell (who had been his history professor at Michigan) and from him to the president of Berkeley, who offered him the chairmanship of its English Department. It would seem that Gayley belonged to what we call an old boys' network, but it was actually a new boys' network. Berkeley was only twenty years old in 1889 when he arrived there, the same age as Cornell. Between 1889 and 1892, Clark, Stanford, and the University of Chicago opened their doors, and Columbia started a major expansion. In the nineties, university departments were beginning their modern formation, and young men capable of running them were at a premium. By 1891, the leaders of the new academic profession were under thirty-five.[10]

When the thirty-one-year-old Latin teacher began his new job at Berkeley, the first campus of the University of California had only 701 students and a faculty of sixty. The 1890 census listed Berkeley's population as five thousand. Electricity was widely available only in 1892, when electric street cars began running. In the 1880s, although the town already boasted such cultural organizations as a choral society, an orchestra, and the "Longfellow Memorial Society" devoted to papers on literary topics and open discussion, dairy farms were still scattered through it, and gypsies were arrested for theft and domestic disorder.[11] In the English Department, Gayley found his work cut out for him. So hated and despised was the freshman course in English then that it was the custom, at the end of the academic year, for the freshman class to carry in mock-solemn funeral procession two textbooks, one of them William Minto's *Manual of English Prose Literature,* for burial in actual graves, with crosses to mark them, on campus. After "rows of little graves accumulated," cremation was substituted for burial.[12] Gayley revamped not only the freshman year but the entire English curriculum, rationalizing it according to the new German *kulturhistorisch* concept of studying literature in relation to the evolution of culture in general. His training in classics, supplemented by a year's graduate study at a German university, equipped him with the latest ideas for systematizing literary study. In 1895, *The Educational Review* called Berkeley's English curriculum "[t]he most broadly and thoroughly planned scheme" of literary study in the nation and recommended it to all teachers of literature.[13] A year before, five years into his chairmanship, Gayley published an article in the distinguished magazine *The Dial* that laid out the curriculum he had designed. It included preliminary, prerequisite, and advanced courses; there were offerings in English prose style, translations of the "Hellenic, Teutonic, or Romance epics" and other classics, practical rhetoric, English masterpieces, argumentation, and the general history of English literature. He singled out the last as "the *sine qua non* for all higher work," which presented "a synoptical view of English literature as the outcome of, and the index to, English thought in the course of its development" and included "the copious reading of authors illustrative of social and literary movements."[14] Gayley's insistence on system, method, and what he called "literary science" aligned him with the German-trained scholars who had created the model for the new concept of the research university. Yet he stood just as squarely in what Gerald Graff and Michael Warner call the opposing camp: "belletristic critics" who saw literature "as a moral and spiritual force and a repository of 'general ideas' which could be applied directly to the conduct of life and the improvement of the national culture."[15] Indeed, President Sproul's obituary praised Gayley for interpreting literature "not as a philological puzzle but as a contribution to living."[16]

Gayley's first book, which forms the cornerstone of his entire career as an educator, is in fact an attempt to improve the national culture. In 1893, he published *The Classic Myths in Literature and Art,* in response to a request from the university's Academic Council, which had established the study of classical mythology in relation to English literature as an entrance requirement. Used as a textbook in all California high schools, twice reprinted in revised and enlarged editions, and popularly known as "Gayley's Myths," the book was identified with its author. Some students thought he had invented the myths; others, that Gayley's initials, "C. M.," *meant* "classic myths."[17] Steeped in the classics, Gayley saw British literature as the supreme expression of an Anglo-Saxon culture founded on and continuous with those of Greece, Rome, and the Teutonic ancestors of modern Germany. In his preface to *Classic Myths,* he specifies, "No myths save those known to the Greeks, Romans, Norsemen or Germans have been included in the text," for the sake of "emphasizing only such myths as have actually acclimated themselves in English-speaking lands and have influenced the spirit, form, and habit of English imaginative thought."[18] Threaded through the book's 597 pages are examples of how English writers, from Addison to Arnold, wove these myths into their writings. Thus, Gayley acclimates Americans to their legacy as English speakers.

As chair of the English Department at California's only state university, which by establishing university entrance requirements virtually determined the high school English curriculum, "Classic Myths" Gayley had enormous influence over future generations. Furthermore, for more than a decade he annually toured the state to examine and accredit high schools, and many of his students at Berkeley, particularly the women, would return to those schools as teachers. At the same time, as a leading spokesman for the state's first university, he was in an embattled position. On the one hand, he was often called upon to defend higher education before skeptical legislators in Sacramento scrutinizing the university's annual budget allowance. On the other hand, within the university, Gayley quietly carried on a kind of culture war. In 1900, he initiated a course in "Great Books," treating "the masterpieces of Sanskrit, Hebrew, Greek, Roman, medieval, French, Spanish and Italian literature" specifically for engineering students, who were then entirely male.[19] He wanted to insure that "culture" would be carried into the industrial, commercial, and political worlds that men commanded. The course was so popular that it had to be moved to a larger hall, and all nonengineering students—that is, women—excluded.

Gayley was also engaged in a gender war. Along with his famous "Oral Debates on Literary Topics," the prerequisites of which Gayley allegedly used for the purpose of excluding women (he denied it), the Great Books course was one of Gayley's several attempts to resist what he saw as the feminization of literary study. According to Mrs. Gayley, male students tended to avoid English courses, heavily populated by female students, because they thought them "effeminate." Furthermore, Gayley felt that the presence of women prevented him from being sufficiently "severe" with male students.[20] In a 1910 jeremiad against the state of higher education, he argues that the advent of kindergartens, taught by women, has vitiated the "devotion to a higher self" necessary to the inculcation of a manly patriotism. Nor should women teach adolescent boys, because "[o]nly men know the temptations of young manhood."[21] Yet in the same text, he seems to realize that social and economic forces, rather than their gender per se, limit women's educational opportunities, implying that young women, who make up 80 percent of public school teachers and earn an average annual salary of $330, are "starved into matrimony."[22]

The ideological tension between land grant universities and culture, as Gayley and his fellow custodians understood it, was a further source of unease. The Morrill Act, passed by Congress in 1862, had awarded public lands to states to found universities "where the leading object shall be, without excluding other scientific or classical studies, to teach such branches of learning as are related to agriculture and the mechanic arts."[23] It took decades for consensus on whether and how science, the classics, agriculture, and "the mechanic arts" could or should be combined. The more important question as regards Gayley was the conflict between the ethnically specific terms of culture as he conceived it, and the democratic principle of taxpayers financing an education appropriate and useful to the entire population. How technical and vocational, and how "classical" or "scientific" should state-financed higher education be? Did farmers really need to know either the classic myths or chemistry?[24]

For Gayley, there was no conflict, because he believed that the basis of American democracy was to be found in its "Anglo-Saxon" roots. Therefore, all citizens—farmers and mechanics as well as teachers and lawyers—should be educated in Anglo-Saxon culture. The concept of Anglo-Saxon culture originated with Richard Verstegen, who argued in 1605 that the English were descended from the Saxons, a Germanic people that had filtered into early Britain, rather than (as legend and medieval chronicles had it) from the Trojans led by Brutus to Britain after their defeat in the Trojan War. During the English Civil War, interest in the theory burgeoned, as Parliamentarians defended "the immemorial liberties of the English people," allegedly based on a native Anglo-Saxon love of freedom, contrasted to the "Norman yoke" of feudal law imposed in 1066 and culminating in the absolutism of Charles I. The idea of an Anglo-Saxon "race" was also fostered by the Romantic concept of *Volksgeist* and by nineteenth-century nationalism: both conceived of peoples as endowed with innate qualities.[25]

Gayley had already begun to formulate this argument, with Shakespeare as its icon, when his sabbatical and World War I began simultaneously in August 1914. He and his family sailed to England, where he did research for *Shakespeare and the Founders*. When he returned to California in 1915, the passionately pro-British Gayley encountered a volatile mix of pacifist, pro-British, and pro-German sentiments on campus and off. According to Carol S. Gruber, however, in the controversy over where America's allegiance lay, "American Anglo-Saxonists . . . were well represented in the sectors of society that influenced foreign policy opinions and decisions," including the professoriate. Although many American professors, including Gayley, had trained at German universities, they retained the scholarly methods but not the political perspective of their German hosts, and their deepest affinity lay with "the political, legal, economic and cultural accomplishments of the English-speaking peoples."[26] Other distinguished scholars shared Gayley's conviction that America's political and cultural interests stood with those of Great Britain. Arthur O. Lovejoy, professor of philosophy at Johns Hopkins University, declared, "Any serious weakening of the British Empire would be an incalculable and irreparable loss to the material and the higher moral interests of the United States."[27] The Yale historian George Burton Adams stated, "When England falls the doom of the United States is sounded. All our interests, those of language, commerce, civilization, and government, are common with her."[28]

On April 21, 1916, at the Shakespeare Tercentenary celebration on the Berkeley campus, Gayley read aloud his poem, "Heart of the Race," his first attempt to rouse public opinion out of neutrality and advocate America's entry into the war, and a prelude to the more scholarly *Founders*. Conceived as an extended apostrophe to Shakespeare and written in Gayley's customarily lofty and breathless style, the poem first pays the conventional tribute to the poet's creation of realistic characters, "[e]ach in likeness of us." It then portrays him as "[s]haper . . . of the tongue" and "[s]plendid lord of the word"—the virtual creator of the English language itself. After vividly evoking Shakespeare's presence in the British Empire, "[u]nder the Southern Cross" where "[c]hildren are learning thy English and handing the heritage down," its concluding stanza links the empire to America by portraying the poet as spokesman for the English and the Americans as a single race:

> Poet, thou, of the Blood: of states and of nations
> Passing thy utmost dream, in the uttermost corners of space!
> Poet, thou, of my countrymen—born to the speech, O Brother,
> Born to the law and freedom, proud of the old embrace,
> Born of the *Mayflower*, born of Virginia—born of the Mother!

Poet, thou of the Mother! the blood of America,
Turning in tribute to thee, revisits the Heart of the Race.[29]

Referring to Shakespeare as a brother born both "of the Mayflower" and of "the Mother" (England, the mother country), Gayley asserts through this genealogy the kinship and loyalty of his country to Great Britain. He read the poem at Shakespeare celebrations held at the University of Chicago and at the universities of Michigan, Wisconsin, and Minnesota; he also published it in several newspapers and in a prestigious book of tributes to Shakespeare sponsored by the British Academy, *A Book of Homage to Shakespeare*.[30]

In that book, English tribute writers make frequent references to "our race"; Gayley uses the word "race" in the title of his poem, along with "born" (four times) and "blood" (three) in its verses. Although in this period "race" was an unstable term that could designate culture, religion, class, or nation, often in the same writing, in the context of Gayley's interventionist politics, the poem's use of the word and related terms comes close to suggesting that Anglo-Saxon culture is genetically rather than culturally transmitted, echoing the ideas of nativists and the patrician intellectuals mentioned above.[31] Such a stance might have come easily to Gayley, who on his mother's side was descended from a Mayflower voyager and who served as "governor" of the California Society of Mayflower Descendants for twenty-four years. Yet in the poem, a strictly genealogical concept of race is blurred by Gayley's citation of Shakespeare as premier poet of the English language, "born to the speech" as much as "the blood." Implicitly, then, anyone who regards English as his mother tongue and knows Shakespeare might be accepted as American. It is likely that Gayley, who was instrumental in founding the university extension program and who taught a rigorous college-level Shakespeare course in it, might have counted among his adult students (and among his Berkeley students as well) more than one for whom studying Shakespeare represented an act of assimilation into American culture.[32]

The argument of *Shakespeare and the Founders* is based on the claim that Shakespeare was closely acquainted with those whom Gayley calls the "Patriots" or "the liberal faction" of the Virginia Company, which financed and organized the Jamestown colony. At the center of this group was the Earl of Southampton, to whom the poet had dedicated *Venus and Adonis* and *The Rape of Lucrece*. The Patriots also included such men as the Earl of Pembroke and his brother Philip, Earl of Montgomery, to whom Heminge and Condell dedicated the First Folio in 1623; Sir Robert Sidney, patron of Ben Jonson; and Sir

Thomas Gates, whose account of the wreck of his ship in the Bermudas while en route to the colony is thought to have influenced Shakespeare in writing *The Tempest*. Pressing hard on the poet-patron relationship, and portraying as Shakespeare's like-minded friend any "Patriot" who knew someone who might have known Shakespeare, Gayley argues that in the sonnets and plays he wrote before the first Jamestown voyage of 1607, Shakespeare "put forward ideas similar to those which the Patriots sought to realize: ideas of legally constituted authority as opposed to divine right, of monarchical responsibility, of aristodemocratic [*sic*] government, of individual freedom and political duty, of equality before the law."[33]

Evidence that Shakespeare actually knew these "Patriots" is exiguous if not nonexistent. What is known about the governance of the Jamestown colony is that it was a joint stock company, in which the governor was elected by the stockholders, to whom he was responsible for making the colony profitable. The colonists were divided into hired men working under the governor, and gentlemen who didn't work. At the same time, its first charter of 1606 granted to the original colonists and their descendants "all liberties . . . . to all intents and purposes as if they had been abiding and born within this our realm of England."[34] Gayley discusses only the ideology of democratic freedom that he attributes to a faction of the stockholders, while ignoring material and economic factors that nearly destroyed the initial enterprise but also helped save it in the end. Lacking the incentive of private property (stockholders owned the colony), the hired men proved poor workers, although they were marched to the fields by drumbeat twice a day. Disease killed many, the colony struggled to feed itself, the colonists were disorderly and riotous, successive governors failed to show a profit. Finally, in 1619 Jamestown was saved from failure by the development of tobacco as a cash crop and the recruitment of "young and uncorrupt maids" for wives, in concert with the new charter that introduced private property, English common law, and government by representative assembly.[35]

The claim that Shakespeare shared the ideas of individual freedom and equality before the law that Gayley attributes to "the Patriots" is the core of his argument, unfolded in the longest chapter of the book. He supports that argument by ignoring dramatic context in order to interpret brief quotes as expressions of Shakespeare's "articles of faith." Not surprisingly, Shakespeare's beliefs follow the broad lines of Richard Hooker's *Laws of Ecclesiastical Polity* (1594–1651) as Gayley spells them out: all men, endowed by divinely ordered nature with reason, are born free and independent but also subject to the law, which should be ordained and enforced by an "aristodemocratic" form of government. By this slippery coinage, Gayley retains hierarchical class structure while endorsing representative democracy. He argues that Shakespeare's ideal, like Hooker's, is not "flat democracy" but rather government administered through "the free cooperation of distinct classes, according to their several degrees of merit and fitness . . . an aristodemocracy of *noblesse oblige.*"[36] Ranging freely over the Shakespearean canon, Gayley reads Shakespeare's sonnets and plays as documents in a theory of liberal government wholly conformable to the postulates underlying the U.S. Constitution, as though Shakespeare had already understood the English monarchy to be itself a constitutional matter.

In his last two chapters, the custodian of culture brings his argument up to the current moment, to construct "the heritage in common" of England, America, and France that necessitates America's entry into the war:

> One language welded of the Old English, Scandinavian, Gallic, and Latin. . . . One race, one nation, one blood infused of many strains and divers characteristics: of the Anglo-Saxon . . . of the Norman . . . of the Celt . . . one custom . . . of individual prerogative and of obedience to the authority that conserves the prerogative; of fair play and equality of opportunity, of fearless speech for the right . . . for popular sovereignty, for allegiance, for national honor in national fair dealing, for the might that is right; one custom, mother of the law. One common law . . . the law of precedent and of the righteous independence of the courts.[37]

In his final chapter, "The Meaning for Us Today," Gayley opposes this massive commonality of language, custom, and law shared by "the triad of modern democracies" to a German "cult of the acquisitive intellect . . . for the development of technical, professional, commercial, or political efficiency"—thus implicitly repudiating the devotion to research, system, and scientific method that had marked his own scholarship and pedagogy.[38]

Pleading that America "rescue for England" and "consecrate anew for herself, the Anglo-Saxon heritage" of democratic freedom of which Shakespeare is the icon, Gayley slips and slides between an appeal to what he sees as the basic continuity between English and American political culture, and an appeal to what we might call race. Statistically, he claims, the majority of Americans are descended from the British colonists of Plymouth and Jamestown and from British immigrants. As his poem has it, they are "of the Blood." With them he lumps the Dutch, Swedish, and German immigrants who, "accepting British rule and law and speech, became one folk with

the Britons in America." These and "other Europeans . . . have glo-
ried in identifying themselves with the inheritors of Anglo-Saxon
blood and speech, common law, individual freedom and national
responsibility."[39] Notice how "blood and speech" are paired as in
the poem, and smoothly grouped with law, freedom, and responsibility—which are political principles, rather than racial characteris-
tics. Is speech to be identified *with* blood, *as* blood, as synecdoche
for an Anglo-Saxon race? Or can anyone who learns to speak
English—and love Shakespeare—be "identified with," or as, Anglo-
Saxon?

Gayley's book didn't receive universal acclaim. Significantly,
though, the reviews I have been able to find don't object to his passionate arguments for an affinity between Great Britain and America
based on common blood. Rather, they criticize his reading of Shakespeare. In the *Boston Transcript*, "E. F. E." challenges Gayley's
assumption that "whenever characters speak . . . they speak also the
inmost beliefs of the dramatist" and comments, "If Shakespeare was
preaching democracy in his plays then so much the less Shakespeare
he."[40] Sir A. W. Ward, the distinguished literary scholar who delivered the Annual Shakespeare Lecture of the British Academy in
1919, challenged Gayley's claims that Shakespeare personally knew
members of the Virginia Company and charged that, even if he had,
"It would not, of course, follow either that his way of thinking on
political questions and issues was impregnated with theirs or that of
their leaders." Respectfully but relentlessly, Ward moves through
Gayley's readings of the plays, questioning the constitutionalist philosophy that the author claims is woven through the Shakespearean
canon.[41]

Undeterred by such challenges, Gayley delivered a "Thanksgiving
Address" in 1917 asserting the common foundations not only of
British and American liberty but of French liberty as well. That
December, he published an ode, "America to England: 1917," in
which he declared the United States to be "another Anglo-Saxon
state" that should stand "shoulder to shoulder" with Great Britain.[42]
Honors were heaped upon him for these and many other patriotic
activities: he was unanimously elected to the élite Pacific Union Club
of San Francisco in tribute to "the inspiration of his words and
deeds"; in April 1918, he became Dean of the Faculties, second only
to the president of the University of California.[43]

Gayley's defense of the Anglo-Saxon race as the standard bearer
of liberty, then, won widespread assent, and his reliance on Shakespeare's cultural cachet to argue his case surely strengthened it—
while also reinforcing that very cachet. Though Gayley's teaching

and his writings ranged over the English canon, *Shakespeare and the Founders* was the capstone of his career. In it, he made Shakespeare a politically potent icon of America as the successor culture to England. In 1943, for Joseph Quincy Adams, then-director of the Folger Shakespeare Library, that icon was still potent. In a typescript titled "Shakespeare and Virginia," Adams recapitulates the argument of Gayley's book and even quotes from it, without ever mentioning the author. Evidently, by then the book had become so unfamiliar that Adams could pass off its ideas as his own.[44] Amid another world war in which "Anglo-Saxon" culture was again threatened, the poet's alleged connection to the beginnings of democracy on these shores could still be marshaled to bolster the idea that Shakespeare belonged as much to America as to England.

NOTES

1. *The Blue and Gold* (Berkeley: University of California, 1897), 128–29. This description is accompanied by a full-page photograph and biography of Gayley.

2. "Miscellaneous Writings of Charles Mills Gayley," Bancroft Library, University of California, Berkeley, 308x, G287mi.

3. Henry F. May, *The End of American Innocence: A Study of the First Years of Our Own Time 1912–1917* (New York: Knopf, 1959), 30.

4. John Higham, *Strangers in the Land: Patterns of American Nativism 1860–1925,* 2nd ed. (New Brunswick: Rutgers University Press, 1988), 159.

5. Lynn Dumenil, "The Progressive Era Through the 1920's," in *Encyclopedia of American Social History,* ed. Mary Cupiec Cayton, Elliott J. Gorn, and Peter W. Williams, 3 vols. (New York: Scribner's, 1993), 1.181.

6. Philip Gleason, "American Identity and Americanization," in *Harvard Encyclopedia of American Ethnic Groups,* ed. Stephan Thernstrom (Cambridge: Harvard University Press, 1980), 31–58, esp. 32.

7. See Madison Grant's influential anti-immigration treatise, *The Passing of the Great Race; Or, The Racial Basis of European History* (New York: Scribner's, 1916). For a more detailed consideration of Anglo-Saxonism and controversies over immigration and American identity, see Coppélia Kahn, "Caliban at the Stadium: Shakespeare and the Making of Americans," *Massachusetts Review* 42.2 (2000): 256–84.

8. Michael R. Bristol, *Shakespeare's America, America's Shakespeare* (London: Routledge, 1990), 3. Bristol's book provides an excellent theoretical foundation for studies of Shakespeare in American culture.

9. Benjamin P. Kurtz, *Charles Mills Gayley: The Glory of a Lighted Mind* (Berkeley: University of California Press, 1943), 236, 111. See also the essay by Elizabeth Renker in this volume for a profile of the new professors such as Gayley, who displaced the "preprofessional" class of college teachers.

10. Laurence R. Veysey, *The Emergence of the American University* (Chicago: University of Chicago Press, 1965), 263–64.

11. For histories of Berkeley, see Richard D. Schwartz, *Berkeley 1900: Daily Life at the Turn of the Century* (Berkeley, CA: RSB Books, 2000); and Writers' Program of

the Works Progress Administration, *Berkeley: The First Seventy-Five Years* (Berkeley, CA: Works Project Administration, 1941).

12. Interview with Miss Alice Hilgard, Charles Mills Gayley Papers, Bancroft Library, University of California, Berkeley, BANC MSS C-B1030, Box 1.

13. Quoted in Kurtz, *Gayley*, 122.

14. Charles Mills Gayley, "English at the University of California," reprinted in Gerald Graff and Michael Warner, *The Origins of Literary Study in America: A Documentary Anthology* (London: Routledge, 1989), 54–60, esp. 56.

15. Graff and Warner, "Introduction," in *Origins of Literary Study in America*, 6.

16. "Miscellaneous Writings of Charles Mills Gayley," Bancroft Library, University of California, Berkeley, 308x, G287mi.

17. Kurtz, *Gayley*, 130–31.

18. Charles Mills Gayley, *The Classic Myths in English Literature and in Art, Based Originally on Bulfinch's "Age of Fable" (1855)* (1893; repr., Boston: Ginn and Company, 1911), vi.

19. *The Daily Californian*, Charles Mills Gayley Papers, Bancroft Library, University of California, Berkeley, BANC MSS C-B 1030, Box 1.

20. Charles Mills Gayley Papers, Bancroft Library, BANC MSS C-B 1030, Box 1.

21. Charles Mills Gayley, *Idols of Education* (New York: Doubleday, Page and Company, 1910), 122–23, 117.

22. Ibid., 124.

23. Quoted in Frederick Rudolph, *The American College and University: A History* (New York: Knopf, 1968), 252.

24. See Veysey, *American University*, 112–13, on the state universities as "ideologically varied" in their relative commitments to "utilitarian" studies and liberal arts and sciences. At the beginning of the twentieth century, he claims, state universities were "less research-oriented than the major private foundations, but imitating them with great success" (113). See also Henry F. May, *Three Faces of Berkeley* (Berkeley, CA: Center for Studies in Higher Education and Institute of Governmental Studies, 1993). May argues that Berkeley developed into a combination of the three models that, Veysey claims, universities followed as late as the 1920s: the democratic-utilitarian, the polite cultural-liberal, and the research institution conceived along German lines.

25. For accounts of the idea of an Anglo-Saxon culture, see Reginald Horsman, *Race and Manifest Destiny: The Origins of American Racial Anglo-Saxonism* (Cambridge: Harvard University Press, 1981); and Allen Frantzen and John D. Niles, eds., *Anglo-Saxonism and the Construction of Social Identity* (Gainesville: University Press of Florida, 1997).

26. Carol S. Gruber, *Mars and Minerva: World War I and the Uses of the Higher Learning in America* (Baton Rouge: Louisiana State University Press, 1975), 27.

27. Quoted in ibid., 54.

28. Quoted in ibid., 63.

29. Charles Mills Gayley, "Heart of the Race," in *A Book of Homage to Shakespeare*, ed. Israel Gollancz (Oxford: Oxford University Press, 1916), 340–41.

30. For a study of this book and its conflicted constructions of Shakespeare as both a quintessentially English poet and a universal bard, see Coppélia Kahn, "Remembering Shakespeare Imperially," *Shakespeare Quarterly* 52 (2001): 456–78.

31. For studies of discourses of race in the Victorian era, see Shearer West, ed., *The Victorians and Race* (Aldershot, UK: Scolar Press, 1996).

32. Charles Mills Gayley, *University Extension 2, 8* (February 1893), in "Miscellaneous Writings of Charles Mills Gayley," Bancroft Library, University of California,

Berkeley. Gayley describes the extension program as "a movement entirely independent of Eastern influence, molded by considerations peculiar to the isolation, geographical extent and educational conditions of a State in the West" (230). In this account of his first extension course on Shakespeare's tragedies, which he gave in 1891, he states that 160 students were enrolled, for sixteen two-hour sessions.

33. Charles Mills Gayley, *Shakespeare and the Founders of Liberty in America* (New York: Macmillan Company, 1916), 40.

34. Quoted in Samuel Eliot Morison, *The Oxford History of the American People* (New York: Oxford University Press, 1965), 49.

35. Ibid., 49–54.

36. Gayley, *Shakespeare and the Founders*, 144, 160.

37. Ibid., 193–94. I have excerpted from a paragraph of about 360 words.

38. Ibid., 214, 219–20.

39. Ibid., 218, 223.

40. E. F. E., *Boston Transcript*, December 12, 1917, 11.

41. A. W. Ward, *Shakespeare and the Makers of Virginia* (London: Oxford University Press, 1919), 33.

42. Kurtz, *Gayley*, 223.

43. Ibid., 228.

44. Joseph Quincy Adams, "Shakespeare and Virginia," bound typescript dated April 12, 1943, Folger Shakespeare Library, Washington, DC, MS.Add.37.

IV
Back to the Future

Shakespeare Visits the Hilltop: Classical Drama and the Howard College Dramatic Club

Marvin McAllister

In the early twentieth century, Howard University served as an intellectual and cultural oasis for ambitious Negro students in search of unapologetic immersion in a classics-based liberal arts education. Social historian Stephan Talty identifies Howard as one of several African American liberal arts colleges—including Fisk University, Atlanta University, and Morehouse College—that functioned "as temples of high European culture, through which blacks passed on their way to success."[1] African American "passage" into the upper echelons of cultured society was tied to the mastery of ancient languages, as well as the performance of classical and early modern literature, especially Shakespeare.

Founded in 1909 by soon-to-be renowned biologist Ernest Everett Just, the Howard College Dramatic Club used Shakespeare and other established European dramatists to propagate high culture on a Negro campus. This essay examines Shakespeare's curricular and extracurricular impact on Howard University, based on campus and off-campus assessments. Multiple voices—including those of faculty advisors, Dramatic Club student managers, campus journalists, university administrators, Washington, DC's black journalists, and local educators—continually framed and reframed two central questions concerning Negro students and a liberal arts education. First, how might Shakespearean presentations enhance the educational experiences of young African American students? Second, did high culture and refinement have to be associated with universal European masters like Shakespeare, or could Negro students develop more modern and racially expressive cultural representations?

Howard University was born in March 1867 when Congress ratified Senate Bill 529, with a section calling specifically for a "[u]niversity for the education of youth in the liberal arts and sciences."[2] Surprisingly, the official university charter makes no reference to color, thus making Howard University unique among "historically black" colleges and universities because the institution was originally intended to educate Negro men and women alongside white men and women. However, as was the case with most Negro colleges, this institution of higher learning situated on a hilltop made an early and steadfast commitment to meeting as many educational needs as possible. The "youth" in this charter would be broadly served by a Preparatory Department, which provided a secondary or high-school-equivalent education for remedial students interested in advancing to college, and a Normal Department, which offered college-level coursework. This Normal Department would eventually transform into the College of Arts and Sciences and a separate Teachers College.

Building on educational models from New England universities like Harvard, Yale, and Dartmouth, Howard University architects originally envisioned a curriculum rooted in the study of ancient languages and literature, philosophy, and mathematics. By the early 1900s, in the Preparatory Department, Teachers College, and College of Arts and Sciences, Howard's curriculum was still firmly grounded in the classical tradition. A three-year course of study at the secondary level required three years of Latin and two years of Greek. On the collegiate level, a four-year Bachelor of Arts at the "Group A" or "upper-class" rank required Greek and Latin every semester. Interestingly, the curriculum for the "Group A" degree also required English Literature during the junior year, with an emphasis on Shakespeare and other early modern literature. These early modern additions were part of a gradual expansion of Howard's classics-based curriculum, which would include new courses in modern languages, hard and soft sciences, and eventually public speaking.

Traditionally, oratory and rhetoric were major components of a classical education as well as a broader-based liberal arts curriculum. In 55 BCE, Roman philosopher and orator Cicero argued that the "art of speaking" was central to higher education, and mapped out oratorical training in his rhetorical discourse *De Oratore*. In nineteenth-century North American educational institutions, oratory, composition, and literary analysis comprised the rhetorical arts, a field of "efficient communication," which could only be mastered through theoretical study and performance. Also, during the mid-1800s, William Grant Allen, a noted Negro orator and rhetoric professor, advocated public speaking as not only central to a liberal arts education but instrumental to the pursuit of social justice for the American Negro. Like many nineteenth-century Americans, Allen believed oratorical study prepared students for full participation in public life.[3]

At Howard University, extracurricular public speaking activities created the foundation for the study and performance of literature and eventually led to the introduction of elocution courses. In 1870s, various departments in the College of Arts and Sciences sponsored societies that promoted public speaking through campus-wide oratorical contests. According to historian Monroe H. Little, these student-run organizations showcased the rhetorical and dramatic talents of their members through debates, skits, and speeches. The most dynamic college orators were known to attract a large and devoted following, rivaled only by the fame and adulation enjoyed by college athletes on campus.[4] Initially, Howard did not offer academic credit for these highly popular extracurricular events; however, by December 1874, the College of Arts and Sciences began awarding academic credit for participation in the contests. Finally in 1899, the college appointed a teacher of elocution in the English department to supervise the study of public speaking as a legitimate art form, with an emphasis on breathing, tone inflection, modulation, and other oratorical techniques. By 1911, public speaking courses were compulsory for all Howard University students.[5]

Following the lead of early liberal arts advocates like William Grant Allen, nationally prominent academicians like W. E. B. DuBois continued to extol the educational, civic, and political benefits to African Americans studying science, literature, philosophy, history, and languages. Liberal arts advocates at Howard University and other Negro institutions would encounter formidable resistance on two fronts. The first source of opposition was Booker T. Washington, a widely respected and powerful educational leader who preferred agricultural, industrial, domestic, and commercial educational fields for Negro students. In his famous 1895 "Atlanta Compromise Speech," Washington conceded that as Negroes transitioned from slavery to freedom, they incorrectly focused on positions atop America's cultural and political hierarchies. Many educated American Negroes misguidedly pursued positions in Congress and the state legislature or attempted to master poetry and other artistic letters. The ultimate pragmatist, Washington assured his audience of southern and northern industrialists that African Americans should start at the bottom of the economic structure and learn to live by the production of their hands, learn to value common labor.[6]

The second educational battle front developing on Howard's campus pitted the university's original classics-based curriculum against a more modern liberal arts agenda. The first successful challenge to the classical curriculum was the introduction of an English course in the junior year of the "Group A" liberal arts degree. As the departments in the College of Arts and Sciences developed, Howard's classics-based approach was continually reconsidered by progressive-minded professors. Academically and socially committed intellectuals such as Kelly Miller embraced modern languages like French and German, as well as the study of modern social sciences like sociology.

Ernest Everett Just and Benjamin Brawley were two professors fully committed to the university's original classics-based curriculum, and both scholars would make significant contributions to the development of dramatic arts at Howard. According to Rayford Logan, Howard University president Wilbur P. Thirkield's two most important academic appointments were Just as an English instructor in 1907 and Brawley as acting associate professor of English in 1910. When Just arrived on campus with a zoology degree from Dartmouth University and a passion for English dramatic literature, he was surprised by the paucity of cultural activity on Howard's campus and was especially disappointed by the lack of a drama society.[7] During his boarding school days at Kimball Union Academy in Meriden, New Hampshire (where he was the only black student in his class), Just had developed a lasting appreciation for the classics, oratory, and dramatic performance. In high school, he completed an intensive four-year classical course of study and excelled in oratory under the guidance of Miss Sawyer, the oratory and physical training instructor. At the culmination of his senior year at Kimball, Miss Sawyer created the minor role of Tom Twist so Just could appear in a graduating-class production of Oliver Goldsmith's *She Stoops to Conquer*. From this point forward, Just was committed to the performance of dramatic literature.[8]

Just's decision to become a classics scholar in high school and his participation in the school's drama-based graduation exercises both illustrate Stephan Talty's notion of immersion in "high European culture" as a necessary component of African American educational progress. At Negro colleges across the nation, black students demonstrated their mastery of European classics at critical moments of passage in their lives. Errol Hill, in his pioneering work *Shakespeare in Sable*, notes that as early as 1905, Atlanta University began presenting Shakespearean dramas as a core feature of graduation exercises. Professor Adrienne McNeil Herndon, trained in elocution at the

Boston School of Expression, directed successive senior classes in elaborately mounted productions of *The Merchant of Venice, The Tempest,* and other Shakespeare texts.[9]

As had Adrienne Herndon of Atlanta University, Just wanted to establish a lively, intellectually vibrant dramatic culture on Howard's campus. In April 1909, he convinced an energetic yet inexperienced collection of college freshmen to launch a dramatic club. Harkening back to his Kimball Union Academy graduation performance, Just elected to debut the club with Goldsmith's *She Stoops to Conquer* at Andrew Rankin Hall.[10] Under his faculty leadership, the Howard College Dramatic Club would articulate two clear missions: (1) "to firmly and permanently establish dramatic work among the students of the University" and (2) "to present each year one of the classic plays of some well known playwright of established fame."[11] Ernest Just functioned as faculty advisor, while a student business manager handled weekly operations and production management duties.

Unfortunately, soon after their first production, the young thespians were forced to continue under new faculty leadership. President Thirkield relieved Just of his English department duties in order to take advantage of the multifaceted professor's zoology degree. Just was reluctant to change course and abandon the English department, but Thirkield insisted because Negro biology professors were rare commodities.[12] Mary Powell Burrill, a graduate of the Emerson School of Expression in Boston and a speech teacher at the local Dunbar High School, stepped in to advise the club. As an instructor and faculty advisor, Burrill concentrated on elocution, public speaking, and dramatics.[13] In April 1910, she trained and directed the Howard College Dramatic Club in their second production, Richard Sheridan's *The Rivals.*

That same year president Thirkield recruited Benjamin Brawley as an associate professor of English and chair of the department of English.[14] As a professor at Morehouse College (formerly Morehouse Academy), Brawley specialized in English literature and Latin; as a published poet, he openly emulated the verse styles of Shakespeare, Milton, and other European literary giants. Brawley's primary contribution to English literary studies was his publication of *A Short History of the English Drama,* a text designed to provide general notes for beginning students of English literature. This brief history devotes a lengthy chapter to Shakespeare, including a survey of the Bard's life, some discussion of Shakespeare's indebtedness to his predecessors, a concise assessment of his dramatic activity divided into four productive periods, and finally Brawley's personal insights on Shakespeare's legacy of greatness.

Brawley replaced Burrill as the Dramatic Club faculty advisor, and his first major decision was to introduce Shakespeare into the club's repertoire with a somewhat surprising production of *The Merry Wives of Windsor*. Brawley's unusual selection premiered in February 1911 at the Howard Theatre, a Negro theatrical house located at 7th and T streets, northwest DC. William Gilbert, Dramatic Club student manager, reported in the campus press that *Merry Wives* was selected after careful consideration by advisor-director Benjamin Brawley and a committee of club members.[15] In *A Short History of the English Drama*, Brawley identified *Merry Wives* as Shakespeare's only comedy primarily situated in England. He also lauded the piece as a relevant and accessible romantic comedy because of its middle-class characters and its prose as opposed to poetic dialogue.[16] With these average subjects and their romantic intrigues, Brawley assumed Howard University's largely middle-class student population could relate to the material.

In terms of comedic style, Brawley remarks in *A Short History* that "if compared with the great comedies that followed it," *Merry Wives* "impresses us as belonging to an entirely different order of work." Brawley characterizes this "different order of work" as "rollicking," "good-natured," and "bordering on farce," and argues that if *Merry Wives* is simply taken for what it is, a middle-class contemporary farce, this comedy represents a "highly successful achievement."[17]

Light farce seems to have been Brawley's intention because his production of *Merry Wives* expanded the play's gender-bending beyond Sir John Falstaff's brief cross-dressing turn in Act 4, scene 2. Brawley cast a young man, Benjamin H. Locke, as Mrs. Ford, one of the plotting merry wives. An unnamed student reviewer for the *Howard University Journal*, initially skeptical of Brawley's casting decision, questioned whether Locke could fully realize this female character. After all, he was a young man and Mrs. Ford was a challenging and pivotal role. Much to the reviewer's surprise, Locke "adulterated his voice and altered his general makeup so successfully that a great many in the audience seemed to forget that he was only a make-believe Mrs. Ford."[18]

As for the new challenge of performing Shakespeare, business manager William Gilbert boasted in a preproduction publicity article that many club members had already handled important dramatic roles at their previous schools. Therefore, he expected the entire cast to meet the demands of Shakespeare and make "this the crowning point in the endeavors of the Club."[19] But apart from the mildly subversive amusement furnished by a cross-dressing Benjamin Locke or a buffoonish Falstaff deftly executed by E. Clayton

Terry, the student reviewer was underwhelmed by the amateur cast and declared the fledgling Shakespeareans "raw material."[20] With some empathy, the reviewer explained how long and hard Brawley had labored to edit the early modern text for a college production. His dramaturgy involved "pruning," "lopping-off," and "substituting" sections to mold the piece into the proper shape for his young charges. The review closed with what seemed like an apology for the production, "It should be remembered that it is no mere play to put anything Shakespearean on the amateur stage successfully."[21]

The Dramatic Club appeared to take this candid yet sympathetic review to heart, and after four years of regrouping and retraining, they returned to the Bard in April 1915. The retooled amateur thespians staged *The Merchant of Venice,* again premiering off-campus at the Howard Theatre. For their second Shakespearean production, the club recruited a professional director and assembled a more experienced cast. Equally important, to increase popular interest in classical performance, the club selected a more cross-culturally significant and politically charged Shakespearean text.

In the recent past, on both sides of the Atlantic, *The Merchant of Venice* had seen major revivals. In December 1901, at the People's Theatre in New York and later on Broadway, Jacob Adler starred in a Yiddish-language version of *Merchant* purposefully retitled *Shylock.* Revisioning Shakespeare's money lender from an explicitly Jewish perspective, Adler and his production team crafted one of the most culturally grounded Shylocks ever seen on the American stage. *Shylock* was an especially unique restaging because Adler performed his "Jewish Jew" completely in Yiddish, while the rest of the ensemble performed their roles in English.[22] Across the pond, another important revival surfaced in April 1908, when Sir Herbert Beerbohm Tree mounted *Merchant* at His Majesty's Theatre in London. Writing nearly one hundred years after this revival, John Shipley interpreted Tree's more humane treatment of the infamous Shylock as an "exercise in political Shakespeare" and "an attempt to influence public opinion at a time of acute Jewish-Christian hostility."[23] According to Shipley, Tree viewed modern theater as the ideal cultural and social forum for confronting racism and reevaluating age-old misrepresentations of minority groups.

Apparently the Howard College Dramatic Club and another colored dramatic society in Washington, DC shared Beerbohm Tree's vision of theater as a powerful civic and cross-cultural forum. In late May 1913, the Washington Dramatic Club, a predominately Negro dramatic society, produced *The Merchant of Venice* at the Howard Theatre, with local actor/director Nathaniel Guy starring as Shylock.

The Washington Dramatic Club had been established in 1912 by prominent classicist Anna Julia Cooper "for the purpose of studying and presenting annually some play of classical rank."[24] In 1887, Cooper entered the District of Columbia public school system as a Latin teacher; by 1902, she was appointed principal of the M Street High School, originally founded as the Preparatory High School for Colored Youth. As a Latin teacher and M Street principal, Cooper prepared Negro high school students for Ivy League universities by exposing them to Greek, Latin, and Shakespeare.[25] Cooper's impact on Negro students in Washington reached beyond the high school level. Howard University thespians gravitated to her dramatic club; in particular, an undergraduate actor named Merrill Curtis played both the Prince of Morocco and Solanio in the Washington Dramatic Club's production of *Merchant*.

Two years after Anna Julia Cooper's production, the Howard College Dramatic Club hired Nathaniel Guy to train and direct the club members in their production, and Guy cast Merrill Curtis as his Shylock. Unfortunately, the University Journal for April 1915 has been lost, so we have no critical record of Nathaniel Guy's impact on the student ensemble. Based on the production program, we do know that under Mr. Guy's "skillful and efficient direction" the company intended "to give a vivid portrayal of this historical comedy, depicting every character as closely as Shakespeare paints it."[26] In the same program, club manager A. H. Tavernier announced that despite being over three hundred years old, *The Merchant of Venice* was a play "not for an age, but for all times."[27] Guy and Tavernier steadfastly believed in Shakespeare's ability to bridge ages—specifically, the early modern and the modern. They lauded Shakespeare for his skill at illustrating for contemporary audiences "the ill treatment which the Jews have undergone in Europe from the earliest time." Unlike Professor Brawley, who extensively edited *Merry Wives*, Guy and Tavernier trusted that *Merchant*, "with little alterations to suit the whims and idiosyncrasies of his critics, still keeps alive in our minds the noble lesson which the Father of English drama strove so diligently and so incessantly to impart to posterity."[28] The program notes explain Shakespeare's "noble lesson" as "the power of endurance and perseverance of a people whom neither time, nor scorn, nor political oppression could subdue."[29]

This timeless lesson spoke directly to Jewish and African American experiences, and black-Jewish parallels were plentiful in Renaissance and modern American culture. In her analysis of *The Merchant of Venice*, Kim F. Hall emphasizes the connections drawn between the racial difference of blacks and the religious difference of Jews. Hall finds that in Renaissance culture and beyond, both Jewish and African imagery are often associated with "filial disobedience."[30] The featured outsiders in Shakespeare's *Merchant of Venice* and *Othello* illustrate Hall's argument because the European nobility view both title characters as immediate threats to the dominant, natural order. Furthermore, in his late nineteenth-century essay on the inescapable racial prejudices endured by American Negroes, Frederick Douglass quotes Shylock's Act 3, scene 1 "Hath not a Jew eyes?" speech in order to make a case for the Negro's basic humanity. Douglass believed that despite his eloquence, Shylock is unable to secure lasting respect in a Christian-dominated society, much like the Negro is denied dignity in nearly every aspect of American public life.[31] So in early twentieth-century America, it was not a stretch to assume Nathaniel Guy, his cast of Negro college students, and large segments of colored Washington would identify with Shylock and his daughter.

Cross-cultural identifications and noble lessons aside, what were the perceived curricular and extracurricular benefits of Howard students producing Shakespeare? Consistent with the Dramatic Club's original mission, Benjamin Brawley viewed live performance as a way to permanently establish dramatic work as an essential component of campus culture. For Brawley, theatrical production was a means of studying Shakespeare that was gaining "a high place in colleges and high schools in the United States." He also believed that in the future Shakespeare was "destined to be a force linking the culture of America with that of England and the world."[32] But the key was live performance, not simply reading the Bard in a classroom or parlor, but staging his dramatic texts so Shakespeare could truly live in twentieth-century America and effectively link the United States to a world community. Brawley's vision of a fully contemporary and breathing Shakespeare was shared by other Washington, DC, classicists like Anna Julia Cooper. Her Washington Dramatic Club was committed to the same kind of Shakespearean study through production and equally interested in bringing African Americans into shared cultural conversations across the globe.

Of course, extracurricular, fully realized Shakespeare still depended on a proper curricular introduction to Europe's master dramatists, their texts, and early modern culture. In the classroom, Brawley exhibited a nearly religious devotion to all things Shakespearean. According to course guides in the English Department archives, Brawley's English Literature I class dedicated substantial curricular space to the Bard of Avon's work, rotating selections like *The Two Gentlemen of Verona* and *King Lear* each semester. In an attempt to provide a balanced portrait of Shakespeare's age, Brawley also included early modern contemporaries like Ben Jonson and Thomas Middleton.[33] However, in *A Short History of the English Drama*, Brawley identified Shakespeare as representative of his age yet "at the same time universal in his appeal."[34] He further proclaimed Shakespeare "the poet incomparable not only of England but of all ages and the world. He has his own distinctive note, and he is master of all the sources of his instrument." Brawley was convinced students of literature, history, and the human condition in any age could learn a great deal from studying the Bard's work because "he 'knows all qualities with a learned spirit, of human dealings.' With him we live and love and dream and hope. He beckons us to all things beautiful—and to God."[35]

Similar to Brawley's praise for England's divine poet, Anna Julia Cooper glowingly explained in her memoir *A Voice From the South* why Shakespeare is "pre-eminent as the photographer of the human soul" and worthy of both rigorous classroom study and live performance. Cooper believed Shakespeare's unparalleled compassion allowed him to understand and generate sympathy for marginal figures like Othello and Shylock, thus proving himself the ultimate artist. Like Brawley, Cooper maintained an unwavering confidence in the Bard's ability to connect with and enrich any reader or auditor, regardless of race, class, or era. She believed Shakespeare resonated with Negroes in the District of Columbia and spoke the language of early twentieth-century America because of his "infinite receptivity" and his "all-comprehending appreciation which proved a key to unlock and open every soul that came within his radius."[36] Historian Stephan Talty found that DuBois and other educated Negroes were drawn to European texts like *Hamlet* because the great authors provided a "full breadth of character and emotion" and helped African Americans feel a sense of "full inclusion in the human," which they so desperately sought.[37] Through Shakespeare, both Cooper and Brawley aspired to move Negro students beyond the perceived limits of class and race and position these young minds to commune with like-minded classicists around the world.

Based on their immersion in European classical traditions, Brawley and Cooper would be labeled elitist, bourgeois, and culturally conservative throughout their careers. However, both intellectuals cultivated a fairly complex program of racial uplift that cannot be reduced to a simple obsession with high culture. Beyond English literary studies, Brawley authored several volumes on African American arts and history. In 1921, he published a groundbreaking study titled *A Social History of the American Negro*, which traced African

American history from slavery through the early twentieth century and included a chapter on the colonization and settlement of Liberia. In two different texts, *Early Negro American Writers* (1935) and *The Negro Genius* (1937), Brawley analyzed black writers, orators, and other artists from three different centuries.[38] Granted, Brawley assessed these Negro writers based on European cultural standards, but his scholarship helped recover many forgotten African American artists.

Although an ardent classicist, Cooper was also a leading black spokeswoman in her era, a feminist who believed black women would play a major role in the political and social progress of Afro-America and America. Very active in the Washington, DC community, Cooper helped organize the Colored Women's YWCA in 1905, and she used the proceeds from the Washington Dramatic Club's production of *The Merchant of Venice* to support the Colored YWCA and its social settlement house. Additionally, in the 1930s, Cooper worked to meet the educational needs of colored Washingtonians as president of Frelinghuysen University, a night school committed to adult education in liberal arts, trades, and religious studies.[39]

As educational and racial role models, Brawley and Cooper were both fully impressed by Shakespeare's range and radius, but were Howard students developing the same intense attraction? How did they view their academic and practical interactions with the early modern "photographer of the human soul?" Student manager A. H. Tavernier, in a persuasive article on the Dramatic Club, explained the educational benefits of studying the classics and, more specifically, the importance of performed Shakespeare. Beyond giving public speaking students an opportunity to hone their elocution techniques, Tavernier argued the club allowed undergraduates to develop a "keen appreciation for both classical and modern literature—an appreciation which they are unable to develop in any other society of the university." Campus literary societies may have incorporated dramatic recitations into their annual oratorical contests, but isolated speeches could never match fully realized production.

On a more personal level, Tavernier declared the Dramatic Club an "unsurpassed opportunity for self-intellectual development" because theatrical performance allowed students to embody or inhabit complex dramatic characters. In a vintage defense of drama's power to uplift, the manager claimed club productions provided young actors with an outlet for building strong moral character. Tavernier reasoned that the "delineation of the characters in the drama offers an opportunity for the members of the club to view human life and human society. Thus they shape their own lives accordingly."[40] By performing Shakespeare's impressive range of humanity, with all their tragic flaws and comic foibles, Dramatic Club members could reevaluate and enhance their own personal characters.

Tavernier assumed academic enrichment and personal moral development would be enough to draw enthusiastic new members to the Dramatic Club, but other Howard students discovered more superficial benefits to performing Shakespeare on campus, advantages related to social status and reputation. Consistent with Talty's characterization of Negro colleges as "temples of high European culture," some Howard coeds promoted the Dramatic Club productions as positive reflections on the entire student body, the faculty, and the university administration. After the inaugural performance of *She Stoops to Conquer,* an unnamed student reviewer called the debut performance "the most stupendous undertaking ever entered into by the students of the University" and noted that President Thirkield received letters from "people of reputation throughout the city" who were astonished to witness a company of student amateurs stage such an impressive production. The reviewer also anointed *She Stoops to Conquer* the "greatest success ever attained on the hill" because the theatrical performances demonstrated "the possibilities that lie dormant around Howard."[41] In a follow-up article on the club's premiere production of *She Stoops,* the *Journal* confidently proclaimed that such sophisticated entertainments would raise the entire school in the "estimation of the best thinking men and women in the community."[42]

The same student desire to impress on campus and in the extended Washington, DC, community was equally apparent when Brawley introduced Shakespearean productions to Howard University. Even in the *Merry Wives of Windsor* review, which branded the cast "raw material," the anonymous *Journal* reviewer boasted that this "play has reflected great credit upon all who are connected with it, upon the School of Liberal Arts, upon the student body and upon Howard University as a progressive institution."[43]

For colored and white Washingtonians, the "people of reputation" or "best thinking men and women in the community" were broadly educated, well-read citizens who demonstrated their intellectual curiosity and elevated their social status by supporting high culture. Talty interpreted DuBois's "Talented Tenth" as this kind of special cadre of black middle-class leaders educated in the classical European tradition.[44] Organizations like Cooper's Washington Dramatic Club were the products of a growing community of literary and cultured colored elites. In advertisements, Cooper boldly referred to her dramatic club as "composed of the best talent of the race."[45] Howard College Dramatic Club members and the student press believed staging Shakespeare and other revered dramatists reaffirmed the university's commitment to a liberal arts curriculum and legitimized this predominately Negro school as a progressive institution committed to the highest quality of learning.

Ernest Just's decision to introduce cultured dramatics to Howard University was quickly recognized and endorsed by local Negro elites. In his "This Week in Society" column, W. Calvin Chase, editor of *The Bee*, inserted a brief mention of *She Stoops to Conquer* at Andrew Rankin Chapel. As the primary Negro daily, *The Bee* was responsible for determining or at least tracking cultural trends among the colored citizens of the District. Editor Chase was surprised by the impressive turnout for the Dramatic Club's premiere production, and he remarked that the society crowd in attendance declared the dramatic performance completely "creditable."[46]

However, far from aggrandizing DC's local "Talented Tenth," Chase and his *Bee* staff seemed more interested in exploiting and perhaps intensifying a "popular" versus "high-brow" schism among black Washingtonians. In a May 1912 article titled "Footlight Flashes," a *Bee* columnist writing under the pseudonym "Artie" applauded an up-and-coming Negro theater manager, S. H. Dudley, who decided to open the brand-new Minnehalia Theatre as a rival to the more established Howard Theatre. Parenthetically, the Howard Theatre, managed by W. H. Smith, was relatively new to the city as well, having only opened its doors in August 1910. But the Howard Theatre had rapidly earned a reputation for hosting Shakespeare and other cultivated productions, supported by DC's smart set of educated Negro men and women.

As an alternative to the Howard Theatre's more cultured entertainments, Dudley's Minnehalia Theatre planned to showcase "broad-gauged" material, the kind of mass appeal extravaganzas perfected by musical theater pioneers like George Walker, Aida Overton Walker, Ernest Hogan, and Bob Cole.[47] A year later in June 1913, a *Bee* writer named R. W. T. authored a theatrical trends article which mentioned how the Howard Theatre, perhaps in response to Dudley's challenge, now planned to offer "popular attractions" like Aida Overton Walker's musical revue *Porto Rican Girls,* widely considered the "race's biggest act."[48] Yet to close his theatrical update, R. W. T. remarked that cultivated audiences would still be served this season. Anna Julia Cooper's Washington Dramatic Club intended to

stage *The Merchant of Venice* at the Howard Theatre, and their production was billed as a "society event."

The Bee's distinct separation into "society" and "broad-gauged"
entertainments was an accurate reading of the growing class stratifi-
cation among colored Washingtonians, and the shrewd W. H. Smith
of the Howard Theatre devised a strategy to capitalize on both
demographics. A third *Bee* correspondent, R. C. Byars, reported that
Monday and Friday nights at the Howard Theatre were dedicated to
refined artistic expression, while Tuesday, Wednesday, Thursday,
and Saturday nights were reserved for more popular material and
even catered to particular DC quadrants, like southwest or northeast
Washington. As an unapologetic people-watcher, Byars was thoroughly impressed with "society nights" at the Howard. On these evenings, DC's colored elites or aspiring glitterati turned out to
experience the finer entertainments, and according to Byars, one
could witness "some of the most refined and cultured young men
and women in the world."[49]

The Howard College Dramatic Club's managerial leadership was
keenly aware of the class and cultural politics framed by the local
media and exploited by leisure outlets like the Howard Theatre. Faculty advisors and student members wanted to be embraced by DC
cultural elites, yet they also represented that original university on
the hilltop committed to enriching and educating the broadest public possible. As previously mentioned, the club selected *Merry Wives*
and *Merchant* because both were accessible Shakespearean texts that
showcased the Bard's contemporary and cross-cultural appeal. For
Merry Wives of Windsor, club manager William Gilbert devised an
explicitly populist ticket policy; the club would keep admission
prices for their Howard Theatre performances "within the reach of
all." Gilbert, Brawley, and the club members wanted to ensure this
important dramatic production would be financially available to the
middle-class smart set, as well as working-class residents throughout
the District.[50]

The club's initiative to popularize Shakespeare and other European dramas met with limited success. On campus, even after overwhelmingly positive responses to *She Stoops to Conquer,* the Howard
College Dramatic Club did not enjoy sustained support from the student body or the administration. In October 1913, concerned manager A. H. Tavernier worried that too few Howard students truly
understood the club and its many cultural advantages. Tavernier
also lamented how university administrators showed "little or no
appreciation for the club," while on any other campus such an
ambitious dramatic society would have been regarded as an "indis-

pensable organization of student activity, without which student life would be monotonous."[51] In a sympathetic *Journal* article, G. David Houston, a faculty member on the Dramatic Club's advisory committee, acknowledged Tavernier's disappointment and frustration. Houston admitted that he knew "only too well the discouragements that threatened to overwhelm the manager; but Mr. Tavernier laughed to scorn every menacing obstacle, and worked patiently and persistently for the success, which he has a right to enjoy."[52] There was no mention of the specific obstacles threatening to overwhelm Tavernier, but apparently the organization's efforts and capacity to generate favorable press for Howard University did not earn the club permanent respect on campus.

This unsustainable enthusiasm for the Dramatic Club may be linked to the second major question relative to classical dramatic production and educational agendas on The Hilltop. On a predominately Negro campus in the early 1900s, was it prudent and progressive to associate art, culture, and society primarily with universal European masters like Cicero, Goldsmith, and Shakespeare, or was there more immediate and relatable cultural literature for black students to embrace or perhaps create?

At Howard University and other Negro colleges, this culture question was often answered in the context of a larger African American political and educational debate framed by W. E. B. DuBois's liberal arts and equal rights advocacy versus Booker T. Washington's industrial and agricultural agenda. When engaging the legendary DuBois-Washington divergence, scholars tend to focus narrowly on these great men and their theories on Negro education and national race relations. However, on the local level, white and black voices expressed their opposition or support of classically educated Negroes and sometimes openly questioned the usefulness of Negro college graduates.

Denny B. Goode, editor of *The Focus,* a political weekly published in Louisville, Kentucky, summarized white opposition in a February 1909 editorial titled "The Negro College." This editorial was reprinted in *The Bee* and drew heated reactions in the nation's capital. Basically, Goode was objecting to a recent proposal to establish a Negro liberal arts college in Louisville on the grounds that "educated Negroes think themselves superior to many white people" and "Negroes who have a classical education, yearn more and more for race equality."[53] Unwittingly, Mr. Goode articulated DuBois's exact position that a broad-based liberal arts education, as opposed to a strictly technical or agrarian course of study, was the ultimate training ground for a new generation of civil rights warriors committed to racial equality. Goode further characterized Afro-America's quest for equality as "the Black Plague" and specifically identified the growth of classical education among Negroes as the cause of current racial tensions.

One primary contributor to Goode's "Black Plague" was Anna Julia Cooper, who lost her position as M Street High School principal in a local manifestation of the DuBois-Washington conflict. During her time as principal, from 1902–6, Booker T. Washington's vocational and industrial training program was the preferred model for educating black children in the District. This pragmatic model, advocated by black and white educators, was based on the assumption that an intensive liberal arts curriculum would be wasted on Negro students. As Washington argued in his 1895 Atlanta speech, African Americans would be better served by learning to work with their hands and not by studying rhetoric or politics. Cooper refused to accept this assumption and refused to use the textbooks authorized by the DC Board of Education. In response to Cooper's unwavering commitment to a classics-based education at the high school level, the Board of Education forced her to resign as principal and used an alleged personal indiscretion to justify her dismissal. This major scandal came to be known as the "M Street School Controversy," and Cooper would not return to the DC school system until a new superintendent of schools reinstated her in 1910. Cooper returned as a Latin teacher at the M Street School, now named Dunbar High School, and she resumed her mission of exposing Negro students to Cicero, Virgil, and Shakespeare.[54]

While Cooper graduated well-educated, college-bound Negro seniors, Kelly Miller, Howard University sociology professor and dean of the College of Arts and Sciences, was committed to guiding black undergraduates through a rigorous and rapidly changing liberal arts curriculum. In April 1915, Miller was invited to the Bethel Literary Society to deliver a paper on the merits of Negro college graduates. Miller argued sociology students in his relatively new department, as well as college graduates from other departments, could have a most productive impact on the African American masses, especially by working in the nation's public schools.[55]

In a response to Kelly's appearance at the literary society, *Bee* editor W. Calvin Chase berated colored college graduates, "From the standpoint of *The Bee* Colored college graduates to some extent are failures. And this is an asylum for such individuals . . . .There are many puffed-up popinjays who would have better success upon a cornfield than they would in our schools. . . . The alleged social Colored man or woman are social shams. Give the sham social colored individual an opportunity to dance his time away, he cares but little what becomes of his future welfare."[56] The "asylum" to which Chase referred was the DC public school system. Although institutions like Howard University were originally designed to supply teachers for public schools, Chase believed Negro colleges were failing in their mission. These institutions had been reduced to breeding grounds for useless colored social climbers. Chase's "puffed-up popinjays" and "social shams" referred to the colored Washingtonians who appeared in *The Bee*'s "This Week in Society" column or frequented the Howard Theatre on "society nights." Without reservation, Chase declared the current crop of college graduates disconnected, if not wholly disinterested in the economic or political progress of the race.

Progressive professors like Kelly Miller were committed to modernizing Howard's traditionally classics-based curriculum while discovering practical solutions to meet national needs. One graduate who grew to exemplify the balanced Howard student was E. Franklin Frazier. Frazier studied Latin, Greek, German, and mathematics while devoting his extracurricular time to serving consecutive terms as class president and performing with the Howard College Dramatic Club. Under the direction of Nathaniel Guy, Frazier assumed the role of Lorenzo in the 1915 production of *Merchant*. After graduating from Howard in 1916, Frazier studied at the New York School of Social Work, earned a doctorate in sociology from the University of Chicago, and authored the Marxist-inspired critique of America's black middle class titled *The Black Bourgeoisie* (1955).[57] As a sociologist dedicated to the systematic study of African American families and communities, Frazier negated Chase's blanket denunciation of colored college graduates and proved a liberal arts curriculum could produce socially responsible Negro scholars.

The Washington-DuBois debate exerted a major influence on Howard University and other Negro campuses. Historian Rayford Logan characterized DuBois's promotion of liberal arts study as "The Revolt of Negro Intellectuals" and pronounced this campus uprising "against the educational, social, economic and political ideas of Booker T. Washington" the most significant development on the African American academic scene in the early 1900s.[58] At Howard, the administration, faculty, and students understood the DuBois-Washington schism as a fundamental choice between an expansive education in languages, mathematics, history, literature, and sciences or a more applied course of study rooted in vocational, industrial, or agrarian training. In purely economic terms, Washington argued a marketable trade or well-honed technical skill better positioned a college-educated Negro to secure solid employment and become a contributing member to society. By contrast, DuBois claimed a liberal arts education better prepared African Americans to question, reevaluate, and potentially transform their national citizenship.

From the first year of the Dramatic Club's existence, the university administration and faculty members found themselves on both sides of this educational divide, sometimes caught squarely in the middle, and occasionally forced to reshuffle the debate. Howard presidents like Wilbur P. Thirkield and college deans like Kelly Miller were in delicate positions because Booker T. Washington actually served on the Howard University Board of Trustees during the early 1900s. Howard trustees represented one of the most powerful university boards in the country because they reserved the power to directly hire and fire all university personnel.[59] Although Washington consistently advocated for vocational training, he also encouraged the university trustees to open a medical school to create professional opportunities for Negro graduates in the medical, dental, and nursing fields. During his administration, president Thirkield was a Washington supporter and considered various plans to increase industrial training on campus. He once remarked that "[i]f I could, I would immediately install a technical plant in Howard University worth a half million dollars."[60] Thirkield was especially interested in the monetary infusion a plant might generate, and he was not alone: subsequent Howard presidents also explored industrial projects, from farming to manufacturing.[61]

A major force preventing Thirkield from actually installing such a plant was his faculty. Howard professors and instructors were less than thrilled with the administrators when they made overtures, real or theoretical, toward the Washington program. In the opinion of university historian Walter Dyson, Howard professors feared if students realized they could earn more money through industrial training, they would no longer enroll in classical courses or pursue careers as schoolteachers. Therefore, Dyson contends, the faculty intentionally scheduled the limited number of industrial courses for late afternoon hours or on Saturdays, in hopes of discouraging enrollment.[62] Such internal sabotage probably dissuaded Thirkield and other presidents from emphatically promoting industrial training at Howard University.

Beyond undermining Booker T. Washington's vocational agenda, Howard's liberal arts revolutionaries were also advocating a "new education" rooted in modern languages, history, the natural and social sciences. As early as November 1909, a fully embattled *Howard*

University Journal editor H. L. Cox warned of this "ominous" alternative to the classics, "In the presence of the rapid development of natural sciences and modern languages and paralyzed perhaps by the evolution of the doctrine of industrial education, many of our educators are taking every opportunity to denounce the study of the classics. In Howard University, this disposition is becoming so common that a student of the upper classes, can't attend his usual round of daily lectures without having his respect for the importance of Greek and Latin in a liberal education taken to task."[63] By "upperclasses," Cox was referring not to economic class or social status but to highly motivated students who were seeking the "Group A" liberal arts degree, which, as previously stated, required Greek or Latin every semester.

Mr. Cox further defended a classics-based education against the "so called 'new education'" on the grounds of adaptability: "[t]his superior disciplinary value of classical education, of necessity, means the superior ability to adapt oneself to [one's] environments, and this is the end to be desired in all education."[64] Essentially fighting educational alternatives on two fronts, the industrial and liberal arts proponents, Cox ridiculed a lecturer who remarked that it is more important for Negroes to "be familiar with tools and workshop appliances" than the rhetorical discourse of Cicero.

In support of Cox and the classics, Brooklyn citizen George Miller penned an open letter to the *Howard University Journal* in which he explained how intellectual training far surpassed industrial training. His essential argument was that the vocational student is fashioned into a "machine of industry" who can be directed. By contrast, the student trained in grammar, literature, and culture is capable of making finer distinctions and can, as a result, direct the course of his or her life.[65] Miller's thoughts on the lifelong benefits of a classical education were later echoed by Dramatic Club student manager A. H. Tavernier in 1913, when he identified two advantages of staging classical dramas: the ability to make ethical distinctions and the potential to improve moral character through performance.

While *Journal* editor H. L. Cox, private citizen George Miller, and Dramatic Club manager Tavernier all articulated sound defenses for classicism on campus and beyond, influential Howard academicians such as sociologist Kelly Miller and philosophy professor Alain Locke were actively and effectively reconsidering classicism's relevance in a modern age. Like the champions of classics-based study, the "new education" proponents ranked independent thinking as a primary concern in their search for educational alternatives. In August 1922, Alain Locke wrote an article for the NAACP's *Crisis* magazine that astutely outlined Shakespeare's limits on a Negro campus. While visiting Stratford-upon-Avon, Shakespeare's birthplace, Locke boldly called for the Negro's cultural independence from the Bard and other European masters.

Locke opened his article with an objective assessment of the Howard College Dramatic Club's history, and he pessimistically concluded that to this point Negro drama and theater has "struggled up on the crumbs of the University Dramatic Club. One recalls the lean and patient years it took to pass from faculty advice to faculty supervision and finally to faculty control . . . from hackneyed 'stage successes' to modern and finally original plays, and hardest of all progressions, strange to relate, that from distant and alien themes to the intimate, native and racial."[66] Locke placed quotation marks around "stage successes" because he doubted whether the club's initial productions of well-worn European classics like *She Stoops to Conquer* or *The Merchant of Venice* were in fact commendable and truly advanced club members or the race artistically. The phrase "modern and finally original plays" alluded to the new experiments in dramatic construction and race drama which another Howard professor Thomas Montgomery Gregory envisioned for the Dramatic Club (more on Gregory to come). Unlike the enthusiastic student reviewers who equated Shakespearean productions with progressiveness, Locke believed race drama was the future of Negro artistic expression and that "the vehicle of all sound art must be native to the group—our actors need their own soil, at least for sprouting."[67]

Locke understood how much Shakespeare mattered to world cultures, and he conceded, "[m]usic in which we have so trusted may sing itself around the world." Yet Locke feared Shakespeare offered only foreign soil for Negro artists because the Bard's most masterful work "does not carry ideas, the vehicle of human understanding and respect; it may pierce the heart, but it does not penetrate the mind." Anyone interested in Shakespeare and American education might dispute or dismiss Locke's evaluation of the Bard's capacity for transmitting ideas. Furthermore, as this essay has shown, Anna J. Cooper, Benjamin Brawley, Nathaniel Guy, and various Dramatic Club managers all defended Shakespeare as a universal catalyst for global understanding and respect. But to close his article, Locke used Shakespeare's very own words to highlight where this European master's capacities ended and how the Negro artist must begin. Locke writes, "'I saw Othello's visage in his mind,' says Desdemona explaining her love and respect, so might, so must the world of Othello's mind be put artistically to speech and action."[68] Locke steadfastly believed black educational centers like Howard

University needed to move beyond the artifice of Shakespeare's marginal Moor or the loving warrior-husband produced by Desdemona's deep adoration in order to truly appreciate, understand, and ultimately stage the vastness of Othello's mind and soul.

In the late 1910s, Harvard-educated English professor Thomas Montgomery Gregory assumed faculty control over the Howard College Dramatic Club and implemented an ambitious plan to fully realize the Negro's true speech and action. Gregory aggressively answered the classical/early modern versus modern culture question by igniting a "race" drama revolution. Gregory's major shift in cultural emphasis would relegate Shakespeare to the margins of curricular and extracurricular dramatic activity at Howard, all in the name of unlocking the expressive soul of Afro-America. Montgomery began articulating his plan for a national Negro theater in a literary magazine titled *The Citizen*, first published out of Boston and edited by Charles Lane. In its January 1915 inaugural issue, Gregory linked overall advancement of the race to measurable success in the fine arts, claiming that in order for African Americans to ascend social and cultural hierarchies in the United States, they must develop a significant quota of exceptional artists. Gregory's plan for racial uplift directly contradicted Washington's 1895 Atlanta position. Although vocational, industrial, and professional training was necessary for collective progress, those benchmarks were not enough; the "heroes of the fine arts" would win the Negro much needed respect.[69]

In a second article for *The Citizen*, titled "Race in Art," Gregory identified the current problems hindering Negro art, and one major impediment was the confused racial consciousness produced by a classics-based liberal arts education. From Gregory's perspective, dead languages and Shakespearean comedies were estranging Negro students from the truest sense of themselves. Among the educated and cultured classes, including students at Howard University, Gregory noticed "a regrettable tendency to imitate slavishly the Anglo-Saxon, and this imitation is little better than mimicry . . . [w]e are being educated out of ourselves, out of our race."[70] He further explained how African Americans "have sought to un-race ourselves, to avoid whatever might definitely associate us with the Negro race."[71] Gregory was fundamentally and perhaps unfairly indicting the missions of classicists like Just, Cooper, and Brawley, who associated racial uplift with intellectual and theatrical mastery of established European dramatists. His envisioned shift to the modern and the racial would destabilize nearly four decades of classical emphasis at Howard. Fortunately for Gregory, some Howard students were equally disturbed by this tendency to "un-race" and were ready for a liberal arts curriculum culturally identified as Negro.

The student call for race expression as an alternative to immersion in European high culture appeared in *The Stylus,* a campus literary magazine advised by Thomas Montgomery Gregory. In the June 1916 debut issue, an undergraduate named Campbell Johnson published an article titled "Our Opportunity in Literature" in which he argued that despite advances in education and social refinement, modern Negro literature lacked real soul and substance. He warned, "[i]f the Negro continues to study and attempt the imitation of the literature of other races exclusively . . . he will eventually grow out of himself and lose his race identity."[72] Johnson did not completely reject the study of other literary cultures but rather viewed Shakespeare and Sheridan as starting points to help Negro students appreciate and articulate their daily lives.

Regrettably, many of Johnson's fellow students were not advancing beyond a cultivated, perhaps affected indulgence in all things European. Similar to Locke and Montgomery, Campbell Johnson believed, "[n]o matter how keen the Negro's appreciation of Shakespeare, Dante and Goethe may become, he will never be able to experience the personal pride and receive the inspiration from their genius which the white man receives. It is as if these spirits are members of another household."[73] For young black artists and audiences in search of personal pride and real substance, Johnson figuratively recommended that they "stay at home." To our twenty-first-century ears, Johnson's suggestion may sound dangerously separatist, especially in light of our current postpositivist, nonessentialist, culturally fluid understandings of race and representation. We should bear in mind that Johnson, along with professors Locke and Gregory, was promoting race expression before the invention of the aesthetically redefining Harlem Renaissance or the convergence of social and political unrest later labeled the Civil Rights Movement. At a time when Negro students and professors could find themselves trapped in unproductive exercises in literary imitation, Johnson simply advised black writers to stop measuring themselves against high culture temples erected elsewhere and begin exploring their own ample racial storehouses.

Returning to the significance of staging Shakespeare on a Negro campus, Thomas Montgomery Gregory considered elite Afro-America's devotion to European models another major obstacle to the full flowering of American Negro drama and theater. Prior to launching his national Negro theater agenda, Gregory conducted an informal survey of the "leading dramatic organizations" in black communities. He noticed that many Negro dramatic club leaders harbored a strong prejudice against race plays, and only allowed classical dramas and comedies to be staged. In his "Race in Art" article from *The Citizen,* Gregory lamented that cultured Negroes "love to masquerade as Falstaff, Hamlet or Macbeth and thus they strut about in parts utterly alien to their real selves."[74] I suspect Gregory would concede African Americans could find some aspect of their "real selves" in Shakespearean figures like Hamlet, Othello, and Shylock. Gregory never questioned the intellectual and aesthetic value of European dramatic literature, but he simply objected to so many dramatic societies choosing exclusively to "bedeck" themselves in "borrowed finery" instead of developing a "more vital type of play." By "vital," Gregory envisioned plays firmly rooted in Negro experiences and more specifically theater concentrated on modern issues to which a black majority, not just the college-educated elite, could relate. His primary concern was that the Negro's "slavish imitation" of privileged European culture almost ensured Afro-America would never develop thoroughly liberated and socially relevant artists. Gregory, Locke, and Campbell Johnson all agreed art was fundamentally rooted in individual self-expression and not simply a function of racial or group identity. Yet at this critical moment in early twentieth-century America, they also agreed the true and vital Negro "self" would only be discovered through shared race-expression, and progressive African American artists should elect to join this emergent movement.

Gregory's ambitious plan for a racially rooted dramatic literature and a socially relevant theater answered the culture question by declaring classical literature limited in its ability to cultivate the souls, minds, and hearts of an African American majority. Under his leadership, the curricular and extracurricular agendas of Howard University performance shifted significantly from glorifying established dramatic giants like Shakespeare to nurturing new plays and exploring experimental playmaking approaches. Along the same line as George Pierce Baker's drama workshops at Radcliffe and Harvard, Gregory envisioned Howard University as a laboratory for modern dramatic techniques where the artistic and social potential of Afro-America could be fully realized. To ensure permanent respect for modern drama on campus, Gregory created a Department of Dramatics within the English department, which offered credit and granted degrees in playwriting, acting, and modern dramatic production. Ignoring the skepticism of local critics like *Bee* editor W. Calvin Chase, Gregory structured his college dramatic pro-

gram as a training ground for "the necessary leaders" who could
work productively among the masses.[75]

The Howard College Dramatic Club, renamed the Howard Players, was now committed to staging original works by current undergraduates, alumni, nationally known white playwrights, and even
local writers. Such diversity was all part of Gregory's initiative to create a storehouse of "race" plays to be produced in African American
communities throughout the nation. Although modern dramas constituted the bulk of their new repertoire, the Department of Dramatics and the Howard Players had no plans to completely abandon the
Bard or their former patron base. According to promotional material for the 1922–23 season, written by a faculty member named
Marie Moore-Forrest, the department planned to mount *Othello,*
Shakespeare's racially charged master tragedy. Moore-Forrest and
Gregory selected *Othello* because it had been so infrequently produced in the United States, and a revival would be sure to draw interest from fans of classical drama. In keeping with their early modern
lineage, the Howard Players promised to produce *Othello* "under
conditions closely approximating the Elizabethan theatre."[76]

Archival material on the *Othello* production is sparse, perhaps a
sign that the new department, students, and the entire university
community were emerging out of the initial fascination with European drama. The Howard Players seemed more interested in show-
casing original work like *As Strong as the Hills,* an exotic, gorgeously
staged play written by a fourteen-year-old Washington high school
student named Matalee Lake, or the latest race drama by noted
white playwright Ridgely Torrence. The department planned to conclude its 1922–23 season with a "danse-pantomime" created by Torrence, set in the "creole atmosphere of New Orleans" during
annual Mardi Gras festivities.[77]

When I first began researching early dramatic efforts on "the Hilltop," I never imagined writing an essay that closed with Shakespeare's diminishing curricular and extra-curricular impact on
Howard University. However, such an assessment seems unavoid-
able. Productions of *She Stoops to Conquer, The Merry Wives of Windsor,*
and *The Merchant of Venice* initially generated positive press for this
Negro institution, but this dramatic activity ultimately proved to be
only a preparatory stage in the full development of theatrical performance at Howard. Building on the foundation laid by Just and
Brawley, Thomas Montgomery Gregory expanded the objective of
university theater to developing original dramas which directly
served America and Afro-America. The new degree-granting program and the revamped student dramatic society turned to progres-

sive, yet popular, dramas, some of which addressed pressing social issues only Negro intellectuals and artists could dramatize. Perhaps at odds with the passionate, classicist agendas of past club mentors and managers, Gregory now declared the acclaimed work of a timeless poet too alien, too distant, and too disconnected for Howard's modern age.

NOTES

1. Stephan Talty, *Mulatto America: At the Crossroads of Black and White Culture. A Social History* (New York: Harper Collins, 2003), 96–97.

2. For the origins and early academic structure of Howard University, see Rayford Logan, *Howard University: The First Hundred Years, 1867–1967* (New York: New York University Press, 1969); and Walter Dyson, *Howard University: The Capstone of Negro Education, A History 1867–1940* (Washington, DC: Graduate School of Howard University, 1941).

3. See Nan Johnson, *Nineteenth-Century Rhetoric in North America* (Carbondale: Southern Illinois University Press, 1991); and Philip S. Foner and Robert James Branham, eds., *Lift Every Voice: African American Oratory, 1787–1900* (Tuscaloosa: University of Alabama Press, 1998), introduction.

4. Monroe H. Little, "The Extra-Curricular Activities of Black College Students, 1868–1940," *Journal of Negro History* 65:2 (1980): 137.

5. Dyson, *Howard University: The Capstone*, 146.

6. Washington's September 1895 speech to the Cotton States and International Exposition in Atlanta can be found in Louis R. Harlan, ed., *The Booker T. Washington Papers*, Volume 3 (Urbana: University of Illinois, 1974), 583–87.

7. Kenneth Manning, *Black Apollo of Science: The Life of Ernest Everett Just* (New York: Oxford University Press, 1983), 40.

8. Ibid., 25–26, 40.

9. Errol Hill, *Shakespeare in Sable* (Amherst: University of Massachusetts Press, 1984), 83–84.

10. "She Stoops to Conquer," *Howard University Journal*, April 23, 1909.

11. William Gilbert, "*The Rivals*, Howard College Dramatic Club," *Howard University Journal*, April 18, 1910; and William Gilbert, "The Howard College Dramatic Club," *Howard University Journal*, November 11, 1910.

12. Bishop Wilbur P. Thirkield, "Doctor Just," *Afro-American*, June 16, [1930s?] clipping, Box 16, Ernest Everett Just Folder, Biography File, University Archives, Howard University, Washington, DC.

13. *The Rivals*, program, April 12, 1910, Box 31, Programs Folder 1910–1924, Howard Players File, University Archives, Howard University; and Kathy Perkins, ed., *Black Female Playwrights: An Anthology of Plays before 1950* (Bloomington: Indiana University Press, 1990), 55–56.

14. "Sketch of Benjamin Brawley" typescript, 1989, Box 2, Benjamin Brawley Folder, Biography File, University Archives, Howard University.

15. Gilbert, "The Howard College Dramatic Club."

16. Benjamin Brawley, *A Short History of the English Drama* (London: George G. Harrap, 1921), v, 71.

17. Ibid.

18. "The Merry Wives of Windsor," *Howard University Journal*, March 10, 1911. The cross-dressing Benjamin Locke and the rest of his *Merry Wives* cast were captured in a photograph by famed Washington, DC, photographer Addison N. Scurlock. This image can be seen online at *http://sirismm.si.edu/archivcenter/scurlock/618ps0229585-01hu.jpg*. The image is part of the Scurlock Studio Records, Archives Center, National Museum of American History.

19. William Gilbert, "*The Merry Wives of Windsor*," *Howard University Journal*, February 3, 1911.

20. "*The Merry Wives of Windsor*," *Howard University Journal*, March 10, 1911.

21. Ibid.

22. Joel Berkowitz, "'A True Jewish Jew': Three Yiddish Shylocks," *Theater Survey* 37 (1996): 75–76.

23. John Ripley, "Sociology and Soundscape: Herbert Beerbohm Tree's 1908 Merchant of Venice," *Shakespeare Quarterly* 56 (2005): 385–410, esp. 385, 388.

24. *The Merchant of Venice*, program, May 30, 1913; *A Midsummer Night's Dream*, program, May 31, 1912, Box 164–169, Folder 12, Alain Locke Papers, Moorland-Spingarn Research Center, Howard University.

25. This discussion of Cooper comes from Mary Ellen Washington's introduction in Anna Julia Cooper, *A Voice from the South* (New York: Oxford University Press, 1988), xxxiii–iv.

26. *The Merchant of Venice*, program, April 17, 1915, Box 31, Programs Folder 1910–1924, Howard Players File, Howard University Archives, Howard University.

27. Ibid.

28. Ibid.

29. Ibid.

30. Kim F. Hall, "'Guess Who's Coming to Dinner?' Colonization and Miscegenation in *The Merchant of Venice*," in *New Casebooks: "The Merchant of Venice*," ed. Martin Coyle (New York: St. Martin's Press, 1998), 105.

31. Frederick Douglass, "The Color Line," *North American Review* 132:295 (1881): 568. For more discussion of similar appropriations of Shylock in this collection, see Heather Nathans's "'A course of learning and ingenious studies': Shakespearean Education and Theatre in Antebellum America"; Jonathan M. Burton's "Lay On, McGuffey: Exerpting Shakespeare in Nineteenth-Century Schoolbooks"; and Sandra M. Gustafson's "Eloquent Shakespeare."

32. Brawley, *A Short History of the English Drama*, 89.

33. "English Course Offerings," 1910, Box 18A, Department of English Course Files Folder, English Department File, University Archives, Howard University.

34. Brawley, *Short History*, 59.

35. Ibid., 89.

36. Cooper, *A Voice From the South*, 114–15.

37. Talty, *Mulatto America*, 89.

38. "Sketch of Benjamin Brawley," typescript, 1989, Box 2, Benjamin Brawley Folder, Biography File, University Archives, Howard University.

39. See Mary Helen Washington's introduction to Cooper, *A Voice from the South*; and *The Merchant of Venice*, program, May 30, 1913, Box 164–169, Folder 12, Alain Locke Papers, Moorland-Spingarn Research Center, Howard University.

40. A. H. Tavernier, "The Advantages of the Dramatic Club," *Howard University Journal*, October 10, 1913.

41. "She Stoops to Conquer," *Howard University Journal*, April 23, 1909.

42. "'She Stoops to Conquer' Cast Entertained," *Howard University Journal*, May 7, 1909.

43. "Merry Wives of Windsor," *Howard University Journal*, March 10, 1911.

44. Talty, *Mulatto America*, 84.

45. *The Merchant of Venice*, advertisement, May 30, 1913, Box 164–169, Folder 12, Alain Locke Papers, Moorland-Spingarn Research Center, Howard University.

46. "This Week in Society," *The Bee*, April 24, 1909.

47. Artie, "Footlight Flashes," *The Bee*, May 4, 1912.

48. R. W. T., "Theatrical Chit-Chat," *The Bee*, June 7, 1913.

49. *The Bee*, March 27, 1915.

50. Gilbert, "The Merry Wives of Windsor," *Howard University Journal*, February 3, 1911.

51. A. H. Tavernier, "The Advantages of the Dramatic Club," *Howard University Journal*, October 10, 1913.

52. G. David Houston, "Richelieu," *Howard University Journal*, February 27, 1914.

53. "Educated Negro Women Are Assailed," *The Bee*, April 19, 1909.

54. This discussion of the "M Street Controversy" comes from Mary Helen Washington's introduction in Cooper, *A Voice From The South*.

55. "College Graduates," *The Bee*, April 17, 1915.

56. Ibid.

57. For a brief biography of E. E. Frazier, see the Howard University Social Work Library website at http://www.howard.edu/library/Social_Work_Library/Franklin_Frazier.htm. Also see *The Merchant of Venice*, program, April 17, 1915, Box 31, Programs Folder 1910–1924, Howard Players File, University Archives, Howard University.

58. Logan, *Howard University: The First Hundred Years*, 139.

59. Ibid., 21, 156.

60. Ibid., 154–55.

61. Dyson, *Howard University*, 109–111.

62. Ibid., 112.

63. H. L. Cox, "Classics at Howard," *Howard University Journal*, November 26, 1909.

64. Ibid.

65. George Frazier Miller, "A Reply to 'Classics at Howard,'" *Howard University Journal*, December 10, 1909.

66. Alain Locke, "Steps Toward a Negro Theatre," *Crisis* 25:2 (1922): 67.

67. Ibid., 66–67.

68. Ibid., 68.

69. T. Montgomery Gregory, "The Fine Arts and Race Ascendancy," *The Citizen* 1:1 (1915): 3–4.

70. Montgomery Gregory, "Race in Art," *The Citizen* 1:2 (1915): 46.

71. Ibid.

72. Campbell Johnson, "Our Opportunity In Literature," *Stylus Magazine* 1:1 (1916): 9, Box 18B, Department of English Publications/Stylus Folder, English Department File, University Archives, Howard University.

73. Ibid.

74. Gregory, "Race in Art," 48.

75. Montgomery Gregory, "Drama at Howard University—A Vision," *The Howard University Record* 14, no.8 (1920): 441. Also see Howard University Department of Dramatics, "The Negro Theatre," brochure, Box 37–3, Folder 9; and Kenneth MacGowan, "Negro University has Dramatic Department on Lines of Harvard's Play-Acting Toward a Degree," *New York Globe*, March 26, 1921, clipping, Box 37–3, Folder 97, both in the Thomas Montgomery Gregory Collection, Moorland-Spingarn Research Center, Howard University.

76. Marie Moore-Forrest, "The Department of Dramatic Arts at Howard University, A Significant Experiment in American Drama," typescript, 1922, Box 37–3, Folder 80, Thomas Montgomery Gregory Collection, Moorland-Spingarn Research Center, Howard University.

77. See "Howard Players Stage Torrence's New Race Drama," *Chicago Defender*, December 24, 1921, clipping, Box 37–3, Folder 95; and Moore-Forrest, "Department of Dramatic Arts at Howard University," typescript, 1922, Box 37–3, Folder 80, both in Thomas Montgomery Gregory Collection, Moorland-Spingarn Research Center, Howard University.

Outdistancing the Past:
Shakespeare and American Education at the 1934 Chicago World's Fair

Rosemary Kegl

IN 1934, DURING THE SECOND YEAR OF THE CHICAGO WORLD'S FAIR, FAIR organizers introduced to their Street of Villages a concession variously entitled the English Village, Old England, and Merrie England. Throughout the five months of the 1934 season, Merrie England advertised among its attractions Ruth Pryor and her Chicago-based ballet company; madrigal singers; mummers; morris dancers; Elizabethan pageants; acrobats; ping-pong tournaments; a small and scantily clad fan-dancing monkey named Jimmie; horses, dogs, and clowns from the Royal English Circus; jugglers; a strolling gypsy; a trained bear act; and, for an additional charge, forty-minute productions of Shakespeare's plays staged throughout the afternoon and evening in the village's reconstructed Globe Theatre.[1] Between the Globe's inaugural performance of *The Taming of the Shrew* on May 27 and the performance of *A Midsummer Night's Dream* that ended only moments before the World Fair's closing on Halloween night, the Old Globe Players offered fairgoers over one thousand performances from a repertoire that included—in addition to *Taming of the Shrew* and *A Midsummer Night's Dream*—*All's Well That Ends Well, As You Like It, The Comedy of Errors, Julius Caesar, King Lear, Macbeth,* Marlowe's *Doctor Faustus,* and Shaw's *Dark Lady.*[2]

The Chicago World's Fair, more commonly known as the Century of Progress Exposition, was devoted to the scientific and technological advances that had transformed the lives of fairgoers over the last hundred years and that would continue to "outdistance anything of the past." Efforts to justify the Globe's presence in terms of progress over the last century, or futuristic claims about the next, inevitably sounded a bit strained. During the Globe Theatre's opening ceremonies on May 8, Thomas Wood Stevens, who had overseen the reconstruction of the Merrie England's Globe and would produce its abbreviated plays, explained that "our goal is to adhere to the progress that has been made in the rediscovery of the Elizabethan method of production, and a more authentic treatment of Shakespeare. Throughout the nineteenth century Shakespeare's plays were merely vehicles for stars of the stage. But now we are exhibiting plays strictly along the line of the discoveries made by the Elizabethan Stage Society—and that is progress."[3] In spite of this and other similarly inauspicious attempts to use progress and Shakespeare in the same sentence, Merrie England and its plays were well suited to the fair. Fair officials estimated that over 1.23 million fairgoers entered Merrie England during the five months of the 1934 World's Fair, and that over 331,000 of Merrie England's visitors, including at least 17,000 children, attended performances at the Globe. Among the visitors was a young Sam Wanamaker, who credited the village with providing childhood inspiration for his adult commitment to reconstructing the Globe Theatre in England.[4] Stevens and his Old Globe Players later brought their abbreviated plays to a short-lived double bill with Hollywood films at Chicago's McVickers Theater and, with more success, to engagements at Chicago's Studebaker Theatre, at theaters in over thirty other Midwestern cities and university towns, and at expositions in San Diego, Cleveland, and Dallas.[5] Between 1934 and 1937, twelve abbreviated Shakespeare plays—the eight produced at the Chicago World's Fair and four added to the Old Globe Players' repertoire—were printed and distributed by Samuel French "as an assistance to producers of amateur performances where the facilities for giving the play in its entirety are not available."[6]

This essay focuses on the aspirations and everyday realities that linked the Century of Progress, the Chicago public schools, and the tradition of "Elizabethan staging" to which both the Merrie England productions and the Samuel French publications were indebted. I find these connections a compelling antidote to the usual characterization of the late nineteenth- and early twentieth-century "Elizabethan staging" of Shakespeare's plays as eccentric. When fair organizers reviewed applications for concession space at the 1934 exposition, they were receptive to an English Village that promised to convey an "atmosphere of dignity, peace, quiet and repose, and have no exhibits, side-shows, nor entertainment which could be regarded as offensive to good taste and decency." Its "high standards" and "decency" offered an alternative to the Live Models exhibit and the Sally Rand fan dances that had been controversially successful during the 1933 fair: Merrie England was advertised as possessing so enviable a civilizing capacity that, less than a month after the fair's closing, the village's president, William E. Vogelback, would recall that "on children's day, when hundreds of thousands of children were let loose, they damaged other concessions in a ruthless fashion—but when they came into the English Village they were as well behaved as in a Sunday School class." And yet, although Vogelback also would recall with satisfaction the long lines of theatergoers that waited to see Merrie England's abbreviated Shakespeare plays, he had been advised during the initial planning for the village that the Old Globe and its "Elizabethan method of production" would be "out of place"—an eccentric choice for a world's fair. The skeptics suggested, instead, Gilbert and Sullivan, music hall vaudeville, or single acts from classical plays. Critics now often claim that the "discoveries made by the Elizabethan stage society" under the direction of William Poel in the late nineteenth and early twentieth centuries contributed to the fashioning of contemporary theatrical practices by helping us to re-envision the production of Shakespeare's plays. And yet even those who would allow Poel a central place in theater history tend to agree with Vogelback's skeptical advisors that Poel's productions were eccentric by design— marginal, experimental, archaeological, scholarly, not terribly lucrative—and, what is more crucial for my purposes, tend to overlook their intersection with more mainstream cultural and social phenomena.[7]

In the first section of this essay, I argue that the fair's "Elizabethan staging" of Shakespeare's plays was quite compatible with very specific contemporary trends in Chicago public school education, including the use of visual materials and the use of Shakespeare throughout the curriculum. I begin by charting how the fair, local schools, and the abbreviated Shakespeare plays eventually settled into what best might be described as a mutually beneficial coexistence. Both the settling and the bumpy road along the way provide a glimpse into the pressures and ambivalences that defined the national project of public school education in the 1930s. This section of the essay then considers, through the lens of those pressures and ambivalences, the long deferred inclusion of Merrie England and its abbreviated productions in the fair's educational brochures and high school tour information. In the final section of this essay, I shift my attention from these mutually beneficial everyday practices and extend my analysis of the intersections among the fair's "Elizabethan staging" and more mainstream phenomena by examining the curious combination of conviction and reticence shared by fair organizers, public school educators, and the proponents of

"Elizabethan staging" when they imagine the effects of their work in the future.

As early as 1931, fair organizers began to promote the "greatest collection of study and teaching material ever assembled" by announcing a "series of small books on scientific subjects" that were to be "popularly and non-technically styled for general reading," and by publishing a weekly promotional magazine called *Progress*. *Progress* described coming attractions and showcased the can-do attitude of fair employees whose knowledge of scientific discoveries and their industrial applications made staging the World's Fair possible.[8] World's Fair organizers were zealous in their attempts to extend the benefits of their "twenty-five million dollar entertainment and educational venture" into elementary and secondary school classrooms without violating their general policy that the fair never pay for publicity.[9] In the two years before the fair opened in spring 1933, organizers placed articles and photos in a number of national publications for educators, including *Practical Educator, Progressive Education,* and *United Educator.* In 1931 the managing editor of the *Chicago Schools Journal,* the official board of education organ for the Chicago public school system, promised to bring to the attention of the city's fourteen thousand teachers the "possibility of correlating and coordinating their class room work with the development of the World's Fair."[10] After protracted wrangling, fair representatives secured a free booth at the February 1933 meetings of the National Education Association in Minnesota. That same year, the Progressive Educators of America promised to advertise the fair during their March meetings in Chicago. Fair representatives previewed fair exhibits at teachers' clubs, in classrooms, and at school assemblies. They responded to requests from schools for library copies of *Progress* and from teachers for information that might supplement classroom curricula—on Europe, on Asia, on home life in different countries—that were linked to proposed exhibits. And they invited school groups throughout the Chicago area, and teachers and administrators attending local meetings of the National Association of Public School Officials, the National Education Association, and the Progressive Educators of America to visit their fair-in-process.[11]

The narrative offered over the last paragraph conveys something of the urgency that tends to accrue, even after several decades, to the fair's interoffice memos, press releases, and everyday correspondence. The archives of the Chicago Board of Education in the 1930s, on the other hand, provide only glancing references in a few yearbooks to the Century of Progress Exposition.[12] Instead the archived collection of school board minutes and the local newspapers under-score a conspicuous twist in the story of the fair's attempt to partner with Chicago public school teachers. In the weeks immediately pre-ceding the 1933 opening of the fair, the teachers repeatedly used the Century of Progress Exposition to draw attention to several years of irregular paychecks followed by, as of that April, eight and a half months without any pay at all. In early April, "one thousand unpaid teachers" disrupted the fair's first flag-raising ceremony by "clamor-ously marching in circles around the open-air platform." A few weeks later over twenty thousand teachers, pupils, and parents formed a "Mile-Long Parade" through the city's downtown streets, one group carrying a "small crepe-lined coffin on which was a sign bearing the words 'Public Education in Chicago—As Some Would Have It.'" The protestors paused in Grant Park to haul down the Century of Progress flag and replace it with an American flag.[13]

The shift in flags drew attention to one of the protestors' recur-rent themes: that the local plight of Chicago's teachers indicated the more general desire, or at the very least, willingness of legislators and businessmen to cripple the nascent system of free universal pub-lic education on which a healthy American democracy depended. In this context it is not surprising that the Century of Progress Exposi-tion—already conveniently in the public eye—merited the teachers' special attention. The exposition's president, Rufus Cutler Dawes, and its general manager, Lennox Lohr, were quoted widely on the business acumen and applied engineering skills that allowed them, in the midst of the Depression, to organize the first fair that was shielded from indebtedness by a combination of industry- and gov-ernment-sponsored exhibits, self-supporting concessions, a favor-able Depression-era labor market, creative practices for reimbursing the fair's workers, ticket sales, and fair bonds purchased by wealthy individuals.[14] And yet, protesters emphasized, the same industries and individuals who mustered the political will and economic wherewithal to support Chicago's fair seemed all too willing to let its public school system falter and, should their gamble on the fair's beneficial effect on the local economy pay off, certainly could not be depended upon to extend those benefits to public school teachers.

Bankers were among those singled out for ire as "men of large consequence" whose fortunes hinged on federal intervention and yet who were reluctant to extend loans to the teachers or to support their efforts to lobby the Senate's banking and currency committee for shifts in loan regulations. At the end of April, a day-long Pay Demonstration of five thousand teachers targeted five Chicago banks unwilling to assist public school teachers. The president of

one of those banks, the Central Republic Bank and Trust Company
of Chicago, was Charles Gates Dawes, former Vice President of the
United States and former director of the federal Reconstruction
Finance Committee through which his struggling bank had recently
received a well-publicized $90-million loan. He was also brother to
the Century of Progress's president, Rufus Cutler Dawes, and chairman of the fair's finance committee. Relations between teachers and
the fair were not improved when Charles Dawes, never a man to
shrink from quotable lapses in public tact, shouted to the assembled
crowd, "To hell with the trouble-makers." Over the next several
months, newspaper stories inevitably mentioned Dawes's sentiment
as they chronicled the effects of "delayed pay" on Chicago's public
school employees, including the protestors' claims of bankruptcies,
nervous diseases, insanity, and the malnutrition-induced death on
the job of a school custodian. A few weeks after Dawes's outburst,
five thousand schoolchildren, accompanied by their teachers,
marched to Grant Park where they burned "Banker Dawes" in
effigy.[15] Teachers from Minnesota, Missouri, New York, Ohio, Virginia, Wisconsin, and New Brunswick wrote in outrage to a fair that
they pledged to boycott in solidarity with their Chicago colleagues,
and the National Education Association announced that it had been
flooded with letters demanding that their summer meetings no
longer be held in conjunction with the World's Fair.[16]

Several educational organizations eventually did meet at the fair
that summer of 1933, including, at the urging of Chicago public
school teachers, the National Education Association.[17] Their members were invited to visit the Social Sciences Building where the fair's
permanent displays depicting key educational transformations over
the last century in curriculum, enrollment, facilities, textbooks, and
student demographics temporarily included two operating junior
high and high school classes whose discussions and lectures were
broadcast over the radio for fifteen minutes every hour; the teachers
and their students, fifty-four boys and girls of "diverse stocks," spent
eight weeks modeling to fairgoers and radio audiences the effects of
those educational transformations in classrooms that used the
"exposition as their textbook."[18] The model classes demonstrated
the shifts in public education over the past one hundred years that
brought this particular combination of students together, offered
them a free high school education, included courses in social science and art within the curriculum, and understood the pedagogical value of educational motion pictures, radio programming, and
field trips. These emphases were in keeping with the permanent
educational exhibits whose "century of public school progress"

unfolded through "charts showing the national increase in school enrollment from 13,000,000 to 28,000,000 in the last forty years, and the doubling of the high school enrollment in the last twelve," "lighted transparencies depicting the present-day activities of the Chicago schools, ranging from music appreciation and creative art through shop work, school gardens and adult education to individual training for the handicapped," and a "model of the log school house of 1833, set beside one of the palatial schools covering acres and accommodating thousands, typical of the modern city . . . [and] paralleled by a similar expansion of the curriculum to suit thousands of varying childish needs."[19] During the same summer weeks that the fair's model classes were in session, the Chicago Board of Education recommended higher student-teacher ratios, suspended the purchase of textbooks and musical instruments, dismissed or reassigned several thousand teachers and administrators, and cut or severely curtailed—under the rubric of "so-called 'extra-curricula' activities, embellishments, or 'fads and frills' "—the very programs most often associated with the schools' transformed and expanded responsibilities, including music classes, orchestra, band, fine arts, industrial arts, visual education, physical education, household arts, vocational guidance, kindergarten, continuation school, parental schools, adult lectures, and education for students with physical or learning disabilities. The irony was not lost on commentators, one of whom noted that a "reversal to medievalism in education methods is a strange and sad accompaniment to Chicago's celebration of a Century of Progress."[20]

Even as their attempts to partner with local educators suffered repeated setbacks, fair organizers remained determined to attract children and teachers to the Century of Progress Exposition. Children visited the fair in large numbers in 1933 and in the spring and summer of 1934, taking advantage of reduced admission and concession fees on the weekly Children's Day, participating in contests (for the healthiest children, the most freckled children, the most accomplished whistlers and pie-eaters, the owners of the most impressive dolls and buggies), and entering essay competitions sponsored by the Keep Chicago Ahead Committee.[21] Educators were well-publicized guests at the fair throughout its 1933 and early 1934 incarnations. The fair cohosted the "largest and most comprehensive scientific meeting of its kind to be held anywhere" when the summer session of the American Association for the Advancement of Science and its forty affiliated societies convened in Chicago in June 1933, offered a symposium on progressive education sponsored by the Chicago Woman's Club in September 1933, coordi-

nated with the American Association for the Advancement of
Science in announcing an Engineers' Day at the fair in the summer
of 1933, coordinated with the Education Emergency Program of the
Civil Works Educational Service in announcing an Adult Education
Day in the summer of 1934, and sponsored during that same summer an International Typing Contest for students enrolled in commercial schools in the United States and Canada.[22]

But it was not until a $22.5-million federal loan resolved the press-
ing problem of the teachers' salaries during the summer of 1934
that fair officials saw an opportunity to launch an ambitious program of autumn school tours that would transform their exposition
"into one big classroom" where students might exchange "chalk
and text-books for an intensive course of visual instruction." Chicago public school teachers found enclosed in their first paycheck a
complimentary ticket to the Teachers' Jubilee Day at the Century of
Progress. The eight thousand teachers who attended the Jubilee Day
in early August enjoyed reduced prices throughout the fair; free
pamphlets explaining "exhibits in simple terms which are especially
suitable for classroom use"; open entry to one concession, Merrie
England; and preliminary information about the school tour program that would begin in September. Fair organizers asked a committee composed of representatives from elementary schools,
secondary schools, technical schools, universities, museums, the Illinois State Emergency Relief Commission, and the exposition's contributing departments and exhibits to survey the fair's exhibits and
concessions with an eye to coordinating school tours with ongoing
classroom instruction. Over the next few weeks, teachers in public
and private schools, in Chicago and across the country, received
educational brochures, suggested itineraries, and sample syllabi that
would allow them to craft, in consultation with fair representatives,
individualized fair tours. Although press releases announcing the
tours included instances of the fair's characteristic overreaching—
claiming, for instance, that "one such well planned efficient tour is
worth a semester's work in the school room"—they more typically
struck the mildly deferential tone of a knowledgeable junior partner, describing the fair's educational niche as "supplementing class
room work" by providing "visualized material in the basic fields of
knowledge."[23]

The fair's promotional materials were quick to point out that
schools across the nation participated in the tour program and that
the tours' appeal in the Chicago area extended throughout the city
and suburbs among students and teachers affiliated with public
schools; with private Catholic schools administered by the Archdio-
cese of Chicago; and with smaller private schools, including those

associated with the Progressive Education movement. Even so, the Chicago public schools constituted the largest and most visible portion of a local constituency that was disproportionately represented in the tour program. Their superintendent, William J. Bogan, was everywhere present in the educational activities of the fair, from the earliest pre-fair planning through the designing of the school tours. The media coverage of their financial crises had discussed, in the same breath, the fate of the schools and the financing and marketing of the fair. And the newspaper articles that depict the early fraught relations between the fair and the Chicago public schools and the Board of Education's subsequent "reversal to medievalism" provide, at least in the aggregate, a relatively textured record of the range of contemporary wisdom about the ingredients necessary for a sound public education under the twin pressures of democracy and the unprecedented growth and perceived disparities in capacities, experiences, and needs of the students now occupying the desks of the nation's classrooms. The fair's persistent emphasis on exchanging textbooks for visual instruction, like its more fleeting references to "project learning" and school assembly presentations, announces the school tours as in keeping with a widespread acceptance by elementary and secondary public school teachers of the techniques—or, at least, the language—associated with a number of educational initiatives developed in response to those pressures.[24]

The use of visual materials tended to straddle two pedagogical impulses—responding to the multiple and idiosyncratic educational needs of an individual child, and ensuring that the curriculum was commonly, if not identically, accessible to students who were entering the public schools with an increasingly disparate set of academic and non-academic experiences. The practices grouped under the rubric of "visual learning" in the Chicago schools included an assortment of materials and teaching strategies. An essay on visual instruction included in the 1937 Annual Report of the Superintendent of Schools claims that "pictorial material" produces an "increase of educational efficiency, ranging from 10 percent to 35 percent" and that visual materials like slides and films have replaced single textbooks, especially in rapidly changing fields like the sciences. A few years earlier, Bogan adopted an even more pervasive impressionistic language when he advised elementary school educators to "use visual material—slides, motion pictures, films, museum materials—to awaken imagination." In Chicago's primary and secondary classrooms, visual instruction included exercises in composing, acting in, viewing, and responding to drama. Bogan suggests that teachers incorporate dramatics into their kindergarten through

third-grade curricula and compiles extensive lists of grade-appropriate anthologies with titles like *A Book of Plays for Little Actors, Children's Classics in Dramatic Form, Little Plays for Little Players,* and
Dialogues for Little Folks. In his advice for teaching slightly older primary school students, "dramatizations," "dramatic sketches," and
pantomimes appear among suggested individual or group exercises
and "attending plays, special programs, or entertainments" among
suggested class excursions. The use of drama as a form of visual
instruction in primary school was continuous with Chicago School
Board advice about how best to teach plays to high school students.
Bogan's 1932 "Course of Study in English Literature in Senior High
Schools, Grades XI–XII," suggests as "further enrichment" during
the ten-week drama unit "dramatization of scenes or parts of
scenes," writing a one-act play, or interpreting difficult passages by
using pictures, drawings, or puppet shows. A school board publication by the Committee on the Course in Dramatics demonstrates
how a more intensive study of drama would fulfill required and elective portions of the high school curriculum. In keeping with its
three-part mantra that a "play is (1) a story devised to be presented
(2) by actors (3) on the stage," the committee suggests individual
and group exercises in pantomime and short class performances,
and, if possible, a field trip to a Shakespearean play.[25] The fair followed the schools' lead in using theatrical techniques—the continuous marionette productions of the history of food preservation
come to mind—to enliven and make commonly accessible even the
most unpromising of topics. It directed those elementary school students and teachers interested in drama and able to afford the fees
associated with fair concessions to the children's exhibits on the
Enchanted Island whose attractions included a dramatization of the
Buck Rogers comic strip and marionette productions of Peter Rab-
bit, Winnie the Pooh, and Punch and Judy. And it directed secondary school students and teachers to a number of pageants, including
the popular "Wings of a Century," and the productions in Merrie
England.[26]

The Globe Theatre productions had a modest presence in the
educational materials and press releases that eventually brought
between 250,000 and 300,000 elementary and secondary school students to the fair in September and October of 1934. Free exhibits
predominated over concessions like Merrie England, and given the
fair's focus, those exhibits disproportionately focused on the sciences and social sciences. Even the reduced fees available to students and teachers touring the fair and to those entering Merrie
England were never extended to the Globe's productions.[27] The

record of direct contact between the schools and the Merrie England productions is concentrated during the high school tours scheduled during the final few weeks of the 1934 fair—a query from one ninth-grade teacher, the inclusion of Merrie England and its Globe productions among the paid exhibits in the History and Civics syllabus and the Geography and History section of the fair's educational brochure, a promise from the English Village to reserve seats for high school tour groups at the 2 p.m. Globe performances, the claim in one promotional article that English teachers and high school principals hoped to see the abbreviated plays produced in Chicago after the fair's closing, and newspaper articles announcing a village-sponsored essay contest on the plays of Shakespeare at the Old Globe whose submissions would be judged on their "originality, power of expression, and evident personal reaction to the performances at the Globe theater."[28]

Teasing out the implications of this relatively sparse but suggestive record requires a brief review of the "Elizabethan method of production" that students and teachers would have encountered at the fair. In claiming that Merrie England would be "exhibiting plays strictly along the line of the discoveries made by the Elizabethan Stage Society," Stevens located the village's Globe productions within a theatrical tradition most closely associated with William Poel. Poel had established the Society in 1894 in an effort to revive the "masterpieces of the Elizabethan drama upon the stage for which they were written, so as to represent them as nearly as possible under the conditions existing at the time of their first production— that is to say, with only those stage appliances and accessories which were employed during the Elizabethan period"; when Merrie England opened its gates in 1934, he had been advocating the use of Elizabethan stage techniques for over half of the fair's Century of Progress. Poel was convinced that the "stage for which Shakespeare had written was radically different from that of [his] own era, and that those differences had determined the audience's perceptions of Shakespeare's plays." Although Poel's productions did reduce and rearrange the texts of Renaissance plays, he resisted nineteenth-century editing practices that envisioned plays as a series of tableaus or isolated speeches that favored a highly bankable star system. He insisted on intralinear editing that retained what he called the "fable," the dialogue and interactions among characters that he interpreted as most crucial to an experience of the play as a whole. He trained his actors to speak swiftly and to rely on an elaborately worked out "Elizabethan" pattern of modulation and inflection that approximated a chant. He argued for a continuity of action, without interruption between scenes or acts. He eliminated the contemporary cluttering of the stage with props and scenery and was particularly resistant to the costume dramas of his day whose productions of Shakespeare's plays would attempt to recreate not the Elizabethan dress of the original productions but Macbeth's Scotland or Julius Caesar's Rome. And, when possible, he preferred a platform stage that brought the actors closer to the audience and a set with upper, lower, outer, and inner playing spaces.[29]

Both Stevens and his assistant during the fair, Ben Iden Payne, had collaborated with Poel earlier in their careers. In 1916, while serving as the first chair of the drama program at the Carnegie Institute of Technology, Stevens had invited Poel to introduce the Institute's students to his Elizabethan methods for three weeks in the early summer and then to direct a production of *The Poetaster* the following autumn. During Payne's tenure as stage director for Manchester's Gaiety Theatre, he had arranged for Poel to work with the repertory company, first as the director of their 1908 production of *Measure for Measure,* in which Payne played the role of Lucio and Poel the role of Angelo, and then, two years later, as an actor in the company's production of *The Cloister.* For the production of *Measure for Measure,* Poel supervised the building of an Elizabethan stage inside the proscenium arches of the Gaiety Theatre and introduced the then-skeptical Payne to his repertoire of Elizabethan stage techniques.[30]

The Merrie England productions followed from Poel's efforts to convey the vitality of a drama neither designed for nor suited to the modern theater and yet differed from his Elizabethan methods of production in at least three crucial ways. First, they numbered among Payne's experiments with a "modified Elizabethan staging," designed to be less off-putting than Poel's methods to a modern audience. Mindful that he had initially considered Poel's staging of *Measure for Measure* a "pedantic archaism," Payne advocated a less thoroughgoing immersion in the past. His productions observed two essential theatrical practices—swift and continuous performances, uninterrupted by breaks between acts or scenes, and the strategic use of what he called the six playing "zones" of an upper stage, an inner "discovery" stage, and a lower stage divided into the foreground, middle, and two sides. Second, unable to raise the funds necessary for a reconstructed theater, Poel had to be content with, when fire regulations permitted, the "Fortune fit-up," a collapsible and portable set, based loosely on the Fortune contracts and Swan drawings, and inserted within a theater's existing proscenium arches. The Merrie England productions—at least those at the expositions in Chicago, San Diego, Cleveland, and Dallas—took place in well-publicized miniature Globes, inspired by the Vissher and Hollar illustrations and the contracts for the Fortune theater. The Chicago Globe was an octagonal building that seated roughly four hundred spectators and featured a blue star-studded ceiling in order to convey the effect of an open-air theater. A few weeks before the opening of the 1934 fair, Stevens and Marc T. Nielson, general manager of the fair's Globe Productions, announced:

> Here we have for the first time a real Elizabethan stage and a practical entire theater such as was used in Shakespeare's day. The so-called Elizabethan methods have always been makeshift. . . . But now, for once, an Elizabethan stage is being built that will permit us to give short, carefully worked-out versions of Shakespeare—not individual scenes or acts, but versions so constructed that they will present the highlights and motifs of the essential characters presented. We shall at last be able to present Shakespeare in the Elizabethan method and in a theater especially designed for that purpose.

As these remarks suggest, the Merrie England plays did follow Poel's rough editing guidelines, presumably reinforced by Payne's general policy as a director that "dialogue may be judiciously cut" as long as "sense and meter," the "'melodic line' of action, as well as the pace" were respected. And yet—and this is the productions' third divergence from Poel's stage practices—the editors of the much-abbreviated Merrie England plays were necessarily much more ruthless than Poel in their decisions about eliminating entire acts and scenes. For instance, the 36-minute *Taming of the Shrew* omits the framing device of Christopher Sly and ends after Petruchio explains to the audience his plan to "kill a wife with kindness"; the 45-minute *A Midsummer Night's Dream* focuses on the Interlude; the 45-minute *Julius Caesar* ends with Marc Antony's speech at Caesar's funeral. Even *Macbeth,* the longest of the Merrie England productions at 60 minutes and, as the prefatory note explains, "one of the shortest plays of Shakespeare, and hence [requiring] less cutting than the others in the Globe repertory," eliminates a number of scenes and passages, including the scene in which Macduff's young son is murdered.[31]

The fair's "modified Elizabethan staging" of abbreviated Shakespeare plays was entirely compatible with the emphasis on visual learning and, at the high school level, the use of Shakespeare throughout the curriculum in the Chicago public schools. For instance, the Merrie England productions dovetailed quite nicely

with Chicago School Board publications recommending that secondary school teachers assign, as the basis of interpretive readings
or acting exercises, brief excerpts from Shakespeare's plays to convey the expectations of Renaissance audiences and the history of literary styles, dramatic forms, theatrical spaces, and stage practices.
Poel believed that, in addition to illuminating the history of literature and theater, the "conventions of the Elizabethan stage emphasized the beauty of the language, continuity of the action, and clarity
of the story line . . . Poel's premise was that Shakespearean criticism
and production are inseparable." In his 1898 *An Account of the Elizabethan Stage Society,* Poel recalls that the Stage Society performed
Twelfth Night, The Comedy of Errors, and *The Tempest* "at St. George's
Hall to students of the High Schools, who assembled there to the
number of six or seven hundred, when the play was one they had
prepared for the Cambridge Local Examination. Text-books are not
sufficient for the study of Shakespeare. Much that is obscure in the
dialogue becomes intelligible when action is added." When complete Shakespeare plays appeared on required and recommended
Chicago high school reading lists beginning in the ninth grade, students were asked to develop a number of analytic and expressive
skills, including several that Poel's Elizabethan stage techniques, the
Old Globe Players' "carefully worked-out versions of Shakespeare,"
and the village's essay contest aspired to reinforce: analyses of plot,
diction, and character; an ability to imagine the visual and auditory
traits of the plays on stage; and an appreciation of literature that
involved reflecting on the pleasures of reading and interpretation.[32]
Finally, the fair's high school tour information located the Globe
productions among Merrie England's many attractions, and the village itself appeared among the "History" offerings in the tour program's "History and Civics" syllabus; the syllabus directs teachers
interested in the Globe productions and pageants on the village
green to the "Geography and History" section of the fair's educational brochure, where they would learn that the "village portrays
life of the time of Queen Elizabeth" and that the Globe's plays, like
the pageant "trial of Mary Queen of Scots, before Queen Elizabeth"
on the village green, contribute to the "atmosphere of old
England." It is doubtful that a village whose "Elizabethan focus"
extended to reconstructions of Samuel Johnson's and James Bos-
well's Cheshire Cheese Inn, Charles Dickens's The Old Curiosity
Shop, and Robert Burns's cottage would have provided a solid foundation for an English history syllabus. On the other hand, the village's pageants (including the trial of Mary Queen of Scots, an
encounter between Queen Elizabeth and Sir Walter Raleigh, the

return of Sir Francis Drake to England from the Americas, and a yuletide play of "St. George and the Dragon" presented before Queen Elizabeth and her court) might have been attractive to those Chicago high school teachers who followed Bogan's general advice to incorporate visual learning into their lesson plans. The pageants would also have reinforced the more particular advice to use excerpts from Shakespeare's plays to make vivid the "historical background" of English literature, including the intellectual and cultural effects of Puritanism, the defeat of the Armada, and the European exploration of the Americas. And the village's yuletide play—like its morris dancers, mummers, and madrigal singers— would have complemented the Globe productions' emphasis on the history of dramatic forms and theatrical practices.[33]

Samuel French's editions of the twelve abbreviated Shakespeare plays presented by the Old Globe Players during the fair and over the next few years would have been particularly appropriate for those high school teachers in Chicago's public schools who, again in keeping with contemporary advice, arranged dramatic exercises in class as a supplement to discussions of theater history and to the reading of complete Shakespeare plays, to high school drama clubs whose productions for assemblies and for the public seem to have been shielded somewhat from the schools' financial pressures, and to audiences unaffiliated with secondary schools, including those amateur university and community drama groups that were devoted, on the balance, less to study and declamation than to the acting of plays. By the 1930s, French had established a longstanding reputation as a publisher of affordable short plays for classroom productions and of affordable acting editions for amateur theater groups; the advertisements that accompany French's 1959 reprint of Merrie England's *Julius Caesar* and 1962 reprint of Merrie England's *The Comedy of Errors* suggest the endurance of that reputation. Although the wording of the editions' copyright notices vary slightly, they generally permit the plays to be "presented by amateurs without payment of royalty." The Note pages that preface each edition tend to mention the length of the performance, the nature of the deletions (with occasional tips for accommodating weak casts and, in the case of longer plays like *King Lear,* for further cutting), and, referring to the "Stage at the Globe Theatre" illustration that appears in the editions' front matter, the traits crucial to a successful staging with particular emphasis on the "Elizabethan" methods associated with the fair's productions (use of stage zones, rapid and continuous action, minimal props and scenery, Renaissance costuming).[34]

The sorts of amateur groups that would have found French's Merrie England editions compelling also are prominent in the varied careers of Poel, Stevens, and Payne. In a 1918 essay, "Children as Actors," Poel recalls with enthusiasm his experimental production of *The Comedy of Errors* in which all of the actors were young boys and girls from a London school. The student performance was the logical extension of Poel's insistence that "textbooks are not sufficient for the study of Shakespeare" and of his preference for amateur actors, a preference shaped by both the financial limitations and the artistic aspirations of his projects. The Elizabethan Stage Society, with which Poel staged some of his best-remembered productions— including *The Comedy of Errors* at Gray's Inn, *Twelfth Night* at the Middle Temple, *Doctor Faustus* at St. George's Hall, and *Everyman* at the Charterhouse—was also an amateur group. It emerged, in conception and partly in composition, from the Shakespeare Reading Society, which had been organized by students from London University College and whose recitals and directed readings Poel had overseen as early as 1887. Amateur productions also figure in the developing mission of the Carnegie Institute of Technology drama program under the leadership of Stevens and Payne. Stevens had founded and chaired at the Carnegie Institute the first drama program to award a university degree. Payne worked with Stevens at the Institute and, when Stevens resigned in 1925 to manage Chicago's Goodman Theatre, served as the drama program's second chair. In his memoir, Payne recalls that, although a number of Carnegie students eventually established distinguished careers as professional actors, he and Stevens placed two students as directors of high school productions as early as the year of their first graduating class; the program's eventual emphasis not only on acting but on the "technical side of production" is a testament to their students' success in this high school placement.[35]

Over the last many pages, I have traced the aspirations and everyday realities of the Century of Progress, its Old Globe productions, and the Chicago public school curriculum with an eye to their intersecting everyday practices. In the final section of this essay, I extend my remarks about the intersection of the fair's "Elizabethan staging" with more mainstream cultural and social phenomena by examining the curious combination of conviction and reticence that characterizes the claims of fair organizers, the plays' producers, and public school educators when they describe the intensity and endurance of the experiences they offer their audiences and when they imagine the effects of those experiences in the future.

In his 1950 memoir, *Fair Management,* Lohr describes the improbable transformation of the Century of Progress into a scene from *Mac-*

beth when "pandemonium broke loose" after the closing of the fair's gates for a final time on Halloween night:

> Everything that could be moved was taken: signs, some with letters six feet tall, light fixtures, benches . . . anything which they could pick up, reach or climb to. . . . Guards at the gates made those leaving deposit all bulky objects on the ground, and nearly an acre was covered. Great Birnam wood shall come to Dunsinane. Hundreds of small trees and shrubs were pulled up by the roots and carried as far as the gates where they were reluctantly left. There was literally a small forest around each exit the next morning.
>
> The most interesting part of the whole proceeding was the fact that the destruction was done by well-meaning, peaceful citizens. . . . And, after all, who is to blame them for wanting to show a souvenir of their beloved Fair to their grandchildren many years later.[36]

Lohr's unruffled response to the reforesting of the fairgrounds is not particularly surprising—the fair's destruction on the final night was expected, and he is writing from the vantage point of almost twenty years—but his interpretation of the vandals' motives is a bit strange. He imagines them as devoted fairgoers to the end, attempting to acquire a souvenir of their experience at the fair, and in the process, hoping to create the possibility for another experience many years later with grandchildren who presumably do not yet exist.

When Lohr published this account of the closing night, he had been president of Chicago's Museum of Science and Industry for approximately a decade. The Chicago World's Fair and the Museum of Science and Industry shared exhibits and publicity from the earliest days of the fair's construction. After the fair closed, a number of its exhibits were housed at the museum, including industry-sponsored models and dioramas, and the towers of the giant sky ride. Several exhibits added to the museum over the next many years were inspired by the popularity of their fair counterparts—the microvivarium, the transparent man, human body sections, and human embryos. In 1940, Lohr resigned as president of NBC to return to Chicago where he succeeded Rufus Cutler Dawes as president of the Museum of Science and Industry; local newspaper articles cite Lohr's reproducing the fair's spectacular and engaging combination of education and entertainment as decisive in the museum's newly appealing exhibits and dramatically increased attendance.[37] This account of the museum's appeal, like Lohr's account of the reforesting of the fairgrounds, echoes one version of the fair's pervasive emphasis on "entertainment and education," privileged by fair organizers, defined not by the particular reaction (mental shock, an attention captured, an imagination awakened) but by the intensity and endurance of the experience, and by its irreducibility to the immediate acquisition of any particular piece of information or the immediate impulse to any particular behavior. Even the fair's signature futuristic architecture is not predictive but affective, compelling not as a blueprint for the future but in its startling proximity both to the "old world buildings" in the Street of Villages and to the contemporary Chicago skyline.[38]

This emphasis is striking because the fair was devoted to the practical applications of science and technology and because its promoters did not otherwise tend to false or even prudent displays of modesty. After all, in the years before the fair's opening, they considered seriously a proposal celebrating Chicago as the birthplace of the folding classroom partition.[39] It is not that I expected an announcement that their ideal fairgoer would leave the Century of Progress inspired by its "great educational project" to purchase a box of Clorox, a Frigidaire, and a ticket to the Old Globe Theatre. But I did expect fair organizers to sustain the can-do attitude that marked their early promotional materials or, failing that, to muster the grudging if belated acceptance of their limitations that marked their dealings with the Chicago public schools in 1933, or the dogged persistence that marked their renewed outreach in 1934. Instead, even when fair organizers and their admirers discuss the successful management of the fair and subsequently of Chicago's Museum of Science and Industry, they are fascinated with how best to convey a "real grasp" of the material on display, a relationship both tenuous and tenacious, whose acquisition and whose educational afterlife is subject to the sorts of unpredictable social and personal circumstances that define and will come to define an individual's needs.[40]

Payne shares this fascination with the intensity and durability of experiences produced, in his case, by "modified Elizabethan staging" and with the unpredictability of their future effects. Locating "modified Elizabethan staging" within his long career in English and Irish repertory theaters, the Stratford Festival, professional theaters in New York and Chicago, and university drama programs at the Carnegie Institute and the University of Texas at Austin, he describes in his memoirs the "enthusiastic response" elicited from a modern audience for whom Shakespeare is a "living experience," including the audiences immersed in the "carnival atmosphere of world's fairs." Pausing to discuss at greater length his first effective "modified Elizabethan production," a production of *Hamlet* at the

Carnegie Institute, he intersperses his response "from the point of view of a spectator" with his observations of the responses of other audience members. The "quality of audience reaction" is "impossible to describe, but unmistakable." He models the intensity and unpredictable effects of that reaction when he describes the influence of this production on his future work and characterizes his own response as "memorable" both for a "resurgence of feeling that can be described only as a kind of illumination—an ineffable stirring of aesthetic dynamics, as it were—which I remembered from the early days at the Gaiety Theatre in Manchester during productions of Ibsen, Shaw, and Galsworthy plays," and for a "strange and wholly unexpected experience" during which he was "suddenly transfused . . . with a feeling that Shakespeare himself was present." The "intensity" of this latter experience is not easily diminished: even after it apparently dissipates over a long walk home, it lingers like the Gaiety Theatre memories, resurfacing and reaffirming his faith in the stage techniques he has developed and will continue to refine until the end of his career.[41]

This emphasis on eliciting an intense experience, unpredictable in its future effects, is reinforced by the shared narrative impulses of Payne and Lohr. Each hesitates to fully inhabit the sorts of abstractions that academic articles, educational policy, and their own formulations about theatrical production and fair and museum management require. As Raymond Williams writes, "our normal public conception of an individual person, for example, is 'the man in the street'. But nobody feels himself to be only the man in the street; we all know much more about ourselves than that."[42] Although the memoirs' tones vary considerably, each focuses on the experimentation that allows its author to develop a technique—Payne's "modified Elizabethan staging," Lohr's brand of showmanship—that is significant within his profession because it produces intense responses in its audiences. These memoirs are not at all inclined to attempt a precise accounting of the cognitive or aesthetic dimensions of audience members' various responses. Instead, Payne and Lohr are much more interested in detailing their experimentation and techniques, explaining their goals, and describing their short-term successes. And yet they are considerably less confident about precisely how today's intense response to their work will affect an audience member in the future. As they meditate on their professional lives, Payne and Lohr are drawn to the experiences—quirky and quotidian, sought out and unexpected—whose intensity is not always immediately apparent and whose full effects often are deferred for a good number of years. Using the unexpected turns of their own professional lives as a narrative template, they are acutely aware that, particularly over time, the intense experiences they offer their audiences are a shaping, not an absolutely determining, influence.

This awareness is also a pervasive theme in the contemporary documents cited detailing the effects of visual learning, including the use of drama, and the use of Shakespeare throughout the Chicago public school curriculum. In fact, for the public school educators and for Lohr during his tenure as president of the Museum of Science and Industry, an emphasis on the transformative but not absolutely determining influence of the experiences they create is a professional requirement. The teachers and administrators cited earlier in contemporary Board of Education materials and in articles and press releases stress not only the difficulties inherent in developing teaching strategies suited to the particular needs and capacities of each child in schools with a rapidly expanding demographic, but also the difficulties inherent in educating children for a world that does not yet exist and whose precise contours the schools cannot possibly expect fully to predict or produce. For his part, Lohr envisions the Museum of Science and Industry as a "mammoth loose-leaf encyclopedia of the achievements of man, changing as the scope of man's knowledge increases," a place where, in his words, the "past rubs elbows with today and treads on the heels of tomorrow."[43]

The Century of Progress Exposition, Chicago public school education, and the "Elizabethan staging" of Shakespeare's plays in Merrie England were associated with disparate, intermittently overlapping short-term goals: civic-minded members of the local community; avid and willing consumers of mass-produced products and services; repeat fairgoers; creative participants in a thriving theater culture; productive, hygienic members of society; inventors and admirers of tomorrow's technologies; reasoning, informed citizens. Yet fair organizers, local educators, and the plays' producers shared a conviction that they had developed a technique that had, at the very least, the potential to exceed their short-term goals by producing a compelling experience, one that might lie dormant for a long while until its residue is summoned or appears unbidden when theatergoers, fairgoers, and students need to organize specialized knowledge, connect apparently disparate professional enterprises, or respond to the changes in circumstance that come to define their everyday lives. However disparate the personal and professional impulses that lead to that conviction, each displays an orientation to the future that is both respectful in its deference to the unknown and committed to generating experiences whose afterlife will allow their audiences to inhabit a permanent present progressive—always outdistancing the past.

NOTES

I completed the research for this essay with the generous assistance of a Folger Shakespeare Institute Short-Term Fellowship and presented a short version at the March 2007 "Shakespeare in American Education, 1607–1934" conference at the Folger Shakespeare Library; the conference was part of the National Endowment for the Humanities "We the People" initiative. I am grateful to the Institute and the National Endowment for the Humanities for their support, and to the conference organizers, conference participants, and librarians in the archives of the Chicago Board of Education, Chicago History Museum, Folger Shakespeare Library, Newberry Library, and University of Illinois at Chicago for their thoughtful responses to this project.

Archives and periodicals frequently cited are identified by the following abbreviations:

ACB	Archives of the Chicago Board of Education
FSL	Folger Shakespeare Library
CDN	*Chicago Daily News*
CDT	*Chicago Daily Tribune*
CJC	*Chicago Journal of Commerce*
CSM	*Christian Science Monitor*
CST	*Chicago Sunday Times*
NYT	*New York Times*
SC	A Century of Progress Records, Special Collections and University Archives, University of Illinois at Chicago
WP	*Washington Post*

1. *CDN*, May 8, 1934, May 26, 1934, July 28, 1934, August 21, 1934, September 7, 1934, and September 13, 1934; *CJC*, June 19, 1934, and June 20, 1934; *Chicago Loop News*, June 10, 1934; *CST*, September 9, 1934; *Highlights of the Educational Exhibits, Chicago World's Fair, Compiled for School Teacher Conductors for Student Tours, September–October, 1934* (Chicago: A Century of Progress Exposition, 1934), 22–23; William Vogelback, "Outline for Address by William E. Vogelback, President, Merrie England, On the Occasion of the Testimonial Dinner to Mr. and Mrs. William E. Vogelback by the Cordon Club of Chicago, December 4, 1934," 3–4, Archives and Manuscripts, Chicago History Museum; Robert Pollack, *CST*, 29 July 1934; " 'Round an' About the World's Fair," *CST*, September 9, 1934; Press Releases, Villages Concessions, June 18, 1934, and June 28, 1934, 23:14–174, SC; and English Village, Villages Concessions, June 28, 1934, 23:14–174, SC.

2. The schedule of the Globe performances is listed in several promotional articles and guidebooks, including *Highlights*, 26. Opening and closing performances at the Old Globe are described in Charles Collins, "Shakespeare Done at Fair Is Roaring Fun: *Taming of the Shrew* Played with Elizabethan Gusto," *CDT*, May 28, 1934; Claudia Cassidy, "On the Aisle: Stellar Petruchio Tops Rollicking Inaugural

Performance in Old Globe Theatre at the Fair," *CJC*, May 28, 1934; and 159th and Final Day, Daily Programs, October 31, 1934, 21:14–138b, SC.

3. *Progress* 1, no. 10 (June 3, 1931): 2. Stevens is quoted in Villages Concessions, May 8, 1934, 23:14–174, SC.

4. These attendance figures are cited, ten days before the fair's closing, in "Thousands See Shakespeare in Tabloid at Fair," *CDT*, October 21, 1934. See also "Sam Wanamaker," interview by Graham Holderness in *The Shakespeare Myth*, ed. Graham Holderness (Manchester, UK: Manchester University Press, 1988), 21–23.

5. Collins, "Movie Theater Will Offer Old Globe Players," *CDT*, November 9, 1934, announces the Old Globe Theatre Company's plans for performances in Grand Rapids, Battle Creek, Detroit, Lansing, and Milwaukee, and, subsequently, the company's engagement at McVickers. Collins writes that the McVickers engagement promises to feature an "exact reproduction of the stage of the Old Globe at the Fair." C[harles?] C[ollins?], "Renaissance Of Art In Chicago," *NYT*, January 13, 1935, explains that as of January 11 the Old Globe Theatre Company had abandoned what proved to be an unsuccessful McVickers engagement three weeks earlier and moved to the Studebaker Theatre where they performed once each afternoon and evening; the Studebaker repertory featured, in addition to the Century of Progress productions of Shakespeare's plays and Marlowe's *Dr. Faustus*, a new *Twelfth Night* and a new 90-minute *King Lear*. Collins, "Globe Players Will Appear at San Diego Fair," *CDT*, May 14, 1935, announces the closing of the Old Globe Theatre Company's successful postexposition tour of the Midwest and its plan to perform for the San Diego exposition during the summer of 1935 at a "reproduction of their Chicago playhouse." Ben Iden Payne, *A Life in a Wooden O: Memoirs of the Theatre* (New Haven: Yale University Press, 1977), 187, describes the rebuilding of the Chicago Globe at the Pacific National Exposition in San Diego and the Globe Theatre's continued prominence in the San Diego National Theatre Festival. "The Stage," *CDT*, April 18, 1936, announces the Old Globe Theatre Company's plan to spend the summer of 1936 at the Great Lakes exposition of Cleveland where a "special Elizabethan theater will be built for their use." For a discussion of the Old Globe's 1934 appearance in Chicago and 1936 appearance in Dallas, see "Sam Wanamaker," in *The Shakespeare Myth*, 21–23. John Rosenfield Jr., "Of Broadway and Main Street," *NYT*, December 12, 1937, describes the influence of William Poel on the stage practices that informed Stevens's productions in the reconstructed Globes of Chicago, San Diego, Cleveland, and Dallas.

6. The quote appears in *Globe Theatre Versions, Shakespeare's "The Comedy of Errors"* (New York: Samuel French, 1935). French's editions of Merrie England's eight Shakespeare plays predict playing times as short as 36 minutes (*Taming of the Shrew, Comedy of Errors*) and as long as an hour (*Macbeth*); with the exception of *Macbeth*, all aimed to play between 36 and 45 minutes. French's editions of the four Shakespeare plays later added to the Old Globe Players' repertoire (*Hamlet, Romeo and Juliet, Tempest, Twelfth Night*) suggest typical playing times of no less than an hour. French's edition of *King Lear* corresponds to the 90-minute Old Globe Players' production at the Studebaker soon after the fair's closing. French's edition of *Taming of the Shrew* offers both the 36-minute Merrie England version and a longer 55-minute version as played in San Diego and Dallas. The Folger Shakespeare Library and Newberry Library archives contain partial collections of the French editions.

7. For the quotes describing the village proposal and the well-behaved children, see Vogelback, "Outline for Address," 1, 4. For descriptions of the long line of theatergoers and the advice to avoid producing abbreviated Shakespeare plays, see

Vogelback, "Globe Theatre—A Rambling Account," manuscript, 1950, pp. 2–3, Archives and Manuscripts, Chicago History Museum, and "Outline for Address," 2; for "out of place" quotation see "Globe Theatre—A Rambling Account," 2. These critics include Rinda F. Lundstrom, *William Poel's Hamlets* (Ann Arbor: UMI Research Press, 1984); Marion O'Connor, *William Poel and the Elizabethan Stage Society* (Cambridge: Chadwyck-Healey, 1987); Payne, *Life;* Robert Speaight, *William Poel and the Elizabethan Revival* (Melbourne: William Heinemann, 1954).

8. Events—Student Tours, September 11, 1934, 26:14–205, SC; *Progress* 1.2 (April 8, 1931): 2.

9. Charles W. Duke, "Science Unfolds its Mysteries," *WP,* May 28, 1933.

10. For fair correspondence with the *Practical Educator, Progressive Education,* and *United Educator,* see General Correspondence, November 25, 1932, and May 12, 1934, 386:1–12318; February 13, 1933, 390:1–12395, SC; and December 30, 1932, 462:1–4876, SC. For *Chicago Schools Journal* in 1931, including the quote, see General Correspondence, 116:1–3261, SC.

11. For National Education Association meetings, see General Correspondence, January 19, 1933, and February 15, 1933, 343:1–10967, SC. For correspondence about visiting speakers or printed materials, see General Correspondence, December 20, 1932, January 19, 1933, February 17, 1933, February 20, 1933, February 28, 1933, 181:1–5291, SC; and February 7, 1933, and February 24, 1933, 485:1–15660, SC. On November 23, 1931, the principal of the West Pullman School finalized arrangements for 150 students to visit the fair-in-process on their way to the Adler Planetarium (General Correspondence, 478:1–15504, SC). For invitations to the National Association of Public School Officials, National Education Association, and Progressive Educators of America, see General Correspondence, May 14 and May 15, 1931, 340:1–0881, SC; December 17, 1932, and February 6, 1933, 343:1–10967, SC; and January 25, 1933, 390:1–12395, SC.

12. The glancing references include brief mentions of the fair in two editions of the *Bowenite* (one edited by the class of February 1933, the other by the class of June 1934), yearbook, Bowen High School in Chicago, ACB.

13. For the April 8 flag-raising ceremony, see "Corr Acts to Hurry Mayor's Election," *CDT,* April 9, 1933, and S. J. Duncan-Clark, "Chicago Teachers to Get Some Pay," *NYT,* April 16, 1933; quotes are from Duncan-Clark. For the teachers' April 15 "Mile-Long Parade" and the coffin quote, see "Teachers Helped by Chicago Parade," *NYT,* April 16, 1933.

14. In 1933, Dawes described the fair's financing in Duke, "Science Unfolds its Mysteries." Over the next several decades, Dawes and Lohr continue to explain how they ensured the fair's financial success. See Rufus Cutler Dawes, "Report of the President of A Century of Progress to The Board of Trustees, March 14, 1936" (Chicago: A Century of Progress, 1936), 22, 27, 35, 51, 53, 54, 55, 72–75, 85, Archives and Manuscripts, Chicago History Museum; Lennox Lohr, *Fair Management: The Story of A Century of Progress Exposition* (Chicago: Cuneo Press, 1952), 163–70, 239–40, 254; and Clay Gowran, "Lenox Lohr: Genius in Museum, Fairs," *CDT,* December 9, 1962. The fair's creative reimbursement practices included substituting fair bonds for a portion of the workers' salaries.

15. "Chicago Is Cited in Plea to Boost Federal Relief," *CDT,* February 3, 1933, outlines the connections among Dawes, protestors, the Chicago banks, and federal loan regulations and is the source for the paragraph's first quote. "Chicago Schools May Be Closed May 12; 5,000 Teachers Besiege Five Loop Banks," *CDT,* April 25, 1933, describes in detail the April 24 demonstration, including its targeting of five banks and Dawes's comments. "Teachers Helped by Chicago Parade" cites the pro-

testors' claims as broadcast from a bus by the leaders of the April 15 demonstration. For the parade of five thousand schoolchildren and their burning of Dawes in effigy, see "States and Cities: Chicago's Party," *Time,* May 22, 1933, 14. "Chicago Teachers to Get Some Pay" and "Chicago Schools May Be Closed May 12" offer longer accounts of the pay crisis, including the effect of a shift in Chicago mayors, the new mayor's securing a portion of the back pay (paying the teachers' salaries through the end of June 1932), the mayor's and bankers' roles in various plans for extending loans to the teachers and lobbying the federal government, and the growing financial crisis for firemen, policemen, and other city employees who had not been paid since the end of October 1932.

16. Spring 1933 letters collected in Teacher Protests, 2:4–14, SC. "Chicago Boycott Urged on Teachers," *NYT,* April 28, 1933, quotes at length from a letter written by three Columbia professors, urging the National Education Association to boycott A Century of Progress, noting that Chicago's "civic leaders . . . have not failed to come to the aid of their banks. It is high time that they showed equal concern for Chicago children and teachers." Both "Dawes' View on Teachers May Stop Chicago Session," *WP,* May 3, 1933, and "Dawes Is Told to Pay Teachers or Lose N.E.A. Convention," *NYT,* May 3, 1933, quote from National Education Association secretary J. W. Crabtree who questions the bankers' hesitation to assist Chicago's teachers and claims that the National Education Association has received thousands of letters urging a change in its summer meeting venue.

17. See "NEA—The Educators Take Heart," *Hartford Courant,* July 15, 1933.

18. Eunice Barnard, "Schools' Progress Revealed at Fair," *NYT,* July 2, 1933.

19. See ibid. for quotes about permanent educational exhibits. For additional information about these exhibits, see *Highlights,* 18, which provides the phrase "a century of public school progress," and Lohr, Social Science Exhibits, manuscript for *Fair Management,* 1952, 19:15–262, SC. Lohr explains that the permanent educational projects were designed by colleges, secondary schools, the U.S. Bureau of Education, Phi Delta Kappa, and the Educational Exhibit Committee for A Century of Progress.

20. The Chicago Board of Education's characterization of the facilities and programs targeted for reduction and its recommendations are outlined in the Official Report of the Proceedings of the Board of Education of the City of Chicago, Regular Meeting, July 12, 1933, pp. 24–25, ACB. The Official Report of the Proceedings of the Board of Education of the City of Chicago, Regular Meeting, July 26, 1933, pp. 30–31, ACB, outlines, with slight modifications and clarifications, the recommendations as adopted. The quote is from the July 12 Official Report, 24, ACB. The paragraph's closing quote is excerpted from Dr. Roy O. Billet's remarks at a Conference on the National Survey of Secondary Education at George Washington University as cited in "Chicago School Slash Evokes Criticism Here: Conference Speaker Says Progress of 25 Years May Be Lost," *WP,* July 21, 1933. For similar comments, see Grace E. Benjamin, "The School Budget," *CDT,* July 16, 1933; and William H. Holmes, Superintendent of the Schools in Mount Vernon, NY, in his address to the High School Teachers Association of New York City as cited in "Schools Held Key to Full Recovery," *NYT,* October 8, 1933.

21. Miscellaneous Contests, press releases throughout 1933 and 1934, 25:14–195, SC. These events generally were scheduled for the weekly Children's Day (Fridays in 1933, Thursdays in 1934) when the fair reduced its admission fees for children under the age of twelve, from 25 cents to 5 cents (Attendance Tables, 1933 and 1934, 17:15–228 and 229, SC).

22. For the American Association for the Advancement of Science meeting and

the June 28 Engineers' Day, see William L. Laurence, "Scientists to Hold Longest Session," *NYT*, June 18, 1933; and Philip Kinsley, "Great Science Conclave Will Be Part of Fair," *CDT*, 22 May 1933; the quote is from Laurence. For the symposium on progressive education, see "Schools Shedding Old Skins, Women Say, for Modern Garb," *CSM*, September 20, 1933. Adult Education Day included pageants and "short talks on adult education" by representatives of the Chicago public schools, the Illinois Emergency Relief Commission, and the University of Chicago (Events—Special Days, August 7, 1934, 26:14–204, SC). For the International Typing Contest, see Miscellaneous Contests, June 25, 1934, June 27, 1934, and June 29, 1934, 25:14–195, SC.

23. For details about the federal loan, see "Hail Teachers' Loan as Great Recovery Step," *CDT*, August 7, 1934. For details about paychecks, Teachers' Jubilee Day at the fair, and Merrie England's involvement, see "Teachers Cheer Mayor Kelly at Pay Celebration," *CDT*, August 11, 1934. For more details about Teachers' Jubilee Day and the fair's preliminary attempts to promote student tours, see Events—Special Days, August 7, 1934, August 9, 1934, and August 9, 1934 (for release in afternoon papers), 26:14–201, SC; this paragraph's quote about exhibits is from the August 7, 1934, press release. For student tour information, see Events—Student Tours, August 30, 1934, September 3, 1934, September 6, 1934, September 11, 1934, September 18, 1934, September 20, 1934, September 24, 1934, September 25, 1934, October 8, 1934, and October 13, 1934, 26:14–205, SC. The first two quotations in this paragraph are from the September 24, 1934, and September 25, 1934, press releases; the final three quotations are from the August 30, 1934 (repeated September 6, 1934), October 8, 1934, and September 10, 1934, releases.

24. For running comparisons between local and national participation in the school tours, see Events—Student Tours, October 8, 1934, and October 13, 1934, 26:14–205, SC. For the 1934 fair's general emphasis on the local audience, see Lohr, Social Science Exhibits, manuscript for *Fair Management*, 1952, 19:15–275, SC. Useful early newspaper articles include Barnard, "Boys' Plea to R. R. C. Told to Teachers," *NYT*, July 6, 1933; Benjamin, "The School Budget"; "Chicago School Slash Evokes Criticism Here"; "NEA—The Educators Take Heart"; and "Schools Held Key to Full Recovery." Although Century of Progress publicity is understandably keen to link the tours to "progressive" educational methods, the influences on and practices in public school education in 1934 were actually a bit more varied. For an overview of public school education in the 1930s (including responses to progressive education, Kilpatrick's project method and the Chicago Normal School, and the varied significance of visual materials), see Arthur N. Applebee, *Tradition and Reform in the Teaching of English: A History* (Urbana, IL: National Council of Teachers of English, 1974), 107–38; Samuel Engle Burr, *An Introduction to Progressive Education* (Cincinnati, OH: C. A. Gregory, 1933); Charles Frey, "Teaching Shakespeare in America," *Shakespeare Quarterly*, Special Issue: Teaching Shakespeare, 35.5 (1984): 546–48; Carl H. Gross and Charles C. Chandler, eds., *The History of American Education through Readings* (Boston: D. C. Heath, 1964), 335–99; Stuart G. Noble, *A History of American Education*, rev. ed. (New York: Rinehart, 1954), 392–493; and the remarks during a symposium at the fair by the director of the Francis W. Parker School (a Chicago-area school dedicated to Progressive Education) as cited in "Schools Shedding Old Skins, Women Say, for Modern Garb." For the fair's emphasis on visual learning, see Events—Student Tours, September 20, 1934, September 24, 1934, September 25, 1934, October 8, 1934, and October 13, 1934, 26:14–205; for the mention of project learning, see September 20, 1934. For the mention of school assemblies, see Events—Student Tours, September 6, 1934, 26:14–205.

25. For the quotes and information on visual instruction, see "Much Instruction Is Now Given Visually," in Annual Report of the Superintendent of Schools for the Year Ending June 11, 1937, Board of Education, Chicago, 95, 143, ACB. For the language advising elementary school educators to awaken students' imagination with visual material, see Bogan, Superintendent of Schools, Course of Study in Composition, Grades 4–6, Bulletin E-C-456, adopted February 27, 1929, Board of Education, Chicago, 17, ACB. For advice to teachers of young primary-level students and for grade-appropriate anthologies, see Bogan, A Course of Study in English, Chicago Public Schools, Grades 1–3, Bulletin L-E-125, adopted February 13, 1929, Board of Education, 44, 65, 72, 94, appendices, ACB. For advice to teachers of slightly older primary-level students, see Course of Study in Composition, Grades 4–6, pp. 55–56, 92. For the quotes and information describing the ten-week drama unit, see Bogan, A Course of Study in English Literature in Senior High Schools, Grades XI–XII, 1932, pp. 2–3, ACB. A model for incorporating intensive study of drama into both required and elective portions of the secondary school curriculum is developed in Chicago Public Schools, A Course of Study in Dramatics, I–II, for Senior High Schools, 1931, produced by the Committee on the Course in Dramatics, 5, 15–19, ACB.

26. See *Highlights,* 14, for one listing of the food preservation events. For events on Enchanted Island, see Daily Programs, October 1, 1934, 21:14–138a; and Enchanted Island—Theatre Memos, August 6, 1934, SC. In Chicago's elementary classrooms, as on the Fair's Enchanted Island, drama exercises and field trips tended not to include Shakespeare's plays; the Island's well-stocked library, Story Cove, included no editions of Shakespeare. See *On the Shelves of the Story Cove* (Chicago: Library of International Relations, 1934).

27. The estimated and projected attendance figures are cited in fair press releases throughout the weeks of the school tours; projected student attendance declines from over 300,000 in the September 11 and September 24 press releases to nearly 250,000 in the October 13 press release. Events—Student Tours, September 3, 1934, September 6, 1934, September 11, 1934, and October 13, 1934, 26:14–205, outline pricing, during school tours, for the fair, Merrie England, and the Globe performances. Students in school tour groups (defined as ten or more students no older than eighteen years of age) were admitted to the fair for 5 cents between 8 a.m. and 4 p.m. Their teacher was admitted at no charge; other chaperones paid the full 50-cent adult fair admission fee. Merrie England reduced its admission fee from 25 to 10 cents for students in school tour groups (a number of comparable concessions had reduced to 5 cents); the cost of seeing a Globe production was not reduced. Eventually Merrie England reduced its village admission fees to 5 cents between 10 a.m. and 4 p.m. for those high school students on tours that attended its 2 p.m. Globe performances (at full price).

28. For the ninth-grade teacher's inquiry, see Events—Student Tours, October 10, 1934, 26:14–205. For references to the English Village and its Old Globe Theatre see Syllabus G, History and Civics, 7, in Itinerary and Syllabus, 21:14–139; and the Geography and History section of *Highlights,* 22. For the 2 p.m. Globe performances, see Events—Student Tours, October 12 and October 13, 1934, 26:14–205. The October 12, 1934, press release announced that the October 15 production at 2 p.m. was already sold out and conveyed the sentiments of English teachers and high school principals. With the exception of *Highlights,* all of these materials are in SC. For the village's essay contest, see "World's Fair Notes," and "Globe Theater Offers Prizes to Essayists," *CDT,* September 16, 1934, and September 23, 1934; the quote is from the second of these articles.

29. The first quote is from William Poel, *Shakespeare in the Theatre* (London: Sidgwick and Jackson, 1913). The second is Lundstrom's account of Poel's aims in *William Poel's Hamlets*, 43. Poel offers accounts of his "Elizabethan" stage techniques, including his editing practices and his characteristic pattern of modulation and inflection, in *An Account of the Elizabethan Stage Society*, June 1898, pp. 6–9, Sh. Misc., 1115, FSL; "The Great Tragedian, 1916," "Spoken Verse, 1923," "The Platform Stage, 1912," "In the Playhouse, 1918," "On Writing Verse-Plays, 1918" in *Monthly Letters*, selected and arranged by A. M. T. (London: T. Werner Laurie, 1929); and *Shakespeare in the Theatre*. For responses of scholars and Poel's contemporaries to his techniques, see Lundstrom, *William Poel's Hamlets*, 4–10; O'Connor, *William Poel and the Elizabethan Stage Society;* Payne, *Life*, 86–91; Speaight, *William Poel and the Elizabethan Revival;* and Thomas Wood Stevens, in his short publication for the Century of Progress Exposition, *The Globe Theatre* (Chicago: Colortext Publications, 1934), 7–8, and in *The Theatre: From Athens to Broadway* (New York: D. Appleton, 1932), 88–89.

30. Payne, *Life*, discusses Poel's work at the Gaiety Theatre and his visit to the Carnegie Institute's drama program, 84–92, 110–12, 151. Speaight, *William Poel and the Elizabethan Revival*, describes in more detail Poel's visits to the Carnegie Institute, 225–26. Poel's *Monthly Letters* includes "USA, 1916," the commencement address that he delivered at the Institute during his first visit.

31. See Payne, *Life*, 162–83, for descriptions of "modified Elizabethan staging"; 103, 166–67, 190, for descriptions of editing practices; 189, for the "pedantic archaism" quote; and 190, for the quotes about editing. O'Connor describes Poel's Fortune fit-up in *William Poel and the Elizabethan Stage Society*, 28–32, including its running afoul of London County Council fire regulations, 36. Descriptions of the Chicago Globe appear in *CDN*, May 8, 1934; *Chicago Herald and Examiner*, May 5, 1934; Clara E. Laughlin, *So You're Going to Merrie England* (Chicago: Colortext, 1934), 18; Events—Student Tours, October 12, 1934; Lloyd Lewis, "Stage Whispers," *CDN*, May 8, 1934, and May 9, 1934; Stevens, *Globe Theatre;* and Vogelback, "Globe Theatre—A Rambling Account," and "Outline for Address," 2. Estimates of the Chicago Globe's seating capacity range between 400 and 450. Neilson and Stevens are quoted in *Chicago Herald and Examiner*, May 5, 1934. For the quote from the French edition's prefatory note, see *Globe Theatre Versions, Shakespeare's "Macbeth"* (New York: Samuel French, 1935).

32. The first quote is Lundstrom, *William Poel's Hamlets*, 6, 10; the second is Poel, *Account*, 10. For a sampling of how district administrators suggested that Shakespeare's plays fit within the recommended Chicago high school literature and drama curricula in the 1920s and 1930s, including the suggested pedagogical methods and goals, see Peter A. Mortenson, Superintendent of Schools, Board of Education, City of Chicago, The Education Division, High School English Syllabus, October 1920, pp. 17–25, 37; Bogan, A Course of Study in English Literature in Senior High Schools, 1–3; and A Course of Study in Dramatics, 3–9, 12, 15–19.

33. Syllabus G, History and Civics, 7, and *Highlights*, 22. See Mortensen, High School English Syllabus, 25, for the usefulness of Malvolio when teaching about Puritanism in Elizabethan society and literature, and A Course of Study in Dramatics, 15–16, for the usefulness of *Edward II, King John, Henry IV, Richard III* when impressing upon students the interest in English history that followed the defeat of the Spanish Armada, and for the usefulness of *The Tempest* when discussing the "interest in foreign lands" that followed from European exploration in the Americas.

34. *Globe Theatre Versions, Shakespeare's "The Taming of the Shrew"* (New York: Samuel French, 1937); *Globe Theatre Versions, Shakespeare's "The Comedy of Errors."* The

slender collection of high school yearbooks in ACB continue to document relatively inexpensive student drama clubs and theatrical productions throughout the 1930s. See the *Bowenite,* Bowen High School, 1932, 1933, 1934, 1935; the *Red and Black,* DuSable High School, 1936, 1937, 1939; and the *Temulac,* Calumet High School, 1939. The FSL archives include several of titles from the long-running "French's Acting Edition" series and, published by French earlier in the century, "American Academy of Dramatic Arts' Edition of Standard Plays" series. A number of French plays (some designated "budget plays") appear in the play production book list in both the "Long Plays" and "One Act Plays" categories of Dorothy Dakin, *How to Teach High School English* (Boston: D. C. Heath, 1947), 572–74. The *Globe Theatre Versions, Shakespeare's "Julius Caesar"* (1935; repr., New York: Samuel French, 1959), includes advertisements for a collection of lectures on method acting and for several affordable editions of farces, comedies, and melodramas requiring between eight and sixteen cast members. The *Globe Theatre Versions, Shakespeare's "The Comedy of Errors"* (New York: Samuel French, 1935; in renewal, B[en] Iden Payne, 1962), includes advertisements for *Here's How: A Basic Stagecraft Book* and for three affordable editions of plays advertised as requiring between thirteen and fifteen cast members, promising very little technical difficulty in the staging and, in two instances, a starring role that "every young girl will adore playing" and "good clean fun." Both reprinted editions are in FSL.

35. Poel, "Children as Actors, 1918," *Monthly Letters,* 22–24. He emphasizes the importance of amateurs throughout *Account, Monthly Letters,* and *Shakespeare in the Theatre,* an emphasis stressed by Lundstrom, O'Connor, Payne, and Speaight. See O'Connor, *William Poel and the Elizabethan Stage Society,* 26–45, for Shakespeare Reading Society and its links to the Elizabethan Stage Society; Payne, *Life,* 123–24, 150–51.

36. Lohr, *Fair Management,* 261.

37. John A. Maloney, "The Museum of Science and Industry," *CDT,* July 10, 1933; Raymond Clapper, "Machine Age Mecca Has Drawn Millions," *WP,* June 24, 1934; "Famous Diorama Given to Chicago Museum," *WP,* December 10, 1934; "Working Models," *CSM,* February 20, 1935; "Science Museum May Add Exhibit of Micro Life," *CDT,* July 4, 1935; "Maj. Lohr Returns to Chicago," *CDT,* January 10, 1940; Kinsley, "City's Century of Progress in Healing Hailed," *CDT,* January 10, 1940; and "Fun of 1933–34 World's Fair Is Re-Created," *CDT,* May 28, 1958. For a description of fair exhibits whose success inspired later additions to the museum, see *Highlights,* 6–7.

38. See Lohr, *Fair Management,* 153–58, for information about the fair's topography, including the wariness of foreign governments and the decision to run the villages as concessions; the quotation is on 157.

39. "Model School at the World's Fair to Present Novel Aids for Teaching," *NYT,* March 20, 1932.

40. For the "great educational project" quote, see Events—Student Tours, September 20, 26:14–205. For accounts of the successful management of the fair and museum, see Duke, "Science Unfolds its Mysteries"; Gowran, "Do-It-Yourself Museum," *CDT,* July 8, 1962; "Lenox Lohr: Genius in Museum, Fairs"; Lohr, *Fair Management;* Marcia Winn, "Know Your Chicago," *CDT,* December 14, 1941. The "real grasp" quote is Duke, 4. In describing the link between education and entertainment, these sources stress the visual character of the fair's exhibits and the hands-on activities at the museum.

41. See Payne, *Life,* 184, for general quotes about the audience response to modified Elizabethan staging; 189, for quote about world's fairs; and 171–72, for quotes

about the audience's response to and his experiences during the production of *Hamlet* at the Carnegie Institute.

42. Raymond Williams, "The Masses," *The Raymond Williams Reader,* ed. John Higgins (Oxford: Blackwell, 2001), 45.

43. Winn, "Know Your Chicago," summarizing Lohr's sentiments; Lohr, as cited in Gowran, "Do-It-Yourself Museum."

Afterword

Theodore Leinwand

The essays gathered together in *SHAKESPEAREAN EDUCATIONS: POWER, Citizenship, and Performance* make the first sustained attempt to describe how Shakespeare fared in diverse North American educational settings from the eighteenth century through to the 1930s.[1] They reveal ways in which Shakespeare pedagogy has varied over parameters that include race and ethnicity, gender, class, geography, age, and institutional setting. Indeed, historical recovery of the sort that fills these pages inevitably reminds us how much the not-so-distant past, not just the rather-distant past, differs from the present.

In this afterword, I have tasked myself to take seriously a number of the aims and approaches that these essays disclose. I conduct (and I ask the reader to join me in conducting) a thought experiment. The prevailing questions that I ask are, "What if we were to try something like what 'they' were doing then?" and "How would we go about it?" At moments, this exercise may seem willful, maybe even perverse. But this is by no means my intention. I simply know of no better way to connect present with past practices, to test our own best intentions against those of our predecessors, than to determine what they can tell us, better still teach us, best of all inspire in us.

From one section to the next, I take my cues from topics that arise in the essays in this volume. While some of these essays may implicitly or explicitly criticize what they describe, I try not to. Instead, I consider what might be gained by adopting or adapting pedagogies that in some cases have been disregarded, in others rejected. Even though my conjectures are meant to be useful, certainly not everything that I suggest will be deemed so. If what I recommend is merely intriguing or if it simply gives pause, that too may prove useful although not necessarily practical. Either way, for those who teach Shakespeare, these essays may stimulate us to think about our own pedagogies.

276

Majors and/or Citizens

Shakespeare's enlistment as an agent in the formation of American citizens and American culture is discussed in several of essays collected here (Renker, Gustafson, Burton, Kahn, McAllister, Kegl). Jonathan Burton writes that long before the late twentieth-century culture wars in the United States, the *McGuffey Readers* "culled and expurgated [Shakespeare excerpts] to shape a citizenry" (96). Coppélia Kahn describes the ways that Shakespeare buttressed Charles Mills Gayley's conviction that "all citizens . . . should be educated in Anglo-Saxon culture" (207). I am reminded of Julia Reinhard Lupton, who describes her book *Citizen-Saints: Shakespeare and Political Theology* as an "extended midrash on citizenship" and concludes it with a "Humanifesto" in which she encourages academics in the humanities to find places for themselves in the public sphere (a call that to some extent was anticipated by Esther Cloudman Dunn in her 1939 *Shakespeare in America*).[2] I myself often conceive of Shakespeare's plays as having many of the hallmarks of Montaigne's probative essays. If I am correct, then they model deliberation and negotiation over consequential issues faced by nation states, governors, citizens, minorities, and the like. Active citizenship entails a recurring, interminable cycle of informed analysis and responsible action. To teach *Coriolanus,* as many do, as a prismatic essay on a polity in crisis, as a fair-minded but skeptical account of every interest group and faction that sets foot on stage, is to offer up one lesson in citizenship. *Measure for Measure* is another thinking-through of styles of governance—administrative, therapeutic, carceral, libertarian—hence it, too, speaks to a long and uneven history of restraints on, and expectations for, (American) citizens right up to the present. Every member of every outlying (or mainstream) identity group in Shakespeare, be it Gower, Fluellen, MacMorris and Jamy, Autolycus, Shylock, Aaron, or Caliban, poses questions about the availability and the contours of a meeting ground upon which distinction can be respected and equality acknowledged.

However, this is to confine Shakespeare to the realm of analysis. It hardly gets students or teachers up on their feet and it stops conveniently short of action. Real citizens, like their fictional counterparts, make choices and then act on them. If Hamlet is famous for anything, it is for the way he does, and keeps doing, the work of analysis. But come Act 5, he makes good on "The readiness is all" (5.2.200),[3] choosing to act brutally and decisively. Enobarbus presents us with a more subtle example, one that bears more closely on the lives of students. Caustic, ironic, detached commentator that he is, he finds himself caught in an exquisite dilemma when it is time to act. Whose interests ought he to serve; to what man, woman, or state does he owe his fealty; is there even a compromise, let alone a right decision, available to him? Enobarbus discovers the necessity of choice and of action, and their almost certainly unhappy upshot. But much more importantly insofar as citizenship is concerned, he learns that there are moments when quiescence is not an option. Like Enobarbus, we and our students live a fair portion of our lives in the public domain. Like him, we require expertise in the realm of evaluation, but also like him, we can escape participation—action—for only so long. Portia recognizes an obligation to enter the civic arena in Venice. She too makes choices, choices that have grave consequences. And so does *Measure for Measure*'s Provost, who agrees to contravene his "oath," to substitute Barnardine's or Ragozine's head for Claudio's. If I seem to have strayed some distance from the "American" in "American citizens," then it need only be pointed out that Hamlet, Enobarbus, Portia, and even the Provost have national, territorial, or what Lupton might call tribal allegiances (the Duke demands of the Provost, "Were you sworn to the duke or to the deputy?" [*Measure for Measure*, 4.2.179]). We have them too, and as Shakespeare seems to me to insist, there is no more reason to (think that we can) set aside such affiliations ("This blows my heart," says Enobarbus [*Antony and Cleopatra*, 4.6.34]) than there is to subject ourselves to them ("This is I, / Hamlet the Dane" [*Hamlet*, 5.1.247–48).

Reading and/or Reciting

The examples that I have just offered suggest a kind of literary praxis for American citizenship. However, a number of the essays in *Shakespearean Educations* remind us that Shakespeare typically entered American classrooms not so much as literature—as text for reading—as a vehicle for instruction in recitation (Johnson, Gustafson, Haskin, McAllister). Nan Johnson discusses "speaker-reciters in the 1890s and the early twentieth century" who turned to Shakespeare, not for "training for the professional stage," but in "preparation for the general rhetorical literacy needed in public speaking and self-presentation" (120–21). Sandra M. Gustafson reminds us that "Shakespeare's eloquence . . . made his words central to American . . . civic rhetoric" (89). While my own children's secondary education confirms for me that this usage persists in some measure to this day, I am certain that I am not alone among my university colleagues in having all but stopped asking my students to recite from Shakespeare. For one thing, I find that it takes quite a bit of energy on their part just to get the reading done. I suppose that I also am prone to excuse myself by allowing as how my university has a drama department, anyway. Let them handle memorization and recitation and expression. Still, I do feel negligent. Even guilty, when I think about the woefully neglected but remarkably diverse "somato-psychic dimensions" of Shakespearean soundplay that Charles H. Frey has analyzed.[4]

So rather than enroll students in "Introduction to Shakespeare" only to spring memorization and recitation assignments on them, we might consider offering whole classes in "Speaking Shakespeare." This would be to advertise up front what we are asking and aiming for. It might also make space in our curricula for something like "Civic Rhetoric through Shakespeare" (not, that is, "Civic Rhetoric *in* Shakespeare"). No less old-fashioned an aim than learning through elocution to manage the passions in the midst of public discourse could still conceivably be a use to which we might put Shakespeare instruction. It would hardly be the first time that Shakespeare was used to teach diction, figurative language, and the like. Or civic rhetoric through and, in this case, *in* Shakespeare could dwell specifically on persuasion and feature the likes of Petruchio, Viola, Helena, Angelo, Hal, Richard III, Ulysses, Antony, Iago, Edmund, and Paulina. It may be too far-fetched to argue that there is still a place for a class devoted to Shakespeare and gesture (Harvard was not alone in offering such classes); but I can imagine a course in Shakespeare and eloquence that guaranteed from the start that it would cure students of every last "like" and "you know." Even though it has probably never even occurred to me to use a Shakespeare class to explore self-presentation—even though self-absorption is probably something from which I think most of us try to wean our students—it seems obvious that our understanding of self-presentation in the plays bears on our own styles of self-presentation. Into such a class, we could easily introduce Harry Berger Jr.'s bracing analysis of characters' exculpations and evasions. Still another elocution or speaking Shakespeare course might conduct cognate experiments in the reduction and enhancement of class and regional identifications by means of speech. On the one hand, students could strive to "speak the speech . . . trippingly on the tongue" in standard spoken English. This would be a way to explore the long-standing American pedagogical aspiration to forge a uniform, national citizenry. On the other hand, students could try to top one another by declaiming in regional or street accents.

Of course, as nineteenth-century American schools of oratory well knew, to deliver a speech written by Shakespeare was to interpret it. Hence, if by "reading" I cannot help but mean interpreting, then the binary at the start of this section is factitious. It also obscures something that just about every instructor at every level relies on: reading aloud. Momentarily to dwell on reading aloud versus recitation might help students and teachers decide just how much attention they want to give to the former. I, for one, never have found a satisfactory way to manage this business.[5] When it comes time to discuss a passage, how much should I read aloud and how much should I delegate to students? Should I allow students to distort line after line or should I stop them, again and again and again? The essays in this volume implicitly recommend that we take seriously the benefits of paying sustained attention to speaking Shakespeare.

MEN AND/OR WOMEN

These essays also remind us that boys and girls often were asked to recite from different plays. We learn that Shakespeare was taught differently to young men and women (Albanese, Haskin, Kahn, Nathans). Heather S. Nathans describes the subtle ways that "female educators could give their young [female] pupils unique ownership of Shakespeare's texts (but still within the 'respectable' confines of a female education)" (65). Denise Albanese has discovered that when "women were first admitted to Columbia as special certificate students in 1887–88 . . . they were given *Love's Labor's Lost* to study . . . rather than the *Macbeth* typically assigned to male students" (162). Shortly thereafter, Barnard College was established, and the "women are reading *Macbeth*—but the men have moved on to *Othello*" (162). Since none of us can deny that canons of respectability (what might be called prudery and prurience thresholds) are still with us and since, at least in part, they may be plotted on the axis of gender, we might experiment with turning our pedagogy on that same axis. I cannot be the only professor—male or female—who is taken aback by the number of undergraduate women who describe Cleopatra as a "bitch." A helpful discussion among a group of women (only women) might ensue were they to put some pressure on this designation. It might even be interesting to see what would happen were such a discussion to be led by a man and then a woman, or were discussion of Cleopatra's fainting to be confined to a group of men. Nothing of the sort that I am proposing need be confused with assumptions about essentialist notions of masculinity or femininity. Nor should we ignore transgendered students. And surely, coeducated student populations still present us with a variety of pedagogical advantages when conducting such discussions. Nevertheless, gender-segregated discussion might prove surprising and fruitfully dis- or reorienting, even if this were to mean nothing more than commencing with separate breakout groups for men and women and then reconvening as a whole. Consider a format of this sort for a discussion of *Julius Caesar*. Were a divided and then reunited class to follow Gail Kern Paster's lead, it could focus on bleeding Caesar, menstruation, masculinity, and shame. I suspect that ideas and opinions would surface that a mixed-gender cohort might be unwilling or unready to admit into discussion.

A case for targeting student reading according to gender might also be made. And in this instance, too, I am not prepared to say that propriety is merely an eighteenth- or nineteenth-century sticking point. It is not just that some of our deeply religious students, or our exceptionally bashful students, find some of the typical Shakespeare classroom sex talk improper. After all, some Shakespeare sex talk itself is improper. Hamlet taunting Ophelia about "nothing" and "country matters" (3.2.112–13) is a case in point. So too is my vivid memory of a morning when I learned that two of three orthodox Jewish women had dropped my "Late Works of Shakespeare" class. The woman who stuck it out told me that it was both what we had been discussing and that our discussions included both men and women that led her friends to part company with us. So might we not ask ourselves what could transpire if we were to give over two weeks in a semester-long class to the women reading *Othello* while the men read *Hamlet?* I am often struck by how many women in classes I teach profess themselves Emilia-ists: they are alert to the implications of her marriage to Iago, but they are either oblivious or sympathetic to her cynicism. Class discussion without men *might* lead more women to recognize Desdemona's courage.

PART AND/OR WHOLE

If gender appropriateness was formerly a criterion for exclusion, it might, I am suggesting, be a criterion for exploration. Now, I want to propose that we consider loosening what I take to be our prevailing commitment to teaching Shakespeare's plays whole. What pedagogical opportunities might arise were we to return to Shakespeare in fragments, to partial texts extracted from their contexts? Several essays in this volume (Johnson, Gustafson, Burton, Haskin, Albanese) remind us that Shakespeare's plays entered early American curricula only in fragments—and remained there in this form until well into the nineteenth century. Jonathan Burton's essay on the *McGuffey Readers* is part of a story that "features Shakespeare recalled in fragments," in brief excerpts that exemplified "rhetorical modes and principles of elocution" (95). Denise Albanese describes the role that college entrance exams began to play, particularly the way they "necessitated the reading of whole plays rather than selected speeches" (170). Reading the essays in this volume made me realize just how liberating, even exhilarating, I find the prospect of teaching a class on a Shakespeare scene, line, speech, or fragment. Do such classes still exist?

Of course, Shakespeare arrived on the pedagogical scene in pieces because, as I have noted above, he was recruited for training in oratory. But it is salutary to consider the possibilities of excerpting. I am confident that a fair number of students at the University of Maryland, where I teach, would jump with me at the chance to enroll in a class taught by George T. Wright or Russ McDonald on Shakespearean metrics, that is to say, a class that in good measure eschewed dramaturgy, character, and plot. If we were to spend a number of weeks on single lines, at what point would we be ready for entire soliloquies, and what might we have to say about verse at the level of a scene? If we taught classes on faith and on doubt, on property or wealth or thrift, on the expression of emotion, would we need whole plays? We could teach a class on affect synchronically, working with selections from Middleton and Jonson, Donne and Herbert. Those of us who try to nudge students beyond character analysis might find it to our advantage to deprive them of crucial props to the understanding of character—plot, for example. If we often talk about characters across plays, for instance, affiliating Portia and Rosalind and Viola, we certainly could try a week on couplets, starting with the sonnets and then canvassing the plays.

Fragments are obviously conducive to intensive scrutiny, whole plays to a broad brush. What sort of preparation would such pedagogy require and what sort of preparation would it provide? If I find it difficult to imagine the discussions we would be having in an upper-level Shakespeare seminar populated by the beneficiaries of the Wright class that I have imagined, it is because I rarely have worked with students equipped with such expertise. It seems inarguable that a metrics class would benefit them in the ways music theory classes improve performance classes. But metrics are not the only way to end-run scene- and character-centered pedagogy. A week of classes might be spent on dilation (Patricia Parker to the rescue), another on the Shakespearean prose or poetry of moodiness, and still another on what Shakespeare does with sententiae.

Hypothesizing like this calls to mind colleagues of mine who assign whole plays in act or scene sequence. In almost thirty years of Shakespeare instruction, I have always, always asked students to read the whole play prior to our first class on it. Some students no doubt fail to comply; however, my expectation is that we should be able to talk about Act 5 from the get-go. But even if sequential scene analysis is for many teachers—I imagine high school teachers and introductory-level college instructors, in particular—a familiar pedagogy of one kind of fragment, I still commend other, seemingly stingier, fragments. Imagine classes devoted to Shakespearean hendiadys, informed by Wright, with an added dollop of Frank Kermode and a pinch of Ted Hughes. The pages in *Shakespeare and the Goddess of Complete Being* that Hughes devotes to his understanding of this figure are by turns madcap and electrifying.[6] In very short order, Hughes passes from unpacking the mechanics of a literary figure to arguing that it reveals Shakespeare's political commitment to both the galleries and the pit at the Globe. If it were to turn out that we can guide students to a political Shakespeare via a route that bypasses character and plot, then we will have done them a good turn.

REWRITING AND/OR TEXTUAL ACCURACY

The extremely popular *McGuffey Readers* expurgated and rewrote Shakespeare, and they presented passages entirely out of context (Burton). Aside from expurgation, to which I turn in the next paragraph, I think that we should probably do more of this. And do it transparently, of course. The least objectionable version of this would be to introduce courses that pair rewritings or adaptations of Shakespeare plays with the plays themselves, better still with both the plays and Shakespeare's sources for them. One version of such a course begins with *Amleth* and *The Hystorie of Hamblet*, moves on to Kliman and Bertram's *Three-Text Hamlet*, and concludes with "The Love Song of J. Alfred Prufrock" or Charlotte Jones's *Humble Boy*. Given the editions now in print and the availability of texts on the Internet, an entire syllabus easily can be devoted to multiple text plays—the *Hamlet*s, *Lear*s, *Othello*s, *Henry V*s, and the like. Having already mentioned Ted Hughes, this might be the time to plug his anthology, *A Choice of Shakespeare's Verse*. Here is how Hughes begins his introduction to the later edition:

> It has never been easy to settle Shakespeare into the succession of poets in English. According to most anthologies, he wrote only sonnets and songs. The reasons for this reluctance of anthologists to break into the sacred precincts of his drama and start looting portable chunks from the holy structures would make a curious chapter in the history of England's attitude toward its national hero.
>
> Yet when the great speeches of his plays are taken out of context they are no more difficult to understand and appropriate than poems by other great poets. In many cases they are very much easier.[7]

Readers of the essays in *Shakespearean Educations* will find amusing any talk of sacred precincts and portable chunks, given the extent to which these essays document the persistent looting of the temple. Still, a Shakespeare course that adopted Hughes's anthology as its text would make known and available for study a "Shakespeare" quite distinct from the familiar *play*wright.

If I am uncomfortable with expurgation, I am in no way against the study of the expurgation of Shakespeare, starting in Shakespeare's own day or with John Benson's 1640 edition of the *Poems* and continuing to the present. What in the way of racial or sexual reference has been (and continues to be) deemed worthy of censorship? Some portion of the fates of *Othello* and *The Merchant of Venice* is discussed in the present volume. More radical and more objectionable would be to endorse expurgation. Burton reports that school editions of *The Merchant of Venice* typically "cut any reference to Launcelot's affair with a Moor" (107). Disturbing racial and sexual matters were expurgated on behalf of "'the most fastidious Teacher'" and "'the most refined and pure-minded Family'" (107). But surely we too draw lines when we decide whether or how to discuss sensitive passages with our students. On their own, how do college, let alone high school, students absorb phrases like "the rank sweat of an enseamèd bed" or "honeying and making love / Over the nasty sty" (*Hamlet*, 3.4.92–94)? Not to address these lines with our students may be to tolerate passive pedagogical expurgation. Carefully to address these lines with them (a son's compulsion to imagine his mother's lovemaking) may be to uncover whether we, if not Shakespeare, expurgate our own imaginings. For years, every bone in my body has told me that Shakespeare is not only the ideal vehicle (mature, explicit, intensive, trustworthy), but perhaps one of the few still safe vehicles, that allows us to discuss and debate the

history behind, and the currency of, the very matters that are so susceptible to expurgation. But I cannot be alone in my transient
doubts. Of this much I am certain: many of us who teach Shakespeare censor the text and censor ourselves, silently monitoring the
hot spots where we will not tread. I do. With admirable honesty, Stephen Greenblatt concludes his well-known essay, "Invisible Bullets,"
with an adaptation of a remark that Kafka made to Max Brod:
"There is subversion, no end of subversion, only not for us."[8] For
"subversion," we might try substituting "expurgation."

LOCAL AND/OR GLOBAL

Once whole-play Shakespeare began to take hold in college curricula, professors had to decide how they would analyze each play
(Haskin). One possibility, the one that we take for granted, was to
discuss or lecture on theme, character, and plot. Another possibility
was to gloss words, to spend entire lectures on unfamiliar words and
familiar words put to unfamiliar uses. Dayton Haskin tells us that at
Harvard, Francis Child never "devoted a sustained patch of lecturing to anything like a theme, a character, or a plot" (181). For F. A.
March, at Lafayette College, the "idea was to get the students to rivet
their attention on words and speeches that, with a gradual unfolding
of their perceptions of what Shakespeare had made the words do,
would remain lastingly memorable" (181). It is my impression that
very few twenty-first-century Shakespeare classes are concerned
either intensively or pervasively to acknowledge the philological
component of their pedigree. Glossing is relegated to what editors
make available to students in the margins and to passing comment
in lecture halls or classrooms. Some students do seem to perk up at
etymological excursions and it does not take much to get them to
acknowledge the telling ways that a word, say, "invention," has
evolved; but I know of no student who walks into Shakespeare class
expecting fifty minutes of word-by-word or line-by-line sense making. For one thing, such a procedure is too slow for most of them.
And if they are not bored by it, then students complain (perhaps
legitimately) that they cannot make out the forest for the trees. For
another thing, prior classroom experience with the plays has led
them to expect global, thesis-driven, "what it all means" lectures.
They assume that this is exactly what they are paying for: it is not
their job to cobble together an hour's worth of glosses into a coher-
ent thesis.

So maybe this is a division of labor issue. I use the indecorous example provided by an early *Saturday Night Live* routine to illustrate just how important it is for students to be wary of editors' glosses and so to grapple with words for themselves. At Pre-Chew Charlie's, a steak house for people with dentures, waiters come to the table and pre-chew food for patrons . . . who then eat something like vomit. I tell my students that unless they have mind-dentures, and unless they are content to eat vomit, that they themselves ought to chew for themselves on Shakespeare's words—especially the familiar words that editors resolutely gloss for them. Students should not too readily accept that "made of truth" (Sonnet 138) means "utterly faithful." It is a splendid, evasive phrase for them to digest on their own. I cannot help but wonder what would ensue were we, like George Lyman Kittredge, stubbornly and steadfastly to restrict ourselves to helping students unpack what words mean. Would this equip them to formulate their own theses and generalizations? It is not difficult to construe our penchant for theme-mongering as a sign of hubris not expertise, distrust not good faith. An entire semester of word work on clusters such as "policy / politic / politician" and "witch / weird / weyard / weyward" and "gentle / gentry / gentle-(wo)man / gentility" might be a fine sign of our respect for our students' intelligence. Or it might drive them batty.

High and / or Low

Where in college and university curricula should we locate Shakespeare classes and who should teach them (Renker, Haskin)? Elizabeth Renker notes that in the late nineteenth century, Shakespeare's "primary curricular location was the less serious and less prestigious" element of the curriculum, the "'English minor class'" (148). Until well into the second decade of the twentieth century, Shakespeare was absent from advanced classes. According to Renker, "labor stratifications" corresponded with curriculum placement: Hopkins's "Collegiate Professor of English" taught Chaucer, Spenser, Shakespeare and Milton, but he did not get to teach Hopkins's highest level classes (149). Assuming that we will continue to teach Shakespeare and assuming nothing about making Shakespeare an English major requirement, what (if any) prerequisites ought there to be for Shakespeare classes? Here are some hundred-year-old curricular ladders: rhetoric and composition, then Old and Middle English, then Shakespeare, then Milton to the present; rhetoric and composition, then Shakespeare, then Old and Middle English; rhetoric and composition and Shakespeare at the same time, then Milton to the present; Shakespeare and American literature before Old and Middle English; Shakespeare as a free-floating radical, open to students at any time, or after rhetoric and composition, or after a survey of English literature?

I do not know what it would be like to teach Shakespeare to students versed in Old and Middle English, and I cannot imagine that many university professors today do either. Few of my students have completed a survey of literature from *Beowulf* to Virginia Woolf. Still, I can imagine offering a Shakespeare class open only to students who have taken Latin literature classes, to students who have taken a class in Middle English, or to a room full of students who have taken an early modern English history class. I wonder about Shakespeare for neuroscience students, for architecture students. Most schools offer science courses for humanities students. Who offers Shakespeare for science students? Given the number of students who would probably enroll in such classes, these are almost certainly going to remain fantasies. But there is another reason, too. I am not a Latinist and my knowledge of Old English dates back to a two-semester, introductory-level graduate-school class. So it is not just that I would be disqualifying many students. I would be disqualifying most professors, myself included, which recalls the question of who should teach Shakespeare (and at what levels) in colleges and universities. This has everything to do with economics, prestige, seniority, and specialization, and there is no way to do justice to it here. Should graduate students teach introductory or upper-level Shakespeare classes? Should our most experienced and most senior faculty teach our introductory-level (Shakespeare) classes? Per force and per choice, colleges are much better at deterritorializing literature classes than are universities. At colleges, there is a fair chance that a Henry James scholar will teach Shakespeare or a Shakespeare scholar Henry James. Miltonists teach Shakespeare all the time, but how many classicists teach Shakespeare? Rhetoricians should teach Shakespeare. Amateurs should teach Shakespeare! I doubt that very many, if any, colleges and universities would allow the uncredentialed to teach Shakespeare, but what if Thelonious Monk or Emily Dickinson were available for a guest lecture?

THEN AND / OR NOW

Taken together, the essays in *Shakespearean Educations* prompt us to reconsider a good deal more about Shakespeare pedagogy than I have addressed or know how to address. The uses to which Shakespeare was put in American education need not be replicated today, but they ought not to be written off, either. Although I have not included a "Student and / or Consumer" section, we still should investigate the ways classroom and consumer exigencies intersect with one another (Kegl). Something ought to be said about "Relevant and / or Irrelevant." For example, should students who concentrate in African-American literature be required to read Shakespeare (McAllister)? Should every Shakespeare class require each student to act out part of a scene (Mylander, Nathans, Gustafson)? If there is much to learn about what was done differently, there is also much to learn about what we might yet do differently.

NOTES

1. "The 1930s" because the essays in this volume were first written for a conference, "Shakespeare in American Education, 1607–1934," organized by the Folger Shakespeare Library in conjunction with the seventy-fifth anniversary of its founding in 1932. I am happy to have this opportunity to thank Barbara Mowat and Kathleen Lynch for asking me to help organize this conference. Their wisdom and expertise, and that of many others on the Folger Library staff (Owen Williams, in particular), along with the invited speakers' wonderful collegiality and impressive archival skills, made this meeting a very great success.

2. Julia Reinhard Lupton, *Citizen-Saints: Shakespeare and Political Theology* (Chicago: University of Chicago Press, 2005), 15; and Esther Cloudman Dunn, *Shakespeare in America* (New York: MacMillan, 1939).

3. Citations of Shakespeare's works are taken from *The Complete Pelican Shakespeare*, Stephen Orgel and A. R. Braunmuller, gen. eds. (New York: Penguin Books, 2002).

4. See Charles H. Frey, *Making Sense of Shakespeare* (Madison, NJ: Fairleigh Dickinson University Press, 1999), 25 et passim.

5. But see Frey, *Making Sense of Shakespeare,* 130–37.

6. Ted Hughes, *Shakespeare and the Goddess of Complete Being* (New York: Farrar, Straus, and Giroux, 1992).

7. Ted Hughes, ed., *A Choice of Shakespeare's Verse* (1971; repr., London: Faber & Faber, 1991).

8. Stephen Greenblatt, *Shakespearean Negotiations: The Circulation of Social Energy in Renaissance England* (Berkeley: University of California Press, 1988), 39 and 65.

Bibliography

Archives and Manuscript Collections

A Century of Progress Records. Special Collections and University Archives. University of Illinois–Chicago.

Alain Locke Papers. Moorland-Spingarn Research Center. Howard University, Washington, DC.

Annual Reports of the President and Treasurer of Harvard University. Harvard University Archives, Cambridge, MA. Online at http://hul.harvard.edu/huarc.

Annual Reports of the President and Treasurer of Radcliffe College. Harvard University Archives, Cambridge, MA. Online at http://hul.harvard.edu/huarc.

Archives and Manuscripts. Chicago History Museum, Chicago, IL.

Archives and Special Collections. Mount Holyoke College, South Hadley, MA.

Archives, City University of New York, New York, NY.

Archives of the Chicago Board of Education, Chicago, IL.

Bentley Historical Library, University of Michigan, Ann Arbor.

Biography File, Howard University Archives. Howard University, Washington, DC.

Board of Education Archives, Municipal Archives, New York, NY.

Charles Mills Gayley Papers, Bancroft Library. University of California, Berkeley.

Columbia University Archives. Columbia University, New York, NY.

Curtis-Stevenson Family Papers Collection. Massachusetts Historical Society, Boston, MA.

English Department File, Howard University Archives. Howard University, Washington, DC.

Ferdinand Hamburger Jr. Archives. Johns Hopkins University, Baltimore, MD.

Folger Shakespeare Library, Washington, DC.

Harvard University Archives, Cambridge, MA.

Howard University Archives, Moorland-Spingarn Research Center, Howard University, Washington, DC.

Jerome Tarver Collection, Richmond, VA (private collection).

Kemble Letters. Folger Shakespeare Library, Washington, DC.

L. Clark Seelye Papers, Smith College Archives. Smith College, Northampton, MA.

Massachusetts Historical Society, Boston, MA.

Newberry Library, Chicago, IL.

Radcliffe College Archives, Harvard University, Cambridge, MA.

Special Collections, Kentucky Historical Society. Frankfort, KY.

Special Collections and Archives. Transylvania University, Lexington, KY.

Stanford University Archives, Stanford University, Stanford, CA.

Thomas Montgomery Gregory Collection. Moorland-Spingarn Research Center. Howard University, Washington, DC.

University Archives, University of Kentucky Libraries, Lexington, KY.

University of Virginia Archives, Charlottesville, VA.

PERIODICALS

American Museum, Philadelphia, PA.

Bee, Washington, DC.

Boston Transcript.

Boston Weekly Magazine.

Chicago Daily News.

Chicago Daily Tribune.

Chicago Defender.

Chicago Herald and Examiner.

Chicago Journal of Commerce.

Chicago Loop News.

Chicago Sunday Times.

Christian Science Monitor, Boston, MA.

Citizen, Boston, MA

Colored American, New York, NY.

Crisis, New York, NY.

Daily Californian, Berkeley, CA.

Freedom's Journal, New York, NY.

Hartford Courant.

Howard University Journal, Howard University, Washington, DC.

Howard University Record, Howard University, Washington, DC.

Ladies' Literary Cabinet. New York, NY.

Ladies' Port Folio, Boston, MA.

Liberator, Boston, MA

National Era, Washington, DC.

New York Times.

Philadelphia Repository and Weekly Register.

Proceedings of the Massachusetts Historical Society, Boston, MA.

Time.

Washington Post.

Weekly Advocate, New York, NY.

BOOKS AND ARTICLES

"AP Subjects: English Literature," College Board. Online at http://www.college-board.com/student/testing/ap/sub_englit.html.

Adams, Joseph Quincy. "Shakespeare and American Culture." *Spinning Wheel* 12 (June–July 1932): 212–15, 229–31.

———. "Shakespeare and Virginia." Bound typescript dated April 12, 1943. MS.Add.37, Folger Shakespeare Library, Washington, DC.

———. *Shakespeare for Students.* New York: Houghton Mifflin, n.d.

Amory, Hugh. "Appendix 1: A Note on Statistics." In *The Colonial Book in the Atlantic World,* edited by Hugh Amory and David D. Hall, 504–18. Cambridge: Cambridge University Press, 2000.

———. "Printing and Bookselling in New England, 1638–1713." In *The Colonial Book in the Atlantic World,* edited by Hugh Amory and David D. Hall, 83–116. Cambridge: Cambridge University Press, 2000.

———. "Reinventing the Colonial Book." In *The Colonial Book in the Atlantic World,* edited by Hugh Amory and David D. Hall, 26–54. Cambridge: Cambridge University Press, 2000.

Andrews, Charles C. *The History of the New-York African Free-Schools.* New York: M. Day, 1830.

Applebaum, Robert, and John Wood Sweet, eds. *Envisioning an English Empire: Jamestown and the Making of the North Atlantic World.* Philadelphia: University of Pennsylvania Press, 2005.

Applebee, Arthur N. *Tradition and Reform in the Teaching of English: A History.* Urbana, IL: National Council of Teachers of English, 1974.

Armitage, David, and Michael J. Braddick, eds. *The British Atlantic World, 1500–1800.* New York: Palgrave Macmillan, 2002.

Atherton, Frederic. "A Suggestion to the English Department." *Harvard Monthly* 22 (March 1896): 10–14.

Bacon, Delia. *The Philosophy of Shakespeare's Plays Unfolded.* Boston: Ticknor and Fields, 1857.

Baldwin, Neil. *Henry Ford and the Jews: The Mass Production of Hate.* New York: Public Affairs, 2001.

Ball, W. W. Rouse, and J. A. Venn. *Admissions to Trinity College, Cambridge.* London: Macmillan, 1913.

Barber, Jonathan. *A Practical Treatise on Gesture, Chiefly Abstracted from Austin's Chironomia; Adapted to the Use of Students, and Arranged according to the Method of Instruction in Harvard University.* Cambridge: Hilliard and Brown, 1831.

Baxter, Maurice G. *One and Inseparable: Daniel Webster and the Union.* Cambridge: Belknap Press of Harvard University Press, 1984.

Benzie, W. *The Dublin Orator: Thomas Sheridan's Influence on Eighteenth-Century Rhetoric and Belles Lettres.* Menston, UK: University of Leeds Press, 1972.

Berkowitz, Joel. " 'A True Jewish Jew': Three Yiddish Shylocks." *Theater Survey* 37 (1996): 75–98.

Bicks, Caroline. *Midwiving Subjects in Shakespeare's England.* Burlington, VT: Ashgate, 2003.

———. "Planned Parenthood: Minding the Quick Woman in *All's Well.*" *Modern Philology* 103 (2006): 299–331.

Blair, Hugh. *Lectures on Rhetoric and Belles Lettres.* Edited by Harold F. Harding. 2 vols. Carbondale: Southern Illinois University Press, 1965.

The Blue and Gold. Berkeley, CA: Junior Class of the University of California, 1897.

Boas, Frederick S. *University Drama in the Tudor Age.* New York: Arno Press, 1978.

Bond, W. H., and Hugh Amory. *The Printed Catalogues of the Harvard College Library, 1723–1790.* Boston: Colonial Society of Massachusetts, 1996.

Booth, Julia E. "The Teaching of Shakespeare." *English Journal* 9.4 (1920): 219–23.

Botein, Stephen. "The Anglo-American Book Trade before 1776: Personnel and Strategies." In *Printing and Society in Early America*, edited by William L. Joyce, David D. Hall, Richard D. Brown, and John B. Hench, 48–82. Worcester, MA: American Antiquarian Society, 1983.

Bourdieu, Pierre. *Distinction: A Social Critique of the Judgement of Taste.* Translated by Richard Nice. London: Routledge and Kegan Paul, 1984.

Brawley, Benjamin. *A Short History of the English Drama.* London: George G. Harrap, 1921.

Brereton, John C., ed. *The Origins of Composition Studies in the American College, 1875–1925: A Documentary History.* Pittsburgh, PA: University of Pittsburgh Press, 1995.

Bristol, Michael D. *Shakespeare's America, America's Shakespeare.* London: Routledge, 1990.

Brownson, Orestes. "Specimens of Foreign Standard Literature." *Boston Quarterly Review* (1838), reprinted in *Americans on Shakespeare 1776–1914*, edited by Peter Rawlings, 72. Aldershot, UK: Ashgate, 1999.

Brousseau, Elaine. "'Now, Literature, Philosophy, and Thought, Are Shakspear-ized': American Culture and Nineteenth Century Shakespearean Performance, 1835–1875." PhD diss., University of Massachusetts–Amherst, 2003.

Brown, Matthew P. *The Pilgrim and the Bee: Reading Rituals and Book Culture in Early New England.* Philadelphia: University of Pennsylvania Press, 2007.

Brown, Victoria Bissel, ed. "Introduction." In *Twenty Years at Hull-House, with Auto-Biographical Notes by Jane Addams.* New York: Bedford / St. Martin's Press, 1999.

Bruce, Philip Alexander. *Institutional History of Virginia in the Seventeenth Century.* New York: G. P. Putnam's Sons, 1910.

Bryson, Anna. *From Courtesy to Civility: Changing Codes of Conduct in Early Modern England.* Oxford: Clarendon Press, 1998.

Bulman, James. *"The Merchant of Venice": Shakespeare in Performance.* New York: Manchester University Press, 1991.

Bunker, Frank Forest. *The Functional Reorganization of the American Public School System.* PhD diss., New York University, 1913. Washington: Government Printing Office, 1916.

Burr, Samuel Engle. *An Introduction to Progressive Education.* Cincinnati, OH: C. A. Gregory, 1933.

Bushman, Richard L. *The Refinement of America: Persons, Houses, Cities.* New York: Alfred A. Knopf, 1992.

Butler, Jon. "Thomas Teackle's 333 Books: A Great Library on Virginia's Eastern Shore, 1697." *William and Mary Quarterly* 49 (1992): 449–91.

Carlson, Marvin. *Theories of the Theatre: A Historical and Critical Survey, from the Greeks to the Present.* Ithaca: Cornell University Press, 1984.

Carr, Jean Ferguson, Stephen L. Carr, and Lucille M. Schultz. *Archives of Instruction: Nineteenth Century Rhetorics, Readers, and Composition Books in the United States.* Carbondale: Southern Illinois University Press, 2005.

Carson, Jane. *Colonial Virginians at Play.* Charlottesville: University Press at Virginia, 1965.

Cartelli, Thomas. *Repositioning Shakespeare: National Formations, Postcolonial Appropriations.* London: Routledge, 1999.

Casper, Scott E., Joanne D. Chaison, and Jeffrey D. Groves, eds. *Perspectives on American Book History: Artifacts and Commentary.* Amherst: University of Massachusetts Press, 2002.

Chaplin, Joyce E. "Race." In *The British Atlantic World, 1500–1800,* edited by David Armitage and Michael J. Braddick, 154–72. New York: Palgrave Macmillan, 2002.

Chubb, Percival. "What the Shakespeare Tercentenary Celebration Might Mean for the Schools." *English Journal* 5.4 (1916): 237–40.

Clark, Gregory, and S. Michael Halloran, eds. *Oratorical Culture in Nineteenth-Century America.* Carbondale: Southern Illinois University Press, 1993.

Cliff, Nigel. *The Shakespeare Riots: Revenge, Drama, and Death in Nineteenth-Century America.* New York: Random House, 2007.

Connors, Robert J. *Composition-Rhetoric: Backgrounds, Theory, and Pedagogy.* Pittsburgh, PA: University of Pittsburgh Press, 1997.

———. "Crisis and Panacea in Composition Studies: A History." In *Composition in Context: Essays in Honor of Donald C. Stewart,* edited by W. Ross Winterowd and Vincent Gillespie, 86–105. Carbondale: Southern Illinois University Press, 1994.

Cook, A. S. "English at Yale University." In *English in American Universities, by Professors in the English Departments of Twenty Representative Institutions,* 29–39. Boston: D.C. Heath, 1895.

Cooke, Increase. *The American Orator; or, Elegant Extracts in Prose and Poetry.* New Haven: Sidney's Press, 1818.

———. *Sequel to The American Orator, Or, Dialogues for Schools.* New Haven: Increase Cooke and Sidney's Press, 1813.

Cooper, Anna Julia. *A Voice from the South.* New York: Oxford University Press, 1988.

Cordasco, Francesco. *The Shaping of American Graduate Education: Daniel Coit Gilman and the Protean Ph.D.* Totowa, NJ: Rowman and Littlefield, 1973.

Coyle, Martin, ed. *New Casebooks: "The Merchant of Venice."* New York: St. Martin's Press, 1998.

Cressy, David. *Coming Over: Migration and Communication between England and New England in the Seventeenth Century.* Cambridge: Cambridge University Press, 1987.

Curry, S. S. *Classical Selection from the Best Authors Adapted to the Study of Vocal Expression.* Boston: Expression Company, 1888.

Dabbs, Thomas. "Shakespeare and the Department of English." In *English as a Discipline Or, Is There a Plot in This Play?* edited by James C. Raymond, 82–98. Tuscaloosa: University of Alabama Press, 1996.

Dakin, Dorothy. *How to Teach High School English.* Boston: D. C. Heath, 1947.

Davidson, Cathy N., and Jessamyn Hatcher. *No More Separate Spheres!* Durham, NC: Duke University Press, 2002.

Davis, Peter A. "Puritan Mercantilism and the Politics of Anti-Theatrical Legislation in Colonial America." In *The American Stage: Social and Economic Issues from the Colonial Period to the Present,* edited by Ron Engle and Tice L. Miller, 18–29. Cambridge: Cambridge University Press, 1993.

Davis, Richard Beale. *Intellectual Life in the Colonial South 1585–1763*. Knoxville: University of Tennessee Press, 1978.

Dawes, Rufus Cutler. "Report of the President of A Century of Progress to the Board of Trustees, March 14, 1936." Chicago: A Century of Progress, 1936.

Deetz, Patricia Scott, Christopher Fennell, and J. Eric Deetz. *The Plymouth Colony Archive Project, 2000–2006*. Online at http://etext.virginia.edu.

Detroit Training School of Elocution. *Questions on the Plays of Shakespeare*. N.p., 1888.

Dollimore, Jonathan, and Alan Sinfield, eds. *Political Shakespeare: New Essays in Cultural Materialism*. Manchester: Manchester University Press, 1985.

Donnelly, Ignatius. *The Great Cryptogram: Francis Bacon's Cipher in the So-Called Shakespeare Plays*. Chicago: R. S. Peale, 1888.

Douglass, Frederick. "The Color Line." *North American Review* 132 (1881): 567–78.

———. "The Meaning of July Fourth for the Negro." *The Life and Writings of Frederick Douglass*. Volume 2, edited by Philip S. Foner. New York: International Publishers, 1950.

Dowden, Edward. *Shakspere*. Literature Primers. 1875. Reprint, New York: D. Appleton, 1882.

Duane, Anna Mae. "Performing Freedom in Antebellum New York: The New York African Free School." Unpublished paper delivered at Luce Hall, Yale University, November 13, 2006.

Dudden, Faye E. *Women in the American Theatre: Actresses and Audiences, 1790–1870*. New Haven: Yale University Press, 1994.

Dumenil, Lynn, "The Progressive Era through the 1920's." In *Encyclopedia of American Social History*, 3 vols., edited by Mary Cupiec Cayton, Elliott J. Gorn, and Peter W. Williams,1.173–88. New York: Scribner's, 1993.

Dunn, Esther Cloudman. *Shakespeare in America*. New York: Macmillan, 1939.

Dyson, Walter. *Howard University: The Capstone of Negro Education. A History, 1867–1940*. Washington, DC: Graduate School of Howard University, 1941.

E. F. E. [Untitled article.] *The Boston Transcript*, December 12, 1917, 11.

Edelstein, Barry. "To Get Out of Those Damned Spots." *New York Times*, April 26, 2009.

Edwards, Richard. *Analytical Sixth Reader*. New York: Mason Brothers, 1866.

Eliot, Charles William. "The New Education: Its Organization, Part 1." *Atlantic Monthly* 23 (February 1869): 202–20.

———. "The New Education: Its Organization, Part 2." *Atlantic Monthly* 23 (March 1869): 358–67.

Emerson, Ralph Waldo. "Shakespeare: Or, the Poet." In *Essays and Lectures*, edited by Joel Porte, 710–26. New York: Library of America, 1983.

Engle, Ron, and Tice L. Miller, eds. *The American Stage: Social and Economic Issues from the Colonial Period to the Present*. Cambridge: Cambridge University Press, 1993.

English Short Title Catalogue. Online at http://estc.bl.uk (accessed January 10, 2008).

Evans, G. Blakemore, ed. *The Riverside Shakespeare*, 2nd. edition. Boston: Houghton Mifflin, 1997.

Farish, Hunter Dickinson, ed. *Journal & Letters of Philip Vickers Fithian, 1773–1774: A Plantation Tutor of the Old Dominion*. Williamsburg, VA: Colonial Williamsburg, Inc., 1943.

Farmer, Alan B., and Zachary Lesser. "Canons and Classics: Publishing Drama in Caroline England." In *Localizing Caroline Drama: Politics and Economics of the Early Modern English Stage, 1625–1642,* edited by Adam Zucker and Alan B. Farmer, 18–41. New York: Palgrave Macmillan, 2006.

———. "Vile Arts: The Marketing of English Printed Drama, 1512–1660." *Research Opportunities in Renaissance Drama* 39 (2000): 77–165.

———. *DEEP: Database of Early English Playbooks.* Online at http://deep.sas.upenn.edu.

Felker, Christopher D. "The Print History of *The Tempest* in Early America." In *The Tempest: Critical Essays,* ed. Patrick M. Murphy, 482–508. New York: Routledge, 2001.

Ferington, Esther, ed. *Infinite Variety: Exploring the Folger Shakespeare Library.* Washington, DC: Folger Shakespeare Library, 2002.

Fisher, Judith, and Stephen Watt, eds. *When They Weren't Doing Shakespeare: Essays on Nineteenth-Century British and American Theatre.* Athens: University of Georgia Press, 1989.

Fitz Gerald, Ellen. "Shakespeare in the Elementary School." *English Journal* 3.6 (1914): 345–53.

Foner, Philip S., and Robert James Branham, eds. *Lift Every Voice: African American Oratory, 1787–1900.* Tuscaloosa: University of Alabama Press, 1998.

Ford, Worthington Chauncey. *The Boston Book Market 1679–1700.* New York: Burt Franklin, 1918.

Franklin, Benjamin, ed. *Boston Printers, Publishers, and Booksellers: 1640–1800.* Boston: G. K. Hall & Co., 1980.

Franklin, Phyllis. "English Studies: The World of Scholarship in 1883." *PMLA* 99 (1984): 346–70.

Frantzen, Allen J. *Desire for Origins: New Language, Old English, and Teaching the Tradition.* New Brunswick, NJ: Rutgers University Press, 1990.

Frantzen, Allen, and John D. Niles, eds. *Anglo-Saxonism and the Construction of Social Identity.* Gainesville: University Press of Florida, 1997.

Frey, Charles H. "Teaching Shakespeare in America." *Shakespeare Quarterly* 35 (1984): 541–59.

Frey, Charles H. *Making Sense of Shakespeare.* Madison, NJ: Fairleigh Dickinson University Press, 1999.

Frink, Henry Allyn. *The New Century Speaker.* 1898. Reprint, New York: Books for Libraries, 1971.

Fuess, Claude M. *The College Board: Its First Fifty Years.* New York: Columbia University Press, 1950.

Fulton, Robert I., and Thomas C. Trueblood. *Choice Readings from Standard and Popular Authors Embracing Complete Classification of Selections, a Comprehensive Diagraph of the Principles of Vocal Expression, and Indexes to the Choicest Readings from Shakespeare, the Bible, and the Hymn-Book.* Boston: Ginn, 1898.

Games, Alison. "Migration." In *The British Atlantic World, 1500–1800,* edited by David Armitage and Michael J. Braddick, 31–50. New York: Palgrave Macmillan, 2002.

Garvey, Ellen Gruber. "Scissoring and Scrapbooks: Reading, Remaking, and Recirculating." In *New Media, 1740–1915,* edited by Lisa Gitelman and Geoffrey B. Pingree, 207–28. Cambridge: MIT Press, 2003.

Gayley, Charles Mills. *The Classic Myths in English Literature and Art, Based Originally on Bulfinch's "Age of Fable" (1855), Accompanied by an Interpretive and Illustrative Commentary.* Boston: Ginn & Company, 1893.

———. "English at the University of California," Reprint, in *The Origins of Literary Study in America: A Documentary Anthology,* edited by Gerald Graff and Michael Warner, 54–60. London: Routledge, 1989.

———. "Heart of the Race." In *A Book of Homage to Shakespeare,* edited by Israel Gollancz, 340–41. Oxford: Oxford University Press, 1916.

———. *Idols of Education.* New York: Doubleday, 1910.

———. *Shakespeare and the Founders of Liberty in America.* New York: Macmillan, 1917.

———. *University Extension 2,* 8 (February 1893). Miscellaneous Writings of Charles Mills Gayley, Bancroft Library. University of California, Berkeley, CA.

Genung, John Franklin. *The Practical Elements of Rhetoric.* Boston: Ginn, 1886.

———. *The Working Principles of Rhetoric.* Boston: Ginn, 1900.

Gildrie, Richard P. *The Profane, the Civil, and the Godly: The Reformation of Manners in Orthodox New England, 1679–1749.* University Park: Pennsylvania State University Press, 1994.

Gilmore-Lehne, William J. *Reading Becomes a Necessity of Life: Material and Cultural Life in Rural New England, 1780–1835.* Knoxville: University of Tennessee Press, 1989.

Gleason, Philip. "American Identity and Americanization." In *Harvard Encyclopedia of American Ethnic Groups,* edited by Stephan Thernstrom, 31–58. Cambridge: Harvard University Press, 1980.

Gollancz, Israel, ed. *A Book of Homage to Shakespeare.* Oxford: Oxford University Press, 1916.

Gorn, Elliott J., ed. *The McGuffey Readers: Selections from the 1879 Edition.* New York: Bedford / St. Martin's, 1998.

Graff, Gerald. *Professing Literature: An Institutional History.* Chicago: University of Chicago Press, 1987.

Graff, Gerald, and Michael Warner, eds. *The Origins of Literary Study in America: A Documentary Anthology.* London: Routledge, 1989.

Grant, Madison. *The Passing of the Great Race; Or, The Racial Basis of European History.* New York: Scribner's, 1916.

Greenblatt, Stephen, gen. ed. *The Norton Shakespeare, Based on the Oxford Edition.* New York: W. W. Norton & Company, 1997.

———. "Shakespeare and the Uses of Power." *New York Review of Books* (April 12, 2007): 75–77, 81–82.

———. *Shakespearean Negotiations: The Circulation of Social Energy in Renaissance England.* Berkeley: University of California Press, 1988.

Greene, Jack P. *Pursuits of Happiness: The Social Development of Early Modern British Colonies and the Formation of American Culture.* Chapel Hill: University of North Carolina Press, 1988.

Greenlaw, Edwin, and Dudley Miles. *Teaching Literature: A Handbook for Use with the Literature and Life Series.* Chicago: Scott, Foresman, 1926.

Greenlaw, Edwin, and James Holly Hanford. *The Great Tradition: A Book of Selections from English and American Prose and Poetry, Illustrating the National Ideals of Freedom, Faith and Conduct.* Chicago: Scott, Foresman, 1919.

Griffin, Eric. "The Spectre of Spain in John Smith's Colonial Writing." In *Envisioning an English Empire: Jamestown and the Making of the North Atlantic World*, edited by Robert Applebaum and John Wood Sweet, 111–34. Philadelphia: University of Pennsylvania Press, 2005.

Grimsted, David. *Melodrama Unveiled: American Theatre and Culture, 1800–1850*. Berkeley: University of California Press, 1968.

Gross, Carl H., and Charles C. Chandler, eds. *The History of American Education through Readings*. Boston: D. C. Heath, 1964.

Gross, John. *Shylock, A Legend and Its Legacy*. New York: Simon and Schuster, 1992.

Gruber, Carol S. *Mars and Minerva: World War I and the Uses of the Higher Learning in America*. Baton Rouge: Louisiana State University Press, 1975.

Guillory, John. "Preprofessionalism: What Graduate Students Want." *ADE Bulletin* 113 (1996): 4–8.

Gummere, Francis. "A Day with Professor Child." *Atlantic Monthly* 103 (March 1909): 421–25.

Gummere, Richard M. *The American Colonial Mind and the Classical Tradition*. Cambridge: Harvard University Press, 1963.

Hackel, Heidi Brayman. *Reading Material in Early Modern England: Print, Gender, and Literacy*. Cambridge: Cambridge University Press, 2005.

Hackett, James Henry. *Notes, Criticisms, and Correspondence upon Certain Plays and Actors of Shakespeare*. New York: Carleton, 1863.

Hakluyt, Richard. *The Principal Nauigations, Voyages, Traffiques and Discoueries of the English Nation*. London, 1599–1600.

Hall, David D. "Introduction." In *The Colonial Book in the Atlantic World*, edited by Hugh Amory and David D. Hall, 1–25. Cambridge: Cambridge University Press, 2000.

———. "The Uses of Literacy in New England, 1600–1850." In *Cultures of Print: Essays in the History of the Book*, 36–78. Amherst: University of Massachusetts Press, 1996.

Hanson, John Wesley, Jr., and Lillian Woodward Gunckel, eds. *The Ideal Orator: And Model of Elocution, Containing a Practical Treatise on the Delsarte System and Physical Culture and Expression, Including Valuable Instructions and Rules for the Cultivation of the Voice and the Use of Gestures, Together with Choice Selections for Readings and Recitations Now Used in the Leading Schools of Oratory*. Chicago, 1895.

Harlan, Louis R., ed. *The Booker T. Washington Papers*. Vol. 3. Urbana: University of Illinois Press, 1974.

Hatfield, April Lee. *Atlantic Virginia: Intercolonial Relations in the Seventeenth Century*. Philadelphia: University of Pennsylvania Press, 2004.

Haven, E. O. *Rhetoric: A Text-Book Designed for Use in Schools and Colleges, and for Private Study*. New York: Harper & Brothers, 1873.

Hazlitt, William. *Characters of Shakespeare's Plays*. 1817. Project Gutenberg, 2002. Online at http://www.gutenberg.org/dirs/etext04/chrsh10.txt.

Hecht, Stuart. *Hull-House Theater: An Analytical and Evaluative History*. Ann Arbor, MI: University Microfilms International, 1991.

Higham, John. *Strangers in the Land: Patterns of American Nativism 1860–1925*. 2nd ed. New Brunswick, NJ: Rutgers University Press, 1988.

Highlights of the Educational Exhibits, Chicago World's Fair, Compiled for School Teacher

Conductors for Student Tours, September–October, 1934. Chicago: A Century of Progress Exposition, 1934.

Hill, Adams Sherman. *The Principles of Rhetoric.* New York: American, 1895.

Hill, David J. *The Elements of Rhetoric.* New York: Shelton, 1878.

———. *The Science of Rhetoric: An Introduction to the Laws of Effective Discourse.* New York: Shelton, 1877.

Hill, Errol. *Shakespeare in Sable: A History of Black Shakespearean Actors.* Amherst: University of Massachusetts Press, 1984.

Hinks, Peter P. *To Awaken My Afflicted Brethren: David Walker and the Problem of Antebellum Slave Resistance.* University Park: Pennsylvania State University Press, 1997.

Holderness, Graham, ed. *The Shakespeare Myth.* Manchester: Manchester University Press, 1988.

Hopkins, James F. *The University of Kentucky: Origins and Early Years.* Lexington, KY: University of Kentucky Press, 1951.

Horsman, Reginald. *Race and Manifest Destiny: The Origins of American Racial Anglo-Saxonism.* Cambridge: Harvard University Press, 1981.

Howe, Daniel Walker. *What Hath God Wrought: The Transformation of America, 1815–1848.* New York: Oxford University Press, 2007.

Hows, John. *Shakspearian Reader.* New York: D. Appleton & Co., 1849.

Hoyle, Francis P. *The Complete Speaker and Reciter for Home, School, Church and Platform.* Philadelphia: World Bible House, 1905.

Hudson, Henry N., ed. *The Merchant of Venice, by William Shakespeare.* 1879. Reprint, Boston: Ginn & Co., 1903.

———. *Shakespeare's "Merchant of Venice."* Boston: Ginn, 1893.

———. *The Works of Shakespeare: The Text Carefully Restored According to the First Editions.* Boston: J. Munroe and Co., 1851.

Hughes, Ted, ed., *A Choice of Shakespeare's Verse.* 1971. Reprint, London: Faber & Faber, 1991.

———. *Shakespeare and the Goddess of Complete Being.* New York: Farrar, Straus, and Giroux, 1992.

Humphreys, W. R. "The Department of English Language and Literature." In *The University of Michigan: An Encyclopedic Survey in Four Volumes,* 7 vols. edited by Wilfred B. Shaw, 3.545–87. Ann Arbor: University of Michigan Press, 1942–81. Available online at http://quod.lib.umich.edu/u/umsurvey/.

Hyder, Clyde Kenneth. *George Lyman Kittredge: Teacher and Scholar.* Lawrence: University of Kansas Press, 1962.

Jackson, Shannon. *Lines of Activity: Performance, Historiography, Hull-House Domesticity.* Ann Arbor: University of Michigan Press, 2000.

Johns Hopkins Half-Century Directory. Compiled by W. Norman Brown. Baltimore: Johns Hopkins University Press, 1926.

Johnson, Nan. *Gender and Rhetorical Space in American Life: 1866–1910.* Carbondale: Southern Illinois University Press, 2002.

———. *Nineteenth-Century Rhetoric in North America.* Carbondale: Southern Illinois University Press, 1991.

Johnson, Odai. *Absence and Memory in Colonial American Theatre: Fiorelli's Plaster.* New York: Palgrave Macmillan, 2006.

Johnson, Odai, and William J. Burling. *The Colonial American Stage, 1665–1774: A Documentary Calendar*. Madison, NJ: Fairleigh Dickinson University Press, 2001.

Jordan, David Starr. *The Blood of the Nation: A Study of the Decay of Races through the Survival of the Unfit*. Boston: American Unitarian Association, 1902.

———. *The Voice of the Scholar: With Other Addresses on the Problems in Higher Education*. San Francisco: Paul Elder and Company, 1903.

Joyce, William L., David D. Hall, and Richard D. Brown, eds. *Printing and Society in Early America*. Worcester: American Antiquarian Society, 1983.

Kahn, Coppélia. "Caliban at the Stadium: Shakespeare and the Making of Americans." *Massachusetts Review* 42.2 (2000): 256–84.

———. "Remembering Shakespeare Imperially: The 1916 Tercentenary." *Shakespeare Quarterly* 52. 4 (2001): 456–78.

Kahn, Edward. "Desdemona and the Role of Women in the Antebellum North." *Theatre Journal* 60.2 (2008): 235–55.

Keller, Helen. *"The Story of My Life" with Her Letters (1887–1901)*. Edited by John Albert Macy. New York: Doubleday, Page, & Co., 1903.

Kelley, Mary. *Learning to Stand & Speak: Women, Education, and Public Life in America's Republic*. Chapel Hill: University of North Carolina Press, 2006.

Kidd, Robert. *New Elocution and Vocal Culture*. New York: American Book Company, 1883.

King, Stanley. *Recollections of the Folger Shakespeare Library*. [Ithaca, NY:] Published for the Trustees of Amherst College [by] Cornell University Press [1950].

Kupperman, Karen Ordahl. "Fear of Hot Climates in the Anglo-American Colonial Experience." *William and Mary Quarterly* 41 (1984): 213–40.

Kurtz, Benjamin P. *Charles Mills Gayley: The Glory of a Lighted Mind*. Berkeley: University of California Press, 1943.

Lauck, John Hampton. "The Reception and Teaching of Shakespeare in Nineteenth and Early Twentieth Century America." PhD diss., University of Illinois at Urbana–Champaign, 1991.

Laughlin, Clara E. *So You're Going to Merrie England*. Chicago: Colortext, 1934.

Leef, George C. *Becoming an Educated Person: Toward a Core Curriculum for College Students*. Washington, DC: American Council of Trustees and Alumni, 2003.

Lehmann-Haupt, Hellmut. *The Book in America: A History of the Making, the Selling, and the Collecting of Books in the United States*. New York: R. R. Bowker, 1939.

Leipziger, Henry. *Annual Report of the Supervisor of Lectures to the Board of Education, 1911–1912*. New York: Department of Education, 1912.

Lepore, Jill. "Literacy and Reading in Puritan New England." In *Perspectives on American Book History: Artifacts and Commentary*, edited by Scott E. Casper, Joanne D. Chaison, and Jeffrey D. Groves, 17–46. Amherst: University of Massachusetts Press, 2002.

———. *The Name of War: King Phillip's War and the Origins of American Identity*. New York: Alfred A. Knopf, 1998.

Levine, Lawrence W. *Highbrow/Lowbrow: The Emergence of Cultural Hierarchy in America*. Cambridge, MA: Harvard University Press, 1988.

———. "William Shakespeare in America." In *Popular Culture in American History*, edited by Jim Cullen, 32–49. New York: Blackwell, 2001.

Lindberg, Stanley. *The Annotated McGuffey*. New York: Van Nostrand Reinhold, 1976.

Little, Monroe H. "The Extra-Curricular Activities of Black College Students, 1868–1940." *Journal of Negro History* 65 (1980): 135–48.

Littlefield, George Emery. *Early Boston Booksellers 1642–1711*. New York: Club of Odd Volumes, 1900.

Logan, Rayford. *Howard University: The First Hundred Years, 1867–1967*. New York: New York University Press, 1969.

Lohr, Lennox. *Fair Management: The Story of A Century of Progress Exposition*. Chicago: Cuneo Press, 1952.

Lott, Eric. *Love and Theft: Blackface Minstrelsy and the American Working Class*. New York: Oxford University Press, 1993.

Lumm, Emma Griffith. *The Home School Speaker and Elocutionist*. New York: Boland, 1899.

———. *The Twentieth Century Speaker*. New York: Boland, 1899.

Lundstrom, Rinda F. *William Poel's Hamlets*. Ann Arbor, MI: UMI Research Press, 1984.

Lupton, Julia Reinhard. *Citizen-Saints: Shakespeare and Political Theology*. Chicago: University of Chicago Press, 2005.

Malone, Kemp. "Historical Sketch of the English Department of the Johns Hopkins University." *Johns Hopkins Alumni Magazine* 15 (1926–27): 116–28.

Manarin, Louis H., and Clifford Dowdey. *The History of Henrico County*. Charlottesville: University Press of Virginia, 1984.

Manning, Kenneth. *Black Apollo of Science: The Life of Ernest Everett Just*. New York: Oxford University Press, 1983.

March, F. A. "English at Lafayette College." In *English in American Universities, by Professors in the English Department of Twenty Representative Institutions*, 74–85. Boston: D. C. Heath, 1895.

Marshall, Dorothy. *Fanny Kemble*. New York: St. Martin's Press, 1977.

Martin, Jerry L., Anne D. Neal, and Michael S. Nadel. *The Shakespeare File: What English Majors Are Really Studying*. Washington, DC: American Council of Trustees and Alumni, 1996.

Matthiessen, F. O. *American Renaissance: Art and Expression in the Age of Emerson and Whitman*. New York: Oxford University Press, 1941.

Maxcy, Carol. "Teaching Shakespeare." *School Review* 1.2 (1893): 105–8.

May, Henry F. *The End of American Innocence: A Study of the First Years of Our Own Time 1912–1917*. New York: Knopf, 1959.

———. *Three Faces of Berkeley*. Berkeley, CA: Center for Studies in Higher Education and Institute of Governmental Studies, 1993.

McAllister, Marvin. *White People Do Not Know How to Behave at Entertainments Designed for Ladies and Gentlemen of Color: William Brown's African and American Theater*. Chapel Hill: University of North Carolina Press, 2003.

McConachie, Bruce A. *Melodramatic Formations: American Theatre and Society, 1820–1870*. Iowa City: Iowa University Press, 1992.

McDougall, Hugh. *Racial Myth in English History: Trojans, Teutons, and Anglo-Saxons*. Montreal: Harvest House, 1982.

McGuffey, Alexander. *McGuffey's Fifth Eclectic Reader: Selected and Original Exercises for Schools.* Cincinnati, OH: Sargent, Wilson & Hinkle, 1857.

———. *McGuffey's New Fourth Eclectic Reader: Instructive Lessons for the Young.* Cincinnati, OH: Wilson, Hinkle & Co., 1866.

———. *The New McGuffey's Fifth Reader.* New York: American Book Company, 1837.

McMurtry, Jo. *English Language, English Literature: The Creation of an Academic Discipline.* Hamden, CT: Archon, 1985.

Melville, Herman. "Hawthorne and His Mosses, by a Virginian Spending a July in Vermont." *Literary World* 7 (1850), reprinted in *Americans on Shakespeare 1776–1914,* edited by Peter Rawlings, 165. Aldershot, UK: Ashgate, 1999.

Miller, Tice L. *Entertaining the Nation: American Drama in the Eighteenth and Nineteenth Centuries.* Carbondale: Southern Illinois University Press, 2007.

Monaghan, E. Jennifer. *Learning to Read and Write in Colonial America.* Amherst: University of Massachusetts Press, 2005.

Morison, Samuel. *The Oxford History of the American People.* New York: Oxford, 1965.

Murphy, Andrew. *Shakespeare in Print: A History and Chronology of Shakespeare Publishing.* Cambridge: Cambridge University Press, 2003.

Mylander, Jennifer. "Early Modern 'How-To' Books: Impractical Manuals and the Construction of Englishness in the Atlantic World." *Journal for Early Modern Cultural Studies* 9 (2009): 123–46.

Nash, Gary. *Forging Freedom: The Formation of Philadelphia's Black Community, 1720–1840.* Cambridge: Harvard University Press, 1988.

Nash, Margaret A. *Women's Education in the United States, 1780–1840.* New York: Palgrave Macmillan, 2005.

Nathans, Heather S. *Early American Theatre from the Revolution to Thomas Jefferson: Into the Hands of the People.* Cambridge: Cambridge University Press, 2003.

———. "A Much Maligned People: Jews On and Off the Stage in the Early American Republic." *Early American Studies* 2.2 (2004): 310–42.

———. *Slavery and Sentiment on the American Stage, 1787–1861: Lifting the Veil of Black.* Cambridge: Cambridge University Press, 2009.

National School of Elocution and Oratory. Catalogue, 1875. Philadelphia: National School of Elocution and Oratory, 1875.

Neal, Anne D., and Jerry L. Martin. *Defending Civilization: How Our Universities Are Failing America and What Can Be Done about It.* Washington, DC: American Council of Trustees and Alumni, 2001.

The New Oxford Annotated Bible, ed. Bruce M. Metzger and Roland E. Murphy. New York: Oxford University Press, 1991.

New York City Superintendent of Schools. *Annual Report, 1899–1900.* New York: Board of Education, 1899.

Newcomer's School of Expression. *Annual Catalog, 1902–03.* N.p., 1902.

Newman, Samuel P. *A Practical System of Rhetoric.* New York: Dayton, 1842.

Nichols, Charles Washburn. "Teaching Shakespeare to Engineers." *English Journal* 2.6 (1913): 366–69.

Noble, Stuart G. *A History of American Education.* New York: Rinehart, 1938; rev. 1954.

Northrop, Henry Davenport. *The Peerless Reciter or Popular Program.* Chicago: Monarch, 1894.

O'Connor, Marion. *William Poel and the Elizabethan Stage Society.* Cambridge: Chadwyck-Healey, 1987.

Odell, George C. *Annals of the New York Stage.* 15 vols. New York: Columbia University Press, 1927–49.

On the Shelves of the Story Cove. Chicago: Library of International Relations, 1934.

Orgel, Stephen, and A. R. Braunmuller, gen. eds. *The Complete Pelican Shakespeare.* New York: Penguin Books, 2002.

Payne, Ben Iden. *A Life in a Wooden O: Memoirs of the Theatre.* New Haven: Yale University Press, 1977.

Payne, William Morton, ed. *English in American Universities, by Professors in the English Departments of Twenty Representative Institutions.* Boston: D. C. Heath, 1895.

Peckham, Howard Henry. *The Making of the University of Michigan, 1817–1967.* Ann Arbor: University of Michigan Press, 1967.

Perkins, Kathy, ed. *Black Female Playwrights: An Anthology of Plays before 1950.* Bloomington: Indiana University Press, 1990.

Peterson, Merrill D. *The Great Triumvirate: Webster, Clay, and Calhoun.* New York: Oxford University Press, 1987.

Poel, William. *Monthly Letters.* Selected and arranged by A. M. T. London: T. Werner Laurie, 1929.

———. *Shakespeare in the Theatre.* London: Sidgwick and Jackson, 1913.

Pollock, Thomas Clark. *The Philadelphia Theatre in the Eighteenth Century, Together with the Day Book of the Same Period.* New York: Greenwood Press, 1968.

Porter, Dorothy B. "The Organized Educational Activities of Negro Literary Societies, 1828–1846," *Journal of Negro Education* 5 (1936): 556–66.

Price, Thomas R. *The Construction and Types of Shakespeare's Verse as Seen in "Othello."* New York: Press of the New York Shakespeare Society, 1888.

Probate Records of Essex County Massachusetts. 3 vols. Salem, MA: Essex Institute, 1916–20.

Rankin, Hugh F. *The Theater in Colonial America.* Chapel Hill: University of North Carolina Press, 1965.

Raven, James. "The Importation of Books in the Eighteenth Century." In *The Colonial Book in the Atlantic World,* edited by Hugh Amory and David D. Hall, 183–98. Cambridge: Cambridge University Press, 2000.

Rawlings, Peter, ed. *Americans on Shakespeare 1776–1914.* Aldershot, UK: Ashgate, 1999.

Raymond, James C., ed. *English as a Discipline or, Is There a Plot in This Play?* Tuscaloosa: University of Alabama Press, 1996.

Reese, William J. *The Origins of the American High School.* New Haven: Yale University Press, 1995.

Renker, Elizabeth. *The Origins of American Literature Studies: An Institutional History.* Cambridge: Cambridge University Press, 2007.

Ripley, John. "Sociology and Soundscape: Herbert Beerbohm Tree's 1908 *Merchant of Venice.*" *Shakespeare Quarterly* 56 (2005): 385–410.

Rolfe, William J., ed. *Shakespeare's Tragedy of Romeo and Juliet.* New York: American Book Company, 1898.

Rudolph, Frederick. *The American College and University: A History.* 1962. Reprint, Athens: University of Georgia Press, 1990.

———. *The American College and University: A History.* New York: Knopf, 1968.

———. *Curriculum: A History of the American Undergraduate Course of Study since 1636.* San Francisco: Jossey-Bass, 1978.

Santayana, George. *The Middle Span.* Vol. 2, *Persons and Places.* New York: Charles Scribner's Sons, 1945.

Saunders, D. A. "Social Ideas in the McGuffey Readers." *Public Opinion Quarterly* 5.4 (1941): 579–89.

Saxton, Alexander. *The Rise and Fall of the White Republic: Class Politics and Class Culture in Nineteenth-Century America.* London: Verso, 1990. Reprinted with a forward by David Roediger. London: Verso, 2003.

Scanlan, Thomas. *Colonial Writing and the New World 1583–1671: Allegories of Desire.* Cambridge: Cambridge University Press, 1999.

Schaffer, Jason. "'Great Cato's Descendants': A Genealogy of Colonial Performance." *Theatre Survey* 44 (2003): 5–28.

Schneider, Gary. *The Culture of Epistolarity: Vernacular Letters and Letter Writing in Early Modern England, 1500–1700.* Newark: University of Delaware Press, 2005.

Schwartz, Richard D. *Berkeley 1900: Daily Life at the Turn of the Century.* Berkeley, CA: RSB Books, 2000.

Scott, William. *Lessons in Elocution: Or, A Selection of Pieces in Prose and Verse, or the Improvement of Youth in Reading and Speaking.* 4th ed. Boston: Isaiah Thomas, Jun., 1814.

Shakespeare, William. *Globe Theatre Versions, Shakespeare's "Julius Caesar."* 1935. Reprint, New York: Samuel French, 1959.

———. *Globe Theatre Versions, Shakespeare's "Macbeth."* New York: Samuel French, 1935.

———. *Globe Theatre Versions, Shakespeare's "The Comedy of Errors."* New York: Samuel French, 1935.

———. *Globe Theatre Versions, Shakespeare's "The Comedy of Errors."* New York: Samuel French, 1935; in renewal, B[en] Iden Payne, 1962.

———. *Globe Theatre Versions, Shakespeare's "The Taming of the Shrew."* New York: Samuel French, 1937.

Shaw, Wilfred B. ed., "The Department of English Language and Literature." *The University of Michigan: An Encyclopedic Survey in Four Volumes.* Ann Arbor: U of Michigan P, 1951. 2:545–557.

Sheldon, Henry D. *Student Life and Customs.* New York: Appleton, 1901.

Sheridan, Thomas. *British Education: Or, the Source of the Disorders of Great Britain.* Dublin: George Faulkner, 1756. Facsimile reprint, New York: Garland, 1970.

Sherman, Stuart. *Life and Letters of Stuart P. Sherman.* Edited by Jacob Zeitlin and Homer Woodbridge. Vol. 1. New York: Farrar & Rinehart, 1929.

———. "Professor Kittredge and the Teaching of English." In *Shaping Men and Women: Essays on Literature and Life,* ed. Jacob Zeitlin. Garden City, NY: Doubleday, Doron, 1928.

Shoemaker, J. W. *Practical Elocution: For Use in College and Schools and by Private Students.* Philadelphia: National School of Elocution and Oratory, 1883.

Simon, Henry W. *The Reading of Shakespeare in American Schools and Colleges: An Historical Survey.* New York: Simon and Schuster, 1932.

———. "Why Shakespeare?" *English Journal* 23.5 (1934): 363–68.

Sinfield, Alan. "Give an account of Shakespeare and Education, showing why you think they are effective and what you have appreciated about them. Support your comments with precise references." In *Political Shakespeare: New Essays in Cultural Materialism,* ed. Jonathan Dollimore and Alan Sinfield, 134–57. Ithaca: Cornell University Press, 1985.

———. "How to Read *The Merchant of Venice* without being Heterosexist." In *Alternative Shakespeares 2,* edited by Terence Hawkes, 122–39. London: Routledge, 1996.

Smith, Craig R. *Daniel Webster and the Oratory of Civil Religion.* Columbia: University of Missouri Press, 2005.

Smith, Susan Harris. *American Drama: The Bastard Art.* Cambridge: Cambridge University Press, 1997.

Smith, Winifred. "Teaching Shakespeare in School." *English Journal* 11.6 (1922): 361–64.

Smith College *Annual Circulars* no. 1 (1873). Smith College Archives, Northampton, MA.

Snyder, William Lamartine. *The Geography of Marriage: Or, Legal Perplexities of Wedlock in the United States.* New York: G. P. Putnam's Sons, 1889.

Speaight, Robert. *William Poel and the Elizabethan Revival.* Melbourne: William Heinemann, 1954.

Stahl, Donald E. *A History of the English Curriculum in American High Schools.* Chicago: Lyceum Press, 1965.

Stanard, Mary Newton. *Colonial Virginia: Its People and Customs.* Philadelphia: J. B. Lippincott, 1917.

Stevens, Laura M. *The Poor Indians: British Missionaries, Native Americans, and Colonial Sensibility.* Philadelphia: University of Pennsylvania Press, 2004.

Stevens, Thomas Wood. *The Globe Theatre.* Chicago: Colortext Publications, 1934.

———. *The Theatre: From Athens to Broadway.* New York: D. Appleton, 1932.

Sturgess, Kim C. *Shakespeare and the American Nation.* Cambridge: Cambridge University Press, 2004.

Sullivan, Dolores P. *William Holmes McGuffey, Schoolmaster to the Nation.* Rutherford, NJ: Fairleigh Dickinson University Press, 1999.

Sweet, John Wood. "Introduction: Sea Changes." In *Envisioning an English Empire: Jamestown and the Making of the North Atlantic World,* edited by Robert Applebaum and John Wood Sweet, 1–21. Philadelphia: University of Pennsylvania Press, 2005.

Swinton, William. *Studies in English Literature Being Typical Selections of British and American Authorship, from Shakespeare to the Present.* New York: Harper & Brothers, 1881.

Talty, Stephan. *Mulatto America: At the Crossroads of Black and White Culture. A Social History.* New York: Harper Collins, 2003.

Tawil, Ezra. *The Making of Racial Sentiment.* Cambridge: Cambridge University Press, 2006.

Taylor, Gary. *Reinventing Shakespeare: A Cultural History from the Restoration to the Present.* New York: Oxford University Press, 1989.

Teague, Frances. *Shakespeare and the American Popular Stage.* Cambridge: Cambridge University Press, 2006.

Tennenhouse, Leonard. *The Importance of Feeling English: American Literature and the British Diaspora, 1750–1850*. Princeton: Princeton University Press, 2007.

Trachsel, Mary. *Institutionalizing Literacy: The Historical Role of College Entrance Examinations in English*. Carbondale: Southern Illinois University Press, 1992.

Tufts, John. *A Compendium of Logick According to ye Modern Philosophers Extracted from Legrand and Others Their Systems: by Mr. Brattle*. 1705. Harvard University Archives_Vault_HUC 8705.351.

Tyack, David. *The One Best System: A History of American Urban Education*. Cambridge: Harvard University Press, 1974.

Uricchio, William, and Roberta E. Pearson. *Reframing Culture: The Case of the Vitagraph Films*. Princeton: Princeton University Press, 1993.

Van Cleve, Charles. "The Teaching of Shakespeare in American Secondary Schools." *Peabody Journal of Education* 15.6 (1938): 333–50.

Vaughan, Virginia Mason, and Alden T. Vaughan, eds. *Shakespeare in American Life*. Washington, DC: Folger Shakespeare Library, 2007.

Verplanck, Gulian Crommelin. "Preface." *The Illustrated Shakespeare*. 3 vols. New York: Harper and Brothers, 1847.

Veysey, Laurence R. *The Emergence of the American University*. Chicago: University of Chicago Press, 1965.

Wallace, Karl R., ed. *History of Speech Education in America: Background Studies*. New York: Appleton-Century-Crofts, 1954.

Ward, A. W. *Shakespeare and the Makers of Virginia*. London: Oxford University Press, 1919.

Ward, William S. "The English Department University of Kentucky: An Informal History, with Personal Recollections. The First Hundred Years 1865–1964." Department of English, University of Kentucky; University Archives, University of Kentucky Libraries, Lexington, KY.

Warner, Michael. *The Letters of the Republic: Publication and the Public Sphere in Eighteenth-Century America*. Cambridge: Harvard University Press, 1990.

———. "Professionalization and the Rewards of Literature: 1875–1900." *Criticism* 27 (1985): 1–28.

Webster, Daniel. "The Constitution and the Union." In *The Works of Daniel Webster*, 5.325–66. Boston, C. C. Little and J. Brown, 1851.

———. "Second Speech on Foot's Resolution." In *The Works of Daniel Webster*, 3.270–342. Boston: C. C. Little and J. Brown, 1851.

Webster, Noah. *An American Selection of Lessons in Reading and Speaking*. Philadelphia: Young and M'Culloch, 1787.

Welles, E. G. *The Orator's Guide; or Rules for Speaking and Composing; From the Best Authorities*. Philadelphia: G. L. Austin, 1822.

Welter, Barbara. "The Cult of True Womanhood, 1820–1860." *American Quarterly* 18 (Summer 1966): 151–74.

Wendell, Barrett. *English Composition*. New York: Scribner's, 1891.

Wendell, Barrett. *A Literary History of America*. New York: Charles Scribner's Sons, 1900.

———. "The Relations of Radcliffe College with Harvard." *Harvard Monthly* 29 (October 1899): 1–10.

———. *William Shakspere: A Study in Elizabethan Literature*. London: Dent, 1894.

————. *The Temper of the Seventeenth Century in English Literature*. New York: Charles Scribner's Sons, 1904.

Wesley, Dorothy Porter, and Constance Porter Uzelac, eds. *William Cooper Nell, Nineteenth-Century African American Abolitionist, Historian, Integrationist: Selected Writings 1832–1874*. New York: Black Classic Press, 2002.

West, Shearer, ed. *The Victorians and Race*. Aldershot, UK: Scolar Press, 1996.

Whitman, Walt. *Specimen Days*. Boston: David R. Godine, 1971.

Wiebe, Robert H. *The Opening of American Society: From the Adoption of the Constitution to the Eve of Disunion*. New York: Random House, 1984.

Williams, Raymond. *The Raymond Williams Reader*. Edited by John Higgins. Oxford: Blackwell, 2001.

Willis, Eola. *The Charleston Stage in the XVIII Century: With Social Settings of the Time*. Columbia, SC: State Co., 1924.

Willoughby, Edwin Elliott. "The Reading of Shakespeare in Colonial America." *Papers of the Bibliographical Society of America* 31 (1937): 45–56.

Wilmeth, Don B., and Tice Miller. *Cambridge Guide to American Theatre*. Cambridge: Cambridge University Press, 1996.

Winterowd, W. Ross, and Vincent Gillespie, eds. *Composition in Context: Essays in Honor of Donald C. Stewart*. Carbondale: Southern Illinois University Press, 1995.

Wood, John. *Mentor, or the American Teacher's Assistant: Being a Selection of Essays, Instructive and Entertaining, from the Most Approved Authors in the English Language*. New York: John Buel, 1795.

Wright, John D. *Transylvania: Tutor to the West*. Lexington: University Press of Kentucky, 1975.

Wright, Louis B. "The Purposeful Reading of Our Colonial Ancestors." *English Literary History* 4 (1937): 85–111.

Wright, Thomas Goddard. *Literary Culture in Early New England 1620–1730*. New York: Russell & Russell, 1966.

Writers' Program of the Works Progress Administration. *Berkeley: The First Seventy-Five Years*. Berkeley, CA: James J. Gillick, 1941.

Zeitlin, Jacob, ed. *Shaping Men and Women: Essays on Literature and Life*. Garden City, NY: Doubleday, Doran, 1928.

Zucker, Adam, and Alan B. Farmer, eds. *Localizing Caroline Drama: Politics and Economics of the Early Modern English Stage, 1625–1642*. New York: Palgrave Macmillan, 2006.

Contributors

DENISE ALBANESE is Associate Professor of English and Cultural Studies at George Mason University in Fairfax, Virginia. Author of *New Science, New World* (1996) and contributor to an edition of Jean Luis Vives's *Instruction for a Christen Woman* (2001), she has also published on Tudor-Stuart mathematics and Shakespeare in film and popular culture. The essay in this collection is part of her recent book on Shakespeare in perimillennial culture, *Extramural Shakespeare* (2010).

JONATHAN BURTON is Woodburn Associate Professor of English at West Virginia University. He is currently working on a book entitled *High School Shakespeare*. His previous publications include *Traffic and Turning: Islam and English Drama, 1579–1624* (2005) and *Race in Early Modern England: A Documentary Companion* (2007).

MIMI GODFREY is Managing Editor of *Shakespeare Quarterly*, Folger Shakespeare Library.

SANDRA M. GUSTAFSON is the author of *Eloquence is Power: Oratory and Performance in Early America* (2000) and has published essays on William Apess, James Fenimore Cooper, Jonathan Edwards, and Margaret Fuller and on subjects such as "American Literature and the Public Sphere" and "Histories of Democracy and Empire." She is presently completing a monograph, *Imagining Deliberative Democracy in the Early American Republic* (forthcoming, 2011). She is coeditor, with Caroline F. Sloat, of *Cultural Narratives: Textuality and Performance in American Culture before 1900* (2010) and is editor of the journal *Early American Literature*. She teaches in the English Department at the University of Notre Dame.

DAYTON HASKIN is Professor of English at Boston College. Past president of the Milton Society of America, he is the author of *Milton's Burden of Interpretation*. He has also written *John Donne in the Nineteenth Century* (2007), documenting the avid interest in early modern literature that developed at Harvard during the period surveyed in his essay for this volume. A contributing editor to the *Variorum Edition of the Poetry of John Donne* and a member of its advisory board, he recently completed the chapter on love poetry for the 2011 *Oxford Handbook of John Donne* and an essay called "Donne's Afterlife" for the *Cambridge Companion to John Donne*.

NAN JOHNSON is Professor of English at the Ohio State University, where she teaches the history and theory of rhetoric, rhetorical criticism, feminist rhetoric, American studies, and writing. Johnson is the author of *Nineteenth-Century Rhetoric in North America* (1991), *Gender and Rhetorical Space in American Life* (2002), and numerous articles and book chapters on rhetorical theory and the history of American rhetorical practices.

COPPÉLIA KAHN, Professor of English at Brown University, is author of *Man's Estate: Masculine Identity in Shakespeare* (1981) and *Roman Shakespeare: Warriors, Wounds, and Women* (1997). She has also coedited anthologies on feminist literary criticism, psychoanalytic interpretation of Shakespeare, and Renaissance literature. She has published articles on Shakespeare, gender theory, early modern drama, and questions of race and nation in twentieth-century constructions of Shakespeare. In 2008–9, she was president of the Shakespeare Association of America.

ROSEMARY KEGL is Associate Professor of English at the University of Rochester, where she teaches courses in sixteenth- and seventeenth-century English Renaissance literature and culture. She is the author of *The Rhetoric of Concealment* (1994) and is currently working on two book manuscripts, *Revisiting Death in English Renaissance Drama: Apostrophe, Tragicomedy, and Utopia* and *Tabloid Shakespeare at the 1934 Chicago World's Fair*. The essay in this volume is part of that second book project.

THEODORE LEINWAND is Professor of English at the University of Maryland. He is the author of *The City Staged: Jacobean Comedy, 1603–1613* and *Theatre, Finance and Society in Early Modern England*. His edition of *Michaelmas Term* appears in the Oxford *Thomas Middleton: The Collected Works* (2008). His ongoing series of essays on readers of Shakespeare (Keats, Coleridge, Virginia Woolf, Ted Hughes, and John Berryman) may be found in the *Kenyon Review, Studies in Romanticism*, the *Yale Review*, the *Hopkins Review*, and the *New England Review*.

MARVIN MCALLISTER is the author of *"White People Do Not Know How To Behave At Entertainments Designed For Ladies and Gentlemen of Colour": William Brown's African and American Theater* (2003), a history of the first known African American theater company. His current projects include an analysis of whiteface minstrelsy and stage Europeans in African American performance and a book-length study of the Howard College Dramatic Club / Howard Players. He has taught theater history at various universities across the country and has worked as a dramaturge for theaters in Seattle, Cleveland, Chicago, and Washington, DC.

JENNIFER MYLANDER is an Assistant Professor of English at San Francisco State University, teaching courses on both early modern Britain and the early Atlantic world. Her publications include a study of early national discourse in seventeenth-century English husbandry and medical manuals that appeared in the *Journal for Early Modern Cultural Studies* and an essay on the circulation and reading of Faust tales in the Atlantic world, forthcoming in *Connected by Books*, edited by James Raven and Leslie Howsam.

HEATHER S. NATHANS is an Associate Professor of Theatre at the University of Maryland, where she is also Associate Chair of Theatre and an Associate Dean for the College of Arts and Humanities. Her publications include *Early American Theatre from the Revolution to Thomas Jefferson* (2003) and *Slavery and Sentiment on the American Stage, 1781–1861* (2009). She is a contributing author to *Weyward Macbeth: Intersections of Race and Performance* (2009) and *Theatre Historiography: Critical Interventions* (forthcoming, 2010). She has guest-edited the *Journal of American Drama and Theatre* and the August Wilson issue of the *New England Theatre Journal.* She has published in *Theatre History Studies, New England Theatre Journal, Journal of American Drama and Theatre, Early American Studies,* and the *Pennsylvania History Journal.* Nathans is President of the American Theatre and Drama Society.

ELIZABETH RENKER is the author of *The Origins of American Literature Studies: An Institutional History* (2007); *Strike Through the Mask: Herman Melville and the Scene of Writing* (1996); numerous essays on American literature and culture, the history of higher education in the United States, American poetry between the Civil War and World War I, and effective teaching; and the introduction to the Signet classic edition of *Moby-Dick.* She is Professor of English at the Ohio State University, where she won the 2008 Alumni Distinguished Teaching Award and the 2006 Rodica C. Botoman Award for Distinguished Undergraduate Teaching and Mentoring. Her work on Shakespeare and curricular history brings together her work on American culture, the history of education, and the history of poetry in America.

Index

Breinigsville, PA USA
24 January 2011
253986BV00003B/2/P